Edmund Spenser: A Reception History

David Hill Radcliffe

Edmund Spenser
A Reception History

CAMDEN HOUSE

Copyright © 1996 by
CAMDEN HOUSE, INC.

Published by Camden House, Inc.
Drawer 2025
Columbia, SC 29202 USA

Printed on acid-free paper.
Binding materials are chosen for strength and
durability.

ISBN: 1–57113–073–x

Library of Congress Cataloging-in-Publication Data

Radcliffe, David Hill.
    Edmund Spenser, a reception history / David Hill Radcliffe.
        p.   cm. -- (Studies in English & American literature,
    linguistics, and culture)
    Includes bibliographical references and index.
    ISBN 1–57113–073–x
    1. Spenser, Edmund, 1552?–1599 -- Criticism and interpretation -
    -History. 2. English literature -- History and criticism – Theory,
    etc.   I. Title.   II. Series: Studies in English and American
    literature, linguistics, and culture (Unnumbered) Literary criticism in
    perspective.
    PR2364.R33   1996
    821'.3 -- dc20
                                                96–1890
                                                CIP

375-97-27

Contents

For James Nohrnberg

Preface

If English poetry does not begin with Edmund Spenser, a case could be made that English *literature* does. Spenser made two important decisions that set his poetry apart from earlier verse: he chose to imitate vernacular as well as classical writers, and he elected to market his works in printed books rather than circulate them in the more prestigious form of manuscript. By taking English Chaucer as his master, he paid deference to national past; by circulating his poems in durable print, he set the precedent for a future literature that would be public and national, not merely courtly or academic. Spenser's historical importance results from this confluence of the old technology of poetic imitation and the new technology of printing books. The basis of both technologies was repetition, which proved vital to the formation of British literature; among the hundreds of later writers who learned to write by imitating Spenser's poems were Milton, Dryden, Pope, Thomson, Collins, Gray, Coleridge, Wordsworth, Keats, Shelley, and Tennyson. In the famous phrase attributed to Charles Lamb, Spenser became "the poets' poet." If repetition is one component necessary to establishing a literature, change is another: Spenser's imitators carried on the initiative begun by Colin Clout by refining and modifying it; the concept of a "British" literature began evolving right from the start. Criticism had much to do with this, of course; repetition and change are dimensions of criticism as much as poetry. The chapters that follow will show that Spenser has proved to be no less important as "the critics' poet." On four occasions – in Spenser's lifetime, in the Augustan era, in the romantic period, and in the founding of English studies at the turn of the century – criticism of Spenser's poems played a significant part in redefining the aims and identity of British literature. Over the last century Spenser's importance has gradually diminished, yet his works have continued to be read and have been the subject of scores of scholarly books and several thousand critical essays.

Why concern ourselves with the history of Spenser criticism? Why should outmoded modes of criticism be any more useful for comprehending the *Faerie Queene* then Ptolemaic astronomy is for understanding the motions of the planets? For several reasons. In order to participate in a critical conversation, one needs to know how the discussion arrived at the point where it now stands. Those whose business it is to interpret poems or conduct experiments will also research the literature on their subject because it has obvious value as a repository of facts and observations. For those seeking to challenge conventional wisdom, outmoded work is sometimes useful because it frames questions in ways that violate the consensus view. As one reads farther back into the record, discussions of astronomy or poetry begin to appear in unexpected contexts and to assume odd forms; one encounters challenging ideas about just what constitutes a scientific fact or a figure of speech and how facts and figures might be used in an argument. It is not common to grant serious attention to exploded notions in science or literature, and often enough they lead nowhere. Yet experience certainly indicates that important innovations in both science and literature can result when scholars return to the historical record: in the Renaissance, for example, both the new science and the new poetry took rise from careful reexamination of the documents of pagan antiquity. Much of importance in Spenser's poetry is simply not discussed in modern criticism, and much of importance in Spenser criticism requires some knowledge of the traditions that criticism sustains and contests.

Volumes in the *Literary Criticism in Perspective* series are addressed to several kinds of reader; to students, professional scholars, and anyone with an interest in literature. The story to be told in these pages should interest to a broad spectrum of readers concerned about literature, history, criticism and education. But different readers bring different kinds of expectation and degrees of familiarity to the subject; because of the difficulties involved, serious scholarship and literary history is seldom addressed to a general readership. I have tried to enliven the summary and argumentative portions of this book by integrating them into a sustaining narrative; for their part, Spenser's critics have said some pretty lively things. Footnotes have been rejected as inappropriate to a small book that addresses many of the central issues in literary criticism, but there is a bibliography of works cited at the back of each chapter and a general bibliography of Spenser criticism at the back of the book. A great deal has been written not only about Spenser but about the history of Spenser's reception; for those who wish to read further I have included a selected list of such titles at the back. Works cited in the text are listed chronologically at the end of each chapter. For the general reader, I have tried to place four centuries of remarks and arguments about Spenser in the larger context of the history of literary criticism; because of his foundational role in British literature, to write a history of Spenser criticism is to verge on writing a history of criticism itself. Specialists will find material discussed here that will not be familiar to most Spenser scholars, and students of other periods will probably find things of interest as well. While the vast body of writing about Spenser has been more thoroughly documented elsewhere in bibliographies, dissertations, and specialized studies, of course I have added my own mote or two to the canons of criticism.

Because reception histories are written for different purposes, they take different forms. In part this is dictated by the writer in question, and in part by the readership being addressed. Most reinforce the norms of contemporary criticism by focusing on major writers and limiting themselves to articles and monographs in the scholarly literature. Other reception histories make a case for writers ignored or undervalued by academic scholarship; they examine book reviews and allusions found in poems, letters, biographies, and prefaces. In such cases reception histories themselves enter actively into the process of reception; more than a few important noncanonical writers have been reprinted in response to the labors of feminists and others seeking to "open up the canon." While this study is concerned with a major writer, it will venture beyond the scholarly literature and consider other kinds of criticism that were important in shaping Spenser's reputation before it became largely an academic matter.

If reception histories differ in the materials they consider, they differ also in the way they organize and present their material: some attend to the vagaries of taste or the imperatives of history; others emphasize the authority of the best readers or the consensus of the many; sometimes critical views are presented as products of individual insight, sometimes as products of anonymous social forces. Reception histories can be explanatory, judgmental, or simple efforts at documentation. This discussion of Spenser criticism trims between several of these kinds of reception history, discussing landmark comments about Spenser's poetry along with other kinds of evidence. I have tried to give major critics their due, recognizing their insights and innovations for what they were. At the same time, I have tried to underscore the social and institutional basis of criticism, for without some such understanding the remarks of critics writing two or three centuries ago often seem trivial or unintelligible. In this I depart from earlier treatments of Spenser criticism, which, despite their many virtues, have been sparing of contextualization and analysis. Anthologies of Spenser criticism, while they have often included material from earlier centuries, have generally limited themselves to discussions of Spenser that resemble modern criticism or have a direct bearing on twentieth-century concerns. While this is not an unreasonable approach, the result of such selections has been to narrow the canon of criticism and to misleadingly present Spenser criticism as a progression toward modern views. Coleridge and Hazlitt, foundational figures for twentieth-century academic criticism, loom large in such accounts, while imitations in verse and discussions of Spenser in school texts – vital matters – are not considered.

Where they have expressed judgments, previous discussions of Spenser criticism have tended to distribute praise and blame according to whether a writer respects historical standards – getting at what Spenser meant – or respects the standards of taste common to our time – arriving at a just evaluation of the poetry as such. Since both historicism and aestheticism are relatively recent developments, these approaches ignore or devalue much that was written about Spenser before modern times, for criticism before the nine-teenth-century was frequently concerned with other matters, like whether or not Spenser was a good man or whether he resembles Virgil more than Homer. While the great romantic critics of Spenser have received the attention they deserve, Augustan and Victorian critics, often just as important in the greater scheme of things, have been unjustly neglected throughout the twenti-eth century. I have tried to redress this balance, at the risk of becoming some-thing of an advocate for alternative forms of criticism. This history was not written in a vacuum, and it does respond, implicitly or explicitly, to what ear-lier historians have said about the criticism. One thing I learned in researching this book is that histories of criticism that attempt to present "the facts" inde-pendently of judgment or interpretation can be just as misleading as those that make less pretense of objectivity. I was not unaffected by what Spenser's critics have written, and from time to time this book will become engaged in their conversation. That said, I have tried to steer between the two extremes of normative evaluation and unadorned documentation, with what success the reader may judge.

Any attempt to make sense of premodern criticism requires considering the social basis of earlier critical practices, particularly a book like this one, which discusses materials often very remote from what is to be found in mod-ern academic journals. One simply cannot understand seventeenth-century epigrams, eighteenth-century imitations and burlesques, or nineteenth-century periodical essays without reference to changes in the social context of criticism. This is not to say that the value of a critical statement is simply reducible to the place of the writer in society or history. While criticism is obviously better or worse judged even by the standards of its time, comments about Spenser by expert witnesses such as Jonson, Dryden, and Coleridge transcend those stan-dards; through constant repetition in prefaces, notes, and appendixes they all but became part of the poetry itself. But to weigh the intrinsic merit or external significance of even these remarks requires a degree of familiarity with changes in critical norms. Such norms are most clearly expressed in the kinds of writ-ing adopted by critics – genres that have been known to alter, along with their implicit social norms, under pressure from the works being criticized. From the very first, the *Shepheardes Calender* and the *Faerie Queene* have presented daunt-ing challenges to the prevailing norms of criticism. As we shall see, they often had their largest impact on the practice of criticism at the very times when Spenser was least popular with the general reading public. While criticism of Spenser plainly addresses its immediate social contexts, I will argue that from time to time outmoded elements in Spenser's writing – his imagery, his alle-gory, his teachings – have challenged the prevailing norms of literary dis-course and entered directly into the writing of later criticism. In this sense, I offer Spenser as the critics' poet.

Books published in the *Literary Criticism in Perspective* series are meant to be
narrative histories rather than annotated bibliographies. Narrative history is a
genre of criticism that opens up possibilities and imposes constraints. Part of its
attractiveness is its emphasis on character. Just as Spenser was a writer distinct
from Sidney or Shakespeare, so the character of his reception differs from
theirs; all three figure prominently in the complex story of critical responses to
Elizabethan literature, which is further shaped by the political character of
Queen Elizabeth. Narrative history also encourages an emphasis on continuity
amid change. For the last century English studies has been increasingly domi-
nated by the period specializations encouraged by sociological approaches to
literary study; the result has been to efface traditions in favor of organizing
writers by schools or subcultures. Or where period approaches are resisted,
modern critics have neglected differences among competing traditions in con-
structing that transhistorical thing called British literature. It is worth recalling
that at most times over the past four centuries, Spenser, neglected though he
may have been, had more readers than all but a handful of period poets: he
was a very active presence in seventeenth-, eighteenth-, and nineteenth-century
literature. At the same time, one needs to recognize that Spenserianism is but
one of several distinct, long-running, and contrary traditions in English poetry
and criticism: by no means is all of later English poetry "British literature" in
the sense of participating in the canon-building process initiated by Spenser.
Spenser's contribution to novelism – the new standards of probable represen-
tation that dominate modern literature and criticism – was small and not easy
to document. By attending to these continuities and discontinuities, a narrative
study of Spenser criticism can complicate our understanding of literary history
in useful ways.

Narrative history also imposes difficulties of selection, presentation, and
organization. For the sake of coherence and readability, only a small number
of the several thousand critics who have written about Spenser can be dis-
cussed here, and most of those in no great detail. The volume of Spenser criti-
cism is huge; the dissertations by Vondersmith and Burgholzer covering early
twentieth-century and mid-twentieth-century Spenser criticism each run to
hundreds of pages and neither is comprehensive. Selection is a necessary but
risky business; while I have read most of the Spenser criticism written prior to
the nineteenth century, for the more recent material I have often relied on sec-
ondary works cited below: annotated bibliographies, reference guides, vari-
orum editions, prefaces, anthologies of criticism, and the recent *Spenser
Encyclopedia*. For recent decades, I have selected for discussion some representa-
tive works to illustrate how Spenser criticism engages the broader trends in
twentieth-century criticism and how Spenser's academic readers handle the
themes discussed in the earlier chapters. Rather than organize this history
around commentary on particular poems, I have followed the critical consen-

sus in emphasizing the *Faerie Queene* and its continuing significance for British literature. No doubt some of my choices have led to eccentricities of judgment and emphasis, though I hope that the long perspective I bring to the subject will have corresponding strengths. In discussing twentieth-century criticism I have perhaps given disproportionate space to North American scholars; they tend to be the more distinctive voices, and there are certainly more of them. I have tried to improve on earlier work in the field, but I happily concede that the history of Spenser criticism can and should be told in more than one way.

There is no comprehensive history of Spenser criticism, though readers who would like a more comprehensive history than I offer here can assemble something like a multivolume history by reading Herbert E. Cory's *The Critics of Edmund Spenser* (1917) and Harko G. De Maar's *A History of Modern English Romanticism* (1924) on the period to 1800, followed by three unpublished dissertations: David Hal Evett, "Nineteenth-Century Criticism of Spenser" (Harvard, 1965), Bernard J. Vondersmith, "A History of the Criticism of the *Faerie Queene*, 1910–1947" (Duquesne University, 1971) and Carolyn Burgholzer, "Edmund Spenser's the *Faerie Queene*: A History of Criticism, 1948–1968" (Duquesne University, 1970). Those who are working up a particular theme or issue in Spenser criticism might begin with *The Spenser Encyclopedia*, edited by A. C. Hamilton (1990), which summarizes recent research and debate on a wide range of topics. Anyone researching Spenser's reception will find Frederick Ives Carpenter's *A Reference Guide to Edmund Spenser* (1923) and *Edmund Spenser: A Bibliographic Supplement*, by Dorothy F. Atkinson (1937) particularly useful. R. M. Cumming's *Spenser: The Critical Heritage* (1971) gives a selection of the criticism to 1715 that is well-edited, accessible, and thorough. There is even more material in *Spenser Allusions in the Sixteenth and Seventeenth Centuries* (1972), edited by William Wells, which attempts to collect every mention of Spenser; several classic essays are assembled in Paul Alpers, ed. *Edmund Spenser: A Critical Anthology* (1969). Since much of the earlier criticism is not otherwise conveniently accessible, I have cited passages from these texts. For those going further afield, the Johns Hopkins variorum *Works of Edmund Spenser* (1932–55) and the earlier variorum edited by Henry J. Todd (1805) index and reprint much valuable criticism. I am at work on a hypertext catalogue-cum-anthology of imitations and criticism covering the period down to 1830, which I hope to make available sometime in the next ten years.

Sayre Greenfield was kind enough to share with me his research on early editions of Spenser's *Works*. I would like to acknowledge debts to several of my teachers. Edward Tomarken read an early version of the manuscript and has given me advice and encouragement. Alastair Fowler has patiently listened to my rantings about Spenserianism for several years. Ralph Cohen, who taught me to love literary history, pioneered modern reception history at a time when it was thoroughly unfashionable. Leo Damrosch helped me to get this project underway during a summer seminar at Harvard, and James Nohrnberg taught me Spenser in graduate school. Indebtedness to teachers can take unpredictable turns; the complexities of working within a tradition, which is a theme to which I will return, have been borne out in writing the book itself. I have not discussed Alastair Fowler's writings on Spenser, but my account of seventeenth-century criticism owes much to his more recent work. Ralph Cohen taught me to think critically, which I have perversely done by turning humanist in some of my criticisms of academic literary history. In his courses on eighteenth-century literature, Leo Damrosch sometimes offended me by putting a romantic construction on eighteenth-century poetry, which is just what I have done in this book. I remember being rather annoyed by the lack of historical context in James Nohrnberg's remarkable lectures on the *Faerie Queene*. I respectfully and humbly dedicate this book, which consists of little else, to him.

Abbreviations

Citations, by signature or page number, are to the books or journals listed chronologically in the general bibliography; for the earlier criticism I have given citations to the most readily available anthologies, using the following abbreviations:

CH   *Spenser: The Critical Heritage, ed. R. M. Cummings. New York: Barnes and Noble, 1971.*

SA   *Spenser Allusions in the Sixteenth and Seventeenth Centuries, ed. William Wells. Chapel Hill: U of North Carolina P, 1972.*

Spingarn: *Critical Essays of the Seventeenth Century, ed. J. E. Spingarn. 3 vols. Bloomington: Indiana UP, 1957.*

ES   *Edmund Spenser: A Critical Anthology, ed. Paul J. Alpers. Harmondsworth: Penguin, 1969.*

1: Ancients and Moderns

Contemporary Criticism of the
Shepheardes Calender and the *Faerie Queene*

Twentieth-century writers have been preoccupied with staging the *deaths* of romanticism, modernity, patriarchy, philosophy, history, and literature; Elizabethan writers were just as fascinated with the problems of orchestrating opening moves. Their challenge was to establish proper and authoritative origins for Protestantism, empire, and serious writing in the vernacular language. Spenser and his contemporaries opened up British literature with a rhetorical strategy oddly similar to those now used for closing it down. Just as moderns and postmoderns have used fiction to deconstruct the novel, philosophy to displace thought, and history to devalue narrative, so Elizabethan humanists boldly embraced paradox by making *imitation* the basis of their claims to originality. "Our new Poete," E. K. announces in the *Shepheardes Calender*, comes into the world "vncouthe" and "vnkiste." Nonetheless E. K. presents his trembling maiden to the world in the full battle-dress appropriate to a grand but difficult Latin classic, with preface, illustrations, commentary, and glossary. The young lady's long pedigree in ancient and modern literatures is pointedly displayed for all to see and admire. It is notable that Edmund Spenser – still anonymous at this point – made his official entrance into the world with criticism already attached.

It is also notable that Spenser's claim to greatness was immediately accepted – no ordeal of trial-by-common-reader was required in his case. Spenser's poems were, however, plainly being discussed, criticized, and revised *prior* to their publication; the sonnets and epistles appended to the *Shepheardes Calender* and the *Faerie Queene* read like a manifesto and suggest something like a collaborative effort. We get just a glimpse of this process in the letters Spenser exchanged with his friend Gabriel Harvey (ca. 1550–1630); these were published in 1580, shortly after *Shepheardes Calender,* and include a catalogue of "lost" titles suggesting a body of work unlike what we see today. As critics early recognized, some of these lost works, like the *Epithalamion Thamesis,* were later incorporated into the *Faerie Queene;* Harvey was likely reading a poem very different from the one we know today. Even Spenser's epistle to Raleigh, printed with the first three books of the *Faerie Queene* in 1590, describes a poem rather different from the one it follows. Raleigh was one of a number of "friends": as a young man, Spenser was associated with the "Areopagus," a coterie of writers led by Sir Philip Sidney and dedicated to the reformation of English letters. Spenser's works were later taken up by another coterie associated with Essex and radical Protestantism. Apparently not one copy of any of the several manuscripts we know were circulating among Spenser's courtly and academic friends has survived, a curious state of affairs considering how highly he and they were regarded. One can only speculate: no doubt something was lost when Tyrone's men burned Spenser out of his house at Kilcolman; other papers may have been consigned to the flames when Queen Elizabeth suppressed the Essex faction. It may be that some deliberate effort was made to obliterate the contingent origins of Spenser's poetry, limiting its public reception to the fixed and monumental form of print presentation. In turning away from the scribal publication favored for courtly writings like Shakespeare's sonnets or Donne's elegies and satires, Spenser and his friends seem to have used the medium of print to lend an air of finality to the new beginning, despite the fragmentary and unfinished state of the *Faerie Queene*. If so, they were certainly successful: by the time of Spenser's death a number of commentators were trumpeting his fame as founder and patriot of a British literature; as such, he belonged to a higher "class" of author than any upstart playwright or courtly sonneteer.

Which is to say that for quite a long time Spenser was more highly esteemed than his younger contemporaries William Shakespeare and John Donne, the two writers we tend to regard as first among the Elizabethans. Consider the importance of print: many of Shakespeare's already much admired plays would have been lost but for that belated, posthumous first folio of 1623. Shakespeare did not prepare his dramatic works for print, and they have suffered accordingly. Most of Donne's poems were not printed until even later; they appeared, also posthumously, in 1633. As highly regarded as Donne's satires and lyrics had once been at court, most seventeenth-century readers seem to have regarded them rather as curiosities of wit than as literature in the grand sense. Shakespeare and Donne did not begin to shape the general perception of British literature and criticism until much later. Spenser, as a heroic poet emulating Virgil and the classics, had a higher status in what was, as we shall see, a very status-conscious age. When one considers that none of Spenser's immediate rivals in heroic poetry outlived their time, or that three generations would pass before Milton published *Paradise Lost*, one begins to understand the kind of pedestal on which our published author was placed. During those years Davenant and Cowley attempted to overgo Spenser in epic and failed; Michael Drayton and Ben Jonson, wiser perhaps, didn't even try. Eyebrows were raised in 1616 when mighty Ben, who certainly appreciated the value of print, published his plays and epigrams in folio and called them "Works." This strategy, which might be construed as an oblique way of emulating Spenser, proved effective: though less a storyteller than Shakespeare, and less a wit than Donne, Ben Jonson became a monument in his own lifetime and a model for others to emulate.

It is necessary to grasp Spenser's monumentality in order to understand why a poet who was seldom genuinely popular has had such an enormous impact on British literature and criticism. Until fairly recently, monuments were very important to civic life generally; in literature, being commemorated in Poets' Corner was no small thing. Persons who might know little enough about the writer in question recognized the marble effigy and the name inscribed below. Because they were a standing invitation to curiosity, monuments preserved a memory when those lacking a monument were simply forgotten. And because monuments commanded respect, that memory could be used to challenge the status quo. Sounding names were always available for use, frequently by parties on both sides of a question; monuments inspired emulation in the double sense of imitation and competition. Monumentality has played a significant part in the history of Spenser criticism: Spenser's authority was such that it could challenge later critical norms opposed to his poetics or his politics; it was such that backward-looking humanists and reform-minded moderns both sought to lay claim to it. Not until our own century have critics argued that the literary canon could and should be reconstructed wholesale in the image of their own norms and beliefs, and not until very recently indeed have scholars argued that a canon could never be anything *but* a product of contemporary norms and beliefs. This was certainly not the view of the Renaissance poet or neoclassical critic looking towards the Latin, Greek, and Hebrew classics with reverence and awe, tinged with a little jealousy and a frustrated desire to compete.

To understand just why E. K. labored so to present his new poet as an instant classic, we might recall the state of literary affairs in 1579. While English *poetry* had been written for centuries, including quite sophisticated and literary poetry, English *literature* might be said to begin with Spenser. It fell to Spenser's generation to construct a substantial body of vernacular poetry self-consciously modeled on the assembled corpus of Latin classics. This was a national undertaking that required, in addition to individual genius, considerable technical resources — in diction and prosody, educational reforms and courtly patronage, even type-founding and paper-making, the latter a late growth in England. A comparison might be made to a space race or an arms race. Tudor writers were very much aware of the fact that Protestant Britain entered the competition for fame among modern literatures far behind its rivals in Catholic Italy, Spain, and France. Relatively few classical authors had been translated or imitated in English (they were well known in the original language, of course), and properly humanist, English poems had yet to be produced in the manner of classical satire, epistle, epigram, georgic, or epic. Critics of Spenser's generation debated whether rhyme or quantitative verse was best for English and even whether important poetry should or could be written in the vulgar tongue. Norms for English prosody, diction, and orthography were far from settled. Chaucer possibly aside, no English writer could claim the status of a Petrarch or a Tasso, much less that of a Horace or a Virgil. E. K. promises a new poet to fill these gaps and settle these questions. As matters turned out, Spenser did fulfill this high promise; in the words of Thomas Lodge, he "brought the Chaos of our tongue in frame" (1593; *CH*, 82). Colin Clout was indeed a founding figure, a "new poet" in the same Machiavellian sense that Elizabeth was a "new prince": both sought to tame the revolutions of Fortuna by creating something new and lasting from the scattered remains of the ancient world.

But since Spenser's originary role depended upon his status as an imitator of classic authors, his opening moves can seem problematic when judged by more modern notions of original genius. The critical apparatus attached to the *Shepheardes Calender* and the *Faerie Queene* presupposes an understanding of imitation foreign to twentieth-century common readers. Its aims were both literary and moral. Humanists like Spenser did not accept the post-romantic distinction between poetry and criticism; for them, the practice of literary imitation was itself the primary critical mode. Composing verse was an act of criticism because it involved selecting, combining, and recasting literary models – originally Latin and Greek, though Spenser encouraged Britons to imitate Hebrew and British models as well. Like the three-faced figure of Prudence, Spenser's treatment of his sources looked backwards to sources of authority, outwards to contemporary reinterpretations of imitation, and ahead to later English poets who might use his own work as the basis for their own writing. As E. K. points out, the new poet situates himself within three traditions: Classical, Italian, and English. From Virgil, Mantuan, and Chaucer he selects and adapts characters, topics, versification, and poetic diction. The new poet was an emulator rather than a mere translator; his poems deliberately repeat their precedents with a difference. To establish a *new* beginning requires a break with the past, which Spenser accomplishes by imitating a vernacular writer – Chaucer – in the manner of Latin humanists. Spenser also strikes an aggressively modern, imperialist, and Protestant posture in his fables and allegories. These were bold and potentially dangerous moves at a time when Elizabeth was resisting political entanglements abroad and controversy at home; E. K. coyly remarks that "as touching the generall dryft and purpose of his Aeglogues, I mind not to say much, him selfe labouring to conceale it" (1579; *CH*, 39). E. K. tends to emphasize the more conservative aspects of the *Shepheardes Calender*, as when he catalogues the flock of poetic birds Spenser is joining: "So flew Theocritus, as you may perceiue he was all ready full fledged. So flew Virgile, as not yet well feeling his winges. So flew Mantuane, as being not full somd. So Petrarque. So Boccace; So Marot, Sanazarus, and also diuers other excellent both Italian and French Poetes, whose foting this Author euery where followeth, yet so as few, but they be wel sented can trace him out" (39). Those "few" would likely recognize the political allegory when they saw it and also recognize that some of these very authorities were being criticized.

If Spenser's pastoral allegory had precedents ancient and modern, E. K. concedes that "many thinges . . . in him be straunge," especially his diction, which at times becomes very rustic indeed. This would prove a sticking point with critics well into the nineteenth century; while Renaissance humanists could readily accept the idea of shepherds discussing theology and politics under the veil of allegory, they did not generally accept the use of "uncovthe" language in ambitious poetry. E. K. anticipates objections sure to come, scrambling to find "auctoritie" for "such olde and obsolete wordes [as] are most vsed of country folke." He finds authority for archaism in Livy and Sallust; while some have criticized such diction, "the best learned" accept archaic language as "an eternall image of antiquitie" (36). As though acknowledging that the point is moot, E. K. appends a more telling argument: Spenser "hath laboured to restore, as to theyr rightfull heritage such good and naturall English words, as haue ben long time out of vse and almost cleane disherited. Which is the onely cause, that our Mother tonge, truely of it self is both ful enough for prose and stately enough for verse, hath long time ben counted most bare and barrein of both. which default when as some endeuoured to salue and recure, they patche vp the holes with peces and rages of other languages." Despite the staid rhetoric of authority and inheritance, here is a radical argument for change: if British literature is to compete with its rivals, it must speak its own language, not a "gallimaufray or hodgepodge of al other speches" (37). To drive home the point, E. K. imitates Spenser's homely diction in his own critical discourse. The extent to which Spenser's diction was archaic or contemporary, regional or national, has been debated by philologists for several hundred years now, but we should not lose sight of the most significant matter, his decision to emulate Italian and French poets by writing and publishing a major poem in a classical genre in the vernacular language.

Spenser's striving to be British extended beyond the use of the English language; even before he published the *Shepheardes Calender* he was hard at work on a romantic poem based on national mythology. This too was the bold choice of an ambitious poet, though again following close on the recent (and hence less than fully authoritative) Italian precedent of Tasso and Ariosto. In the *Three Proper, and wittie, familiar Letters* of 1580 Spenser's correspondent Gabriel Harvey — sometimes thought to be E. K. himself — expressed alarm lest "the Faeyre Queene be fairer in your eie than the Nine Muses, and Hobgoblin runne away with the Garland from Apollo" (*CH*, 52). Why adopt a parochial

mythology in an avowedly modern genre when England still lacked a prop-
erly classical epic? One answer would be that Spenser was more concerned
with entering the literary lists with Catholic Europe than with pagan Rome.

When the first installment of the *Faerie Queene* appeared a decade later, it
was accompanied by Spenser's dedicatory sonnets and explanatory letter to Sir
Walter Raleigh, as well as commendatory verses by other hands, not all identi-
fiable. These courtly overtures link the *literary* emulation of the poem to the
high *political* aspirations the Raleigh faction held for Britain. Spenser's dedica-
tory sonnets to prominent courtiers situate the work in the world and the
world in the work, intertwining the two according to the doctrine of imitation:
just as persons at court have supposedly served as originals for characters in
the poem, so those characters might serve as originals for the court to emulate.
Spenser underscores the same kind of reciprocity in the letter to his friend Ral-
eigh; his purpose "is to fashion a gentleman or noble person in vertuous and
gentle discipline: Which for that I conceiued shoulde be most plausible and
pleasing, being coloured with an historical fiction, the which the most part of
men delight to read, rather for variety of matter, then for profite of the ensam-
ple" (*CH*, 45). On the one hand, "historical" promises a pleasant narrative, re-
plete with eventful matter. On the other, it implies a memorial of significant
events that might serve as an example for modern courtiers to take to heart.
Imitation links literary makers to political doers; both repeat the past with a
difference, becoming models in turn. Spenser and his readers were well aware
that the Arthurian legends had already served as "models" for modern ro-
mances written in Italian, French, and Spanish; the time had come to reclaim
and transform the national mythology in service to the growing Protestant
empire. If the *Faerie Queene* was to usher in a new era of literature and politics,
it must resolutely recreate its sources to meet the present requirements of the
new Troy a-building on the banks of the Thames.

As an ethical practice, imitation implies disciplined doing, the regular and
rule-governed repetition of one's own good actions or those of others until
they become habitual. Discipline is an affair of art rather than nature (though
its results were sometimes described as a "second" nature); Spenser's terms
"fashion" and "fiction" both derive from the Latin *facere*, "to do" or "to make."
The reciprocity between poetic and ethical making and doing, implied in the
commendatory sonnets and underscored in the letter to Raleigh, was central
to Spenser's notion of a national literature and appears repeated and amplified
throughout much of early criticism of the *Faerie Queene*. Over the next two cen-
turies the ethical and political rationale for imitation would slowly recede in the
face of a new set of epistemological concerns. With the passing of Renaissance
humanism, "fiction" lost its original connection with rule-governed imitation;
in postromantic criticism contemporaneous with more modern nationalisms,
poetry is generally thought to originate less from a disciplined and repetitive

making imposed upon previously existing materials than from an untrammeled and unprecedented *seeing*: genius is understood as a kind of creative autonomy that parallels the "constitutionalism" undergirding more liberal understandings of literature and politics. Yet Spenser was himself a romantic, and indeed something like the coming separation of "fact" from "fiction" already appears in his parallel between Plato's fictional *Republic* (fantastic and unprecedented in its very orderliness) and the more prosaic didacticism of Xenophon's *Cyropaedia*. Very possibly Spenser alludes to these rival disciples of Socrates in order to point up his way of sometimes opposing faerie mythology to British history and sometimes assimilating it. In the *Faerie Queene*, imaginary beings and historical personages inhabit the same moral landscape; they are generally indistinguishable as vehicles of instruction by repetition. Of course, such violations of decorum and general unwillingness to discriminate between mortals and monsters can also be regarded as the mark of an undisciplined, romantic genius. Spenser was imitating Italian romance as much as classical epic, itself no model of decorum, for that matter. The instabilities and paradoxes of Spenser's literary and political program were not lost on later readers; the letter to Raleigh, with its teetering balance between humanism and gothicism, worldly Xenophon and visionary Plato, would be construed in many and opposing ways by critics classical and romantical, aesthetical and philological. In this matter as in many others, the seeds of later criticism are to be found within Spenser's poetry itself. Considered in this light, much of the later criticism can itself be regarded as a form of "imitation."

The 1590 commendatory verses explore these themes in their praises of Spenser; they too insist upon the larger ethical and political significance of Spenser's historic acts of poetic imitation. Hobynoll (Gabriel Harvey) notes that Colin has repeated Virgil by lifting his "notes from Shepheardes vnto Kings." By comparing Sidney and Spenser to Ulysses and Achilles, W. I. parallels the deeds of ancients and moderns and implies that the composition of an epic poem is itself an act of epic proportion. R. S. refers to Spenser as "this Bryttane Orpheus," implying that he has political powers as a vatic lawgiver and magical powers as an inventor of "deepe conceites." In a poem that would find many echoes in seventeenth-century criticism, W. R. (Sir Walter Raleigh) praises Spenser's powers of emulation, describing in a vision how "all suddenly I saw the Faery Queene: / At whose approach the soule of Petrarke wept" – high praise indeed, and from a legitimate hero. Raleigh's choice of Petrarch rather than Tasso seems odd on literary grounds, but it makes sense given the project of establishing Spenser as the founding figure of a modern literature. As a group, the commendatory verses announce the larger aim of the new poet: to reconstruct a new Roman polis and literature by the shores of "Fayre Thamis streame, that from Ludds stately towne, / Runst paying tribute to the Ocean seas" (R. S.) (*CH*, 63–68). Spenser's two major poems, in short, were ushered into the world accompanied by a body of criticism stressing how creative imitation might establish a role for a new English poetry in a new English empire. For Spenser and his contemporaries, originality would be all but unthinkable without earlier precedent, an understanding of originality fraught with ethical and political implication. Appearing in such a prominent place, these critical utterances would become themselves objects of imitation in later criticism; they would guide the reception of Spenser's poetry and serve as models for criticism in their own right.

In a 1911 article, Edwin Greenlaw suggested that the *Shepheardes Calender* was not at first very popular, and indeed copies of the book itself are scarce. In 1913 C. R. Baskervill responded in "The Early Fame of 'The Shepheardes Calender'" by collecting a goodly handful of Elizabethan allusions to the poem, launching a decades-long attempt to collect all the early references to Spenser and his poetry, eventually published as *Spenser Allusions In the Sixteenth and Seventeenth Centuries* (1972). Despite the loss of many Elizabethan pamphlets and even more manuscript material, we can now see clearly just how popular Spenser was. References to and imitations of the *Shepheardes Calender* begin immediately, at a time when Spenser was out of England and his identity was known only to a small circle of academic and courtly friends. With the publication of the first three books of the *Faerie Queene* in 1590, Spenser became a national figure; London poetasters celebrated his fame and craved his acknowledgment; by the time of his death, well over a hundred references to Spenser or imitations of his work had appeared. This is a remarkable number; in the 1590s — for the first and last time — Spenser's admirers might boast that he was more popular than Shakespeare. Spenser's minor and occasional verse was then published (his earliest publication, a contribution to Van der Noodt's *Theatre for Voluptuous Wordlings* had appeared anonymously in 1569) — the "Fowre Hymnes," "Mother Hubberds Tale," "Epithalamion," "Prothalamion," and "Amoretti" — a highly diverse body of work written over a long period of time. Critics debate over the extent to which Spenser himself was involved in publishing this work, some of it written two decades earlier; it was now a salable commodity, though in the case of the occasional verse this may have been a matter of more concern to the bookseller than to the poet. In its mixture of high and low genres, and public and private utterances, the minor verse, printed in smaller formats, departs from the carefully crafted character built up in the major poems. "Colin Clouts Come Home Againe," with its tantalizing personal references, deliberately descends from the heights of Parnassus Spenser had worked so hard to scale. In such works the poet displays a fertility of invention, an intricate mastery of craft, and an ability to write across a broad scale of genres, things not unimportant to establishing one's self as a laureate poet as opposed to a polite amateur. On the other hand, Spenser's bitingly satirical verse does not conform to the public persona of the *Shepheardes*

Calender and the first installment of the *Faerie Queene* which are much more circumspect in criticizing the court. Was the poet settling old scores? Were his "friends" taking the initiative while Spenser was away in Ireland? When the second installment appeared in 1596, readers of books 5 and 6 might well have surmised that something odd was taking place in Fairy Land. If so, this does not appear until after Spenser's death, when rumours of poverty and unhappiness began to appear. The reception of the smaller poems was various. The vogue for writing sonnets quickly passed, leaving the *Amoretti* with few admirers. Spenser revived the epithalamium for seventeenth-century poets, though more classical models were generally preferred to his own; *Mother Hubberds Tale*, not much admired today, was read and imitated by neoclassical satirists. It was particularly popular during the reign of James I, when courts became a byword for corruption. Still, it was the public Colin of the first publications that caught the imagination of the first readers; the late work (or later published work), strangely beautiful as it often is, has never received the same kind of attention from critics. On the other hand, poets from Alexander Pope to T. S. Eliot plainly knew the smaller poems.

Whatever Spenser's second thoughts about his role as a court poet, it was his opening moves that ensured that he would be hailed as a founding figure, the Great Shepherd of Britain's poetical flock. Even before Spenser's identity was known, the *Shepheardes Calendar* was praised and imitated. In 1586 young William Webbe (1568–91) lauds "our late famous English poet, who wrote the Shepheards Calender" in *A Discourse of English Poetry* (*CH*, 56); three years later George Puttenham (d. 1590) speaks of "that other Gentleman who wrate the late shepherdes Callendar" (*CH*, 62). In the *Defense of Poesie* Sir Philip Sidney respected Spenser's anonymity: "the sheepheards Kallender, hath much Poetrie in his Egloge." Sidney was also the first on record to object to the "olde rusticke language" (1595; *CH*, 280). In 1593 "Learned Collin" was imitated wholesale by the ambitious Michael Drayton (1563–1611) in the *Shepherds Garland* (*CH*, 78) and in part by several lesser writers. In 1585 Spenser's pastorals were translated into Latin in a manuscript by John Dove, a mark of high approbation. Much early praise of Spenser takes the form of pastoral allegory; the language of shepherds was the language of criticism, at least for such as chose to write criticism in verse. The first professed imitation of the *Faerie Queene*, *Cynthia*, by Richard Barnfield (1574–1627), was published in 1595; in 1598 sixteen-year-old Francis Rous, future speaker of Parliament and provost of Eton College, imitated Spenser in a rambling allegorical narrative, *Thule, or Vertues Historie*. In his collection of sonnets, *Chloris* (1596), William Smith asks "Collin my deere and most entire beloued" to "Give warmth to these yoonghatched orphan things, / Which chill with cold to thee for succor creepe" (*SA*, 52); Thomas Edwards in *Cephalus and Procris* (1595) celebrates "Collyn" as a "mighty swaine, / In his power all do flourish" (*CH*, 87). In *Phillis* (1593) Thomas Lodge beckons poets to "where learned Colin feedes his louely flocke" (*CH*, 82). In expressing deference to the master they imitated, Elizabethan poets were not at all ashamed of presenting themselves as "sillie sheepe."

This posture must have come naturally, for one long-standing pattern was established very early: Spenser's readers and critics tended to be young men at school. While I haven't done the calculation, it appears that the typical age of those who comment on Spenser in the period prior to the twentieth century is likely to be under twenty-five. Long before the appearance of "scholarship" on Spenser, a substantial portion of the criticism is connected in one way or another with young scholars at the public schools, universities, and Inns of Court. An interesting instance of this phenomenon is Abraham Fraunce's *Arcadian Rhetorick: Or the Praecepts of Rhetorick Made Plain by Examples* (1588); the examples of rhetorical figures include passages from both the *Shepheardes Calender* and the *Faerie Queene*. The latter poem had yet to be published, of course, indicating that manuscripts were circulating among the poet's Cambridge acquaintances and were even then being used to instruct students in grammar, rhetoric, and logic. John Milton very likely encountered Spenser at Saint Paul's School, where the master, Alexander Gill, had used the *Faerie Queene* to illustrate rhetorical figures in his textbook, *Logonomia Anglica* (1619). Humanists used poetry to teach their more polite forms of logic than those favored by medieval doctors; Spenser thus appears in Fraunce's *Lawiers Logick* (1588) — might it have been read by John Donne and the other lawyer-wits? In the eighteenth century, college English as a discipline emerged from courses in philosophy taught by logicians like James Beattie. In the early seventeenth century, Spenser enjoyed something like cult status among a group of law students associated with London's Inns of Court: William Browne, George Wither, and Christopher Brooke used allusions to the *Shepheardes Calender* to define themselves as a literary "school." In various guises, Spenser figures in several theatricals performed at both the universities and the Inns of Court. In both "Comus" and "Lycidas" John Milton drew upon Spenser and academic pastoralism to celebrate Spenser's achievements and to define his own neoromantic conception of the greater aims of poetry and education. Although the belated Spenserianism of Milton's 1645 *Poems* attracted little attention from contemporaries, a century later its pastoral allegories served young romantics as object lessons in "how to read Spenser" and led the way to a whole new appreciation of Elizabethan poetry, a phenomenon that was, once again, centered in the schools and universities.

The best evidence for the breadth of Spenser's first readership comes from the drama. George Peele early imitated the *Shepheardes Calender* in *The Araygnement of Paris* (1584); Christopher Marlowe must have seen a manuscript of the *Faerie Queene*, for in *Tamburlaine the Greate* (1590) he imitated passages prior to their publication; W. S. imitates Spenser's *Complaints* in *Locrine* (1595), as does

Robert Greene in *Alphonsus* (1599). Cyril Tourneur imitates Spenser in *The Transformed Metamorphosis* (1600): "Thus (pricking on the plaine) at last he ey'd / The grisly beast as in her den she lay" (*SA*, 81), as does Chapman in *Monsieur D'Olive* (1606). These examples could be multiplied; plainly, Spenser's poetry was a topic of conversation in London and elsewhere. Spenser's pastoral characters appear in several college theatricals – the early, goatish origins of academic criticism. In the anonymous *Returne from Parnassus* (1606) for instance, Ingenioso and Iudicio deliver their "judgement of Spencer":

> Iudicio: A sweeter swan then euer song in Poe,
> A shriller Nightingale then euer blest
> The prouder groues of self admiring Rome.
> Blith was each vally, and each sheapeard proud,
> While he did chaunt his rural minstralsye.
> Attentiue was full many a dainty eare.
> Nay hearers hong vpon his melting tong,
> While sweetly of his Faeiry Queene he song . . . .
>
> Ingenioso: Pity it is that gentler witts should breed,
> Where thickskin chuffes laugh at a schollers need.
> But softly may our [Homer's] ashes rest,
> That lie by mery Chaucers noble chest.

(CH, 116–17)

Whatever his fortunes elsewhere, Spenser has always had friends among the scholars. But he was also well known to pamphleteers and poetasters in the literary underworld in London; a raft of Spenser's characters – Florimell, Paridell, Satyrane – make cameo appearances in Thomas Dekker's *Whore of Babylon* (1607).

Spenser Among the Epigrammatists

Praise and emulation came quickly, yet after the appearance of the first folio edition of Spenser's works in 1617 more than six decades would pass before the next. There were occasional imitations and indeed a Caroline "school of Spenser," yet the quantity of Spenserian verse plainly diminished rapidly after Spenser's death. Does this indicate a decline in reputation? Spenser has always enjoyed more fame than popularity, an important distinction prior to the twentieth century. If popularity were the issue, Shakespeare would have been regarded as much the greater poet, which he was not, at least until comparatively modern times. In Spenser's lifetime and long afterward, literary laurels were not regarded as something to be obtained in the playhouse, despite the heroic efforts of Jonson and Dryden. While poets and critics might argue otherwise, prejudice demanded that fame be won in head-to-head emulation with Homer and Virgil in epic poetry; it would take a work of the magnitude of *Paradise Lost* to change this view. Success or failure in such contests was to be assessed by the few rather than the many; even as Spenser's manner became obsolete, the best judges – Drayton and Jonson, Milton and Cowley, and Denham and Dryden – unanimously marked out Spenser as *the* Modern among Moderns. For the most part, their testimony was ratified by a consensus of lesser judges, those Pope memorably described as "the mob of gentlemen, who wrote with ease." The evidence is there for all to see: if one attends to what was actually written, it becomes obvious that Spenser's fame was never higher than in those decades of the seventeenth century when his "influence" and popularity was slightest. At a time when writing an epic poem was regarded as the highest achievement of the human intellect, the Prince of Poets had no serious rivals – until both he and the national epic were trumped by John Milton, emulating God himself in a poem on the Creation.

The extent and quality of Spenser criticism in the seventeenth century might appear negligible until one realizes that most of it was written in verse, and that often for purposes unfamiliar to us. Before 1750, literary criticism in its now familiar forms hardly existed; seventeenth-century authors did not publish book reviews, interpretive essays, literary biographies, or academic monographs. Most of their criticism was composed in verse because those cultivating English literature did not distinguish between creative and discursive writing. This distinction begins (not coincidentally) with those later genres of criticism. The early critics wrote in verse at least in part because they were more interested in marking general characters than in forming nuanced aesthetic judgments. Poetry was chosen as the proper means of performing an ethical action – celebrating virtue and fame or censuring folly and vice. Only later would poetry become, as in John Keats's "On First Looking into Chapman's Homer," primarily a vehicle for describing an aesthetic response. While Jonson, Milton, Davenant, Cowley, Dryden, Addison, and Pope all made significant comments about Spenser in prose, they were not practicing criticism in our modern sense; as humanists they were more interested in assessing a poet's virtue than in interpreting his poetry. That is why most seventeenth- and much eighteenth-century criticism is written in epigrammatic verse. Epigram was fame's peculiar form; while the popularity of this genre has been taken to mark Spenser's eclipse, epigrammatists of both "the school of Donne" and "the tribe of Ben" were never shy about praising Edmund Spenser, even as they declined to imitate or emulate his more ornate poetical manner.

The substitution of epigram for pastoral allegory in seventeenth-century critical writing deserves some comment. Spenser, who signed himself "Colin Clout," was so closely associated with pastoral verse that in any given era his reputation can almost be measured by the presence or absence of important work in this genre. For more than two centuries, each succeeding Spenserian revival was marked by a new version of pastoral; in the seventeenth century, nothing marks an allegiance to Spenser more clearly than the use of pastoral allegory, "Comus" and "Lycidas" being prime examples. No doubt the demise of Elizabethan pastoral was partly a matter of taste, Moderns of Ben Jonson's generation preferring strong lines and classical simplicity in diction. There were other things involved in this shift in critical modes. In the sixteenth century, wool was where the money came from, and money was concentrated in the court. In the seventeenth century, as fashionable fortunes were being made in mercantile adventures abroad and scientific agriculture at home, the pastoral fantasies of courtly poetry began to yield to epigram and georgic verse.

Georgic (the word is derived from geo) was a genre particularly fruitful in the metaphors that would later coalesce into modern understandings of "culture." Georgic metaphors are prominent in a manuscript (ca. 1628) by the seventeenth century virtuoso and admirer of Spenser, Sir Kenelm Digby (1603–65): "He shall have but a superficial view of the most prominent parts [of a great poet], without being able to make any discovery of into the large continent that lyeth behind those; wherein usually is the richest soyle . . . . [Spenser's] learned workes confirme me in the beliefe that our NORTHEREN climate may give life to as well tempered a brain, and as rich a mind as where the sunne shineth fairest. When I read him methinks our country needeth not envy either GREECE, ROME or TUSCANY . . . . And if at any time he plucketh a flower out of their gardens, he transplanteth it soe happily into his owne, that it groweth there fairere and sweeter then it did where first it sprang up" (*CH*, 148). The presiding classical authorities in epigram and georgic were Martial and Virgil; yet as recreated in Britain both genres were decidedly modern both in their empirical particularity and in their celebrations of personal liberty in the face of courtly deference and corruption. Linking verse to virtue (or vice), epigram became the primary critical medium in the politically fractious Stuart age; through this genre Spenser's authority was defined and promulgated among a more classically minded group of readers in an increasingly less courtly reading public. Such epigrams, of which thousands survive, became the common currency for both Royalists and Parliamentarians. With their emphasis on the characters of virtues and vices, seventeenth-century epigrams praising Spenser might be regarded as extensions of Spenser's poetry itself, unlike as they are in other respects. The differences are telling, however: while the verses attached to the *Faerie Queene* stress the importance of character and the usefulness of poetry for forming ethical judgments, they present highly idealized portraits of their subjects. Epigrams were much more detailed and personal, increasingly so as the century wore on. The definition and expression of moral "types" changed as allegory yielded to the more probabilistic and empirical modes of description that are common to epigram and georgic. In their specificity of language and nuance, seventeenth-century epigrams laid the foundation for both modern poetics and modern literary criticism in prose.

In the earlier epigrams, however, an author's "character" was less a function of his individual manner than of his place on an impersonal grid of traditional names. The word "character" had connotations very similar to "sign"; like signs, characters and marks of character operated within a system constructed around points of affinity and opposition. The epigrams habitually illustrate Spenser's character by locating the poet within a constellation of related figures, as in the lines Samuel Daniel addressed to the countess of Pembroke:

> Whereby great SYDNEY & our SPENSER might,
> With those Po-singers beeing equalled,
> Enchaunt the world with such a sweet delight,
> That theyr eternall songs (for euer read,)
> May shew what great ELIZAS raigne hath bred.
> What musique in the kingdome of her peace,
> Hath now beene made to her, and by her might,
> Whereby her glorious fame shall never cease.
>
> (1594; *CH*, 75)

Daniel compares the renaissance in English poetry to the reconstruction of classical verse by the modern "Po-singers" in northern Italy; rebirth is achieved through emulation among Ancients and Moderns, Italians and Englishmen. The reciprocal relation between rhyming and reigning suggests a further "breeding" of parallels in the character of Elizabeth and her poets: "to her, and by her." In 1614, a generation later, John Norden (1548–ca. 1625), surveyor and topographer, measures the reputation of Sidney and Spenser in a prospect view of English writers:

> Chawcer, Gower, the bishop of dunkell,
> In ages farre remote were eloquent:
> Now Sidney, Spencer, others moe excell,
> And are in latter times more excellent,
> To antique Lauriats paralell.
>
> (*CH*, 130)

Daniel underscores equality, Norden superiority, but both use a "paralell" to define character and chalk off degrees of fame. Such conjunctions of names were standardized in the handbooks employed in grammar schools, like *Palladis Tamia* (1598) by Francis Meres (1565–1647), which is, among other things, a catalogue of catalogues such as this one:

As the Greeke tongue is made famous and eloquent by Homer, Hesiod, Euripedes, Aeschilus, Sophocles, Pindarus, Phoclides, and Aristophanes; and the Latine tongue by Virgill, Ouid, Horace, Silius Italicus, Lucanus, Lucretius, Ausonius and Claudianus: so the English tongue is mightily enriched and gorgeously inuested in rare ornaments and resplendent abiliments by sir Philip Sidney, Spencer, Daniel, Drayton, Warner, Shakespeare, Marlow and Chapman. (*CH*, 96)

When names in catalogues are adorned and amplified with epithets, they sort the poets as well as group them; thus in his *Bumble Bee* (1599) – the title signifies fruitful pollination as well as a sting at the back – the satirist Thomas Cutwode attaches a brief character to each name in a catalogue of Ancients and Moderns: "Virgil, the curious Ape of Homer. Ouid the Amorous, Martiall the lycentious, Horace the mixt betwixt modest & satirique vaine. The flower of our age, sweete pleasing Sidney. Tasso the grave. Pollished Daniel the Historick Spencer the Truthes Faith" (*SA*, 64).

If epigrammatic characters work like signs in a semiotic diagram, they sometimes approach the condition of "types" in the scriptural sense of typology; thus the sense of historical repetition and fulfillment in Sir John Stradling's "To Edmund Spenser, the British Homer" (1607): "Si nos Troiani, noua nobis Troia sit: Ipse / (Vt Gracis suus est) noster Homerus eris" ("If we are Trojans, we have a new Troy. You (as for the Greeks theirs is) shall be our Homer"; 21; trans. Cummings, *CH*, 123). Much as interpreters used typology to integrate the New Testament with the Old, so epigrammatists used types and characters to mark off the rebirth of classical literature. Taking his cue from the dedicatory sonnets in the *Faerie Queene*, in 1596 Charles Fitzgeffrey, singing the exploits of Sir Francis Drake, salutes "SPENSER whose hart inharbours Homers soule," a "Type of true honour" (*CH*, 89). More commonly, Spenser (who follows upon Chaucer-as-Homer) is "the English Virgill," as R. C. expresses it in 1651 with a nod toward Raleigh and Sir Kenelm Digby (*CH*, 189); in 1635 Edmund Johnson suggests a transmigration of souls: "Thus, by Soule-shifting, Virgil's ghost did wend / To Spenser's lodge" (*SA*, 193). The earlier epigrams usually juxtaposed Spenser with the ancients; as the decades passed and English literature became better established, his name was more frequently paired with shifting groups of modern writers, at first with Sidney, Daniel, and Du Bartas. Only much later, in the middle of the eighteenth century, did the canonical quartet of Chaucer-Spenser-Shakespeare-Milton emerge as the final product of all this sorting and shifting. The redundancy of names occurring in georgic and epigrammatic catalogues bespeaks a desire to shape the vernacular canon through repetition and emulation – a procedure not unrelated to the pedagogy of habit formation Spenser outlines in his letter to Raleigh. Spenser's fame, after all, was established through habitual repetition of his name; the appended epithets indicate which of his qualities others might emulate or avoid. Epigrams themselves were known to enter into emulative combat with other epigrams, most notably in Ben Jonson's testy lines on

Shakespeare, appearing in the First Folio published in 1623: "I will not lodge thee by / Chaucer, or Spenser . . . . Thou art a monument without a tomb" (*SA*, 168). Monumentality, that is, is bestowed by appearance in a printed folio.

The concatenations of poetical names, their selection and orders of priority, often positioned the epigrammatist as a member of a group of readers. In *The Purple Island*, by the Cambridge poet Phineas Fletcher (1582–1650) signals allegiance to Spenser and his school by imitating the *Faerie Queene* in modified Spenserians; his poem (written about 1610 and published in 1633) includes stanza-epigrams that make its loyalties even more explicit:

> Two shepherds most I love with just adoring;
> That Mantuan swain, who chang'd his slender reed
> To trumpets martiall voice, and warres loud roaring,
> From Corydon to Turnus derring-deed:
> And next our home-bred Colins sweetest firing;
> Their steps not following close, but farre admiring:
> To lackey one of these is all my prides aspiring.
>
> (*CH*, 167)

Note the pastoral conceits signaling Fletcher's adherence to the school of Colin Clout. There was an art to knowing which authorities to cite and which comparisons to make – ancient or modern, Italian or French, court or country, lyrical or dramatical, epical or epigrammatical – though the aesthetic and political nuances are not always easy to grasp at this distance of time. Then as now there was social pressure to conform, so that Spenser was praised by writers one would hardly identify with the school of Spenser. Cambridge poets, like young Joseph Hall (1574–1656), would be expected to acknowledge their own, which the bishop-to-be does in "His Defiance of Enuy." Yet even in 1597 Hall appears to be practicing the equivocation Milton would later find so reprehensible: Hall ridicules those who write of "rusted swords of Eluish knights, / Bathed in Pagan blood: or sheath them new / In misty morall Types" but makes an exception for "Renowmed Spencer: whom no earthly wight / Dares once to emulate" (*CH*, 91–92). While the latter lines have been used by Thomas Warton and others to enlist Hall among our poet's admirers, and while indeed Hall always speaks *explicitly* in Spenser's praise, one wonders: might *dares* not emulate imply *should* not emulate? Hall's own muse certainly took a different bent. Ben Jonson admired Spenser, though like Hall he was no great admirer of the Elizabethans. Jonson, who was nothing if not a competitive writer, seems to me similarly slippery. An entry in *Timber* (1640) censures Spenser's manner though he "would have him read for his matter"; in conversation Jonson told William Drummond, "Spenser's stanzaes pleased him not, nor his matter" (*CH*, 294, 135). Critics of all schools recognized and praised Spenser's personal achievements.

Epigrams generally speak in the voice of conventional wisdom, by its nature subject to change. As we have seen, the significance of the name "Spenser" varies with the constellations of names in which it appears, at first commonly grouped with Homer and Virgil, later with Ariosto and Tasso, much later with Shakespeare and Milton. In the first instance Spenser is the reincarnation of classical authority, in the second a modern innovator, in the third a compass point for British poetry. As time passes, the epigrams begin to attend less to the public generalities of his matter than to the private particularities of his manner. As that manner began to seem outmoded in the second and third decades of the seventeenth century Spenser was regarded less as a paradigm for contemporary verse than as the initiator of a process of continuing growth and refinement. This kind of perception required a conceptual change, from marking out parallel types on a grid to observing stages in a temporal progression; in consequence, verse criticism underwent a formal change, from collections of single epigrams to concatenations of epigrams interpolated into odes, satires, verse epistles, and georgic poems. The longer forms encouraged more complex thinking about literary history. By the 1650s, for example, Spenser was sometimes regarded as a founder of neoclassicism, sometimes hailed as a native alternative to a slavish imitation of the ancients. In the latter case, as Spenser was diminished in his status as Virgil *redivivus*, he began gaining an even higher reputation as an original genius in his own right. Among those in the former camp, Sir John Denham (1615–69) – Son of Ben – praises Spenser in "On Mr. Abraham Cowley" (1668) as a forerunner of classicism: "Next (like Aurora) Spencer rose, / Whose purple blush the day foreshows" (*CH*, 198). In 1653 Denham took a swipe at an attempt by William Davenant (a belligerent "Modern" of the opposing camp) to overgo both Spenser and the classics; his *Gondibert* "Can silence Tasso, and the Fairy-Queen, / Though all by Will unread, and most unseen" ("To Daphne"; *SA*, 235). At times, mid-century discussions about literary history begin to resemble political debates over the Ancient Constitution, for the problem of conceptualizing identity in time was common to both. Genealogical questions set the stage for a long-running controversy – classic Spenser versus romantic Spenser, Ancients criticism versus Moderns criticism – that sustained Spenser's reputation while eventually rendering his humanist poetics incomprehensible in its own (admittedly equivocal) terms.

Seventeenth-Century Imitations

No doubt seventeenth-century readers pondered the depths of Spenser's reflections on faith, temperance, and chastity; studied his allusions and iconography;

speculated over the historical and political identities of his allegorical person-
ages; and debated the relative merits of Platonic and Aristotelian doctrine in
his philosophy. But because students were not yet writing interpretative essays,
nor scholars publishing learned articles, we are left mostly with the inferences
we can draw from marginalia. The written evidence surviving in abundance –
verse epigrams – suggests that seventeenth-century readers were much more
concerned than we have been about Spenser's status as a classic, his selection
of models, his success in the competition among ancient and modern litera-
tures, and the applicability of his political and theological doctrines to current
affairs. This last was inevitable in the "culture wars" of the Stuart period; the
era yielded both a *Faerie King* (ca. 1655) and a *Faerie Leveller* (1648). The hyper-
monarchical, hyper-Protestant Spenser appealed to both Cavaliers and
Roundheads (though it seems that the court party had more to say about
him). Other sorts of divide were almost as important, such as the choice be-
tween the active and the retired life, forced, at various times, upon members of
either faction. In 1645, Milton's L'Allegro, musing on tilts and fair ladies, rep-
resents one kind of seventeenth-century reader of Spenser, while his antisocial
counterpart, pursuing sage and solemn tunes "Of Forests, and inchantments
drear, / Where more is meant than meets the ear" is yet another (*CH* 162). We
can follow the intricacies of a Penseroso's speculations in the pamphlet pub-
lished in 1643 by Sir Kenelm Digby, *Observations on the 22. Stanza in the 9th Canto
of the 2d. Book of Spencers Faery Queene*. Digby brings all the resources of neopla-
tonic mysticism to bear on a passage "dictated by such a learned Spirit, and so
generally a knowing Soul, that were there nothing else extant of Spencers writ-
ing, yet these few words would make me esteeme him no whit inferiour to the
most famous men that ever have been in any age" (*CH*, 151). This unusual
"close reading" is the exception that proves the rule, for Digby is more con-
cerned with the text of Plotinus than the text of Spenser; this display of wit
made Digby something of a famous man himself, celebrated in epigrams by
Ben Jonson and Thomas May. George Herbert and Richard Crashaw seem
not to have taken an interest in Spenser, but other religious poets of a Platonic
stripe certainly did. Earlier in the century Giles Fletcher (younger brother of
Phineas) sang the mysteries of salvation history in a imitation of Spenserian al-
legory entitled *Christs Victorie and Triumph on Heaven and Earth* (1610). In 1648
Joseph Beaumont of Cambridge University imitated Spenser in a sprawling
religious allegory called *Psyche*; at forty-thousand lines it is longer than the
Faerie Queene itself. Henry More (1614–87), the saintly Cambridge Platonist
and sometime opponent of Beaumont, imitated Spenser in his vast "Platonicall
Song of the Soul" (1642) and alluded to him as a mentor in *Conjectura Cabbalis-
tica* (1653) and other philosophical writings. In 1650 the Welsh magician (and
Oxford man) Thomas Vaughan snapped that "it is suppos'd he [More] is in
Love with his Fairie Queene, & this hath made him a very Elf in Philosophie"

(*SA*, 227). One might expect allegorical interpretation in *Mythomystes, Wherein a Short Survey Is Taken of the Nature and Value of True Poetry*, yet in 1632 Drayton's shadowy friend Henry Reynolds sees only "an exact body of the Ethicke doctrine" (*CH*, 164). And that, ultimately, seems to have been what the Puritanical John Milton valued most; in *Areopagitica* (1644) he lauds "our sage and serious Poet Spencer, whom I dare be known to think a better teacher then Scotus or Aquinas" (*CH*, 163). This is a fine compliment from a poet more learned than Spenser but equally committed to the active life. The republican Milton shared Spenser's conception of a redeeming Protestant mission, even has he rejected Spenser's belief in the divine nature of monarchy.

Perhaps the best evidence for how Spenser was being read lies in the verse imitations themselves. While the epigrams and poetical dictionaries were delivering common sense to common readers, a second generation of Spenserian poets was breaking new ground. These writers – Michael Drayton (1563–1631), Robert Aylett (1583–1655), William Browne (1590–1645), George Wither (1588–1667), Francis Quarles (1592–1644), Phineas and Giles Fletcher (1582–1650; 1585–1623) – were variously clergymen, lawyers, and country gentlemen. Most began their careers by imitating Spenser's imitations of Virgil's pastorals, though only Michael Drayton, the senior member, made a serious attempt to pursue the laurel as Davenant, Milton, and Cowley would later. Satisfied, perhaps, that England had her Virgil, the second-generation Spenserians were largely content to express their lesser ambitions in lesser forms, though they often smuggled great matters into smaller genres. Despite the fact that many of these poets began their careers with formal eclogues, their nod towards Virgil was indirect and superficial; at a time when Ben Jonson was establishing strict norms for imitating classical poets, Jacobean and Caroline Spenserians were more inclined to follow the lead of Spenser and the Frenchman Du Bartas in recasting scripture in nonclassical modes. Confirmed classicists like Jonson set aside earlier traditions in Renaissance humanism and imitated Latin writers directly. The Spenserians not only imitated a Modern, they tried to imitate him in his very modernity, which required that they emulate, amplify, and embellish in original directions. Spenser, after all, was no more a clone of Chaucer than he was a slave to Virgil. Not for them a Colin treading carefully in the steps of Virgil, but the bold Modern who had initiated English Protestant poetry as such. As devoted Moderns, they imitated Spenser's archaisms only fitfully; archaic diction dwindles among seventeenth-century writers until it all but disappears among Restoration Spenserians, Milton included. In one sense, such departures are typical of humanism: imitators were expected to emulate selectively and critically. In another, their unwillingness to adhere to the master's manner looks forward to the cult of originality in the later generations of professedly romantic poets. The more sophisticated thinking about history was beginning to render imitation problematic for poets long before the issues were explicitly formulated by the critics. A brief sketch of Spenserian poetry will indicate how various and critical Moderns' imitation could be.

The imitators chose selectively from the wide range of stylistic features made available to those wishing to represent themselves as specifically British poets. While it would later become a hallmark of romantic Spenserianism, very few seventeenth-century writers actually employed the stanza of the *Faerie Queene*. Giles and Phineas Fletcher imitated Spenser by affixing a concluding alexandrine to other kinds of stanza; John Dryden introduced alexandrines into couplet verse as a "Spenserian" liberty; still later, Matthew Prior added a tenth line to Spenser's stanza to make it more regular. Dryden, Thomson, Beattie, Wordsworth, and Keats selectively plundered Spenser's archaisms, Latinisms, and coinages while adding many newly minted words to the treasury. In the wake of Samuel Butler's *Hudibras* (1663), archaisms became the special province of burlesque; Spenser was lovingly burlesqued by John Gay in *The Shepherd's Week* (1714), Alexander Pope in "The Alley" (1727), and William Shenstone in *The School-Mistress* (1737). Beginning with the Fletchers, decorative "Spenserian" diction (with a boost from Sylvester's Du Bartas) evolved into the painterly language of natural description in philosophical verse by John Milton, James Thomson, Erasmus Darwin, and a host of lesser figures. The difficult form of Spenser's sonnet (developed independently in Scotland) had been adopted occasionally by Daniel and a few other Elizabethans, though the *Amoretti* proved to be the least popular and least respected of Spenser's larger works. Nonetheless, when sonnets began to be written once more, the Spenserian form was the first to be revived by the eighteenth-century romantics Thomas Edwards and Bishop Percy.

With the exception of the special case of formal eclogue, Spenser was seldom imitated in the literal way that Jonson or Pope imitated Horace. Apart from the occasional continuation, modernization, or burlesque, there were no more *Faerie Queenes*. The most common procedure among later Spenserians was to expand an episode into a free standing work in a different kind. Phineas Fletcher, for example, reworks the religious controversy of book 1 into his anti-Jesuit satire *The Apollyonists* (ca. 1610; 1627) and expands the machinery of the House of Alma into his book-length allegory of the human body and soul, *Purple Island*. William Browne trims the pastoral material of book 6 to epic (more properly, georgic) proportions in *Britannia's Pastorals* (1613, 1616). Drayton expands the Marriage of the Thames and Medway into his longer than epic-length *Poly-Olbion* (1612–22). Beginning in 1622, Robert Aylett (ca. 1583– ca. 1655) drew on the House of Holiness for a clutch of devotional meditations written in Spenserians, collected in *Divine and Moral Speculations in Metrical Numbers* (1653). The Bower of Bliss episode became the basis for many later imitations, most notably John Milton's "Comus" (1637) and James Thomson's *The*

Castle of Indolence (1748). Imitating Spenser at greater distance, Pope revived and adapted the quest for the Blatant Beast in his *Dunciad* (1728–42). Spenserian allegory went into remission during the process of seventeenth-century modernizing but made a comeback in the process of eighteenth-century archaizing. The generic heterogeneity of the *Faerie Queene* encouraged selective imitation and ensured the popularity of the poem even as every one of its cardinal features now and again came under strong criticism. That no major writer – Renaissance, Augustan, or romantic – attempted to imitate Spenser's epic wholesale indicates implicit criticism rather than anxiety of influence; heroic verse found new homes in drama, satire and the Pindaric ode, while later writers demoted the tale-weaving techniques of renaissance epic to romances, and – later – novels that were written in prose. Anxiety is more visible in their unwillingness, at times, to criticize Spenser overtly. Poet-critics like Jonson and Wordsworth hesitated to undermine the authority of the acknowledged father of English verse; Dryden went out of his way to praise Spenser. The diminished presence of Spenserianism in Restoration verse – in Cowley's and Milton's epics, or Dryden's satires – is a more telling criticism than any overt complaint about the diction, design, or stanza of the *Faerie Queene.* Jonson, Cowley, Milton, and Dryden knew Spenser intimately and admired him, but as humanist writers who accepted the direct link between literary and ethical imitation, they were bound to reject Tudor poetics along with Tudor politics. Even so, elements of Spenserianism continued to appear, like those of the gothic architecture to which it was later compared.

Spenser among Ancients and Moderns

Changes in the political landscape led to changes in the grounds of criticism and changes in the grounds of criticism led to changes in the genres in which criticism was written. Modern prose criticism took rise from mid-seventeenth century developments in the essay, a word that means "trial" and that was associated with experimentation and the New Science. Like the epigram, the essay was a genre with no specific content of its own. It was an instrument for observation; like contemporary optical devices, it could be used to examine fine details or vast prospects. Before the invention of periodicals, critical essays took the form of prefaces to plays and volumes of poetry. These began as letters such as the ones to Harvey and Raleigh appended to the *Shepheardes Calender* and the *Faerie Queene.* The letter format implied personal relationships among scholars and courtiers, poets and patrons – an intimacy that was gradually abandoned in prefaces as commercial publication displaced manuscript circulation and an anonymous reading public began to develop. The work of creating this public, which might be said to begin with Spenser's decision to circulate his works in print, was a group enterprise self-consciously un-

dertaken by a later generation of epigrammatists and essayists. The familiar
essay expressed its modernity in a desire to fit the language of criticism to the
changing language of the age; to several seventeenth-century essayists, Spenser
appeared as a relic of bygone times. Francis Atterbury's 1690 preface to
Waller's *Poems* takes notice of the change: "in the mean time, 'tis a surprizing
Reflection, that between what Spencer wrote last, and Waller first, there
should not be much above twenty years distance: and yet the one's Language,
like the Money of that time, is as currant now as ever; whilst the other's words
are like old Coyns, one must go to an Antiquary to understand their true
meaning and value" (*CH*, 302–3). As the simile indicates, commerce – literary,
financial, and social – was transforming the practices of criticism. But as far as
Spenser was concerned, this cloud had a silver lining; as his poems lost one
kind of currency, they gained yet another: old coins and medals were never
valued more highly than at the time Atterbury's preface was written.

It was a firm nineteenth-century conviction that neoclassical critics failed to
understand romantic Spenser. In some cases this is true, but it is not difficult to
turn the table and argue that classicists like Jonson and Dryden understood
Spenser better than most of the romantics who idolized him. Spenser's poetry
was criticized *because* it was understood. Sir William Davenant (1606–68), who
had aroused Denham's ire for presuming to better Spenser, is a good case in
point. Davenant began writing court masques, was exiled to France, and after
the Restoration became a playwright and theater manager. As a "modern"
epic, Davenant's heroic *Gondibert* (1651) attempted to do for the reign of Char-
les what Spenser had done for that of Elizabeth, which required rethinking the
presentation of national origins. Davenant attempted to supply the "regularity"
lacking in Spenser by making the design of the poem accord with the Aristote-
lian strictures on tragedy. His preface, the famous letter to his mentor Thomas
Hobbes (1650), imitates Spenser's equally famous letter to Raleigh; it makes
clear that the poet shares Spenser's conception of the larger ethical, political,
and religious functions of heroic poetry. While he finds fault with the *Faerie
Queene*, Davenant holds Spenser in higher regard than later readers who found
only beauties: Spenser has performed a work to "outlast even Makers of Laws
and Founders of Empires"; he has accomplished something that "yeelds not to
any other humane work" (Spingarn, 2:6, 5). As a modern poet, Spenser has
followed the Baconian injunction to sail beyond the Pillars of Hercules into
"untry'd Seas" (2:2). To imitate Spenser, therefore, it is necessary to overgo
Spenser. In a prefatory epistle, Abraham Cowley slyly compares William
Davenant to Spenser's own hero Guyon, who in the name of moderation
overturns Acrasia's Bower of Bliss:

> Methinks Heroick Poesie, till now
> Like some fantastick Fairy land did show;
> Gods, Devils, Nymphs, Witches, & Giants race,

And all but man, in mans best work had place.
Thou like some worthy Knight, with sacred Arms
Dost drive the *Monsters* thence, and end the Charms.

(*CH*, 185)

Cowley might more prudently have invoked the inscription in Busirane's Palace — "Be bold . . . Be not too bold." Spenser, who in the letter to Raleigh deferred to the authority of Plato and Xenophon, is less presumptuous than Davenant, though in its departures from epics ancient and modern, the *Faerie Queene* was doing in fact what Davenant tried and failed to accomplish in *Gondibert*.

Since the very concept of progress implies that later poets should refine and improve upon the work of earlier poets, Davenant finds it necessary to reopen the question of imitation: "For whilst we imitate others, we can no more excel them, then he that sailes by others Mapps can make a new discovery" (2:7). Nonetheless, Davenant alludes with approval to Aristotle's discussion of imitation in the *Nichomachian Ethics*. While imitation can be a hindrance to literary innovation, he concludes, it also serves as a useful check to error and excess. This shared belief in the virtue of literary imitation differentiates Spenser and Davenant from much later criticism of the *Faerie Queene*. For Renaissance humanists, the issue was not whether or not to imitate, but what and how to imitate. The consensus of seventeenth-century readers believed that Spenser's archaisms run contrary to the Modern's dictum that poetry should speak the language of polite society; to imitate Spenser in his rusticity would run counter to the whole project of reforming and refining the language to compete with other literatures. Davenant expresses this in a characteristically georgic metaphor: "It is false husbandry to graft old branches upon young stocks, so we may wonder that our Language (not long before his time created out of a confusion of others, and then beginning to flourish like a new Plant) should as helps to its increase receive from his hand new grafts of old wither'd words." And in an oft-cited passage, Davenant faults Spenser for his stanza: "This vulgar exception, shall only have the vulgar excuse; which is, that the unlucky choice of his Stanza, hath by repetition of Rime brought him to the necessity of many exploded words" (2:6). If the sentiment accords with the New Science, Davenant's metaphor also glances at contemporary politics by alluding to the great theme of Virgil's *Georgics*, which marked the passage from a state of civil war to an age of civility and improvement. The objection to Spenser's archaisms is thus more than merely aesthetic; peace, progress, and commerce require the use of a common language. For similar reasons, as a disciple of Hobbes, Davenant objects to Spenser's allegory, "by many held defective in the connexion, resembling, methinks, a continuance of extraordinary Dreams, such as excellent Poets and Painters, by being over-studious, may have in the beginning of Feavers: And those moral Visions are just of so much use to humane application as painted History, when with the cousenage of lights it is represented in Scenes, by which we are much lesse inform'd then by actions on the Stage" (2:6–7). Progress demands more regular standards of probability – like the scenic machinery Davenant was introducing to the reformed stage: heroic poetry should imitate not feverish visions but "the World's true image" (2:3); its medium should be not painted words but substantive things, the significant actions of men. Because of his failure to imitate properly, Spenser has fulfilled his ethical design imperfectly. The discourse prefaced to *Gondibert* was much the most substantial criticism of the *Faerie Queene* to date and was quoted throughout the eighteenth century, long after Davenant's reputation as a poet had gone into decline.

Thomas Hobbes, philosopher and poetaster, responded with a laudatory letter that takes an even more modern stance. If Davenant's many comparisons of poetry to painting already indicate an interest in the psychology of images, Hobbes's commitment to the new epistemology is even stronger: "Time and Education begets experience; Experience begets memory; Memory begets Judgement and Fancy: Judgement begets the strength and structure, and Fancy begets the ornaments of a Poem" (1650; Spingarn, 2:59). "Poets are Painters" says Hobbes (2:61), and no doubt Spenser would agree. But for Hobbes verbal painting is less a matter of making authority memorable through allegorical signs than of organizing sense data through perspective devices. The furniture of Alma's Castle is thus rearranged: in the *Faerie Queene*, the imagination itself is a rational (though slippery) element of mind; Phantastes, surrounded by "Deuices, dreames, opinions vnsound," has yet "a sharpe foresight, and working wit" (II.ix.49, 51). A potent imaginative faculty can cleverly anticipate events to come, while the judgment proper looks behind, surveying "memorable gestes," which it masters through "continuall practise and vsage" (II.ix.53). In Hobbes's account of the mind, judgment is prior to fancy in order and dignity. The wit requires assistance and supervision from a separate and superior faculty: "he therefore that undertakes an Heroick Poem, which is to exhibite a venerable & amiable Image of Heroicke vertue, must not only be the Poet, to place & connect, but also the Philosopher, to furnish and square his matter" (2:60). Opposing the faculty of imagination to the faculty of judgment would, of course, have large consequences for how Spenser would be read and how Spenser criticism would be written. As the study of poetry in college gradually shifted from courses in philosophy to courses in rhetoric (and as both disciplines were redefined in the later eighteenth century), the successors of Spenser and Milton would find it increasingly difficult to see how Plato, Xenophon, Scotus, Aquinas, and Spenser might be engaged in a common intellectual enterprise.

The consequences of "experimental" criticism begin to appear in a curious passage in which Hobbes uses an optical toy (anamorphic perspective) as a metaphor for the process of squaring the poet's matter by discovering its unity in multiplicity: "I beleeve, Sir, you have seen a curious kinde of perspective, where he that looks through a short hollow pipe upon a picture containing divers figures sees none of those that are there painted, but some one person made up of their parts, conveyed to the eie by the artificial cutting of a glass. I finde in my imagination an effect not unlike it from your Poem. The vertues you distribute there amongst so many noble Persons represent in the reading the image but of one man's vertue to my fancy, which is your own" (2:66–67). The "cousenage of lights" – such as Davenant had criticized in Spenser's poem – is given a positive turn. Hobbes anticipates by more than a century the solution (as it was thought) of the problem of design in the *Faerie Queene*: coherence is to be sought not in the substantive action the poet imitates but in the poet's subjective perceptions and fancies as recreated in acts of interpretative reading and writing. Hobbes has not lost sight of the "vertue" that was the aim of mimetic instruction, but already it is disappearing down the long tube of critical perspectivalism. Does it matter if an action is coherent according to probable standards like those appropriate to the stage? Should romantic epic be judged according to the ethical rules of Aristotle or according to the empirical laws of modern psychology? Theatrical probability aside, neoclassical critics often allowed wide latitude to poetic imagination, if only because in some other kinds the poet's heightened fancy was not expected to render a "true" image of the world. The new generation of critics began to write more of their literary criticism in the *rational* medium of prose.

The Restoration was an adventurous age, perhaps no more so than when in *Spenser Redivivus* (1687) Edward Howard undertook the misguided attempt to rewrite the *Faerie Queene* in decorous heroic couplets:

> A Worthy Knight was Riding on the Plain,
> In Armour Clad, which richly did Contain
> The Gallant Marks of Many Battels fought,
> Tho' he before no Martial Habit sought

(1.1.1–4)

While the premise that Spenser's "Stile seems no less unintelligible at this Day, than the obsoletest of our English or Saxon Dialect" (*CH*, 216) is Howard's self-serving exaggeration, Spenser's stanza, diction, and allegory were indeed coming under sustained criticism. If Spenser is typically Tudor in his crusty gothicism, Howard is typically Stuart in looking to France for the latest in polite refinement and fashionable theory. Edward Howard's desire to bring native poetry up to date is comparable, in intent anyway, to what Dryden was doing when he reconfigured Shakespeare's *Antony and Cleopatra* as *All for Love* (1678). *Spenser Redivivus*, like Howard's much-maligned *British Princes* (1669), is a backhanded testimony to Spenser's high status in the later seventeenth century; in 1679 Spenser's *Works* was reprinted for the first time in many decades, at a time when poets and critics were beginning a century-long struggle to declare cultural independence from France. Spenser appears several times in the Soame-Dryden translation of Boileau's *Art of Poetry* (1683), which asserts British claims to innovation by substituting the names of English writers for the original French:

> Let mighty Spenser raise his reverend head,
> Cowley and Denham start up from the dead,
> Waller his age renew, and offerings bring;
> Our monarch's praise let bright-eye'd virgins sing;
> Let Dryden with new rules our stage refine,
> And his great models form by this design.

(Elledge, 267)

Restoration wits faulted the poets of the "last age," but when competing for literary glory with their neighbors across the Channel they were quick to assert the genius of Chaucer, Spenser, and Shakespeare. Thus the force of the pronoun "our" in the 1675 biographical dictionary of ancient and modern poets compiled by Milton's nephew and student, Edward Phillips: "Edmund Spencer the first of our English Poets that brought Heroic Poesie to any perfection, his Faery Queen begin for great Invention and Poetic height judg'd little inferior, if not equal to the chief of the ancient Greeks and Latins or Modern Italians" (2:34–35).

Unlike their Elizabethan and romantic counterparts, Restoration critics were inclined to temper their praise for Spenser with blame. This should not be mistaken for merely tepid admiration. Twentieth-century readers tend to be thoroughgoing historical relativists, accustomed to making judgments within rather than across periods. Academic critics dismiss Spenser's prolixity, false rhymes, and narrative blunders because he is, after all, an Elizabethan. At the same time, and for the same reason, we lose sight of just how much Spenser did to advance – lastingly – the technical resources of English poetry. Neoclassical wits, who were neither academics nor relativists, were often harsh on Spenser (on whom in some respects they had indeed improved) while at the same time according him the greatest respect as both a great genius and a founder of English poetry. Ironically, in a translation of the Frenchman Rene Rapin's *Reflections* on Aristotle (1674), Thomas Rymer (1641–1713) faults Spenser for following foreign models too closely: "We must blame the Italians for debauching great Spencer's judgement; and they cast him on the unlucky choice of the Stanza, which is in no wise proper for our Language." Rymer, foremost among hypercritics, could describe the *Faerie Queene* as all "fanciful and chimerical, without any uniformity" and still regard Spenser as "the first among our Heroick Poets," "a Genius for Heroick Poesie, perhaps above any that ever writ since Virgil" (*CH*, 207, 206). This willingness to grant latitude to genius accords with the account of poetic fancy we have seen in Hobbes. Moreover, the generation that rediscovered Longinus was capable of admiring poetry because it *was* irregular. Samuel Wesley the elder (1662–1735), in the preface to *The Life of our Blessed Lord* (1697), lauds the *Faerie Queene* for a naturalness already being opposed to French "politesse" as *the* distinctively English virtue: Spenser "comes the nearest Ariosto of any other; he's almost as irregular, but much more Natural and Lovely" (*CH*, 230). Moreover, Spenser had accomplished that most difficult of challenges, making British Arthur the hero of a national epic. Improving upon his example proved to be no easy task: Milton, Dryden, and Pope all considered and rejected Arthuriads; the desirability and danger of such a scheme were made apparent to all when the physician-poet Sir Richard Blackmore (1654–1729) emulated Spenser in his correctly-regular, stillborn political epics, *Prince Arthur* (1695) and *King Arthur* (1697). Later attempts to modernize the *Faerie Queene* were mere exercises; Augustan writers discovered that like Shakespeare, Spenser was, for all his faults, irreplaceable.

John Dryden (1631–1700), who was Edward Howard's brother-in-law, elevated preface writing to new heights, surpassing all others in the fine art of expressing sharp observations in memorable phrases. King Charles's laureate wrote many prefaces over several decades; they do not amount to a systematic body of criticism but treat their topics according to the matter in hand. The selection and priority of the names dotting seventeenth-century epigrams took on new regularity in John Dryden's prose and have remained substantially the same ever since. In the best "essayistic" manner, Dryden's prefaces undertake a sustained, empirical investigation of poetical causes and effects. Whatever its inconsistencies, Dryden's criticism had a profound effect in normalizing both the topics of criticism and the English canon; his comments about Spenser were lifted out of their contexts and repeatedly quoted in articles and biographies well into the nineteenth century. Dryden returned to Spenser again and again; in the dedication to the *Works of Virgil Translated* (1697) he wrote shortly before his death, "I must acknowledge that Virgil in Latin, and Spencer in English, have been my Masters" (*CH*, 302). Dryden did not compose formal imitations of Spenser, though he quarried Spenser's works for materials; the precedent of *Mother Hubberds Tale* is perceptible in *The Hind and the Panther* (1687), which may have contributed to the wrath of the fallen laureate's Protestant critics, who beat him about the head and shoulders in beast fables of their own. While much of Dryden's criticism selectively repeats and amplifies "what oft was said" by lesser-known writers, it was his reformulations of their remarks that set the agenda for Spenser criticism in the Augustan age. At the same time, one recognizes in Dryden's remarks on Spenser a gradual drift away from the prejudices of the age. In the dedication to *The Spanish Fryar*

(1681) he recalled, "I remember, when I was a Boy, I thought inimitable Spencer a mean Poet, in comparison of Sylvester's Dubartas" (Sig. A3); by the end of his long career he had become a firm advocate for the tradition of Chaucer and Spenser.

Dryden's discussion of the design of the *Faerie Queene* follows the bent in which epistemology was leading discussions of poetic probability. The dedication to his translations of Juvenal (1693), like Hobbes's remark on *Gondibert*, raises the question of how one distributes the virtues among different characters in a poem: "There is no Uniformity in the Design of Spencer: He aims at the Accomplishment of no one Action: He raises up a Hero for every one of his Adventures; and endows each of them with some particular Moral Virtue, which renders them all equal, without Subordination of Preference" (*CH*, 203). The new philosophy regarded probable design as a concurrence of signs: in lower forms, a mimetic correspondence between parts of the poem and the world as given to perception; in higher forms a correspondence between parts of the poem and a sublime moral informing its significant action. Allegory and typology were thus recast by psychologizing critics. Dryden, like Davenant and Hobbes, had absorbed some systematizing tendencies from French criticism: a heroic poem was to have one moral, to which the action, characters, speeches, and episodes within the action were to be strictly subordinate. Unlike most of his contemporaries, Dryden does not attribute Spenser's failure to subordinate parts to a whole to the primitive state of poetry or a *furor poeticus*. Since Spenser's narrative structure was obviously not a probable fiction in the manner of a tragedy by Corneille or a canvas by Poussin, Dryden suggests in the dedication that Spenser may have been led by mercenary motives to adopt the lower, more mimetic, kind of design: "The Original of every Knight, was then living in the Court of Queen Elizabeth: And he attributed to each of them that Virtue, which he thought was most conspicuous in them: An Ingenious piece of Flattery, tho' it turned not much to his Account" (203). The allusion, of course, is to the discussion of history and poetry in the letter to Raleigh. Spenser's high notions of ethical imitation were not incomprehensible to Dryden. He knew their force and their limitations all too well: drawing inferences from his own experience as a courtier and a laureate, Dryden offers a "probable" explanation for Spenser's faulty design. It is not the least cogent explanation for some of the puzzling irregularities in the *Faerie Queene*.

As he grew older and was estranged from the court, Dryden's views about Spenser appear to have become more favorable. In the 1685 preface to *Sylvae* he rejects the diction of rustic pastoral: it was "impossible for Virgil to imitate . . . neither will it succeed in English, for which reason I forbore to attempt it" (*CH*, 301). In the 1697 dedication of Virgil's pastorals to Clifford he takes a different view: "Spencer being Master of our Northern Dialect; and skill'd in Chaucer's English, has . . . exactly imitated the Doric of Theocritus" (*CH*,

204). This indicates a shift in position from the Ancients to the Moderns, and with it a shift from cosmopolitanism to nationalism. In the preface to the *Fables* (1700) the work of constructing a strictly British canon is well underway: "Milton was the Poetical Son of Spencer . . . . Spencer more than once insinuates, that the Soul of Chaucer was transfused into his Body; and that he was begotten by him Two hundred years after his Decease. Milton has acknowledged to me, that Spencer was his Original" (*CH*, 205). Despite Milton's several allusions to Spenser, this second transmigration would *not* have been obvious to contemporary readers, partly because they were less familiar with Milton's early poetry but mostly because of their political sense: how could the republican Milton have taken the ultra-royalist Spenser as his original? Moreover, Milton, like Davenant and Cowley before him, had rejected the Spenserian model for modern epic. Of course, by aligning Milton with Spenser (and himself with both), Dryden was doing more than observing stylistic or political affinities; he was formulating a canon of English poets that would bring Milton into the fold and reestablish Spenser as a model to imitate. As a Catholic and a monarchist, Dryden was intensely concerned with traditions and genealogies; if other Restoration writers had located Spenser in a "progress" from Chaucer to present times, Dryden himself was not content with such an arbitrary and contingent form of succession: he wanted "son" and "original" to be understood in an almost literal sense. In this respect he began to resemble modern writers who have treated the canon of British literature as though it were a kind of apostolic succession or a family romance. As early as the preface to *Sylvae* Dryden could even prefer Spenser to Virgil, as in the tempered praise of Spenser's Theocritean diction that would shortly relaunch British pastoral: "Even his Dorick Dialect has an incomparable sweetness in its Clownishness, like a fair Shepherdess in her Country Russet, talking in a Yorkshire Tone" (*CH*, 301). That this foremost of Restoration poets would end his career by imitating Chaucer indicates both the reach of Spenser's authority and the complexity of literary and political affiliations at the beginning of the eighteenth century. After 1689 there is a noticeable uptick in the frequency with which Spenser's name appears in criticism; in 1700 it is frequently paired with Dryden's own in the elegies written for the departed laureate.

Spenser's significance as a *British* poet was always secure, but not every writer was as prepared as Davenant or Dryden to level Virgil and Spenser — or Latin with English poetry. In "Of Poetry" (1690) the statesman and essayist Sir William Temple (1628–99) expresses only slight regard for Spenser: "Spencer endeavoured to supply this with Morality, and to make Instruction, instead of Story, the Subject of an Epick Poem. His Execution was excellent, and his Flights of Fancy very Noble and High, but his Design was poor, and his Moral lay so bare, that it lost the Effect; 'tis true the Pill was Gilded, but so thin, that the Colour and the Taste were too easily discovered" (*CH*, 222). The Ancients-Moderns controversy intensified with the publication of Temple's later essay, "Of Ancient and Modern Learning" (1692). Ostensibly about the achievements of modern writers, the debate turned on the relation of arts to sciences and history to both. The Ancients faction, led by Sir William Temple and his secretary and disciple Jonathan Swift (1667–1745), upheld the traditional humanist position; they insisted that literature differed from other writing: while sciences progressed, the essential truths of an unchanging humanity were known to the ancients and expressed in timeless poetry. The Moderns faction, led by the bellicose Professor Richard Bentley of Cambridge (1662–1742), held that poetry reflects the customs and beliefs of the particular society producing it and that, like science, it progresses with the accumulation of experience. Since the two factions held incommensurable views about what literature is and does, their dispute about the relative worth of ancient and modern poets could not be readily resolved. In *The Battle of the Books* (1704) Jonathan Swift takes aim at Dryden's claim that "Virgil in Latin, Spencer in English, have been my masters"; the ex-laureate appears before Virgil, perspectivally diminished by his vast suit of armor, "like a Mouse under a Canopy of State, or like a shriveled Beau from within the Penthouse of a modern Perewig: And the voice was suited to the Visage, sounding weak and remote. *Dryden* in a long Harangue soothed up to the good *Antient*, called him *Father*, and by a large deduction of Genealogies, made it plainly appear, that they were nearly related" (ed. Guthkelch, 246–47). The famous frontispiece of armor-clad authors tilting in a library ridicules romance as a Moderns genre. This example is one of many in which satirists adapted allegory to the end of ridiculing Spenserian poetry – a backhanded compliment of sorts. At the time Swift was writing, allegory might be regarded as a gothic and hence rustic and satyr-like "satirical" device.

Unlike Davenant and Milton, who openly proclaimed their allegiance to the Moderns' position, Spenser had equivocated by imitating both ancient and modern precedents (as Dryden and Pope would later). But he was still Modern enough to be suspect to tough-minded neoclassicists. Temple's remarks on the gilded pill appear as an aside in a broadside directed against that arch-modern, antipagan poet John Milton. One wonders whether Temple had actually read Spenser; likely not, since this criticism of the *Faerie Queene* had been made before by Henry Reynolds in *Mythomystes* (1632), a work Temple would have consulted: "Some good judgments have wisht (and perhaps not without cause) that he had therein beene a little freer of his fiction, and not so close rivetted to his Morall" (Spingarn 1:147). If Dryden's prefaces represent the strength of essayistic criticism, Temple's ill-advised reliance on prejudice and secondary sources represents the limitations of the "common sense" approach. Richard Bentley's superior learning inflicted severe damage on Temple, or would have, had not the Ancients faction been so very successful at dismissing professional scholarship as inconsequential pedantry. Bentley, a founding (if fallible) figure in modern literary history, was hooted from the stage by Swift and Pope. Temple's criticism is typical, not only of the Ancients' position, but of the Restoration generally in its willingness to admire Spenser's genius while condemning his gothicism.

Whigs and Tories

By the second decade of the eighteenth century, however, the force of opinion was turning inexorably in the direction of Spenser and the Moderns. For this, Joseph Addison (1672–1719) was largely responsible. Of some dozen poets and critics then taking up Spenser's cause, almost all were associated with Addison's "Little Senate." In *A History of English Romanticism* (1899) Henry A. Beers argues that Addison's unflattering remarks in "An Account of the Greatest English Poets" (1694) "probably represent accurately enough the opinion of the majority of [eighteenth-century] readers" (80):

> Old Spencer next, warm'd with Poetick Rage,
> In Antick Tales amus'd a Barb'rous Age;
> An Age that yet uncultivate and rude,
> Where-e're the Poet's Fancy led, pursu'd
> Through pathless Fields, and unfrequented Woods,
> To Dens of Dragons, and Enchanted Woods.
> But now the Mystick Tale, that pleas'd of Yore,
> Can Charm an understanding Age no more;
> The long-spun Allegories fulsom grow,
> While the dull Moral lyes too plain below.
>
> (*CH*, 224)

But Addison's remarks – likely lifted from Temple's recently published essay, even as Temple borrowed from Reynolds – are more typical of seventeenth-century criticism of improbable narratives. Dryden's 1700 preface to *Fables*, with its fulsome praises of "antick tales" by Chaucer and others, seems to have had a profound effect on young writers like Addison – who had yet to read the *Faerie Queene* when he wrote these couplets. Soon enough, Addison and Steele would be extolling Spenser and Milton, while Prior, Pope, and Gay would be imitating Chaucer. In *The Art of English Poetry* (1702), an updated version of Meres's *Palladis Tamia*, Edwin Bysshe does not include passages from writers earlier than Waller, averring that while Chaucer and Spenser are unsurpassed "in Justness of Description, or in Propriety and Greatness of Thought, yet the Garb in which they are Cloath'd, tho' then Alamode, is now become so out of Fashion, that the Readers of our Age have no Ear for them"

(Sig. *2b). With a large assist from Addison, Dryden changed all that; in a slightly later handbook, *The Compleat Art of Poetry* (1718), Charles Gildon boasts that "I have been pretty large in my Quotations from Spenser . . . and . . . Shakespear . . . being satisfy'd that the Charms of these two great Poets are too strong not to touch the Soul of any one who has a true Genius for Poetry, and by Consequence enlarge that Imagination which is so very necessary for all Poetical Performances. And since Milton and Waller were made Poets by Spenser, I do suppose the same Cause may in all Probability have the same Effect" (vol. 1, Sig. a7v). Spenser's stature as the "poet's poet," established by Milton, Cowley, and Dryden, became a commonplace of eighteenth-century criticism.

A new generation of Spenser imitations began in 1706 with Matthew Prior's *An Ode, Humbly Inscrib'd to the Queen,* celebrating Marlborough's victory at Ramillies. No poem written in Spenserian stanzas had appeared since Samuel Woodford's *Paraphrase on the Canticles* in 1679, the year in which the *Faerie Queene* had been last reprinted. In the intervening decades Spenserian imitation largely consisted of a handful of pastoral elegies in which the urge for metrical refinement left any stylistic resemblance remote. It seems to have taken an actual war against France to boost patriotism to the point where Spenser's manner became acceptable again. Even then, Prior constructs his heroic ode on a foundation adapted from Horace: "As to the Style, the Choice I made of following the Ode [of Horace] in Latin, determin'd Me in English to the Stanza; and herein it was impossible not to have a Mind to follow Our great Countryman SPENSER; which I have done (as well at least as I could) in the Manner of my Expression, and the Turn of my Number: Having only added one Verse to his Stanza, which I thought made the Number more Harmonious; and avoided such of his Words, as I found too obsolete" (*CH*, 310–11). Critics of Henry Beer's generation sneered at Prior's "pseudo-Spenserian" modification of the stanza, regarding it as a feeble compromise between Elizabethan exuberance and neoclassical restraint. Constructed of two quatrains and a couplet, Prior's stanza sacrifices Spenserian interlacing for the turns and points of a Shakespearean sonnet, which it resembles. Prior stanzas continued to be used well into the nineteenth century; their stately form made this verse form particularly popular in odes written for dignified public occasions.

Indeed, the reasons for a Spenserian revival during the reign of Queen Anne (1702–14) have much to do with politics. Not only was Prior trimming between Ancients and Moderns poetics; he was trimming between Whig and Tory politics. He wrote in his diary, "The Whiggs, tho' they did not openly censure this poem were no way satisfied that I had writt it; they say'd the Imitation was of a verse now grown obsolete, the Style a little hard, &c" (2:896n). But the Whigs would soon change their mind about "obsolete" poetry, for

Prior's *Ode* demonstrated to Addison and company how to link Spenser's
verse to their own admiration for all things Elizabethan:

> When bright ELIZA rul'd BRITANNIA's State,
> Widely distributing Her high Commands;
> And boldly Wise, and fortunately Great,
> Freed the glad Nations from Tyrannick Bands;
> An equal Genius was in SPENSER found:
> To the high Theme he match'd his Noble Lays:
> He travell'd ENGLAND o'er on Fairy Ground,
> In Mystic Notes to Sing his Monarch's Praise:
> Reciting wond'rous Truths in pleasing Dreams,
> He deck'd ELIZA's Head with GLORIANA's Beams.

(1:232)

In advocating an aggressive policy toward Catholic France, the Whigs of Ad-
dison's generation were acting as the political heirs of Raleigh and Essex a cen-
tury earlier. The Whig place-seeker Samuel Croxall (ca. 1690–1752) followed
Prior in *An Original Canto of Spencer: Design'd as Part of his Fairy Queen, but Never
Printed* (1713), a clever and well executed satire casting Queen Anne as Una
and the Tory prime minister, Robert Harley as Archimago. Anne's death was
mourned in Spenserian allegory by Pope's foe Lewis Theobald (*The Mauso-
leum*, 1714); the new dynasty was saluted in Croxall's *An Ode Humbly Inscrib'd to
the King* (1714), which plainly reworks Prior's *Ode*. In 1715 *Mother Hubberds Tale*
was done over as Jacobite propaganda (in 1773 it would be dusted off by the
Wilkes faction in *A Scourge for False Patriots; or, Mother Hubberd's Tale of the Ape
and the Fox. Part the Second*). Throughout the eighteenth century, Spenser was
invoked in political odes and elegies, pastorals and satires, allegories and birth-
day odes. However slight their literary merits, these occasional works, like
their predecessors during the interregnum, are legitimate descendants of
Spenser's political conception of poetry.

Spenser was familiar with the forms in which these poems were written,
but not their political sentiments; constitutional monarchy, modern statehood,
and the new commercial empire altered court politics almost beyond recogni-
tion. The Addison coterie, devoted Whigs, were in the forefront of these
changes, and they took full advantage of the weakness of the court as a foreign
dynasty prepared to assume the monarchy. Their periodicals, the *Tatler*, the
Spectator, and the *Guardian*, functioned as party organs and often celebrated
"Britishness" at the expense of French absolutism with its cult of the monarch.
A century before Schlegel and Coleridge established Shakespeare as the icon
for romantic totality, the Addison coterie began using Spenser as an icon for
romantic liberty. Addison's widely read *Spectator* essays on the imagination,
Paradise Lost, and ballad poetry made possible a return to gothicism, as did the

enormously popular *A Collection of Old Ballads* (1723, 1723, 1725, 1727, 1738), thought to be edited by Addison's associate and fellow Spenserian Ambrose Philips. This annotated anthology of ballad poetry educated a polite audience in legendary British history, setting the stage for collections later edited by Percy, Ritson, and Scott. Spenser would have approved. But Spenser would not have approved of the larger political objectives pursued by the eighteenth-century Spenserian revivals. As much as the Whigs supported the Hanoverian court (and vice versa), they were upholders of the 1689 settlement that diminished the powers of the monarchy. In place of Spenser's politics of deference, the new Spenserians practiced a politics of consensus that forever changed the ways in which poetry was written and criticism practiced. Tories and Jacobites, not the Whigs, upheld Spenser's belief in the sanctity of absolute monarchy, and they did so in heroic couplets and Latin verse rather than in Spenserian stanzas.

The new periodicals promoted and instated the ideals of consensus and aesthetic education developed by Shaftesbury's *Characteristicks* (1711, 1714). An arch-Whig, Anthony Ashley Cooper, the third earl of Shaftesbury (1671–1713) challenged rote reliance on authority and promoted a literary politics predicated on liberty, commerce, benevolence, and creative genius – the great themes of Spenserian imitation in the eighteenth century. Readers of eighteenth-century poetry are painfully aware of how frequently these themes were handled in allegorical verse: essay and allegory were practiced as equivalent means to the same end, which was to link "common" with "sense." By expressing common sense in common language, periodical essayists undermined the authority held by scholars, priests, and lawyers. In the latter seventeenth century, Spenserian allegory fared badly under this program; in *Paradise Lost*, Milton reserved it for uncouth figures like Chaos, Sin, and Death. To the reformers of the language, allegory suggested hieroglyphics or metaphysics; as we have seen in the remarks of Rymer and Temple, Restoration readers preferred to remain in the probabilistic company of flesh-and-blood characters. But as allegory shed most of what remained of its occult or gothic connotations, it became a staple of Enlightenment criticism, especially in the new periodical essay. In 1715 Spenser's editor John Hughes (1677–1720), a dissenter and a Whig, noted that "with us the Art of framing Fables, Apologues, and Allegories, which was so frequent among the Writers of Antiquity, seems to be, like the Art of Painting upon Glass, but little practic'd, and in a great measure lost" (*CH*, 259). Hughes and his contemporaries sought to revive this lost art because they believed, like Hobbes, that abstract ideas can be made tangible through imaginative fictions. There are many allegories in eighteenth-century periodicals, though any debt to Spenser is not generally obvious since the essayists adhere to the common and polite language of the day.

Spenserian allegory found its way into liberal philosophy because, insofar as images could render ideas self-evident, the authority of traditions and documents (and their official interpreters) could be diminished. John Hughes emphasizes the appeal to the senses in his definition of allegory: "It is a kind of Poetical Picture, or Hieroglyphick, which by its apt Resemblance conveys instruction to the Mind by an Analogy to the Senses" (*CH*, 249). The success of Thomas Paine's *Common Sense* was in large part due to his ability to express political abstractions in concrete images that were at once "sensual" and "consensual": "Government, like dress, is the badge of lost innocence; the palaces of kings are built upon the ruins of the bowers of Paradise" (1776; Foner 1:4–5). The Chinese dissidents who recently signaled their political allegiances by erecting the figure of Liberty rendered mute testimony to the spread of Lockean principles as well as the continuing power of Whig allegory. Augustan imitations of Spenser that champion British liberty by pitting allegory against Bourbon tyranny or gothic "superstition" include John Durant Breval, *Henry and Minerva* (1729), Francis Manning, *The British Hero* (1733); Gilbert West, *A Canto of the Fairy Queen . . . Never before Published* (1739) and *Education: A Poem in Two Cantos* (1751); John Upton, *A New Canto of Spenser's Fairy Queen* (1748), and Thomas Denton, *The House of Superstition* (1762). As the Court Whigs acquired firm control of the patronage system, these political views were taught in rhetoric courses to future gentlemen, clergy, and state officials in schools and colleges throughout most of Britain and the colonies.

In something like a Whig succession, commonsense allegory came to Addison by way of Shaftesbury, who as a boy was tutored by the philosopher John Locke (on record as an admirer of Blackmore's Arthuriads). In "Soliloquy, or Advice to an Author," Shaftesbury uses allegory to illustrate how moral knowledge can do without external authority and yet be founded on something firmer than mere opinion. If writers would examine their own minds, imagining the sources of their passions, Shaftesbury argues, they would discover the foundations of a sensibility truly "common." He illustrates his point by introducing an allegorical pageant into his essay. The passions parade before the inner vision of an aspiring writer; the first, Despair, "appears in a sort of dismal weed, with the most mournful countenance imaginable; often casting up her eyes, and wringing her hands, so that 'tis impossible not to be moved by her, till her meaning be considered and her imposture fully known" (1711; ed. Robertson, 1:202). To visualize an idea is to know it; in the manner of Descartes, Shaftesbury pursues a "first philosophy" of ethics that circumvents textual authority by meditating upon the springs and levers of a universal psychology. Shaftesbury, a Modern who has little favorable to say about modern writers, may or may not have read Spenser. It was left to the Addison coterie to repackage the Prince of Poets in a way that would appeal to the new generation of social and political liberals. This was done in the time-honored way of selectively imitating the *Faerie Queene*. Augustan writers translated the speaking pictures out of heroic romance and into the more humble genres of occasional essay and occasional verse. For example, Addison updates and familiarizes Spenserian allegory in the famous allegory of Public Credit in the third *Spectator* (1711): "I saw . . . a beautiful Virgin, seated on a Throne of Gold. Her Name (as they told me) was Publick Credit. The Walls, instead of being adorned with Pictures and Maps, were hung with many Acts of Parliament written in Golden Letters . . . . The Lady seemed to set an unspeakable Value upon these several Pieces of Furniture, insomuch that she often refreshed her Eye with them, and often smiled with a Secret Pleasure, as she looked upon them; but, at the same time, showed a very particular Uneasiness, if she saw any thing approaching that might hurt them" (ed. Bond, 1:14–15). Allegory is no longer a rusty coin, nor is this new model Philotime a personage to be shunned. Stripping the veil of mystery from modern finance, Addison demonstrates how the liberal state relies upon credit and therefore upon belief in probable fictions; by means of an allegorical fable he underprops the theory by which his government governed. In a very different generic and political register, Addison's allegorical fictions attempt to do for Queen Anne what Spenser's had done for Queen Elizabeth.

In his periodical essays, Addison, following Shaftesbury, several times presents allegory as a useful means for uniting philosophy with manners and virtue with taste. In *Guardian* 152 (1713) he proposes bringing Spenser up to date: "I was once thinking to have written a whole Canto in the Spirit of Spencer, and in order to it contrived a Fable of imaginary Persons and Characters. I raised it on that common Dispute between the comparative Perfections and Pre-eminence among the two Sexes, each of which have very frequently had their Advocates among the Men of Letters" (ed. Stephens, 497). Fashionable women were regarded as the very embodiment of polite commerce, and as such figured largely in Addison's plans for undermining the rituals of deference. In 1723 Addison's narrative would be versified by the younger Samuel Wesley as *The Battle of the Sexes*, but it bore more immediate fruit in the allegorical sylphs and gnomes Alexander Pope added to the 1714 version of *The Rape of the Lock*. Pope's mock-epic machinery, imported from Spenserian and Miltonic epic into the salons of contemporary London, brilliantly fulfills Shaftesbury's and Addison's aim of making good taste the arbiter of ethics. Pope suspected that Addison rejected his expanded version of the *Rape* out of jealousy. He was probably right.

Some Versions of Pastoral

There were other, less personal forces behind the growing rift between Addison and Pope, forces stemming from the unresolved Ancients-Moderns dis-

pute that heated up again in an acrimonious public debate over British pas-
toral. Eighteenth-century pastoral poetry deserves serious attention, for it
marks the fault line dividing Renaissance from modern poetics. We have seen
how Spenserians used pastoral allegory to define their literary theory and po-
etic practice. In Renaissance criticism, this genre derived special status from its
supposed historical precedence; as the earliest form of poetry, it might be
thought to define the essence of poetry as such. Since no examples of ur-
pastoral survive, later poets were always able to define its origins to suit their
own purposes. Spenser, Milton, Pope, and Wordsworth all began their careers
by using versions of pastoral to announce and authorize their innovations. For
neoclassical poets, however, pastoral poetry was foundational in a second
sense. More than any other kind, the formal eclogue was *about* imitation. Like
Spenser himself, aspiring writers used the pastoral to define a relationship to
poetic tradition by selectively imitating and modifying significant precedents –
Theocritus and Virgil, of course, but also a wide range of modern Italian,
French, and British poets whose works and critical views were well known.
After their opposing bents, Moderns would use arguments from origins to his-
toricize the relationship of poetry to nature and society, while Ancients would
use arguments from origins to define a place for poetics outside of history.
Should pastoral *otium* be located in a primitive but innocent realistic present, or
in an artful but innocent idealized past? As this supposedly "simple" genre be-
came a battleground for contending ideas, critics on both sides of the question
could and did cite Spenser as an authority for their position.

    While the art-versus-nature, Virgil-versus-Theocritus opposition was of
long standing, the renewed emphasis on historical criticism in the eighteenth
century gave it unprecedented urgency. Even as belief in the progress of man-
ners and virtue was rendering epic unwriteable, pastoral poetry staged a dra-
matic and unexpected comeback. Restoration poets wrote much in the
pastoral mode, but they seldom composed formal Virgilian eclogues. Ambrose
Philips prefaces his 1709 collection of pastoral eclogues by noting, "it is strange
to think, in an Age so addicted to the Muses, how Pastoral Poetry comes to be
never so much as thought upon; considering especially, that it has always been
accounted the most considerable of the smaller Poems" (*CH*, 238). The
Augustan formal eclogue was not a survival from renaissance poetics; Pope
aside, most of its practitioners were Moderns and innovators. The famous dis-
pute between Pope and Philips unfolded along familiar lines: the Ancients
camp looked to Spenser as a precedent for refining poetry according to the
Virgilian model; the Moderns camp saw in Spenser an attempt to create a
truly British poetry. "British" pastoralists were invariably Whigs; for example,
"Albino," one of four pastorals Philips published in 1708, echoes the senti-
ments of Prior's recent Horatian-Spenserian ode. If Prior can merge Spenser's

manner into that of Horace, Philips can unite Spenser with Virgil by linking "Eliza's Name" to "Anna's Cares":

> Through Anna's cares at ease we live,
> And see our cattle unmolested thrive,
> While from our Albion her victorious arms
> Drive wasteful warfare . . . .

(ed. Griffith, 139)

Notice the plea for patronage built into a complex, three-tiered typology: wars of Augustus, wars of Elizabeth, wars of Anne. Joseph Addison expected great things from young Philips.

The controversy over this supposedly minor genre was carried out in the most prominent publications of the Augustan era and was still being aired by major critics in the nineteenth century – it continued as long as the practice of imitation survived. Philips's poems caught the attention of Jacob Tonson, who reprinted them with additions in *Poetical Miscellanies: Sixth Part* in 1709. Tonson's series of miscellanies, begun under Dryden's supervision, were the premier anthologies of the age; the sixth volume begins with six pastorals by Philips and concludes with Pope's four. Since neither writer had an established reputation at that point, and each had influential supporters, much was at stake in this singing contest. Both poets signal their allegiance to Spenser by imitating the opening of the *Shepheardes Calender*: "A Shepheards boye (no better doe him call)." Philips begins:

> A Shepherd Boy, all in an Ev'ning fair,
> When Western Winds had cool'd the sultry Air,
> When all his Sheep within their Fold were pent,
> Lamented thus his dreery discontent . . . .

(ed. Griffith, 122)

Pope begins:

> A Shepherd's Boy (he seeks no better Name)
> Led forth his Flocks along the silver *Thame*,
> Where dancing Sun-beams on the Waters play'd,
> And verdant Alders form'd a quiv'ring Shade.

(ed. Audra and Williams, 71)

Philips imitates by tentatively introducing Spenserian diction ("dreery discontent") and using English names for his characters; Pope imitates by condensing and refining Spenser's temporal schema and by condensing and refining particular lines, such as "the Woods shall answer, and their Echo ring" from the "Epithalamion." Pope makes no attempt to be either Elizabethan or jingoistic. The presentation in the anthology appears to give Pope the last word; moreover, his pastorals are accompanied by flattering verses suggesting that England had found her new Virgil.

But Philips was not without allies. The critical battle was joined in April 1713, in Addison's and Steele's *Guardian.* Thomas Tickell (1685–1740), deputy professor of poetry at Oxford, uses Philips as his exemplar in an impressive sequence of essays on the history and theory of pastoral. Tickell also nods to his patron, Joseph Addison, on the pleasures of imagination: pastoral "transports us into a Kind of Fairy Land," the fanciful domain of aesthetic contemplation: "An Author, that would amuse himself by writing Pastorals, should form in his Fancy a Rural Scene of perfect Ease and Tranquillity, where Innocence, Simplicity and Joy abound. It is not enough that he write about the Country; he must give us what is agreeable in that Scene, and hide what is wretched. It is indeed commonly affirmed, that Truth well painted will certainly please the Imagination; but it is sometimes convenient not to discover the whole Truth, but that part only which is delightful . . . . When a Reader is placed in such a Scene as I have described, and introduced into such a Company as I have chosen, he gives himself up to the pleasing Delusion" (ed. Stephens, 105). Tickell does not affirm that *all* poetry should delude in this way; long before Southey and Wordsworth, British Spenserians were fond of contemplating pastoral innocence in distress. But the notion of being transported by pleasure steadily migrated from pastoral into other kinds, becoming foundational not only for pastoral but for poetry conceived as an alternative to history, poetry "as such." The "pleasing delusion" formulation differs from the "erected wit" Sir Philip Sidney describes as differentiating poetry from history both in its emphasis on pleasure and its epistemological turn. Insofar as poetry aspires to the happy condition of pastoral, aesthetic contemplation takes another step in the direction suggested by Hobbes, moving toward Kant and romantic understandings of disinterested pleasure.

Tickell's reflections on pastoral suggest another and opposing strand of romantic aesthetics: that rural poetry should accurately (if selectively) represent the country life it describes. He ridicules formulaic Restoration pastoral elegies (Congreve and Dryden both published occasional poems that follow "Astrophel" at a distance), insisting that the poet "may lawfully deviate from the Ancients." While some pastoral elements are universal (country life, innocence, simplicity), "others there are of a changeable kind, such as Habits, Customs, and the like. The difference of the Climate is also to be considered, for what is proper in Arcadia, or even in Italy, might be very absurd in a colder Country" (129). Tickell quotes with approval Philips's catalogue of *British* flowers, and concludes that "changes from the Ancients should be introduced [because] . . . we must take up the Customs which are most familiar, or universally known, since no Man can be deceived or delighted with the Imitation of what he is ignorant of" (130). Spenser's *Shepheardes Calender*, with its depar-

tures from classical and continental models, is an obvious precedent for intro-
ducing local innovations. By mid-century the admixtures of dialect and local
detail in eighteenth-century Spenserian pastoral sometimes render it so
"historically" specific that the verse begins to engage in the kinds of empirical
observation discussed above in connection with georgic – one encounters not
only British pastorals but American, Arabian, and African pastorals in which
the brief narratives of Theocritus and Virgil are recast in the company primi-
tive customs and sublime topography. By way of summary, Tickell introduces
a pastoral allegory of his own, a singing contest in which figures representing
different varieties of pastoral pay court to the fair Amaryllis. The lady is won
by the most "natural" suitor, who founds the tradition in which Spenser
worked: "Amyntas and Amaryllis lived a long and happy Life, and governed
the Vales of Arcadia. Their Generation was very long-lived, there having been
but four Descents in above two thousand Years. His Heir was called Theocri-
tus, who left his Dominions to Virgil, Virgil left his to his Son Spencer, and
Spencer was succeeded by his eldest-born Philips" (137).

The insult to Pope was palpable and deeply felt. He responded in good
Defovian fashion by contributing a sequel to the Guardian series in which,
posing as a Modern, he slyly hoists the opposition by their own petard. Pope's
rhetorical strategy is to extend Tickell's doctrines to illogical conclusions – that
Virgil's eclogues are not pastorals, for instance – thereby pointing up contra-
dictions in the theory. By juxtaposing parallel passages, he illustrates his own
superiority to Philips in points on which both agree. But the nub of the matter
is disagreement over what in Spenser is worthy of imitation. Since Pope's doc-
trines derive from Virgil, Virgil is censured for not writing like Spenser: "I
have frequently wonder'd that since [Virgil] was so conversant in the Writings
of Ennius, he had not imitated the rusticity of the Doric, as well, by the help of
the old obsolete Roman Language, as Philips hath by the antiquated English"
(161). Pope recalls Dryden's comment in *Sylvae*, one of the earlier Tonson
miscellanies: "Dorick Dialect . . . was impossible for Virgil to imitate; because
the severity of the Roman Language denied him that advantage. Spencer has
endeavour'd it in his Shepherds Calendar; but neither will it succeed in Eng-
lish" (*CH*, 301). Spenser's archaisms were a bad idea and not to be imitated.
Pope points out how Philips fails Tickell's standard by introducing continental
wolves into insular England, and then turns to the doctrine of regionalism it-
self: "lastly, his Elegant Dialect, which alone might prove him the eldest Born
of Spencer, and our only true Arcadian; I should think it proper for the several
writers of Pastoral, to confine themselves to their several Counties. Spencer
seems to have been of this Opinion: for he hath laid the Scene of one of his
Pastorals in Wales" (164). Pope quotes "September" ("Diggon Davy, I bid hur
Good-day") and wittily burlesques Spenser in a "Pastoral Ballad" of his own
("Rager go vetch tha Kee, or else that Zun, / Will quite be go . . ."). One won-

ders whether Josiah Relph's pastorals in the Cumberland dialect (posthumously published in 1747) were inspired by misreading Pope's mocking theory of pastoral in the *Guardian*.

Pope defends his own case – the Ancients case – in his elegant "Discourse on Pastoral Poetry," published with the 1717 *Works*. Though a modern writer, Pope regards Spenser as the premier British pastoralist and thus worthy of emulation. Rather than imitate Spenser's deformities (barbarous language, promiscuous versification, obscure political allegory), he has attempted to do with Spenser what Virgil did with Theocritus: to refine, condense, and improve. Very likely, Pope's Catholic faith encouraged a cosmopolitan outlook opposed to the strident nationalism which more than anything in the verse defines Philips as Spenser's legitimate heir. Passing over the local and time-bound, Pope takes up what is most universal in the *Shepheardes Calender*, the comparison of a human life to the passing of the seasons. This theme, as opposed to thinly veiled attacks on particular persons or policies, is the sort of allegory that appealed to Horatian sensibilities. Pope rejects Tickell's notion that pastoral should describe the lives of contemporary laborers, even selectively: "We are not to describe our shepherds as shepherds at this day really are, but as they may be conceiv'd then to have been; when a notion of quality was annex'd to that name, and the best of men follow'd the employment" (ed. Ault, 298). Spenser, of course, sets his "land of Faery" in a remote and idealized past for similar reasons. While Pope seems to have believed that Spenser and Shakespeare themselves lived in such a golden age, they were worth imitating not for their native primitivism, but for their native genius.

Pope would not have imitated Chaucer, Spenser, and Donne had he not sincerely admired their poetry, but neither would he have imitated them if he felt that they were beyond improvement. A parallel if different ambivalence informs John Gay's *Shepherd's Week* (1714), the next important contribution to the Spenser controversy. Though it was published under Gay's signature, the other Scriblerians – Pope, Swift, Arbuthnot – likely had a hand in it. The Scriblerians stood in opposition to Addison's Little Senate, but they too practiced coterie criticism. Like Swift's *Battle of the Books*, *The Shepherd's Week* resorts to parody and satire to ridicule the Moderns' antiquarian tastes and historical approach to literary criticism. But John Gay (1685–1732) was neither a dogmatic Tory like Swift nor a dogmatic Ancient like Pope was at this stage; his satire is genial and often unfocused. Gay's pastorals are notoriously difficult to interpret, since they are at once a parody of Philips, a burlesque of Spenser, and a satire on low life in general. Gay parodies Philips by imitating his poems in a lower mimetic register, including large dollops of obscenity. He snipes at Samuel Croxall (who had placed Archimago's staff in Harley's hands) by saluting "Oxford, who a Wand doth bear, / Like Moses, in our Bibles fair" (1714; 1:95). He burlesques E. K., Bentley, and Tickell by adorning his poems

with the kind of antiquarian lumber Moderns were fond of appending to po-
etic texts. Gay also mimics Philips's remark that pastorals were scarce of late:
"Great Marvell hath it been (and that not unworthily) to diverse worthy Wits,
that in this our Island of Britain, in all rare Sciences so greatly abounding,
more especially in all kinds of Poesie highly flourishing, no Poet (though oth-
erways of notable Cunning in Roundelays) hath hit on the right simple Ec-
logue after the true ancient guise of Theocritus, before this mine Attempt"
(1:90). Gay's burlesque of Elizabethan prose displays more familiarity with
early writing than one finds in most imitations of the period.

Consider how Gay amplifies Jonson's remark in *Timber* that Spenser, "in
affecting the Ancients, had writ no language" (*CH*, 294): "that principally,
courteous Reader, whereof I would have thee to be advised, (seeing I depart
from the vulgar usage) is touching the Language of my Shepherds; which is,
soothly to say, such as is neither spoken by the country Maiden nor the
courtly Dame; nay, not only such as in the present Times is not uttered, but
was never uttered in Times past; and, if I judge aright, will never be uttered in
Times future" (1:92). In one breath, Gay repeats Jonson's censure of Spenser,
accuses Philips of vulgarity, and responds to Tickell by denying that Philips's
poems are accurate depictions of rural life. Gay seems to stand with Jonson
and the neoclassicists in believing that the language of polite poetry should be
the language of contemporary conversation. But neither does Gay limit his
imitations to polite writing; *The Shepherd's Week* yields unexpected homage to
the ballad poetry that Gay would later celebrate in *The Beggar's Opera* (1728).
Perhaps because Gay's own origins were low enough, he does not adopt the
patronizing attitudes typical of sentimental writing for and about the poor. His
not so innocent shepherds display voracious appetites for drink, tobacco, lech-
ery, and laziness. By sending up Tickell's novel argument that pastoral re-
quires detailed specificity, Gay renders his antic louts far more pleasing than
Philips's bloodless creatures. Their very obscenity renders them attractive.
The final eclogue (where Virgilian pastoral traditionally aspires to greater
things) tells of Bowzybeus. Roused from a drunken stupor under a hedge, this
rustic bard performs in an astonishing catalogue of literary kinds, even to ro-
mance-epic itself:

> Why should I tell of Bateman or of Shore,
> Or Wantley's Dragon slain by valiant Moore,
> The Bow'r of Rosamond, or Robin Hood,
> And how the Grass now grows where Troy Town stood?
>
> (1:122–23).

The materials going into this catalogue are those Philips himself would later
collect and publish as *A Collection of Old Ballads*.

In fact, it was not Philips or Pope (or William Diaper, Thomas Purney, Abel Evans, or Moses Browne, who were also composing Spenserian eclogues) but John Gay who established the norms for eighteenth-century pastoral. After Gay, the most successful dialect pastoralist was the Scottish Jacobite Allan Ramsay (1686–1758), author of Scots pastoral elegies for Spenserians Addison and Prior (1719, 1721). Ramsay's pastoral comedy, *The Gentle Shepherd* (1725) was one of the most frequently reprinted works of the century. Dialect pastorals in the manner of Gay and Ramsay were especially popular in Scotland (those by Fergusson and Burns are the best-known), though any direct debt to Spenser is always questionable. Charles Churchill revisits Gay to nail (North) British pastoral in *The Prophecy of Famine* (1763):

> Two Boys, whose birth beyond all questions springs
> From great and glorious, tho' forgotten, kings,
> Shepherds of Scottish lineage, born and bred
> On the same bleak and barren mountains head,
> By niggard nature doom'd on the same rocks
> To spin out life, and starve themselves and flocks,
> Fresh as the morning, which, enrob'd in mist,
> The mountain top with usual dullness kiss'd,
> JOCKEY and SAWNEY to their labours rose;
> Soon clad I ween, where nature needs no cloaths.
>
> (ed. Grant, 202)

But by late in the century Gay's burlesques were no longer read as burlesques. The preface to Robert Southey's radicalizing "English Eclogues" (1799) is typical: "With bad eclogues I am sufficiently acquainted, from Tityrus and Corydon down to our English Strephons and Thirsisses . . . . Gay struck into a new path. His eclogues were the only ones which interested me when I was a boy, and did not know they were burlesque" (183). Southey's efforts inspired the anti-Jacobin "Needy Knife-Grinder," and the whole cycle turned over again.

John Hughes Edits Spenser

The debate over British pastoral illustrates the complexity of literary affairs in the Augustan era. While Ancients and Moderns appealed to different understandings of common sense, they both practiced a criticism that identified manners with taste and virtue. Both factions wrote in the same genres, which indicates at least a degree of consensus about the broad aims of criticism. Consensus, after all, was the object of common sense criticism, though in the event consensus proved elusive. Just as the political settlement of 1689 was rejected by some and variously interpreted by others, so was the parallel reformation of criticism typified by the *Spectator*. The literary kingdom also had its non-jurors, dogmatists like Jonathan Swift who simply refused to modernize. For Ancients like Pope, common sense implied the timeless and cosmopolitan ideals of classical humanism; for Moderns like Addison, common sense implied nationalist ideals of commerce, progress, and statehood. Both parties appealed to Spenser as an authority for their position. If the Moderns held the high ground, the Ancients could usually field the better writers; in the end nothing was settled but Spenser's centrality to British poetry.

Perhaps the greatest achievement of "Queen Anne" Spenserianism is John Hughes's six-volume *Works of Mr. Edmund Spenser* (1715), the first edition since 1679 and the first critical edition ever. The editorial procedures bear witness to the contrary tendencies in Augustan criticism: as an Ancient, Hughes makes inconsistent efforts to improve and regularize the text; as a Modern he uses the apparatus to situate Spenser's work in its historical context. Hughes defends his author by citing, where he can, parallels in classical literature; where he cannot, Shaftesbury's and Addison's doctrines are pressed into service. Moderns could defend allegory as an expression of creative genius: "The Power of raising images or Resemblances of things, giving them Life and Action, and presenting them as it were before the Eyes, was thought to have something in it like Creation" (*CH*, 250). Moderns find room in their criticism to defend personal liberty: Spenser "chose to frame his Fable after a Model which might give the greatest Scope to that Range of Fancy which was so remarkably his Talent" (261). But to defend Spenser's eccentricities by appealing to irregular genius threatens the presuppositions of common sense criticism; this would be the rock on which the Moderns' position would split. By mid-century, "irregularity" would become highly valued in Whiggish celebrations of Spenser, Shakespeare, and Milton; once British nationalism became more secure, desire for consensus yielded to confidence in individual enterprise. Belief in human progress in general and British progress in particular made historicism tolerable to Addison's generation and highly attractive to many romantics later. With Hughes, historicism begins its long march through Spenser criticism: Spenser's "fabulous Descriptions . . . might render his Story more familiar to his first Readers; tho Knights in Armour, and Ladies Errant are as antiquated Figures to us, as the Court of that time wou'd appear, if we cou'd see them now in their Ruffs and Fardingales" (262). The Ancients faction correctly recognized appeals to "first readers" as an affront to "common" sense and resisted it every step of the way. The Moderns seem to have been unaware or unconcerned about the long-term consequences of their critical relativism.

And so, almost casually, Hughes introduces the argument that would knock the props from under humanist criticism and become a foundational assumption of liberal romanticism: "The want of Unity in the Story [of the *Faerie*

Queene] makes it difficult for the Reader to carry it in his Mind, and distracts too much his attention to the several Parts of it; and indeed the whole Frame of it wou'd appear monstrous, if it were to be examin'd by the Rules of Epick Poetry, as they have been drawn from the Practice of Homer and Virgil. But as it is plain the Author never design'd it by those Rules, I think it ought rather to be consider'd as a Poem of a particular kind, describing in a Series of Allegorical Adventures or Episodes the most noted Virtues and Vices: to compare it therefore with the Models of Antiquity, wou'd be like drawing a Parallel between the Roman and the Gothick Architecture" (260). With this statement criticism takes a decisive turn: the issue is no longer one of selecting proper models to emulate, but whether poetry or even criticism may be practiced according to a single set of rules. The Ancients-Moderns controversy set the stage for the Spenserians' most enduring contribution to critical theory, transforming a debate about history into a debate about the ends and principles of *criticism*. It is in this context that Pope's *Essay on Criticism* (1711) needs to be read. It is no accident that the first "art of criticism" would appear during Anne's reign, for until then Pope's belief that nature affords "one clear, unchang'd, and Universal Light" was hardly contested. Whether he was aware of it or not, Hughes violates the common sense underpinnings of both Ancients' and Moderns' positions by proposing that Spenser's design, though not a probable imitation of nature, might be legitimate according to an alternative set of "rules." Spenser's gothicism was proving a more fundamental challenge to humanist criticism than Shakespeare's mere irregularity because the Bard's affronts to Aristotle could be explained "naturally" as experimental corrections to inadequate rules, or as new rules discovered in nature by a "Grace beyond the Reach of Art." Hughes proposes a whole new set of rules, a new critical constitution based on custom rather than nature. While full-blown historicism was still decades away, his passing remark signals the coming change: the *Faerie Queene* would serve as the primary exhibit for eighteenth-century critics attempting to argue that "gothic art" was not an oxymoron.

Works Cited

Addison, Joseph. "An Account of the Greatest English Poets," *The Annual Miscellany for the Year 1694*. London, 1694.

———*Spectator* (1711–14). Ed. Donald F. Bond. 5 vols. Oxford: Clarendon Press, 1965.

Atterbury, Francis. Preface, *The Second Part of Mr. Waller's Poems*. London, 1690.

Aylett, Robert. *Divine and Moral Speculations in Metrical Numbers*. London, 1653.

Barnfield, Richard. *Cynthia; certaine sonnets; the legend of Cassandra*. London, 1595.

Baskervill, C. R. "The Early Fame of the Shepheards Calender," *PMLA* 28 (1913): 291–313.

Beaumont, Joseph. *Psyche, or Loves Mysterie*. London, 1648.

Beers, Henry A. *A History of English Romanticism in the Eighteenth Century*. New York: Henry Holt, 1899.

Blackmore, Sir Richard. *Prince Arthur. An Heroick Poem. In Ten Books*. London, 1695.

———*King Arthur. An Heroick Poem. In Twelve Books*. London, 1697.

Breval, John Durant. *Henry and Minerva*. London, 1729.

Browne, Moses. *Piscatory Eclogues: an Essay to Introduce New Rules, and New Characters, into Pastoral*. London, 1729.

Browne, William. *Britannias Pastorals*. London, 1613–16.

Bysshe, Edwin. *Art of English Poetry*. London, 1702.

R. C. "Epistle Dedicatory," William Bosworth, *The Chast and Lost Lovers*. London, 1651.

Chapman, George. *Monsieur D'Olive: a Comedie*. London, 1606.

Churchill, Charles. *The Prophecy of Famine*. London, 1763. In *Works*, ed. Douglas Grant. Oxford: Clarendon Press, 1956.

Cooper, Anthony Ashley, Lord Shaftesbury. "Soliloquy, or Advice to an Author," *Characteristicks*. London, 1711. Ed. John M. Robertson. Indianapolis: Bobbs-Merrill, 1964, 1:103–234.

Croxall, Samuel. *An Original Canto of Spencer: Design'd as Part of his Fairy Queen, but Never Printed*. London, 1713.

———*An Ode Humbly Inscrib'd to the King, Occasion'd by His Majesty's Most Auspicious Succession and Arrival*. London, 1714.

Cummings, R. M., ed. *Spenser: The Critical Heritage*. New York: Barnes and Noble, 1971.

Cutwode, Thomas. *Caltha Poetarum: or The Bumble Bee*. London, 1599.

Daniel, Samuel. "To the Right Honourable, The Lady Marie, Countess of Pembroke," *Delia and Rosamond augmented*. London, 1594.

Davenant, William. *A Discourse upon Gondibert*. London, 1650.

Dekker, Thomas. *The Whore of Babylon, As it was Acted by the Princes Servants*. London, 1607.

Denham, Sir John. "To Daphne: On his Incomparable In[c]omprehensible Poem Gondibert," Certain *Verses Written By several of the Authors Friends; to be re-printed with the Second Edition of Gondibert*. London, 1653.

———"On Mr. Abraham Cowley His Death and Burial," *Poems and Translations*. London, 1668.

Denton, Thomas. *The House of Superstition. A Poem*. London, 1762.

Diaper, William. *Nereides: or Sea-Eclogues*. London, 1712.

Digby, Sir Kenelm. *Observations on the 22. Stanza in the 9th Canto of the 2d. Book of Spencers Faery Queene*. London, 1643.

Drayton, Michael. *Idea. The Shepheards Garland*. London, 1593.

———*Poly-Olbion*. London, 1612–22.

Dryden, John. Dedication to *The Spanish Fryar*. London, 1681.

———Preface, *Sylvae: or, the Second Part of Poetical Miscellanies*. London, 1685.

———"Dedication To the Right Honourable Charles Earl of Dorset," *The Satires of Decimus Junius Juvenalis. Translated into English Verse*. London, 1693.

———Dedication to Clifford, *The Works of Virgil Translated into English Verse*. London, 1697.

———Preface, *Fables Ancient and Modern*. London, 1700.

Edwards, Thomas. *Cephalus and Procris. Narcissus*. London, 1595.

Evans, Able. "Six Pastorals" (ca. 1710), *A Select Collection of Poems*, ed. John Nichols. 8 vols. London, 1782, 5:87–143.

The Faerie Leveller: or, King Charles his Leveller descried and deciphered. London, 1648.

Fitzgeffrey, Charles. *Sir Francis Drake*. Oxford, 1596.

Fletcher, Giles the younger. *Christs Victorie and Triumph on Heaven and Earth*. London, 1610.

Fletcher, Phineas. *The Locusts, or Apollyonists*. Cambridge, 1627.

———— *The Purple Island, or the Isle of Man: together with Piscatorie Eclogs and other Poetical Miscellanies.* London, 1633.

Fraunce, Abraham. *Arcadian Rhetorick: Or the Praecepts of Rhetorick Made Plain by Examples.* London, 1588.

———— *The Lawiers Logick, Exemplifying the Praecepts of Logicke by the Practise of the Common Lawe.* London, 1588.

Gay, John. *The Shepherd's Week.* London, 1714. *Poetry and Prose,* ed. Vinton A. Dearing. 2 vols. Oxford: Clarendon Press, 1974.

Gildon, Charles. *The Complete Art of Poetry. In Six Parts.* London, 1718.

Gill, Alexander. *Logonomia Anglica. Qua gentis sermo facilius addiscitur conscripta.* London, 1619.

Greene, Robert. *The Comicall Historie of Alphonsus King of Aragon.* London, 1599.

Greenlaw, Edwin. "The Shepheards Calender," *PMLA* 26 (1911): 419–51.

Hall, Joseph. "His Defiance of Enuy," *Virgidemiarum.* London, 1597.

Harvey, Gabriel. *Three Proper, and Wittie, Familiar Letters.* London, 1580.

Hobbes, Thomas. *The Answer of Mr. Hobbes to Sr. Will. D'Avenant's Preface Before Gondibert.* London, 1650.

Howard, Edward. *Spencer Redivivus Containing the First Book of the Fairy Queen.* London, 1687.

Hughes, John, ed. *Works of Mr. Edmund Spenser.* 6 vols. London, 1715.

Johnson, Edmund. "A Quare with a Quare concerning Iohn Quis," John Gower, *Pyrgomachia.* London, 1635.

Jonson, Ben. Untitled, in Shakespeare, *Works.* London, 1623.

————"Timber; or Discoveries," *Works.* 2 vols. London, 1640.

E. K. "Dedicatory epistle," in Edmund Spenser, *The Shepheardes Calender.* London, 1579.

Lodge, Thomas. "Induction," *Phillis: Honoured with Pastorall Sonnets, Elegies, and Amorous Delights.* London, 1593.

Manning, Francis. *The British Hero, or the Vision: A Poem, Sacred to the Immortal Memory of John, Late Duke of Marlborough.* London, 1733.

Marlowe, Christopher. *Tamburlaine the Greate.* London, 1590.

Meres, Francis. *Palladis Tamia. Wits Treasury. Being the Second part of Wits Common wealth.* London, 1598.

Milton, John. *A Maske Presented at Ludlow Castle* ["Comus"]. London, 1637.

————*Areopagitica.* London, 1644.

———"Il Penseroso," *Poems of Mr. John Milton, Both English and Latin, Compos'd at Several Times.* London, 1645.

More, Henry. *Psychodia Platonica: or a Platonical song of the Soul, Consisting of Foure Severall Poems.* London, 1642.

More, Henry. *Conjectura Cabbalistica.* London, 1653.

Mother Hubbard's Tale of the Ape and Fox, Abbreviated from Spencer. London, 1715.

Norden, John. *The Labyrinth Of Mans Life, or Vertues Delight and Envies Opposite.* London, 1614.

Paine, Thomas. *Common Sense.* Philadelphia, 1776. In *Complete Writings*, ed. Philip S. Foner. 2 vols. New York: Citadel Press, 1945.

Peele, George. *The Araygnement of Paris. A Pastorall.* London, 1584.

Phillips, Edward. *Theatrum Poetarum, or A Compleat Collection of the Poets.* 2 vols. London, 1675.

Philips, Ambrose. "Preface to Pastorals," *Poetical Miscellanies: The Sixth Part.* London, 1709. Pastorals, in "A Variorum Text of Four Pastorals by Ambrose Philips," ed. R. H. Griffith, *Texas University Studies in English* 12 (1932): 118–57.

Pope, Alexander. Pastorals in *Poetical Miscellanies: The Sixth Part.* London, 1709. Reprinted in *Pastoral Poetry and An Essay on Criticism*, ed. E. Audra and Aubrey Williams. London: Methuen, 1961.

———An Essay on Criticism. London, 1711. Reprinted in *Pastoral Poetry and An Essay on Criticism*, ed. E. Audra and Aubrey Williams. London: Methuen, 1961.

———*The Rape of the Lock. An Heroi-comical Poem. In Five Canto's.* London, 1714.

———"Discourse on Pastoral Poetry," *Works.* London, 1717. In *Prose Works*, ed. Norman Ault. Oxford: Blackwell, 1936, 297–302.

———*The Dunciad.* London, 1728–42.

Prior, Matthew. *An Ode, Humbly Inscrib'd to the Queen. On the Late Glorious Success of Her Majesty's Arms, 1706. Written in Imitation of Spencer's Stile.* London, 1706.

———*Colin's Mistakes. Written in Imitation of Spenser's Style.* London, 1721.

———*Works*, ed. H. Bunker Wright and Monroe K. Spears. 2 vols. Oxford: Clarendon Press, 1971.

Puttenham, George. *The Arte of English Poesie.* London, 1589.

Ramsay, Allan. *Richy and Sandy: A Pastoral on the Death of Mr. Joseph Addison.* Edinburgh, 1719.

————*Robert, Richy, and Sandy: A Pastoral on the Death of Matthew Prior*. Edinburgh, 1721.

————*The Gentle Shepherd: a Scots Pastoral Comedy*. Edinburgh, 1725.

Relph, Josiah. "Cumberland Pastorals," *A Miscellany of Poems*. Glasgow, 1747.

The Returne from Parnassus. London, 1606.

Reynolds, Henry. *Mythomystes, Wherein a Short Survey Is Taken of the Nature and Value of True Poetry*. London, 1632.

Rous, Francis. *Thule, or Vertues Historie*. London, 1598.

Rymer Thomas. "Preface of the Translator," in René Rapin, *Reflections on Aristotle's Treatise of Poesie*. London, 1674.

W. S. *The Lamentable Tragedie of Locrine*. London, 1595.

A Scourge for False Patriots; or, Mother Hubberd's Tale of the Ape and the Fox. Part the Second. Dedicated without Permission to John Wilkes, Esq. London, 1773.

Sheppard, Samuel. *The Faerie King Fashioning Love and Honovr*. Ca. 1655; ed. P. J. Klemp. Salzburg, 1984.

Sidney, Sir Philip. *The Defence of Poesie*. London, 1595.

Smith, William. "To the Most Excellent and learned Shepheard Collin Clout," *Chloris*. London, 1596.

Soame, William and John Dryden, *The Art of Poetry, written in French by The Sieur de Boileau*. London, 1683. In *The Continental Model*, ed. Scott Elledge and Donald Schier. Ithaca: Cornell UP, 1960.

Southey, Robert. "English Eclogues," *Poems*. Bristol, 1799.

Spenser, Edmund. "Letter to Raleigh," *The Faerie Queene*. London, 1590.

Spingarn, J. E. ed. *Critical Essays of the Seventeenth Century*. 3 vols. Bloomington: Indiana UP, 1957.

Stradling, Sir John. "To Edmund Spenser, the British Homer," *Epigrammatum Libri Quatuor*. London, 1607.

Swift, Jonathan. *A Full and True Account of the Battel. . . Between the Antient and the Modern Books*. London, 1704. In *A Tale of a Tub*, ed. A. C. Guthkelch and D. Nichol Smith. Oxford: Clarendon Press, 1965, 211–58.

Temple, Sir William. "Of Poetry," "Upon the Ancient and Modern Learning," *Miscellanea. The Second Part*. London, 1690.

Theobald, Lewis. *The Mausoleum. A Poem. Sacred to the Memory of Her Late Majesty Queen Anne*. London, 1714.

Thomson, James. *The Castle of Indolence: An Allegorical Poem. Written in Imitation of Spenser*. London, 1748.

Tickell, Thomas. Essays in *Guardian* (1713). Ed. John Calhoun Stephens. Lexington: University of Kentucky, 1982.

Tourneur, Cyril. *The Transformed Metamorphosis*. London, 1600.

Upton, John. *A New Canto of Spenser's Fairy Queen. Now First Published*. London, 1748.

Vaughan, Thomas. "Epistle Dedicatory," *The Man Mouse taken in a Trap*. London, 1650.

Webbe, William. *A Discourse of English Poetrie*. London, 1586.

Wells, William, ed. *Spenser Allusions in the Sixteenth and Seventeenth Centuries*. Chapel Hill: U of North Carolina P, 1972.

Wesley, Samuel the elder. "The Essay on Heroic Poetry," *The Life of our Blessed Lord*. London, 1697.

Wesley, Samuel the younger. *The Battle of the Sexes. A Poem*. London, 1723.

West, Gilbert. *A Canto of the Fairy Queen. Written by Spenser. Never Before Published*. London, 1739.

———*Education: A Poem in Two Cantos*. London, 1751.

2: British Literature

Spenser Challenges the Rules

While the Ancients-Moderns debate would resurface in the "Pope Controversy" involving Campbell, Bowles, and Byron, by the middle of the eighteenth century it was clear that the Moderns had won the Battle of the Books as surely as the Whigs had secured control of the government: Swift and Pope were dead, grammar schools were teaching vernacular poetry, critics were hailing English Shakespeare as the world's greatest playwright or even greatest poet – and another Spenserian revival was under way. This is not to say that the opposition was completely silenced or that the dominant party was completely united. But evidence of the mid-century triumph is compelling: in 1748 appeared the most successful ever formal imitation of the *Faerie Queene*, the *Castle of Indolence*, written by arch-Whig James Thomson, and there were several reprintings of Spenser's poetry: Hughes's edition was reissued in 1750 and excerpted in 1758; the *Faerie Queene* was edited by Birch (1751), Church (1758), and Upton (also 1758). Together with Thomas Warton's *Observations on the Faerie Queene of Spenser* (1754), Upton's notes broached most of the philological and critical issues that would preoccupy Spenser scholars for the next two centuries. All told, the decade 1748–58 was a remarkable event, a high-watermark in the otherwise mostly placid ebb and flow of Spenser's reputation. When Dryden and Addison began to revive Spenser, the *Faerie Queene* was known only to serious readers of poetry (recall that it had been reprinted only once since 1617); in the century following the Hughes edition of 1715 it would be reprinted more than a dozen times. While this is small compared to the number of editions of Shakespeare, Milton, Dryden, and Pope, it is impressive by Spenserian standards. Spenser's reputation has always been more high than broad. To get a sense of just how much the Prince of Poets was esteemed in the eighteenth century we should again turn to the best judges – the poets themselves – as they expressed their opinions in their practice. Consider the rising number of poems written in regular Spenserians: in all of the sixteenth and seventeenth centuries only fifteen were published; eleven more appeared in the next fifty years, followed by nearly ninety between 1750 and 1799 and some three hundred between 1800 and 1830. While none of the seventeenth-century poems were widely read and few were reprinted before modern times, several eighteenth-century poems in Spenserians became instant classics, objects of imitation in their own right. In the first half of the eighteenth century some 25 poems were published in Prior's ten-line, neoclassical variation of Spenser's stanza and another twenty-five between 1750 and 1799. These numbers are indeed small compared to the hundreds of poems published in blank verse and thousands in couplets, but plainly, the time had passed when Thomas Newcomb could joke in *Bibliotheca* (1712) that "Brave Gyon and Sir Britomart, / Instead of nymphs, protect a tart" (Nichols, 3:34). Newcomb was supposedly Spenser's great-grandson. Of the better-known eighteenth century poets, only Johnson and Goldsmith did not imitate or burlesque Spenser in verse. While Shakespeare and Milton had many more readers (as the number of editions indicates), Spenser established himself, in the phrase attributed to Lamb, as "the poet's poet"; in the words of the *Muses' Library* (1737), "no writings have such Power as his, to awake the Spirit of Poetry in others."

Yet such is the complexity of literary history that it remains difficult to assess Spenser's overall significance to eighteenth-century poetry and criticism, or even the significance of that poetry and criticism to the larger sweep of British literature. If Spenser had comparatively few readers, those readers tended be the literary vanguard, which from the time of Dryden's *Fables* (1700) began taking a keen interest in romantic poetry and other things medievally "British." While Spenser was frequently imitated, a high proportion of the imitations were burlesques. In a busy republic of letters, fashions in literary commerce changed so rapidly that most of the imitations quickly dropped from sight; most were not very highly regarded to begin with. Spenser's later champions persuaded generations of later critics that Augustan readers neglected romantic Spenser, misunderstood him, or at any rate failed to appreciate him. When twentieth-century philologists discovered strong evidence to the contrary, some historians went so far as to argue that eighteenth-century Spenserianism should be considered the origin of British romanticism. But Hazlitt's twentieth-century followers, pegging the rise of romanticism to the French Revolution, opposed or ignored this suggestion; with the decline of philological criticism, discussions of influence took a different form and the question was dropped before it could be resolved. Since then, eighteenth-century Spenserianism has received little attention. There can be no doubt that Coleridge and Wordsworth, Byron, Keats, and Shelley read and imitated the minor eighteenth-century Spenserians, but just how important was their work for later developments in poetry and criticism? I will argue that it was of considerable importance, though conceding in advance that in this argument minor poets and critics will loom large – Augustan versions of the earlier epigrammatists. This would only make sense, given the corporate nature of most eighteenth-century poetry and criticism. Seen in Spenserian terms, British romanticism appears less a revolution than an evolution, less the efflorescence of brilliant genius than the collective endeavor of several generations of moderately talented parsons and professors.

A good example of how this evolutionary process worked is supplied by one of the best known and most often imitated imitations of Spenser, *The School-Mistress*, by William Shenstone (1714–63). It began in 1736 as an imitation of Pope's burlesque of Spenser, "The Alley," and was written while the poet was an undergraduate at Oxford. In the dozen years he worked on this poem, Shenstone modified his opinion of Spenser – as is apparent not only from the considerable additions and alterations in his burlesque, but also in a series of letters to correspondents in which the poet described what he was attempting to do. Like Pope, Shenstone originally found Spenser's rustic manner appropriate for a burlesque treatment of a low subject; where Pope had sung of London fishwives, Shenstone describes a country dame school in the style of a Dutch genre painting:

> Lo! now, with State, she utters the command.
> Eftsoons the Urchins to their Tasks repair;
> Their Books of stature small take they in Hand,
> Which with pellucid Horn secured are,
> To save from Finger wet, the Letters fair:
> The Work so quaint, that on their Backs is seen,
> St. George's high Atchievements does declare;
> On which thilk Wight that has y-gazing been
> Kens the forth-coming Rod, unpleasing Sight, I ween!
>
> (1737, 18)

Spenser, of course, had sung didactically the achievements of St. George in a different stylistic register – much of the humor in Augustan burlesque turns on comparing great things with small. The first surviving letter of the correspondence, written five years later in 1741, indicates an equivocal view of Spenser: "Some time ago, I read Spenser's Fairy Queen; and, when I had finished, thought it a proper time to make some additions and corrections to my trifling imitation of him, the Schoolmistress. – His subject is certainly bad, and his action inexpressibly confused; but there are some particulars in him that charm one. Those which afford the greatest scope for a ludicrous imitation are, his simplicity and obsolete phrase; and yet these are what give one a very singular pleasure in the perusal" (ed. Williams, 36). That is to say, pleasure derives not (or not only) from a disproportion between what is found in the object text and the imitation, but from a kind of symmetry: insofar as it was also pleasingly "rustic," a description of children at work and play might be a pleasure in its own right – another version of pastoral: "The true burlesque of Spenser (whose characteristic is simplicity) seems to consist in a simple representation of such things as one laughs to see or to observe one's self, rather than in any monstrous contrast betwixt the thoughts and words" (40). In 1742, as he was preparing for publication a longer, more sentimentalized version of the poem, Shenstone wrote: "I am now . . . , from trifling and laughing at him, really in love with him. I think even the metre pretty (though I shall never use it in earnest); and that last Alexandrine has an extreme majesty" (55). Notice how this growing respect is reflected in a modified treatment of education:

> Yet sprung from Birch, what dazzling Fruits appear!
> Ev'n now sagacious Foresight points to shew
> A little Bench of heedless Bishops here,
> And there a Chancellor in Embryo;
> Or Bard, sublime, if Bard may e'er be so,
> As Milton, Shakespear; Names that ne'er shall die!
> Tho now he crawl all on the Ground so low,
> Nor weeting how the Muse shou'd soar on high,
> Wishes, poor starv'ling Elf! his Paper-Kite may fly.
> (Stanza 23, 1742)

Thomas Gray recalled this passage in his famous *Elegy* (1751) where he hails another country schoolboy as a "mute, inglorious Milton." Shenstone circulated manuscripts of his poem, making minute adjustments of the equivocal tone with the assistance of his correspondents Richard Jago, Richard Graves, and Henrietta Knight – two clergymen and a lady-in-waiting. A final revision appeared in Robert Dodsley's influential and oft-reprinted *Collection of Poems* (1748), which became the source for more than a dozen formal imitations, some written well into the nineteenth century. In pastoral writing, nothing is more complex than simplicity, and in British pastoral, as we have seen, Spenser paved the way to a broad reconsideration of nationalism and the social order. In the concluding stanza of *The School-Mistress*, Shenstone praises an England "Fam'd for a Race of Sons in Battle try'd."

During the years Shenstone was at work on *The School-Mistress*, James Thomson was working on *The Castle of Indolence*, an even more heroic burlesque of Spenser, also written in close collaboration with gentlemen and courtiers. While Thomson's work is less overtly pastoral than Shenstone's poem, the theme of indolence is a pastoral topos and Thomson's formal imitation of the *Faerie Queene* is directly concerned with the social and political value of poetry. Thomson's poem was imitated by many poets, including Coleridge, Wordsworth, and Keats; the theme of indolence was congenial and the Aeolian harp was quickly taken up as a figure for romantic verse. Indeed, Spenser's stock was rising with each passing year. A series of allegorical essays, "The Apotheosis of Milton," was printed in the *Gentleman's Magazine* for 1738. In its willful wildness, this piece conveys something of what Spenser was coming to represent to mid-century romantics: "the Figure that next appeared, struck me with Surprize, Reverence and Dread: it was that of a Man, who seemed about 50; his Eye was remarkably piercing, and his Features most delicately formed; but a deep Anguish seemed to prey upon his Cheek, and Melancholy to settle in his Look: His Robe was wrought with Figures, that looked as if they breathed, intermixed with Landskips, in which the Trees seemed to wave, and the Streams to murmur: The Whole was composed of the most lively Colours, but with an Irregularity that pleased, and a Confusion that gave Delight. All the Assembly expressed the greatest Reverence as he walked up to take his Seat; which he did at the right Hand of the President. That Person, said my Companion, is Spencer, whose Name is his Encomium" (234). Here again, admiration is expressed by means of imitation, the praise of Spenser taking the form of Spenserian allegory, and a mystical one at that. Notice also how much more detailed is this "character" than those in the terser, epigrammatic criticism. While Spenser's "irregularities" had been the subject of positive and negative remarks since the middle of the seventeenth century, it was not until the middle of the eighteenth century that a reverence for Spenser led poets, editors, and critics to study attentively the peculiarities of his allegory, design, and diction, discovering in their very irregularity the basis for a new kind of regularity, a *gothick* poetics. Spenser's authority became a standing challenge to the "rules" adopted by Davenant, Rymer, and their followers. This discovery — perhaps invention would be a more accurate term — properly marks the beginning of the romantic movement with its post-humanist poetics and relativized, "cultural" criticism that remains the norm in academic writing to this day.

Arguably, in the eighteenth century Spenser's example contributed more to shaping romantic beliefs and practices than those of even Shakespeare or Milton. This has much to do with Spenser's status as the national poet: Shakespeare, who merely wrote plays (however excellent) could never be the British Virgil; Milton, who overwent both Virgil and Spenser, presented himself as a Christian rather than a British poet. The multifarious Shakespeare was and is cited as an authority by both sides of any debate; changes in criticism were not required to accommodate an author already popular with readers of every stripe (Voltaire excepted!). His works did not provoke romanticism, though they proved especially amenable to romantic canons of criticism. Much the same was true of Milton, whom Dryden hailed as a founder of a new poetics. Augustan poets regarded Milton, quite rightly, as the leading exponent of their own principles. We tend to forget that most of Milton's verse was composed after the Restoration: he would be back-dated to Renaissance status only after mid-century critics promoting a gothic revival began to discover the Spenserian juvenilia: "Comus," "Lycidas," "L'Allegro" and "Il Penseroso." Unlike Shakespeare and Milton, Spenser proved difficult to accommodate within the norms of neoclassical criticism; as we have seen in Shenstone's attempt to burlesque the *Faerie Queene*, encounters with Spenser might lead to changes in the "rules" that permitted low subjects to receive serious treatment. But a return to the unqualified admiration that typified Elizabethan criticism of Spenser required setting aside Jonson, Milton, Dryden, and Pope, and a further development of the Moderns' position first articulated by Davenant and Hobbes: a turn toward historicism on the one hand and, on the other, towards the "pure" poetry advocated by Joseph Warton and by his followers in the Cockney School, Leigh Hunt and John Keats. These new developments amounted to major changes in the very concept of what poetry is and does, and they can be immediately linked to eighteenth-century readings of Spenser. In *Letters on Chivalry and Romance* (1762), Richard Hurd noted Spenser's priority among poets-as-such: "In spite of philosophy and fashion, Faery Spenser still ranks highest among the Poets; I mean with all those who are either come of that house, or have any kindness for it" (120). Almost explicitly, Hurd is marking off a private domain for poetry separate from the public spheres of intellectual debate and social commerce. The land of faerie was about to be reborn as what Hugh Downman in a 1768 imitation of Spenser would call *The Land of the Muses*.

Literary History: The Wartons

The resulting changes in critical practice are marked by new critical genres developed by a later generation of Moderns. The first book-length study of Spenser was John Jortin's *Remarks on Spenser's Poems* (1734). It consists entirely of detached philological glosses that explicate obscure lines, annotate sources, and criticize beauties and defects. Jortin's Bentleyesque investigations track the wandering paths of words and phrases as tenaciously as later philological descendants would pursue the history of ideas. Jortin and his contemporaries – Theobald on Shakespeare, Bentley on Milton – accumulated a large and valuable body of literary facts that eventually found their way into nineteenth-century variorums and from thence into the apparatus of modern critical editions. Such collections of antiquarian curiosities were first assembled by an earlier generation of Moderns believing that criticism (like poetry) should be empirical, cumulative, and progressive. These themes are sounded in a 1697 verse epistle Lady Mary Chudleigh (1656–1710) addresses to Dryden:

> Such in this Isle was once our wretched State:
> Dark melancholy Night her sable Wings display'd,
> And all around her baleful influence shed;
> From Gloom, to Gloom, with wary'd Steps we stray'd,
> Till Chaucer came with his delusive Light,

> And gave some transient Glimmrings to the Night:
> Next kinder Spencer with his Lunar Beams
> Inrich'd our Skies, and wak'd us from our Dreams
> Then pleasing Visions did our Minds delight . . . .
>
> (1703; Ed. Ezell, 70)

Dryden and modern science have since brought us into the full light of day. By mid-century, however, a new generation of Moderns was sorely tempted to forsake enlightenment, manners, and progress for what Lady Mary describes as "that ancient Rubbish of the Gothick Times" (72). John Jortin's own un-Spenserian imitation of Spenser, *A Hymn to Harmony* (1729), typifies the kind of refinement and polish Chudleigh advocated. In a curious twist, it would be the Moderns who discovered and promoted "the past"; this begins to make sense if we recall that for Ancients like Pope or Swift, the past survives (or ought to survive) as the better part of the present.

This process is clearly under way in Thomas Warton's *Observations on The Fairy Queen of Spenser* (1754, 2 vols, 1762). Thomas Warton the younger (1728–90) was twice Professor of Poetry at Oxford, a chair his father had held before him. Like his father, the younger Warton was a Tory in politics and a Modern in literary taste – rather a contradiction seen in Addisonian terms, but a combination that anticipates the nineteenth-century romanticism of Scott and Wordsworth. In 1706 the elder Warton had addressed the Great Shepherd of the poetical flock in terms that plainly recall Elizabethan verse criticism:

> When rural Spencer sung, the list'ning Swains
> Would oft' forget to feed the fleecy Throng;
> The fleecy Throng, charm'd with the melting Strains,
> Fed not – but on the Musick of his Song;
> His Mulla would in ling'ring Bubbles play,
> 'Till his pleas'd Waters stole unwillingly away.
>
> ("Philander," 1748, 63)

Warton proposes that "A second Colin mourn a second Astrophel." Apart from the prominent participles and regular prosody, the later origin of this poem is betrayed by an elaborate georgic conceit in which rivers become emblematic of literary commerce: "My Lays shou'd more than equal Glory boast, / And the fam'd Mulla be in smoother Cherwell lost" (66) – that is, Spenserian verse should flow once more in the cloistered halls of Oxford. And indeed it did, moreso even than at Spenser's own Cambridge. The several archaizing poems published in this 1748 memorial volume were probably retouched by the elder son, Joseph Warton, who contributed anonymously to it, as did his brother Thomas and their sister Jane. Joseph had already declared the family fealty to renaissance verse in his groundbreaking collection of odes, published in 1746:

There long she [Poesy] wept to darkness doom'd,
'Till COSMO's hand her light relum'd,
That once again in lofty TASSO shone,
Since has sweet SPENSER caught her fire,
She breath'd once more in MILTON's lyre,
And warm'd the soul divine of SHAKESPEAR, fancy's son.

("To a Gentleman," 25)

To single out this particular trio of names – Spenser-Shakespeare-Milton – was unusual at the time and marked the beginning of the romantic reconstruction of the canon of renaissance English poets. The younger Thomas had already signaled his allegiance to Spenser and the Moderns in the usual way, by publishing a collection of "realistic" pastorals in the manner of Ambrose Philips: *Five Pastoral Eclogues: the Scenes of Which are Supposed to Lie Among the Shepherds, Oppressed by the War in Germany* (1745). It was his first publication, though he later disowned it.

The word "observations" in the title of Thomas Warton's book on Spenser indicates a modern, empirical bent. Like Jortin, Warton assembles hundreds of detached philological remarks, but unlike Jortin, he takes Baconian induction a step farther: "These OBSERVATIONS, thus reduced to general heads, form a series of distinct essays on Spenser, and exhibit a course of systematical criticism on the FAERIE QUEENE" (1754, 1762; 2:262). In the two-volume second edition there are eleven essays: "Of the plan and conduct of the FAERIE QUEENE," "Of Spenser's stanza, versification, and language," "Of Spenser's Allegorical Character," and so on. Warton's desire to systematize (one must speak of intentions rather than results) marks a clear departure from the criticism considered thus far; eschewing the politesse of epigram, verse epistle, and periodical essay (all of which he practiced elsewhere), the *Observations* take a form that aspires to science. Warton's contribution to scholarship (as one would say of an equivalent latter-day dissertation) was to discover that the *Faerie Queene* borrows not only from Virgil, Chaucer, and the Italians, but from medieval poets, popular romance, and court spectacles. The range of Warton's reading is remarkable for a man still in his twenties, extending far beyond the bounds of "literature" as understood by Dryden or Pope. Emulating Bacon, this founder of modern academic criticism poked his nose into rotten matter and literary rubbish that more polite readers preferred to leave undisturbed. In a letter of July 16, 1754, Samuel Johnson hailed Warton's diligence as an innovation in English studies: "you have shown to all who shall hereafter attempt the study of our ancient authours, the way to success; by directing them to the perusal of the books which those authours had read. Of this method, Hughes and Men much greater than Hughes, seem never to have thought. The Reason why the authours which are yet read of the sixteenth Century are so little understood is that they are read alone, and no help is borrowed from those who lived with them or before them" (ed. Redford, 1:81). Warton's treatise grew by accretion: he gathered observations into essays and essays into volumes; his oeuvre later expanded to include *The History of English Poetry* (1774–81) and an edition of Milton's minor poems (1785, 1791). Taken together, these three works amount to a running chronicle of English poetry loosely structured around a comparative method and a running thread of digressions. Critical digressions, like their equivalent, the meandering rivers of georgic poetry, are especially characteristic of the Moderns' approach to history: attending little to narrative, Warton examines customs, clothing, architecture, spectacle, the whole detritus of the past. As the critic explains, without the accumulation of facts, "many allusions and many imitations will either remain obscure, or lose half their beauty and propriety" (2:264). In contrast to those "who profess to point out beauties; because . . . they naturally approve themselves to the reader's apprehension" (Pope's *Shakespeare,* as opposed to Theobald's), Warton investigates what is not so obvious or natural, "the peculiarities of his [author's] style, taste, and composition" (2:263–64). Warton's emphasis on "peculiarity" is itself typically Modern, characteristic both of the earlier Baconian science and the romantic poetry yet to come.

The aspirations of the Observations might usefully be compared to those of Polymetis: or, An Enquiry concerning the Agreement Between the Works of the Roman Poets, and the Remains of the Antient Artists. Being an Attempt to illustrate them mutually from one another (1747). This work was composed by Pope's friend Joseph Spence (1699–1768), who was professor of poetry at Oxford between the tenures of the two Thomas Wartons. Spence's method was likewise Baconian, sorting through the physical remains of Roman civilization and constructing from them a classificatory system of the heathen mythology that might be used to interpret Latin literature. Most of this evidence took the form of "rubbish" – the coins, medals, and statuary being dug out of the ground and jealously hoarded by antiquarians and virtuosi. While many of Spence's conclusions proved unreliable – Greece was not yet open to European scholars, and Roman artifacts and mythology could hardly be understood without the Greek precedent – Polymetis made a lasting impression on British literature. William Collins, another Oxford man, surely knew it and made use of it in his allegorical odes; Joseph Warton admired Polymetis and seems to have used an abridgment of it to teach literature when he was headmaster at Winchester School. (Spence himself anticipates Warton in complaining of an "almost a total neglect of that [English studies], which I should think is the most necessary for us, not only in conversation, but in almost all the business of life," 289.) John Keats, one of the most pictorial of English poets, supposedly studied Polymetis before writing such masterful ecphrastic poems as "Ode on a Grecian Urn." It is not insignificant, then, that Joseph Spence would devote a long essay to criticizing Spenser's allegory. Like Warton's Observations, Spence gathers his evidence systematically under "general heads" used to sort likenesses and differences. Spence expresses admiration for Spenser, whom he sometimes imitated in his own verse, while at the same time comparing Spenser's allegories unfavorably to those of the ancients: "this may be sufficient to shew, that where Spenser does introduce the allegories of the antient poets, he does not always follow them so exactly as he might; and in the allegories that are purely of his own invention, (tho' his invention is one of the richest and most beautiful that perhaps ever was,) I am sorry to say, that he does not only fall very short of that simplicity and propriety which is so remarkable in the works of the antients; but runs now and then into thoughts, that are quite unworthy so great a genius" (303). Despite his weight of learning, Joseph Spence had yet to take the historicizing turn – indeed he hardly recognized it as an issue.

It was a daunting and unavoidable issue for Thomas Warton, in whose criticism the opposing claims of science and imagination are notoriously at odds. In the *Observations,* chapter after chapter employs the "reigning maxims of modern criticism" (1762, 2:269) to catalogue solecisms and absurdities in Spenser's grammar, diction, design, and allegory: "I have endeavored to account for these defects, partly from the peculiar bent of the poet's genius [recall Hobbes on *Gondibert*], which at the same time, produced infinite beauties, and partly from the predominant taste of the times in which he wrote" (2:268). The learned professor discovers all the unruly Longinian virtues in Spenser: "His old manners, his romantic arguments, his wildness of painting, his simplicity and antiquity of expression, transport us into some fairy region, and are all highly pleasing to the imagination" (1:197). Warton's other great poetical love, the Greek pastoralist Theocritus, could also be called in as a classical precedent for gothic rusticity. As late as 1782, he was still agonizing over a fondness for historical detritus that he could not square with humanist principles:

> For, long enamour'd of a barbarous age,
> A faithless truant to the classic page;
> Long have I lov'd to catch the simple chime
> Of minstrel-harps, and spell the fabling rime;
> To view the festive rites, the knightly play,
> That deck'd heroic Albion's elder day;
> To mark the moldering halls of barons bold,
> And the rough castle, cast in giant mould;
> With Gothic manners, Gothic arts explore,
> And muse on the magnificence of yore.
> ("Verses on Reynolds's Painted Window," ed. Mant, 1:54–55)

In the last analysis, the painstaking philology undertaken in the *Observations* undermined the claims of both taste and science; to be "transported" into some fairy region is to leave the new empiricism behind, overcoming historical difference through visionary identification with the primitive. Warton boldly declares the pleasure he takes in what Chudleigh dismisses as "pleasing Visions" and "antic Rounds" (1703, 71, 72): "much of the pleasure that Spenser experienced in composing the FAIRY QUEEN, must, in some measure, be shared by the commentator" (2:269). The same pleasure is everywhere apparent in the poetry that Warton later wrote as poet laureate to George III. As knight-errant in the Baconian cause, Warton tilts against the Ancients' prejudices; enthralled by the idols of Tory nostalgia, he at last abandons the Moderns' march of progress to wallow in the Bower of Bliss.

Historicizing Spenser: Upton and Hurd

John Upton (1707–60) was yet another Oxford scholar, though he had resigned his fellowship long before he undertook his landmark edition of the *Faerie Queene*, published in 1758. Unlike John Hughes, Upton attempted to establish an accurate text along the lines of contemporary work being done on Shakespeare. His edition is most remarkable for its copious notes, which differ from Warton's *Observations* in emphasizing classical and Biblical sources, and in their sustained attempt to trace the references in Spenser's poem to contemporary persons and events. This reflects yet another strain in romantic criticism, a growing interest in poetry as a record of personal experience. As Upton expresses it in the opening lines of his preface, "As every original work, whether of the poet, philosopher, or historian, represents, mirrour-like, the sentiments, ideas and opinions, of the writer; so the knowledge of what relates to the life, family, and friendships of such an author, must in many instances illustrate his writings; and his writings again reflect the image of the inward man. What wonder therefore, if our curiosity is excited to get some kind of intimacy with those, whom from their writings we cannot but esteem, and that we listen to every tale told of them with any degree of probability, or even suffer ourselves to be imposed on by invented stories?" (ed. Radcliffe, 1:2). John Upton repeats the legendary stories of Spenser's exchanges with Sidney and Elizabeth (recorded a century earlier by Thomas Fuller) and uses references in the *Shepheardes Calender, Amoretti,* and *Colin Clouts Come Home Again* to construct a love-life for Edmund Spenser. This line of biographical inquiry would gather momentum throughout the romantic era. Upton is equally diligent in making connecting characters in the *Faerie Queene* with historical personages; most of the identifications now accepted by scholars were first made in Upton's edition, though others made by him have since been rejected as wrong or merely speculative.

As a critic, Upton is best remembered for his strenuous defense of Spenser's design against the earlier criticisms of Dryden and Hughes: "In every poem there ought to be simplicity and unity; and in the epic poem the unity of the action should never be violated by introducing any ill-joined or heterogeneous parts. This essential rule Spenser seems to me strictly to have followed: for what story can well be shorter, or more simple, than the subject of his poem? – A British Prince sees in a vision the Fairy Queen; he falls in love, and goes in search after this unknown fair; and at length finds her. – This fable has a beginning, a middle, and an end. The beginning is, the British Prince saw in a vision the Fairy Queen, and fell in love with her: the middle, his search after her, with the adventures he underwent: the end, his finding whom he sought" (1:21–22). It will be noted that this account, constructed out of the letter to Raleigh, does not describe the poem as we find it; Upton almost concedes as much: "'Tis requisite therefore that the several incidental intrigues should be unraveled, as we proceed in getting nearer and nearer to the main plot; and that we at length gain an uninterrupted view at once of the whole." Given the unfinished state of the poem, such a view of the whole is not to be had. Assuming that Spenser was writing an imitation of classical epic, Upton "cannot help admiring the resemblance between the ancient father of poets [Homer], and Spenser; who clearing the way by the solution of intermediate plots and incidents, brings you nearer to his capital piece; and then shows his hero at large" (1:25). Authority for Spenser's use of allegory is found in Hesiod and the Table of Cebes, and authority for using archaisms in Homer, Virgil, and Quintillian, but the same reverence for the ancients leads Upton to criticize Spenser's stanza: "were I an admirer of the jingling sound of like endings (as Milton calls rhyme) I could with better grace endeavour at an apology for that kind of stanza, which our poet has chosen" (1:38). Rather then condemn it outright, Upton historicizes a bit, noting its origin in the *ottava rima* adopted by the Italian poets; since Spenser "intended not to be a servile imitator, he added one verse more to the above-mentioned stanza; and the closing verse, as more sonorous, he made an Alexandrine of six feet" (1:38–39). John Upton was almost unique in insisting that the *Faerie Queene* conformed to Aristotle's "rules"; his arguments were not accepted and indeed seem to have led Richard Hurd to make a final break with what remained of Renaissance humanism.

Tom Warton, known for sharing a pipe and a jest with the Oxford watermen, was no paragon of politeness; Richard Hurd, by contrast, lived more in the world and (with assistance from that mighty prelate William Warburton) successfully scaled the slippery pole to a bishopric. Hurd was a Cambridge man, untainted by belated Jacobitism. The social difference between these two preeminent critics of Spenser is readily apparent in their style of writing; in contrast to Warton's disorderly Baconianism, Hurd produced criticism with a French cut, reasoning from the top down. As Dr. Johnson put it, "Hurd, sir, is one of a set of men who account for everything systematically; for instance, it has been a fashion to wear scarlet breeches; these men would tell you, that according to causes and effects, no other wear could have been at that time chosen" (Boswell, *Life of Johnson* ([1791], ed. Hill 4:219). In *Letters on Chivalry and Romance* (1762) Hurd happily concedes that he has not so much as looked into the barbarous romances that comprise the evidence for his argument; the sequence of polite letters on gothic manners is unsullied by the dust and dirt of antiquarian research. There is more of argument in Hurd's slender octavo than in both of Warton's fat quartos together. Hurd's signal contribution was to import Montesquieu's notion of a "spirit of the laws" into literary criticism, developing from it a highly original argument that laid out the program for a century's worth of Spenser criticism. The assumption behind the *Letters* is that "the only criticism, indeed, that is worth regarding is, the philosophical" (88). By "philosophical" Hurd means methodical. He begins by postulating a "spirit of romance" arising from the feudal constitution and then presents a list of elements common to chivalry and romance: honor, quests for adventure, gallantry, and superstition. One pair of essays outlines points of continuity between the warrior societies presented in classical epic and medieval romance; another, the points of difference arising from "the different humour and genius of the East and West" (40) – principally the greater emphasis on spirituality and romance in modern poetry. Hurd contends that "the *manners* [the Moderns] paint, and the *superstitions* they adopt, are the more poetical for being Gothic" (55, emphasis in original). Hurd uses the new aesthetic terminology – "genius," "spirit," and "romantic" – to indicate how a remodeled Moderns' criticism might overcome both the scorn of Ancients' prejudice and the barbarisms of Moderns' philology.

He begins by tackling the issue of historicism that so bedeviled Warton: "The spirit of Chivalry, was a fire which soon spent itself: But that of *Romance*, which was kindled at it, burnt long, and continued its light and heat even to the politer ages" (3–4, emphasis in original). How does a poetry so rooted in outmoded institutions and beliefs transcend the conditions of its production? Not the least peculiar thing about romantic poetry, Hurd observes, is the fact that its finest achievements come *after* the decline of the institutions it celebrates. For all their accurate depictions of feudal life, the great Italian and English romances are fictions – not historical representations but timeless works of imaginative genius. The best modern romances possess their own kinds of formal qualities, as great or greater than those of the revered classics. To appreciate this, however, readers need to find concepts of probability appropriate to the design and machinery characteristic of romance. Dryden censured the *Faerie Queene* for its lack of probable design, while Hughes protested against applying classical rules to a gothic poem; Warton admired Spenser's irregularity, while John Upton had argued that the several actions of the poem can be regarded as subordinate episodes in the story of Arthur's quest for Gloriana. Hurd, on the other hand, was the first critic to define and illustrate an alternative set of gothic "rules," which he bases on the historical practice of sending knights out on quests. The action of Spenser's poem is regular and methodical, he argues, if measured against such "established modes and ideas of chivalry" (62). The several books should be regarded as so many independent actions, linked together by their common relation to the queen. While not "probable" according to the neo-Aristotelian standards of tragedy, such a design has its own kind of propriety and coherence: it imitates the actions and ideals of feudal society.

To illustrate this properly modern and romantic kind of unity, Hurd compares the several destinations of Spenser's knights to the "crow's foot" of diverging paths in French gardens: the garden is regular and methodical in that its variety is subordinated to "one common and concurrent center" (67). Like Upton, Hurd assumes it is possible to obtain "an uninterrupted view at once of the whole." While his crow's-foot analogy is not a particularly apt description of Spenser's tale weaving — were the action of sending out the knights to appear in the poem, which it does not, it would have occurred only after the several adventures had been completed — this perspectival metaphor is a very apt analogy for Hurd's own revisionary and "modern" understanding of the rules of poetry. He feels comfortable relativizing the several paths of criticism because both classical and gothic alternatives are rationally subordinate to the first principles of his own "philosophical criticism." In Hurd's argument the off-scenes Gloriana supplants Arthur as the chief agent in Spenser's design; just so, the philosophical critic supplants the historically bound poet, discovering "some latent cause" of a design not in the author's explicit statements, or even in his implicit intentions, but in the "modes and fashions of different times" (1–2). That is, Hurd subordinates the differences between classical and gothic rules to a higher criticism that can accommodate both. Hurd's argument is a good example of the reconstruction of a text according to what Hobbes describes as a "curious kinde of perspective"; in Hurd's account, however, the poem is a projection not of the poet's mind but of the spirit of the age.

Such rationalism can accommodate different kinds of systems, but not different kinds within a system — designs should be classical or romantic, but not both. Spenser is faulted for extending characters beyond the bounds of their several legends and for attempting to elevate Arthur above his other heroes (vain gesture toward Virgilian precedent!). Yet what thus appear to be flaws in the action turn out to be necessary parts of what Hurd regards as Spenser's moral argument — the allegorical treatment of psychology. Within this second and different kind of regularity, the action becomes the vehicle for a formal design quite properly centered in a principal character. In contrast to the Guyons and Calidores, the role of Arthur is to exemplify the Aristotelian *via media* – a minor character in the action, he becomes the major character in exhibiting its moral coherence. Hurd concludes that the *Faerie Queene* displays "a unity of design, and not action" (67). Upton tried and failed to link moral to action according to conventional rules for just and probable narrative, but Hurd can make rational sense of Spenser's irregularities – by severing action from allegory, fable from moral: each makes sense on its own terms, but not both together. Hurd thus attempts to save the phenomenon, though at the high cost of sacrificing the moral aims of humanist interpretation to a choice between historicist and formalist alternatives. This is an important moment in the history of criticism, for Hurd's choices define the great fork in the road – with the decline of humanism, ambitious Spenser criticism would henceforth divide between philological and aesthetic approaches. Hurd uses history to explain the peculiar unity of action of the poem, leaving it with little moral sway over readers who don't happen to live in feudal societies; he discovers another, formal unity of thought in its allegory but cannot square this with the story being told. In fact, Hurd makes little attempt to assess any ethical, social, or political significance the poem might hold for modern readers; its value resides in the pleasure it affords to historical curiosity and imaginative fancy. This is very different from Warton and many antiquarians, who traced the origins of contemporary British liberty backward to medieval precedent. Although *Letters on Chivalry and Romance* still employs much of the humanist vocabulary, Hurd's philosophical criticism points directly toward the historicism of Hegel and the formalism of Kant.

Hurd's argument develops an equivalent opposition between historicism and aestheticism in his defense of romance "machinery." He begins with the standard of probability: it is "enough, if [poets] can but bring you to *imagine* the possibility" (89, emphasis in original); fairy fictions accord with what people believe, taking "a countenance from the current superstitions of the age" (90). Poetry does not offer "philosophical or historical truth: All she allows us to look for, is *poetical truth*" (emphasis in original). Here again Hurd adapts a humanist vocabulary to a new kind of argument: "The poet has a world of his own, where experience has less to do, than consistent imagination" (93). This telling phrase recalls Sir Philip Sidney's notion of a Golden World of the poets and later neoclassical doctrines of idealized nature; Upton had used a similar phrase to defend the probability of Spenser's narrative: "To speak out, he is at liberty to lie, as much as he pleases, provided his lies are consistent, and he makes his tale hang well together" (1:23). But there is a subtle difference: by fairy "fiction" Hurd means not some higher or absolute truth but what is peculiar to the genius of a particular writer or a particular age. In his argument, "consistency" loses its older, probabilistic sense of getting one's facts straight, and refers specifically to the formal unity appropriate to a work of art as such.

Hurd cites Spenser to illustrate how, "in the poet's world, all is marvelous and extraordinary; yet not unnatural in one sense, as it agrees to the conceptions that are readily entertained of these magical and wonder-working Natures" (93). Where critics like Dr. Johnson sometimes defended the real-world probability of ghosts, witches, and fairies as objects of vulgar belief, Hurd regards "gothic invention" as essential to "the more sublime and creative poetry[;] . . . it appeals neither to the *eye* nor the *ear*, but simply to the *imagination*, and so allows the poet a liberty of multiplying and enlarging his impostures at pleasure" (95–97, emphasis in original). Imagination loses its basis in *common* sense and opinion; while fairy fictions might be typical of uneducated people in a credulous age, they offer a purely aesthetic pleasure to modern sophisticates willing to suspend their disbelief. We still enjoy romances written in earlier times, though "I would advise no modern poet to revive these faery tales in an epic poem" (101). The humanist doctrine of imitation was itself passing into history.

Imitating Spenser: Pure Poetry

John Upton had tried to accomplish something very like that which Hurd warns against. *A New Canto of The Fairy Queen* (1747) is a diligent and skillful attempt to reproduce Spenser's peculiarities of style – and it fell stillborn from the press. The successful seventeenth- and eighteenth-century Spenser imitations all depart from their original in significant ways, attempting to emulate Spenser rather than merely reproduce him. Yet Hurd's discussion of probabilism does indicate two ways in which Moderns might use historical relativism to tap the wells of romantic poetry. Living in belated times, Spenser was led by "the romantic Spirit of his age" to "hide his faery fancies under the mystic cover of moral allegory" (116). As Hurd was surely aware, such "closet" gothicism was actively and successfully cultivated by eighteenth-century Spenserians like Alexander Pope in *The Rape of the Lock* or Gilbert West in *Education*. Allegory enabled poets and readers to enjoy all the pleasures of gothic machinery without much troubling themselves about believing in improbable fictions. Alternatively, belated moderns might set their improbable narrative in an exotic locale, like Spenser's Land of Faery, or in a credulous age, as in Horace Walpole's superstition-ridden Renaissance in *Castle of Otranto* (1762). A well-made fiction permitted readers to "transport" themselves to credulous times and places – not in spite of the improbable narrative but because of it. In the century following the publication of *Letters on Chivalry and Romance*, scores of poets employed the machinery of superstition in ballad imitations, oriental tales, and gothic romances. That the *Faerie Queene* lent authority to these procedures is apparent from the substantial number of them written in Spenserian stanzas.

In the eighteenth century, as indeed in the seventeenth, extended, formal imitations of the *Faerie Queene* were few, far fewer than imitations of *Paradise Lost*, a sacred poem that did not raise the same spectres of historicism and improbability. The efforts at Spenserian narrative by Breval (1729), Upton (1747), and Downman (1768) aroused little notice, though Thomson's *Castle of Indolence* (1748) and William Julius Mickle's *The Concubine* (1767) were several times reprinted and admired into the nineteenth century. Both of these poems tempered their incipient romanticism with strong admixtures of burlesque irony. One reason for the comparative scarcity of formal imitations is also suggested by Hurd's argument: narrative and allegory were becoming distinct and opposing literary forms. While Spenserian allegory survives in Augustan satires like Pope's *Dunciad* or Thomson's *Castle*, after mid-century, narrative poetry increasingly presented probable characters in novelistically detailed circumstances – even in neogothic romances. Thomas Chatterton's fanciful narratives are crammed with circumstantial detail, as Walter Scott's poems would be later on. Young Walter Scott's response to the *Faerie Queene*, circa 1783, recorded in Lockhart's *Life* (1837), is probably typical of eighteenth-century readers who simply loved a story: "Too young to trouble myself about the allegory, I considered all the knights and ladies and dragons and giants in their outward and exoteric sense, and God only knows how delighted I was to find myself in such society" (1901, 1:30). In Scott's verse romances Spenser's dragons and giants reappear transformed into pikestaffs and pantaloons; avoiding allegory, Scott's poetry remained always outward and exoteric. For its part, allegory migrated from narrative and descriptive verse to take up residence in a new species of ode that attempted to represent universal passions *abstracted* from historical action and the peculiarities of place and time. In the poetry of the first generation of romantics – Akenside, Collins, Mason, the Wartons, and Gray – Spenser's presence is noticeable in epithets, imagery, alternating rhymes, and the adoption of a concluding Alexandrine. The twisted syntax and intellectual difficulty of their "Pindaric" odes depart from the mannerly norms of Augustan critical exchange to return to something closer to the conceitedness of Spenser or Cowley.

To make such innovative poetry acceptable, changes were again required in the content and the forms of criticism. As we have seen, in Augustan epistles, essays, and progress poems, Spenser figures as a way station in the progress towards modern English literature and manners: Pope improves on Dryden, Dryden on Waller, Waller on Spenser, Spenser on Chaucer. As the second writer in this sequence, Spenser was really the one who initiated the process, as described in Samuel Cobb's *Poetae Britannici* (1700):

> Sunk in a Sea of Ignorance we lay,
> Till Chaucer rose, and pointed out the Day,
> A joking Bard, whose antiquated Muse

In mouldy Words could solid Sense produce.
Our English Ennius He, who claim'd his part
In wealthy Nature, tho' unskill'd in Art.
The sparkling Diamond on his Dung-hill shines,
And Golden Fragments glitter in his Lines.
Which Spencer gather'd for his Learning known,
And by successful Gleanings made his own.
So careful Bees, on a fair Summer's Day,
Hum o'er the Flowers, and suck the sweets away.

(*CH*, 231–32)

In sequences of epigrams and epithets, poets like Cobb described how progress was achieved through imitation ("careful Bees"), emulation ("made his own"), and refinement ("successful Gleanings"). But by 1750 a number of critics were beginning to argue that poetry was not in fact progressing and that politeness was leveling important distinctions. Pope seemed to have taken poetic refinement as far as it could go, leaving poetry and criticism in needed of a new direction. Rather than attempting to triumph over Pope as Pope had triumphed over predecessors playing at the same game, mid-century writers elected to change the rules. Joseph Warton, in *An Essay on the Writings and Genius of Pope* (1756, 1782), worried that "we do not, it should seem, sufficiently attend to the difference there is, betwixt a MAN OF WIT, a MAN OF SENSE, and a TRUE POET. . . For one person who can adequately relish, and enjoy a work of imagination, twenty are to be found who can taste and judge of, observations on familiar life, and the manners of the age . . . . Are there so many cordial admirers of Spenser and Milton, as of Hudibras?" (iv, vi). Warton advocated a return to first principles and the "Pure Poetry" of a more innocent age.

A new form of verse criticism was invented to cut through the polite mediations of literary commerce; its object was not to dramatize the rituals of civility but to reproduce and transmit emotive responses to poetry. Descriptive and allegorical odes served this purpose nicely, since they confirmed (or appeared to confirm) the Longinian doctrine that the experience of great poetry could make poets of readers. With the publication of collections of descriptive and allegorical odes by Akenside (1745), Joseph Warton (1746) and William Collins (1746), Milton's long neglected companion poems – which describe the education of an emphatically Modern poet – suddenly became the cynosure of all poetical eyes. Like Hurd, such writers admired the supernatural in poetry and thought of reading as a kind of spiritual possession. Imitating "Il Penseroso," Joseph Warton attempts to conjure up the spirit of Spenser:

Then lay me by the haunted stream
Wrapt in some wild, poetic dream,

> In converse while methinks I rove
> With Spenser thro' a fairy grove;
> Till suddenly awoke, I hear
> Strange whisper'd music in my ear,
> And my glad soul in bliss is drown'd
> By the sweetly-soothing sound!

(7–8)

The mediations of literary commerce (Warton reading Milton reading Spenser) disappear into the immediate experience of a disembodied ineffable, a "whisper'd music in my ear." In a long allegorical poem, *Sickness* (1745), William Thompson, another notable minor Spenserian, pleads in Miltonic blank verse:

> Father of Fancy, of descriptive verse,
> And shadowy beings, gentle Edmund hight
> Spenser! the sweetest of the tunefull throng,
> Or recent, or of eld, Creative bard,
> Thy springs unlock, expand thy fairy scenes,
> Thy unexhausted stores of fancy spread,
> And with thy images inrich my song.

(18)

Enthralled by the "strange music" of Elizabethan poetry, many mid-century writers attempted to turn back the clock by conjuring up the spirit of Spenser even as Spenser himself had invoked the spirit of Chaucer. They cultivated the ode as an appropriate genre for supplicating divinities. In 1751 Thompson, yet another Oxford poet, lost a bid for the poetry professorship. Given the strange ways in which such contests were often decided, his advanced tastes were probably not an issue.

Joseph Warton's friend at Winchester and Oxford, William Collins (1721–59), likewise strives to be original through a Longinian rereading of Renaissance poetry in the famous "Ode on the Poetical Character." From Waller's myrtle shades retreating, the poet uses a syntactically torturous allegory to signal allegiance to "Him whose school above the rest / His loveliest Elfin Queen has blessed" (428). Collins recognizes what no critic had yet explicitly formulated: that in the school of Spenser, pupils are expected to display both intellectual ambition and formal originality. This he allegorizes in an allusion to Florimell's girdle: competitors must somehow emulate Spenser without violating the "chastity" of their invention by imitating too closely. Recalling the deference Spenser expressed toward Chaucer, one cannot but notice the degree of change implied in this remorselessly competitive new emphasis on "originality": it is no longer one for all, but every man for himself. Only one competitor has or could achieve this "ancient trump" – John Milton, who

overgoes Spenser by singing the Creation itself, the ultimate origin of original-
ity. Who could hope to compete with that heroic achievement? Yet Milton's
success in emulating Spenser did suggest to Collins and his contemporaries
something like a new way to be original: by repossessing "the shadowy tribes
of Mind / In braided dance their murmurs joined" (433). Alluding perhaps to
Colin's vision on Arlo Hill, this braid signifies Florimell's girdle, the laurel
crown, and the cycle of allegorical poems of which "Poetical Character" is a
part. Rather than compose humanist epistles on practicing the virtues, Collins
and contemporary Spenserians began composing Neoplatonic odes on con-
templating the passions. Rather than (explicitly) wooing peers, prelates, and
politicians, mid-century lyricists invoked Fancy, Health, Fear, Mercy, Friend-
ship, Liberty, and Genius, eschewing the shallows of politeness and shoals of
patronage in a conceited pursuit of the deep, universal, and abstract principles
underlying human society. While mining the *Faerie Queene* for adjectives and
epithets, such poems separated Spenser's allegory from Spenser's narrative; for
ethical narrative they substitute lyrical evocations of mental powers that owe
little to Aristotle's ethics and much to Shaftesbury's psychology.

In melting hymns and dutiful odes, writers pleaded with the Muses to re-
turn to their belated, benighted society. Like Hurd's *Letters on Chivalry* or
Burke's *Reflections on the Revolution in France*, they appealed to the spirit of ro-
mance, hoping to rekindle the primal erotic bonds in a society far gone in ma-
terialism and corruption. In *The Pleasures of Melancholy* (written in 1745 and
published in 1747) a very young Thomas Warton compares Spenser's Una to
Pope's Belinda, underscoring the loss of spiritual fidelity besetting an age of
common sense:

> Thro' POPE's soft song tho' all the Graces breathe,
> And happiest art adorn his Attic page;
> Yet does my mind with sweeter transport glow,
> As at the root of mossy trunk reclin'd,
> In magic SPENSER's wildly-warbled song
> I see deserted Una wander wide
> Thro' wasteful solitudes, and lurid heaths,
> Weary, forlorn; than when the fated fair
> Upon the bosom bright of silver Thames
> Launches in all the lustre of brocade,
> Amid the splendors of the laughing Sun.
> The gay description palls upon the sense,
> And coldly strikes the mind with feeble bliss.

(Mant, 1:82)

In an essay on taste prefixed to *An Ode on the Powers of Poetry* (1751), Thomas
Cooke praises Spenser's "allegorical Representation of religious Fortitude and

the Virtues of Humanity: his shadowy Scenes are so many enchanted Castles, Palaces, and Bowers, and many of them so divinely adorned as to inspire the attentive Reader with Notions and Desires superior to the Frailty of his Nature" (4). Invoking Spenser in "The Bard" (1757) Thomas Gray expresses the hope that verse will "adorn again / Fierce war and faithful love, / And truth severe, by fairy fiction dressed" (Lonsdale, 198).

This program for achieving originality through imitating Renaissance verse was, strange to say, successful. Perhaps the aroma of incense was sweet to the Muses, though the pressure for change may have had more to do with the same fashionable commerce so often bemoaned in romantic poetry – the new economic order, quite as much as the new literary order, demanded competition, originality, and public displays of taste. In *The Polite Correspondence: or Rational Amusement* (1741) John Campbell declares that "I am naturally fond of such Poets as discover a strong Fancy, and therefore admire Sidney, Spencer, and Drayton, more than many of the Moderns" (236). Gothicism was celebrated in wallpapers, furniture design, and landscape follies. In 1749 William Shenstone wrote to Lady Luxborough: "I am upon the Search for a Motto to my Gothick Building, which I would have consist of a Stanza or two of old English Letters. I've been looking over Spenser, but cannot yet fix upon one to my Mind. Perhaps your Ladyship may chance to find one. I begin to prefer English Mottoes in general. There is scarce one Gentleman or Clergyman in Fifty that remembers anything of Classick Authors" (ed. Williams, 213). William Thompson wrote Spenserian sonnets for use as garden inscriptions; like a holy hermit, "No less the raptures of my summer day, / If Spenser deign with me to moralize the lay" (1763, 8:97). In 1765 Horace Walpole, thinking about adding a labyrinth to his estate at Strawberry Hill, wrote to his antiquarian friend Cole, "in short, I both know and don't know what it should be. I am almost afraid I must go and read Spenser, and wade through his allegories and drawling stanzas to get a picture – but goodnight; you see how one gossips, when one is alone and at quiet on one's own dunghill!" (ed. Lewis and Wallace, 1:91). As early as the 1730s, Stowe, one of the most allegorically complex of landscape parks, had a grotto adorned with scenes from the *Faerie Queene*. In *The English Garden: A Poem* (1772) Gray's friend William Mason included an apostrophe to Colin of "the Dorian mood" who had inspired a taste for nature among the English (1783, 1:438–52). Warton's and Hurd's critical books on Spenser, in combination with Percy's *Reliques* (1765), rode the crest of a general and admittedly diverse interest in the Elizabethans, as witnessed by scholarly editions of Drayton (1748, 1753), Shakespeare (1766), William Browne (1772), Giles and Phineas Fletcher (1783), and anthologies of early poetry by Capell (1760), Bell (1778), Headley (1787), Anderson (1792), Roach (1794), Ellis (1801), and Chalmers (1810). These books were the constant

companions of more than one young romantic poet; there began to be a bur-
geoning market for old verse.

Spenser in School and Salon

One cannot but be struck by how much of eighteenth-century Spenserian writ-
ing is concerned in one way or another with education. This is no accident, for
many minor poets made their living as tutors, schoolmasters, or preachers; the
teachers among Spenser's eighteenth-century imitators include Thomas Black-
lock, John Durant Breval, Samuel Cobb, John Dalton, William Dodd, Elijah
Fenton, Walter Harte, Robert Lloyd, Robert Potter, Josiah Relph, Jerome
Stone, William Whitehead, Wesley the younger, and Samuel Whyte. It is
more than likely that these men, and many others like them, were teaching
Spenser's poems to their pupils despite the fact that English literature was not a
part of the curriculum in either grammar schools or colleges. While the official
canon was strictly classical, students spent considerable time studying and writ-
ing English poetry, as appears from the many anthologies of college verse pub-
lished to mark public occasions. During the reign of Queen Anne such
collections were strictly Latin; by the time of George III, they consisted mostly
of English verse written in the manner Johnson ridiculed as "Trickt in Antique
Ruff and Bonnet, / Ode and Elegy and Sonnet." In addition to publishing
thoughtful criticism of Spenser, two Oxford poetry professors, Joseph Spence
and Thomas Warton, advanced the cause of British poetics by editing and
contributing to such volumes. While patently designed to attract political pa-
tronage to the colleges, such collections were also part of a pedagogical pro-
gram for English poetry: by weeping over the deaths of kings and queens in
the manner of "Astrophel" or "Lycidas," celebrating court weddings in the
manner of Spenser's "Epithalamion," or celebrating the progress of Protestant
arms in allegorical odes and hymns, students were habituated to the patriotic
virtues. Here too, a "modern" and romantic program seems to have been suc-
cessful: having reached something of a nadir in the time of Richard Bentley,
enrollments at the two universities began to swell in the later decades of the
eighteenth century. If some of the enthusiasm expressed in academic Spense-
rian-Miltonic verse seems forced, a check of the *Dictionary of National Biography*
reveals that more than a few of those imitating Spenser and Milton went on to
become leading figures in the church or the government. The training and in-
stitutional bonding of the group Coleridge would later describe as the clerisy
can be easily tracked through neogothic imitations of Spenser and Milton.
These minor poets were the eighteenth-century "gothic" equivalents of the
seventeenth-century epigrammatists, though it could hardly be said that such
anxious suitors after preferment "wrote with ease."

The process of empire building often went hand in hand with the process
of forming British poetry into a teaching canon. This was done off the books,
as it were, but it was being done. Joseph Warton's 1756 *Essay on the Writings and
Genius of Pope* set out to arrange the British poets by "different classes and de-
grees." While those at the bottom of the list are not familiar to modern read-
ers, Warton did fix the classics at the top of the romantic canon: "In the first
class I would place, our only three sublime and pathetic poets; SPENSER,
SHAKESPEARE, MILTON" (1:xii). The omission of Jonson, Dryden, and
Pope is deliberate and significant. At least one telling assignment survives from
Warton's years at Winchester, a Pindaric ode written in 1772 by one Charles
Bathurst: "The Poetical Triumvirate: Spenser, Shakespeare, Milton. Written
as a School Exercise, on this Subject Given," belatedly published in 1849. The
young essayist concludes, no doubt with the approval of his master, that,

> Great Milton sits supreme:
> E'en Shakspeare yields his native fire,
> Nor blushing Spenser dares aspire.
>
> (9)

Where the preceding generation of students weighed the relative merits of
pleasure and virtue by translating and versifying Prodicus's "Judgment of
Hercules," Warton's pupils learned to discriminate degrees of creativity by
weighing the merits of the British poets. Students were known to rebel, of
course. The original version of William Shenstone's *The Schoolmistress* was
probably written to amuse a college tutor, and in "On Rhime: A Poetical Epis-
tle to a Friend" (published in 1774), the rakish William Lloyd, tutor and son of
a schoolmaster, several times ridiculed the academic affectation for the antique:

> Whilom, what time, eftsoons and erst,
> (So prose is oftentimes beverst)
> Sprinkled with quaint fantastic phrase,
> Uncouth to ears of modern days.
>
> (2:113)

Lloyd's choice of genre – the Horatian epistle – was an appropriate instru-
ment for resisting the encroachments of the allegorical ode. But in 1785 John
Pinkerton (1758–1826) warned that "to young writers especially, Imitation
cannot be held out in too just, in too contemptible, a light. They ought even to
be told that there is more applause due to a bad original, than to the best of
copies" (362). In this reforming spirit, Spenser and English studies gained a
toehold as an academic subject.

Neogothicism did not simply sweep the field, however; it existed side by
side with older Augustan modes even in the writings of Collins, Gray, and the
two Wartons. Criticisms of the *Faerie Queene* by Rymer, Temple, and Dryden

were ritually repeated throughout the eighteenth century; it would be easy to
multiply quotations objecting to Spenser's stanza, allegory, machinery, diction,
and design. Throughout the period, and indeed down to our own time,
friends and foes of Spenser alike describe the *Faerie Queene* as out of fashion
and accessible only to scholars. And throughout the eighteenth century
Spenser's claim to be England's great national poet was steadily undermined
by Shakespeare's rising star. Generic differences that had earlier placed the two
poets in separate spheres mattered less to critics who were severing originality
from imitation and beginning to measure literary fame by the approbation of
the "common reader." Then as now, common readers much preferred Shake-
speare. Spenser's eighteenth-century admirers tended to be clerics and univer-
sity men at home with their Hooker and Chillingworth; his detractors tended
to be busy men of affairs committed to the more secular values of polite litera-
ture – readers like Oliver Goldsmith or Horace Walpole with enough educa-
tion to know who Spenser was and social confidence enough (or social
prejudice enough) to express a negative opinion. Authors and readers whose
interests tended toward novels and the London theaters mostly ignored him.

Spenser's popularity with the clerisy was bound to inspire opposition from
the enlightened spirits who were writing in opposition to the institutional status
quo. No doubt David Hume (1711–1776) spoke for many of these when in
the fourth volume of his *History of England* (1759) he brazenly complained of
the "effort and resolution" required to get through the *Faerie Queene*: "This ef-
fect, of which every one is conscious, is usually ascribed to the change of man-
ners: But manners have more changed since Homer's age; and yet that poet
remains still the favourite of every reader of taste and judgment. Homer cop-
ied true natural manners, which, however rough or uncultivated, will always
form an agreeable and interesting picture: But the pencil of the English poet
was employed in drawing the affectations, and conceits, and fopperies of chiv-
alry, which appear ridiculous as soon as they lose the recommendation of the
mode . . . . Spencer maintains his place in the shelves among our English clas-
sics: But he is seldom seen on the table" (ed. Todd, 4:386). In his *Elements of
Criticism* (1762) Henry Home, Lord Kames, though a great admirer of Shake-
speare and Milton, reached a similar conclusion: "However agreeable long al-
legories may at first be by their novelty, they never afford any lasting pleasure:
witness the Faery-Queen, which with great power of expression, variety of im-
ages, and melody of versification, is scarce ever read a second time" (11th ed.,
357). In 1771 John Millar faults the *Faerie Queene* for its allegory: "The writer,
instead of improving upon the Gothic model, has thought proper to cover it
with a veil of allegory; which is too dark to have much beauty of its own"
(1771, 1806; 83); Spenser is mentioned not at all in Hugh Blair's *Lectures on
Rhetoric and Belles Lettres* (1783), the most frequently reprinted handbook of the

period. Tobias Smollett's *Critical Review* was consistently hostile to Spenserian poets.

Johnson and Beattie

But these are the voices of a liberal and pragmatic Scottish Enlightenment at war with a particularly stringent religious moralism. Spenser was viewed more favorably by the English Tory Samuel Johnson (1709–84) and the devout Scottish Presbyterian James Beattie (1735–1803). It may be that the mercenary motives of the booksellers precluded a life of Spenser by Johnson: the *Faerie Queene* was said to have been excluded from the original "British Poets" because it was out of copyright and editions were then abundant. Or it may be that Johnson, whose "Ancient" predilections in poetry are evident throughout his prefaces, was promoting a conception of the canon of British poetry that favored neoclassical writers. Surely, Johnson, who elsewhere displays both a weakness for romance and a nostalgia for feudal institutions, would have composed a pointed and curious commentary on Spenser's writings. We do have a number of scattered remarks. Writing as a patriot or a Christian, Johnson could express great admiration for Spenser, as in the 1755 *Dictionary of the English Language*: "from the authors which rose in the time of Elizabeth, a speech might be extracted adequate to all the purposes of use and elegance. If the language of theology were extracted from Hooker and the translation of the Bible; the terms of natural knowledge from Bacon; the phrases of policy, war, and navigation from Raleigh; the dialect of poetry and fiction from Spenser and Sidney; and the diction of common life from Shakespeare, few ideas would be lost to mankind, for want of English words, in which they might be expressed" (1: Sig. c1r). As a lexicographer, Johnson understood better than most Spenser's foundational role in British poetics; his frequent citations of Elizabethan writers in the *Dictionary* lent authority to the revival of interest in the English "classics." As a moralist, Johnson was also committed to allegory as an effective means of teaching public and private ethics. In *Rambler* No. 102 (1751), for instance, he recasts Guyon's adventures for modern readers: "In the midst of the current of life was the Gulph of Intemperance, a dreadful whirlpool, interspersed with rocks, of which the pointed crags were concealed under water, and the tops covered with herbage, on which Ease spread couches of repose, and with shades, where Pleasure warbled the song of invitation" (ed. Bate and Strauss, 2:182).

Yet Johnson's Tory sentiments also led to unstinting attacks on Spenserians suspected of Miltonic republicanism or Whig sympathies – which is to say the great majority of them. Though Johnson invited Joseph Warton to contribute to the *Rambler*, the Rambler himself did not share Warton's views about the liberty of pure poetry. Responding in No. 121 to the plethora of

Spenser imitations that had recently been appearing in Robert Dodsley's influential *Collection of Poems, by Several Hands* (1748) he snarled, "to imitate the fictions and sentiments of Spenser can incur no reproach, for allegory is perhaps one of the most pleasing vehicles of instruction. But I am very far from extending the same respect to his diction or his stanza. His style was in his own time allowed to be vicious, so darkened with old words and peculiarities of phrase, and so remote from common use, that [Ben] Johnson boldly pronounces him 'to have written no language.' His stanza is at once difficult and unpleasing; tiresome to the ear by its uniformity, and to the attention by its length....Perhaps, however, the style of Spenser might by long labour be justly copied; but life is surely given us for higher purposes than to gather what our ancestors have wisely thrown away, and to learn what is of no value, but because it has been forgotten" (2:285–86). One cannot but believe that such remarks from a scholar who praised Thomas Warton's researches and encouraged Thomas Percy to undertake the *Reliques of Ancient English Poetry* were motivated by distaste for the Whiggish appeals to "ancient" liberty that were such a prominent feature of Spenserian writing. In *The Lives of the Poets* (1779–81) Johnson attacks writer after writer for political unreliability and affectation. Of his friend Collins, he writes, "He affected the obsolete when it was not worthy of revival; and he puts his words out of the common order, seeming to think, with some late candidates for fame, that not to write prose is certainly to write poetry" (ed. Hill 3:341). Johnson's distaste for modern "odes and elegies and sonnets" led to a break with his old friend Thomas Warton. Nonetheless, Warton, who was then George III's official laureate, and Johnson, who was then the king's unofficial propagandist, stand together as the two great Tory voices in what was otherwise a sea of Whig Spenserianism. As such, they form an important intellectual bridge between Renaissance and nineteenth-century romanticism.

Like his mentors Dryden and Pope, Johnson had little original to say about Spenser; he collected the conventional wisdom and expressed it with eloquence and authority. Like Dryden and Pope, he expressed distaste for neogothic conceitedness; like Pope in *The Dunciad,* Johnson in the *Lives* attempted to turn back the tide of modernity. Yet Johnson's critical strictures also contributed much to establishing the precepts that would become the commonplaces of later romantic criticism. Imitators possess, at best, a secondary virtue; Gilbert West's "imitations of Spenser are very successfully performed, both with respect to the metre, the language, and the fiction; and being engaged at once by the excellence of the sentiments, and the artifice of the copy, the mind has two amusements together. But such compositions are not to be reckoned among the great achievements of the intellect, because their effect is local and temporary; they appeal not to reason or passion, but to memory, and pre-suppose an accidental or artificial state of mind. An Imitation of Spenser is nothing to a reader, however acute, by whom Spenser has never been perused. Works of this kind may deserve praise, as proofs of great industry, and great nicety of observation; but the highest prize, the praise of genius, they cannot claim" (3:333). Johnson censures both the "studied barbarity" and artificiality of Spenserian pastoral: "'Diggon Davie, I bid her good-day . . . . ' What will the reader imagine to be the subject on which speakers like these exercise their eloquence? Will he not be somewhat disappointed, when he finds them met together to condemn the corruptions of the church of Rome? Surely, at the same time that a shepherd learns theology, he may gain some acquaintance with his native language" (*Rambler* No. 37; 1:202–03). Held up to a probable, novelistic understanding of Nature, works such as "Lycidas" can only appear ridiculous. Johnson's hostile remarks on pastoral are especially prescient: he criticizes both the evocation of a golden world favored by the Ancients and the condescending rusticity favored by Moderns. Pastoral (and, by extension, poetry itself) should represent, with dignity, the lives of ordinary people: Johnson praises both Shenstone's *School-Mistress* and Gray's *Elegy*. Both poems point the direction that later Spenserian pastoral would take – in the "Moral Pastorals" of Johnson's friend Dr. Dodd (*Poems*, 1767), the dialect verse of Robert Fergusson (1773) and Robert Burns (1786), the *Moral Eclogues* of Scott of Amwell (1778), the "English Eclogues" of Robert Southey (1799), and of course *Lyrical Ballads* (1798). In *Literary Hours* (1798), Nathan Drake censures "translators, imitators, or parodists" and asks, "If rural life no longer presents us with shepherds singing and piping for a bowl or a crook, why persist, in violation of all probability, to introduce such characters?" (1:327). Confounding pastoral eclogue with Virgilian georgic, romantic pastorals celebrate honest labor and frequently offer particularized descriptions of local customs and natural scenery.

The extension of this new conception of pastoral into broad understandings of poetry as such is seen in James Beattie's *The Minstrel; Or, The Progress of Genius* (1771, 1774), probably the most influential Spenserian poem written in the eighteenth century. Beattie was professor of moral philosophy at Marischal College in Aberdeen, a founder of English studies, and Britain's foremost literary critic after the death of Doctor Johnson. His "progress of genius" addresses the question raised a generation earlier by Collins's "Ode on the Poetical Character": where does poetry come from? Like Bishop Hurd, Beattie identifies imagination and superstition as the chief sources of genius, locating a parallel basis for "progress" outside of the classical, humanist tradition. In fact, Beattie's hero Edwin very much resembles the credulous, mediating figure Hurd describes: he is located in a distant place (the Scottish Highlands) and a distant time (the gothic ages); and, as shepherd and child, he is simplicity itself. Edwin is "innocent" not in the condescending, humanist sense of ignorance but in the positive, Rousseauvian sense of being uncorrupted by modernity:

inspired by the "mute inglorious Milton" of Gray's *Elegy Written in a Country Churchyard* (1751), Beattie's shepherd lad ("no better doe him call"!) appears as a kind of Scottish Emile. The Aberdeen professor had written his share of mid-century allegorical odes and elegies; he too had attempted to reform society by addressing apostrophes to the passions. In *The Minstrel* his search for social renewal extends from a conventional moral idealism to an empathetic exploration of the historical past. Like Spenser's faerie land, Beattie's Scotland is an idealizing fiction, a higher norm against which the present can be judged and found lacking. Also like Spenser, Beattie plants one foot firmly in contemporary life; as he later admitted, Edwin is a portrait of himself as a boy. Yet *The Minstrel* makes a different kind of claim on a reader's imagination; it is a probable fiction in a sense that the *Faerie Queene* is not. Beattie elicits historical belief through realistic depictions of peasant society and religious belief through physicotheology. Identifying pastoral simplicity with modern fideism, he hoped to regenerate a moral society in the teeth of materialism, skepticism, and David Hume: in better times, the character of a minstrel "was not only respectable, but sacred" (ed. Dyce, 3).

This ambitious program led to major and lasting changes in Spenserian poetics. Most obviously, Beattie raises rural life to heroic stature, almost as though he were rewriting the *Shepheardes Calender* as the *Faerie Queene*. Britain's poets were beginning to be seen as national heroes: "Colin Clout" could double for "Redcross" because in the nationalist program being pursued in English literature, Spenser, Shakespeare, and Milton were (as in Gray's *Elegy*) beginning to be seen as equivalents to actors on the political stage. Poems like the *Minstrel* could be seen as icons of the political order itself. Rather than using the versatile Spenserian stanza to discriminate between ranks and orders, as in the *Faerie Queene*, Beattie begins to merge high and low matters in a probable, novelistic manner emblematic of the new social order: the Spenserian stanza "admits both simplicity and magnificence of sound and language" (4). For similar reasons, Beattie makes sparing use of archaisms, despite his ostensible subject: "Antique expressions I have avoided, admitting, however, some old words, where they seem to suit the subject: but I hope that none will be found that are now obsolete" (3). Rather than use archaic diction to defamiliarize his subject, as Spenser had, Beattie retains just enough to "suit the subject," that is, a diction naturalized for poetry by Milton, Dryden, Pope, and Thomson, one that enables Moderns to merge themselves imaginatively into a fanciful, rural past:

> And oft he traced the uplands, to survey
> When o'er the sky advanced the kindling dawn,
> The crimson cloud, blue main, and mountain gray,
> And lake, dim-gleaming on the smoky lawn:
> Far to the west the long vale withdrawn,

> Where twilight loves to linger for a while;
> And now he faintly kens the bounding fawn,
> And village abroad at early toil.
> But lo! the Sun appears! and heaven, earth, ocean, smile.
>
> (15)

Such diction had in fact *been* obsolete; several of Beattie's "old words," now the common coin of literary diction, had been glossed in Hughes's Spenser. Beattie's innovations in pastoral writing had a profound effect: Shenstone and Gray understood humanist pastoral and modified it; Johnson understood humanist pastoral and rejected it. In the wake of the *Minstrel,* critics like Nathan Drake repeat Johnson's remarks seeming not at all to understand the rationale behind the artifices of humanist pastoral.

With this new poetic diction – the well of English undefiled – comes a new understanding of decorum, one that integrates ordinary life into poetry even as it uses a specialized diction to mark off subjective, "poetic" experience from the commerce of daily life. Underlying Beattie's resistance to discriminating between high and low or past and present, is a conception of "spirit" with strong social and Christian overtones. Acknowledging the objections of Johnson and others to the Spenserian stanza, Beattie writes, "It pleases my ear, and seems, from its Gothic structure and original, to bear some relation to the subject and spirit of the Poem" (4). Beattie does not spell out what he means by "gothic structure" or "spirit," yet the political and religious themes developed in the poem, and indeed the formal structure of the poem itself, suggest that by spirit he means something like Montesquieu's "spirit of the laws" or Hurd's "romantic spirit" – a structure of feeling underlying a complex whole. Just as Spenser's intertwining rhymes balance variety and unity, so the gothic constitution tempered liberty with order:

> Let thy heaven-taught soul to heaven aspire,
> To fancy, freedom, harmony, resigned;
> Ambition's groveling crew for ever left behind.
>
> (10)

In contrast to the complexity and corruption that commerce and specialization introduce into modern society, gothic institutions were simple, virtuous, and knit together by the traditions of common belief and feeling fostered by the minstrels. Insofar as Beattie's Edwin enables moderns to participate imaginatively in the virtuous passions of simple people, the poem acts as a corrective to the modes of feeling Warton censures in Pope's Belinda. In place of an Augustan commerce of differences, the *Minstrel* expresses nostalgia for an older, less differentiated unity. Much the same ideas were developed in the "heroic pastorals" James Macpherson fathered on Ossian.

Beattie's most lasting contribution to romantic poetics lies in his educational program. In contrast to Spenser's design to "fashion a gentleman or noble person in virtuous and gentle discipline," the *Minstrel* undertakes to fashion a young poet in imagination and Christian faith. Beattie's progress of poetical genius appears to be linked to a parallel regress of political genius: where a society is to be governed by "spirit," the kinds of tasks Spenser expected to be performed by a virtuous court begin to be transferred to the imaginations of unacknowledged poetic legislators. Beattie makes his hero a highland shepherd boy not because of some interest in historical recreation but because he feels that in the corrupt eighteenth century, virtue is most likely to emanate from the margins of society. He rejects Spenserian allegory in order to develop an educational program grounded in human passions accessible to all – in the contemplation of natural beauty, in the mystery of old wives' tales, in the folk wisdom of ballad literature:

> Then, as instructed by tradition hoar,
> Her legend when the Beldame 'gan impart,
> Or chant the old heroic ditty o'er,
> Wonder and joy ran thrilling to his heart;
> Much he the tale admired, but more the tuneful art.
>
> (25)

In the yet unpublished "Superstitions Ode," William Collins had declared that Spenser himself would admire such traditional Scottish minstrelsy, "Taught by the father to his listening son / Strange lays, whose power had charmed a Spenser's ear" (1788; ed. Lonsdale, 504). Beattie puts a firm damper on Edwin's poetical exuberance in his second canto – in the last analysis he was unable to imagine political virtue without something like a humanist education – but he had suggested more than enough to change the way in which romantics would read Spenser and write verse.

The Minstrel was designed to demonstrate to Hurd and others that modern poets could "revive these faery tales in an epic poem." Moreover, Beattie had answered every one of Johnson's objections to Augustan Spenserianism: Spenser's stanza could be used successfully in a long poem, Spenser's diction could be modified to suit modern tastes, Spenser's allegory could be readapted to poetry, and republican sentiments could find a place in a politically reactionary poem. Beattie's fervid Christianity – in marked contrast to the deistical sentiments of Pope and Thomson – suggested how romantic spirituality might be successfully deployed against a new kind of paynim. Beattie's faith also led to important innovations within romantic Spenserianism – in place of pagan gods or allegorical spectacle, the *Minstrel* promotes Christian doctrine through a machinery of sublime landscape description and faux-naive superstition; Christian humility finds expression in a serious treatment of humble life notably lacking in Spenser himself. I have dwelt at length with this poem because it epitomizes and transforms much eighteenth-century criticism of Spenser and because, like any other imitation, it acts as an implicit criticism of its original. The *Minstrel* takes up major themes in mid-century poetics and criticism – speculative interest in origins, natural description, humble life, the supernatural, education, political corruption – and merges them, awkwardly it must be said, into something recalling Spenserian romance. The celebrity of Beattie's poem has more to do with its intellectual than its poetic achievements. The *Minstrel* demonstrated that romance could take on the serious social business hitherto treated in epic and georgic, epistle and satire; it proved to an age obsessed with originality that a poet might imitate without copying, and emulate Spenser in a way that avoided objections to archaism, allegory, and the use of stanzas in a long poem. Beattie did all these things but did them imperfectly. For the next fifty years, romantic Spenserians would retain Beattie's doctrines while refining his poetics.

The Romantic Era

Perhaps only a poem on the order of the *Prelude* could do justice to Beattie's intellectual program. Nor is it accidental that Wordsworth's vocation so resembles Edwin's; Beattie's influence on later romantic poetry was broad and demonstrable, if often intermixed with similar ideas taken directly from Rousseau and Ossian. Most romantic Spenserians imitated Beattie in lesser genres, adapting and refining selectively. Rural life was a particularly popular theme in such poetry; in the wake of Beattie, and with a strong assist from the "Cottar's Saturday Night" by Robert Burns (1786) – which owes much to Shenstone and Beattie – the Spenserian stanza was used in village verse by Gavin Turnbull, John Thelwall, Thomas Dermody, Thomas Bidlake, Thomas Campbell, William Wordsworth, George Crabbe, John Struthers, Alexander Wilson, Bernard Barton, and John Clare. It was used for gothic narratives by John Hoole, Andrew MacDonald, Perdita Robinson, Henry Bland Burges, Hector MacNeil, Henry Boyd, Walter Scott, Margaret Hodson, James Hogg, and in Dudley Fosbrooke's antiquarian curiosity, *The Economy of Monastic Life* (1796). Spenserian stanzas were used to describe the education of poetic sensibilities by Charles Lloyd, Richard Polwhele, John Finlay, John Merivale, William Cameron, Charles Masterton, James Brydges Williamson, J. H. Wiffen, John Wilson, and John Hamilton Reynolds. Notably missing in most of this verse is the allegory that had been so popular in mid-century odes; as *simplicity* became the watchword, allegory was once again consigned to burlesque and satirical poetry. A good example of such burlesque is the advice William Hayley (1745–1820) offers in a verse epistle to his friend the painter George Romney (1778):

> But while the bounds of Hist'ry you explore,
> And bring new Treasures from her farthest shore,
> Still make Simplicity thy constant guide:
> And most, my Friend, a Syren's wiles beware,
> Ah! shun insidious Allegory's snare!
> Here Flattery offers and alluring wreath,
> Fair to the eye, but poisons lurk beneath,
> By which, too lightly tempted from his guard,
> Full many a Painter dies, and many a Bard.
> How sweet her voice, how dangerous her spell,
> Let Spenser's Knights, and Rubens's Tritons tell;
> Judgment at colour'd riddles shakes his head,
> And fairy Songs are prais'd, but little read . . . .
>
> (Epistle 2, ll. 392–404)

Hayley, it should be noted, shortly afterwards published a long didactic allegory, *The Triumphs of Temper* (1781) which was modeled after *The Rape of the Lock*. It was popular for many decades among readers who apparently hadn't been told that Pope was unfashionable and allegory beyond the pale. But Beattie's *Minstrel* is the more exemplary instance of what late-century readers expected from verbal painting; Spenserian stanzas were used in descriptive and topographical poetry by William Combe, William Sotheby, Elizabeth Smith, James Grahame, Lord Byron, George Croly, William Lisle Bowles, William Cullen Bryant, Felicia Hemans, and a host of other very minor poets and anonymous periodical versifiers. Calling the roll of Beattie's imitators, one begins to get a sense of the depth of romantic Spenserianism; its breadth can hardly be measured, for the groundswell of nineteenth-century verse written in Spenserians (most bearing scant relation to Spenser) has been little studied.

By the turn of the century Britain was mad for poetry in a way that it never was before or since; Spenser was imitated by laboring peasants and by peers of the realm – if "imitation" can still be applied to verse so remote from Spenser's beliefs and practices. Humanist poetry, tied to an ethics of imitation practiced at court and college, could not survive the consequences of the commerce and global empire building that Spenser and Raleigh themselves had advocated. As the population of Britain surged, so did the public that was producing and consuming polite literature – perhaps ten times larger in 1800 than it had been in 1700 and a hundred times larger than in 1600. The character of Spenser criticism had changed in 1700 when literary production shifted from court to coffeehouse; it changed again in 1800 as it expanded out of the urban clubs and into a diversified public sphere comprised of lesser gentry, schoolteachers, government and church officials, and persons in trade. By 1800 Dublin and Edinburgh, even Philadelphia and New York, were important centers in an international book trade. Like so much else, literature had become a commodity, changing and diversifying in response to the demands of volatile market forces. As much as poets and critics might deplore these changes, they afforded writers freedom from the moils of patronage and held out the possibility of wealth as well as fame. Accordingly, the genres of criticism changed once more. The needs of a diverse and far-flung readership were best met by a periodical press that could match its product to the various tastes and levels of education of different market sectors, accommodating the interests of specialized readerships of women, clerics, or local populations, or, reaching over their heads, to a more cosmopolitan reading public. Eighteenth-century periodicals like the *Gentleman's Magazine* and *European Magazine* devoted columns to literary criticism and original poetry; after 1790 newer and more specialized literary reviews appeared like mushrooms after a summer rain. In the 1760s the pioneer *Monthly Review* and *Critical Review* offered little more than a paragraph of summary and description to any given poem; by the 1830s journals such as *Blackwood's* or the *Quarterly Review* might devote thirty pages to important new works. The importance of these journals to literary criticism would be difficult to overestimate: if the century following the publication of Warton's *Observations* is now remembered as the golden age of Spenser criticism, that long period can boast not one significant book devoted exclusively to Spenser. Before the rise of modern academic criticism, poems, prefaces, and periodical essays remained the primary media of criticism.

Virtually all of the periodical writing was published anonymously, even when written by the leading lights of the day. This was a nod toward the idea that, in theory at least, all citizens were equal in the republic of letters – though in fact there was a clear pecking order among journals that competed to attract the better-known writers of the day. The reviews had many subscribers and paid well; all but the most popular poets stood to earn more by their prose than by their verse. To really shine, the man of letters would pursue another, related, form of criticism that was anything but anonymous: the public lecture. It is difficult to imagine Dryden, Pope, or even Johnson lecturing about Spenser to an audience of ticket holders. Yet by the early nineteenth century the commercial demand for criticism became such that Coleridge, Hazlitt, and Campbell could speak to packed houses (small, however, compared to what the novelists could command later in the century). Johnson's *Lives of the Poets* was the model and the immediate inspiration for their performances, which would expound the biography and character of a writer, comment on his place in literary history, and offer readings and strictures on familiar passages. Public lectures shared points in common with dramatic performances but also with the sermon: as the vast oeuvre of British poetry was assuming the status of a secular scripture, expositors of a national spirit expressed through poetry were taking on the public roles Coleridge assigned to his clerisy. In 1701 John Dennis had complained that "Moliere, Corneille and Racine, and Boileau, are known in a manner to all the Christian World; whereas Spencer and Milton, Ben Johnson and Shakespear, are Strangers, as it were, to all the World, excepting the Subjects of Great Britain" (ed. Hooker, 1:205); a century later British literature was read all around the world. This had something to do with the quality of the best poetry and the rising stature of literary criticism but also with the burgeoning commercial empire. These factors were very much intertwined.

With the diffusion of literacy and an expanding market for literature, virtually anyone with pretensions to taste could publish poetry and criticism. Many felt that the general run of literary production had declined from earlier standards; it did not help that the poet laureate, Robert Southey, modeled himself on Spenser while turning out epic poems like so many novels. Distanced by time from the gossip, satire, and scandal bedeviling contemporary writers, the revered classics assumed an ever higher status: the British Poets reposed secure in their uniform bindings while the Blatant Beast pursued living quarry through the journals and newspapers. Shakespeare is the obvious example beneficiary of this turn of events, but Spenser also enjoyed a reputation for more-than-mortal genius. Pope and Dryden looked upon Spenser as a fellow writer, fallible to say the least; but to many young romantics he seemed to inhabit a different order of being. In "On First Looking into Chapman's Homer" (published in 1817) young John Keats compared his encounter with Elizabethan literature to Cortez's discovery of the Pacific Ocean (the heroic sentiment more than compensates for the historical error). In 1816 Keats's friend John Hamilton Reynolds, always a good barometer of taste, writes of "superior spirits who survive after the multitude has perished, and thus collectively joining their different eras, form a cloud of witnesses . . . . Their respective times are now *theirs*; – they make them what they seem to us; – they fashion out their epochs, giving them their form and pressure, – and the periods exist in our imaginations modeled according to the greatest minds they produced." The quarrelsome works of Harvey and Nashe, Prynne and Rymer, Dennis and Bentley were not reprinted, possibly lending earlier literature a misleading appearance of Olympian composure. In comparison to the "golden spires and magnificent cupolas" of the ages of Elizabeth and Anne, modern literature seemed to consist of "little narrow dirty streets where dwell the diminutive dealers in small ware" (ed. Jones, 74). Democratizing the republic of letters boosted the reputation of British Spenser, and for a time he seems to have been almost popular.

Romantic critics like Reynolds were particularly prone to discover in past ages the unity and cohesion of "spirit" lacking in their own commercial society, fragmented by professional specialization and rapid social change. The belief that a genial spirit of the age presided over past eras was fostered by confidence in the unifying imagination of their great writers; the gentle spirit

Beattie evoked in Edwin was discovered in Chaucer and Spenser, Shakespeare and Milton. This conjunction of historicism and aestheticism in romantic criticism is the basis of Shelley's claim that poets are "unacknowledged legislators." The proper business of the poet is not to offer high examples of virtue to gentlemen and courtiers but to shape the desires and imaginations of strangers in an anonymous republic of letters. This notion was not entirely foreign to Spenser, who after all published his works so that they might be purchased and seen by all. But in romantic criticism the humanist's emphasis on imitation and discipline yields to a new emphasis on originality and "laws." The republicans Milton and Locke had advocated a rule of law to supplant the monarch as the basis for freedom in modern society; literary critics, both Augustan and romantic, sought an equivalent "law" to regulate the republic of letters. In the 1800 preface to *Lyrical Ballads* Wordsworth looks in one direction, proposing to make "the incidents of common life interesting by tracing in them, truly though not ostentatiously, the primary *laws* of our nature" (ed. Owen, 156). Percy Bysshe Shelley looked the opposite way, regarding the poets themselves as lawgivers. While both Wordsworth and Shelley admired Spenser, they had grave reservations about his courtly ethics of imitation. In the "Defense of Poetry" (posthumously published in 1840), Shelley demotes poetical moralizing to such an extent that he explicitly questions Spenser's stature as a poet: "Those in whom the poetical faculty, though great, is less intense, as Euripides, Lucan, Tasso, Spenser, have frequently affected a moral aim, and the effect of their poetry is diminished in exact proportion to the degree in which they compel us to advert to this purpose" (ed. Clark, 283). Like Hurd's reading of Spenser, the criticism of Wordsworth and Shelley divorces probable moral action from a higher "spirit" of the laws.

Given their inconsistent belief in both the waywardness of genius and the fixed laws of human psychology, one would not expect romantic critics to have much to say about the complex interplay between formal design and ethical teachings in the *Faerie Queene*. The grace beyond the reach of art, the last resort of Augustan critics, became normative in their criticism to such an extent that romantic readers looked with astonished contempt upon their predecessors' attempts to discover a structure of probable morality in Spenser's romantic poetry: "It is ignorant of all artificial boundaries, all material objects; it is truly in the land of Fairy, that is, of mental space," remarked Coleridge in his lectures (posthumously published 1836; *ES*, 144). Ethical matters were better handled in prose by systematic thinkers like Kant or Godwin. The beauty of a *poem* lies less in its moral matter than in its romantic manner, a style expressing the peculiar genius of its creator and (depending on the context) the timeless laws of poetry, the genius of Britain, or the spirit of the Elizabethan Age. As it always had, the *Faerie Queene* continued to challenge and ultimately to influence the forms of criticism used to describe it. The meanderings of

Spenser's narrative, his wallowings in bowers of bliss, his virtuoso powers of character description – in one way or another, all found echoes in high-romantic critical writing about the *Faerie Queene*. One looks in vain for developed, original arguments in later romantic criticism of Spenser. Essayists and lecturers recycled comments lifted from Hughes, Warton, and Hurd, often turning them against the very authors who first uttered them; surely such cold, reptilian neoclassicists could not appreciate Spenser! If the search for a unifying spirit in Spenser's writings inhibited many kinds of critical discrimination, romantic criticism also rewarded readers with rich lodes of personality and connoisseurship. Reviewers of Todd's variorum edition of Spenser (1805) argued that criticism of poetry required a critic who was a poet, and essayists and lecturers devoted considerable energy and skill to describing and dramatizing their imaginative responses to the *Faerie Queene*. Spenser's reputation as a maker of poets began to acquire a secondary sense, as readers encountered Coleridge's Spenser, Hazlitt's Spenser, Hunt's Spenser, "Christopher North's" Spenser – all generally romantic, each colored by the personality and private preoccupations of the commentator. The same phenomenon is apparent in romantic verse: apart from levels of craft, it would be difficult to distinguish imitations by Breval, West, Thomson, and Upton; not so imitations by Wordsworth, Campbell, Keats, and Shelley, all of which display immediately recognizable personal mannerisms.

Spenser's Stanza, Character, and Allegory

In the wake of Beattie, the Spenserian stanza became a perennial subject of comment. In 1820 an irate father wrote to the *Talisman* to complain about how the journals were corrupting his fifteen-year-old son's advanced tastes in poetry. A man of the old school, he cites Johnson's *Rambler* with approval and defines the Spenserian stanza as something that "goes like the quavering of a Scotch bagpipe, and then sinks into a most lamentable long whine at the end" (59). This is an extreme case. Shenstone, Thomson, and Beattie had made Spenser's stanza respectable, but Byron's *Childe Harold*, which began appearing in 1812, made it truly common. Byron had not read Spenser at that point; he was writing after Beattie. As late as 1805 Mary Tighe was still expressing Davenant's old canard in *Psyche*, which was, after *The Castle of Indolence* the most popular formal imitation of the *Faerie Queene* ever written: "the frequent recurrence of the same rhymes is by no means well adapted to the English language, and I know not whether I have a right to offer, as an apology, the restraint which I had imposed upon myself of strictly adhering to the stanza, which my partiality for Spenser first inclined me to adopt" (1811, xiii). In an 1811 letter to her father, Mary Russell Mitford (1787–1855) also commented on the difficulty of the stanza: "[Walter] Scott certainly does not excel in the

Spenser stanza. He has been so long accustomed to make the measure bend to him, that he can not bend to the measure, and a consequence results from it something similar to that in the Taming of the Shrew: 'Why, then, thou canst no break her to the lute? / Why, no; for she hath broke the lute on me!' Messieurs the reviewers are unanimous in the recommendation of the Spenser stanza; but, I don't know how it is, whenever any one writes in it there is some unaccountable fault – a coldness, a stiffness, or an obscurity which spoils the sale of the work. It is the bow of Ulysses, and I shall leave the attempt to bolder suitors" (1:109). Byron changed all that; only a year after Mitford's remarks, in a review of *Childe Harold*, the *British Review* could assert the artless versatility of a stanza "in which the grotesque and the sedate, the lofty and the mean, the sad and the humorous, are so harmoniously blended, that, whether it is the nature of the verse itself, or a consequence of the prejudices connected with it, certain it is, that nothing but the wild, the remote, the allegorical, or the romantic appears in it with becoming effect" (3:275). Byron's poem was, properly speaking, an imitation of Beattie rather than Spenser, as was Wordsworth's brooding political meditation, "Salisbury Plain," the source of "The Female Vagrant" as published in *Lyrical Ballads*. In the *Biographia Literaria* (1817) Coleridge recalled how his original response to Wordsworth's account of poverty and superstition was shaped by Beattie-inspired "prejudices": "The Spenserian stanza, which always, more or less, recalls to the reader's mind Spenser's own style, would doubtless have authorized in my *then* opinion a more frequent descent to the phrases of ordinary life, than could without an ill effect have been hazarded in the heroic couplet" (ed. Engell and Bate, 1:80–81; my emphasis). Such was the legacy of *The School-Mistress, The Minstrel*, and the "Cottar's Saturday Night"; after the appearance of *Childe Harold*, Spenserian stanzas were no longer regarded as best-suited to rustic, grotesque, or antiquarian subjects.

For most of the twenty years since Coleridge first heard "Salisbury Plain," England had been at war with France; indeed, the contest for empire is a dominant theme in both "Salisbury Plain" and *Childe Harold*. During the Napoleonic Wars, as in every war with France since the seventeenth century, "British" Spenser enjoyed a boost in status. This can be seen in Coleridge's attitude toward the Spenserian stanza. Like more than a few romantics before or since, Coleridge learned to write in this form by burlesquing Spenser. His "Effusion XXIV. In the Manner of Spenser" (1796) might have been written by Mickle, Mendez, Shenstone, or any of a number of eighteenth-century imitators:

> But LOVE, who heard the silence of my thought,
> Contriv'd a too successful wile, I ween:
> And whisper'd to himself, with malice fraught –
> "Too long our Slave the Damsel's smiles hath seen:

To-morrow shall he ken her alter'd mien!"
He spake, and ambush'd lay, till on my bed
The morning shot her dewy glances keen,
When as I 'gan to lift my drowsy head –
"Now Bard! I'll work thee woe!" the laughing Elfin said.

(ed. E. H. Coleridge, 74–75)

In such verse the stanza, like the archaisms, is taken none too seriously. By the time of the 1819 lectures, however, the stanza had acquired something like philosophical status; Coleridge prefaces an analysis of "the harmony of [Spenser's] description with the allegorical and activity of the Poem" with a discussion of "the scientific construction of the meter" (*ES*, 142). The lecturer's aesthetic responses to "science" were not so far removed from the philosophical raptures of Beattie's physicotheology; both were concerned with the physical manifestations of an unseen spirit. William Hazlitt's lectures, published in 1818, deliver a less metaphysical response to the stanza with exceptional gusto and connoisseurship: "it is a labyrinth of sweet sounds, 'in many a winding bout of linked sweetness long drawn out,' that would cloy by their very sweetness, but that the ear is constantly relieved and enchanted by their continued variety of modulation, dwelling on the pauses of the action, or flowing on in a fuller tide of harmony with the movement of the sentiment . . . . It has the perfection of melting harmony, dissolving the soul in pleasure, or holding it captive in the chains of suspense" (*ES*, 138). On such occasions the more discriminating verbal criticism of philologists like Jortin, Upton, and Thomas Warton yields to a *spirited* impressionism. In his 1746 ode "To Fancy," Joseph Warton had made a similar point using a similar allusion to Milton; in the intervening decades "romanticism" had migrated from effusions in verse to effusions in prose. The metaphors Hazlitt uses to describe his enthusiasm for Spenser suggest the very effects a good lecturer-rhapsode might produce in an audience; Coleridge in particular was known for enthralling audiences with linked arguments long drawn out.

Common to the public lecture and the *Faerie Queene* itself is an emphasis on "character," a second recurring topic of romantic criticism. Spenser expounded manners, politics, and theology by reducing ideas to types and types to personifications. Eighteenth-century readers were conversant with this kind of allegory, although as we have seen they believed that Spenser failed to subordinate his characters to a probable narrative design, or even to a coherent visual image. Romantic readers, especially those, like Coleridge, touched by German idealism, adopted a more Platonic understanding of types and hence a different concept of allegory; in their criticism "characters" have an existence prior to and sometimes independent of the action in which they appear. Looked at another way, characters in a work were exterior manifestations of the interior character of the author, a poetical character valued, as in Collins's

Ode, for being exceptional rather than normative. In this sense, Coleridge could regard the inventors of truly original figures like Caliban or Talus as themselves all but supernatural. As personality displaced personification, romantic poems, essays, and lectures strove to capture the essentials of Spenser's "character," about which there was surprising consensus. For Nathan Drake in *Shakespeare and his Times* (1817), the *Faerie Queene* and its author are marked by exquisite tenderness: it is "impossible indeed to read it without being in love with the author, without being persuaded that the utmost sweetness of disposition, and the purest sincerity and goodness of heart distinguished him who thus delighted to unfold the kindest feelings of our nature, and whose language, by its singular simplicity and energy, seems to breathe the very stamp and force of truth" (1838, 314). One recognizes behind this formulation and many others like it an approach the *Faerie Queene* mediated by the sentimentalizing imitations by Shenstone, Beattie, Burns, and Tighe.

In his "Specimen of an Induction," also published in 1817, John Keats invokes Spenser's character in similar terms, the young poet adopting a posture of supplication that recalls Collins and the Wartons sixty years earlier:

> Spenser! thy brows are arched, open, kind,
> And come like a clear sun-rise to my mind;
> And always does my heart with pleasure dance,
> When I think on thy noble countenance:
> Where never yet was aught more earthly seen
> Than the pure freshness of thy laurels green.
> Therefore, great bard, I not so fearfully
> Call on thy gentle spirit to hover nigh
> My daring steps . . . .

(ed. Garrod, 10)

In part, the gentleness romantic readers perceived in Spenser developed out of an implied contrast with the sublimity of Shakespeare and Milton. In the *Biographia* Coleridge discovers "a mind constitutionally tender, delicate . . . I had almost said, effeminate" (1:36). In an 1816 sonnet published in *The Champion* and addressed to "sweet" Spenser, John Hamilton Reynolds coos, "Fair is thy record of romantic ages, / And calm and pure the pleasure which it yields" (78); the anonymous author of *The Village Sunday* (1809) praises "Spenser's simplicity and tenderness of description." In 1819 Thomas Campbell describes Spenser's verse as "warmly, tenderly, and magnificently descriptive." The sternness of the "Legend of Justice" is virtually ignored in romantic discussions of character, save in an 1818 swipe by Hazlitt at unromantic Pope, who supposedly "had only dipped into these last" three books (*ES*, 137).

Longinian precepts encouraged critics to seize on "characteristic" fragments without having to consider contrary evidence, but even so, a strong act of will must have been required to ignore Spenser's moralizing. Hazlitt attempted to quash nattering doubts: "the love of beauty, however, and not of truth, is the moving principle of his mind; and he is guided in his fantastic delineations by no rule but the impulse of an inexhaustible imagination. He luxuriates equally in scenes of Eastern magnificence or the still solitude of a hermit's cell, in the extremes of sensuality or refinement" (*ES*, 132). Hazlitt represents the *Faerie Queene* as one continuous Bower of Bliss, entwining its readers haplessly in Acrasia's toils. Thomson's *Castle of Indolence* and Beattie's *Minstrel* had opposed aesthetic to ethical readings of Spenser (their bifurcated forms presenting readers with a Herculean choice between Pleasure and Virtue); romantic readers universally preferred the first to the second cantos of these poems. Keats's early "Calidore, A Fragment" which otherwise recalls both Thomson and Beattie, never gets around to the unpleasant reversal:

> Young Calidore is paddling o'er the lake
> His healthful spirit eager and awake
> To feel the beauty of a silent eve,
> Which seem'd full loath this happy world to leave.
> The light dwelt o'er the scene so lingeringly.
> He bares his forehead to the cool blue sky,
> And smiles at the far clearness all around,
> Until his heart is well nigh over wound,
> And turns for calmness to the pleasant green
> Of easy slopes, and shadowy trees that lean
> So elegantly o'er the waters' brim
> And show their blossoms trim.

(1817; ed. Garrod, 11)

No Palmer sage intervenes to spoil the idyll, nor do these "easy slopes" lead downward to error and entrapment. "Negative capability," as Keats termed the poetical character, is profoundly opposed to Spenser's ethical demands for discipline and restraint. In "The Eve of Saint Agnes" (1820), best-loved of all Spenserian imitations, the seduction described in the narrative appears to be a figure for Keats's own desire to be possessed by Spenser's descriptive gorgeousness,

> At length burst in the argent revelry,
> With plume, tiara, and all rich array,
> Numerous as the shadows haunting fairily
> The brain, new stuff'd, in youth, with triumphs gay
> Of old romance

(ed. Garrod, 196)

Yet there remained a snake lurking in the Spenserian garden, a snake yclept Allegory. In what is probably the most famous passage in Spenser criticism, Hazlitt's lectures chide readers for their timidity: "They are afraid of the allegory, as if they thought it would bite them: they look at it as a child looks at a painted dragon, and think it will strangle them in its shining folds. This is very idle. If they do not meddle with the allegory, the allegory will not meddle with them" (*ES*, 133). But readers *would* meddle with the allegory; no other topic receives such consistent attention from romantic critics. The suicide Henry Neele (1798–1828) voiced the common complaint in another series of published lectures: "Spenser's hero is always honour, truth, valour, courtesy; but it is not man. His heroine is meekness, chastity, constancy, beauty; but it is not woman. His landscapes are fertility, magnificence, verdure, splendour; but they are not nature. His pictures have no relief; they are all light, or all shadow; they are all wonder, but not truth" (1829). The Scottish poet Thomas Campbell uses an allusion to a famous stanza in Thomson's *Castle* to make a virtue of Spenser's dreamy pictorialism: "The clouds of his allegory may seem to spread into shapeless forms, but they are still the clouds of a glowing atmosphere. Though his story grows desultory, the sweetness and grace of his manner still abide by him" (1819). Campbell had emulated this same sweetness of manner (without the allegory) in *Gertrude of Wyoming* (1809), one of the better imitations of Beattie.

Condemnation of allegory was not universal among romantic critics of Spenser, though most voices were raised in protest. Like Joseph Spence in *Polymetis*, an anonymous *Quarterly* reviewer of Mary Tighe's *Psyche* declares in 1811 that "consistency has it claims; nor can any worse accident befall an allegory, than that the war between its direct and its typical signification become so fierce and open, as to force on our attention both of them at once, and that in a state of raging enmity. The lamentable aberrations of Spenser in this respect, are well known" (5:477). Taking another tack, an 1813 review in the *Eclectic* asserts that "we have had no fellow feeling in conversing with such beings, and we suffer no regret when they are vanished: they come like shadows, and so departed. If ever allegorical characters excite either sympathy or affection, it is when we forget that they are allegorical, consequently when the allegory itself is suspended, with respect to them" (9:226–27). In the *Gentleman's Magazine* for 1819, "C. B." reverts to an older probabilism in censuring Spenser's characters: "it is by the feelings of the heart, and the propensities of the soul, that we are enabled to make an estimate of individual character; and therefore to typify any of those properties under a living form, is to destroy all our measures of its actions in the usual occurrences of life" (89:318). In an 1830 review of Robert Southey's edition of *Pilgrim's Progress*, Sir Walter Scott found in Spenser's allegory "the character of a cold and unimpassioned moralist" in comparison to Bunyan (*ES*, 152). Where Hughes and Addison found in

Spenser's pictorial allegory a means by which a society might be united through common sense, the later romantics believed that moral allegory interfered with the sympathetic identification required to unify a society through the apprehension of an uncommon character, genius, or spirit.

Imagination and Morality

Coleridge's criticisms of Spenserian allegory, founded in his distinction between fancy and imagination, have proved more durable than most, deservedly so, for unlike Hazlitt or Campbell, he acknowledges the centrality of allegory to Spenser's poetics. As a young man, Coleridge not only imitated Spenser, but went so far as to adopt "Satyrane" as a pen name. Later in his life, his dramatic readings of Spenser's verse enthralled listeners; much of the *Faerie Queene* reposed in his proverbial memory. Nevertheless, while Spenser remained a great favorite, in his lectures Coleridge was finally unwilling to regard him as a poet of the first rank: "The great and prevailing character of Spenser's mind is fancy under the conditions of imagination, as an ever present but not always active power. He has an imaginative fancy, but he has not imagination, in kind or degree, as Shakespeare and Milton have . . . . Add to this a feminine tenderness and almost maidenly purity of feeling, and above all, a deep moral earnestness which produces a believing sympathy and acquiescence in the reader, and you have a tolerably adequate view of Spenser's intellectual being" (*ES*, 146). Like Joseph Warton damning Pope through faint praise, Coleridge discovers lapses of imagination and poetry that is not pure – purely imaginative, that is. Why would so many writers describe this most goatish of poets as "maidenly" or "feminine"? In the case of Coleridge, this appears to have something to do with idealizing conceptions of unity: "imagination" implies a masculine self-containedness in contrast to a feminine "fancy" dependent on an Other. Allegory is unable to stand alone: "For if the allegoric personage be strongly individualized so as to interest us, we cease to think of it as allegory; and if it does not interest us, it had better be away" (*ES*, 140). Spenser's dualism appears effeminate beside Shakespeare and Milton with their superior, "masculine" powers of integration through symbolism. Even Keats, who pursued unity through a "feminine" power of negative capability, later attempted to leave Spenser behind, taking up Shakespeare and then Milton in a hot pursuit of sublimity. In an 1818 letter to Charles Brown, Keats states his determination to go beyond the poetasters: "Mrs. Tighe and Beattie once delighted me – now I see through them and can find nothing in them – or weakness – and yet how many they still delight! Perhaps a superior being may look upon Shakespeare in the same light – is it possible? No" (ed. Forman, 259).

Such gendered criticisms tell us more about nineteenth-century romanticism than renaissance romance; the poet who created Belphoebe and Gloriana was less inclined to identify femininity with dependence or sensuality, while some of his female characters display an excess of both. Because Spenser understood self-possession as a matter of ethical choice, in his poetry chastity is a less sex-specific virtue. Self-possession is not the same as autonomy, nor does love necessarily imply a loss of self-control. When romantic readers dismiss Spenser's ethical themes as the product of a "cold" moralism, not Arthur's or Britomart's patient questing but the immediacy of possession becomes their ideal: the self-possession admired by Coleridge or the being-possessed admired by Keats. Spenser's frank sensuality was admired by poets who regarded the Bower of Bliss as the archetype of romantic liberation: "Into her dream he melted, as the rose / Blendeth its odour with the violet" ("Eve of St. Agnes"), to which one can only compare Spenser's unforgettable (one would have thought) allegory of ethical laxity: "And through his humid eyes did sucke his spright, / Quite molten into lust and pleasure lewd" (2.xii.73). Maidenly Spenser was ravished by romantic misreaders intent on pleasure, even as masculine Milton was subverted by romantic misreaders intent on displays of less Christian forms of heroism. That readers would object to Spenser's procedure of yoking an extremely sensuous vehicle to an extremely ethical tenor – a criticism not heard before the nineteenth century – also tells us something about how aestheticism was rendering Spenser's moral teachings as incomprehensible as his predilection for allegory. The unusual and much-remarked presence of allegory in Mary Tighe's *Psyche* is the exception that proves the rule, for only she – the rare woman among Spenserian poets – mingles fervent eroticism with the praises of chastity. Tighe's poem grew out of a different, feminine tradition of romanticism: she was emulating William Hayley, who was emulating Alexander Pope, who had first introduced Spenser's erotic combats into the realm of tea tables and drawing rooms.

Spenser's supposed femininity was also bound up with romantic conceptions of poetic imitation, the most literal form of taking possession of an object "arched, open, kind." Milton had always been imitated more frequently than Spenser. But as imitations of *Paradise Lost* proved stubbornly unsuccessful, Milton came to be seen as inimitable, as inviolate. Not so Spenser: Florimell's girdle was worn by each passing knight, sometimes very successfully indeed. Spenser was, in the phrase attributed to Lamb, "the Poet's Poet": the darling of Milton, Cowley, Dryden, and Pope; of Thomson, Collins, and Gray; of Coleridge, Wordsworth, and Southey; of Byron, Shelley, and Keats. Ambitious poets imitated Spenser as preparation for higher things; minor poets imitated the *Faerie Queene* because it was easy. In the words of Washington Irving's Pindar Cockloft (1807):

Dan Spenser, Dan Chaucer, those poets of old,
Though covered with dust, are yet sterling gold;
I can grind off their tarnish, and bring them to view,
New-modeled, new-mill'd, and improved in their hue.

(Works, 16:68).

Poor Spenser! Among the classicists he was censured for ruggedness; among the romantics, he was demoted for femininity. Yet even as those critics used metaphors of sexual filiation to define an upward progress toward commerce and politeness, and these to define a downward regress towards originality and individuation, Spenser's canonical status remained always secure. Because he was the parent of poets, the story of British literature could not be told without him.

There were some romantic readers capable of appreciating Spenser's allegory, even Spenser's ethical concern with chastity. Wordsworth's scattered remarks on Spenser are the products of a long life's reflections, a life quite remote from the marketplace and lecture hall. The comments on allegory in the 1815 "Preface" read like a riposte to Coleridge's philosophical dogmatizing: "Spenser, of a gentler nature [than Milton], maintained his freedom by aid of his allegorical spirit, at one time inciting him to create persons out of abstractions; and at another, by a superior effort of genius, to give the universality and permanence of abstractions to his human beings, by means of attributes and emblems that belong to the highest moral truths and the purest sensations, – of which his character of Una is a glorious example" (ed. Zall, 151). To continue the sexual metaphor, Wordsworth was chaste in imitation, as in most other matters. While young Coleridge was burlesquing the *Faerie Queene* in "Lines in the Manner of Spenser," Wordsworth was conducting a reasoned and sober dissent in "Salisbury Plain," one of the few eighteenth-century "republican" responses to Spenser to openly acknowledge the profound political differences separating Elizabethan from Georgian politics. In "Nutting" (1800) Wordsworth presents himself as a belated Spenserian pilgrim, "Figure quaint, / Tricked out in proud disguise of cast-off weeds" descending into a latter-day Bower of Blisse. In complete contrast to Keats's "Young Calidore . . . paddling o'er the lake . . . eager and awake," Wordsworth's knowing self-portrait as a young man displays an equally sophisticated knowledge of the poems he is imitating – both the naive Beattie in his "eagerness of boyish hopes" and the sophisticated Spenser in the "tangled thicket" of wandering error (ed. Hayden, 1:368). No doubt Wordsworth remembered, as did Beattie, the account in "December" of how, "whilome in youth, when flowr'd my joyfull spring" Colin, "stung by heedlesse lust" would "gather nuttes to make me Christmas game" (ll.19, 28). As poet, critic, and ethical being, Wordsworth followed Guyon's lofty example in taking Temperance as his guide.

Most romantic writers simply visited the *Faerie Queene* as if it were a museum – a glorious gallery of noble pictures, some profane, some sacred in a classical sort of way (in 1819 the "Cave of Despair" was the assigned subject at the Royal Academy). Painterly comparisons became a virtuoso exercise for lecturers and essayists. The high point of such criticism is "A New Gallery of Pictures" (1833) by Keats's friend and mentor, Leigh Hunt (1784–1859). In 1801 Hunt had published *Juvenilia,* a volume crammed with imitations of Spenser and Milton, Collins and Gray; he knew the Spenserian pictorial tradition intimately. His gallery tour through the *Faerie Queene* leads readers impressionistically past a sequence of imbedded Titians, Rafaels, Cuyps, Rembrandts, and Poussins. Here is yet another example of Spenser's poetry entering into criticism, for essays like Hunt's plainly take rise from Spenser's own exercises in ecphrasis, such as Britomart's encounter with Busirane's palace: "That wondrous sight faier Britomart amazed, / Ne seeing could her wonder satisfie" (3.xi.49). Protestant Spenser is alert to the moral perils of idolatry, signalled by the "discolourd Snake" winding its way through the threads of both the magician's tapestries and Spenser's verse (3.xi.28). Like many of his contemporaries, Hunt prefers the seductions of the literal narrative: the "allegorical paintings are . . . sometimes admirable, but . . . generally speaking, they are by no means the best." Spenser's genius "is picturesque, not so much because it can paint abstract moral portraits, as because it overflows with the luxuriousness of every species of beauty and enjoyment, with the picquancies of contrast, and a hearty faith in nature left to herself. Spenser is not half so didactic a personage as he himself thought he was!" (ed. Houtchens and Houtchens, 442). On this point, Hunt is at one with Keats, who in "The Eve of Saint Agnes" mimics Comus in tempting the eye with "candied apple, quince, and plum, and gourd" – a *nature morte,* worthy of a Dutch master, of Mammon's own hoard. Naturally he omits the fly on the jelly, an omission the more striking if one of Keats's literary models was "Christabel" (1816); in Coleridge's profoundly romantic-Spenserian reflections on scopophilia, Geraldine's Duessa-like person remains "a sight to dream of, not to tell" (ed. E. H. Coleridge, 224). Spenser himself was not shy about describing female anatomy, lovely or loathsome; in 1816 John Hamilton Reynolds acknowledges this, while somehow missing the point: "He says more of the persons of women than any other writer, and yet he never says too much. He is always gratifying the senses – but his gratifications serve to purify, by their very refinement" (ed. Jones, 61).

In the 1820s and 30s, as Wordsworth's stature was beginning to rise, one detects the beginnings of a retreat from the hedonistic readings of Spenser we associate with Hazlitt, Hunt, and Keats. In 1826 even the doting connoisseur Charles Lamb (1775–1834) underscores "that hidden sanity which still guides the poet in his widest seeming aberrations." The bewildering transitions in the

Cave of Mammon episode "are every whit as violent as in the most extravagant dream, and yet the waking judgment ratifies them" (ed. Lucas, 2:189). Looking for a "moral center," John Henry Newman (1801–90) anticipated the Oxford Movement when in 1829 he included Spenser in a short list of poets whose "right moral feeling places the mind in the very center of that circle from which all the rays have their origin and range; whereas minds otherwise placed command but a portion of the whole circuit of poetry" (ed. Alden, 321). In 1817 the "Cockney School of Poetry" series in *Blackwood's* was already sneering at a Leigh Hunt who "pretends, indeed, to be an admirer of Spenser and Chaucer, but what he praises in them is never what is most deserving of praise . . . . We can always discover, in the midst of his most violent ravings about the Court of Elizabeth, and the days of Sir Philip Sidney, and the *Faery Queen* – that the real objects of his admiration are the Coterie of Hampstead and the Editor of the *Examiner*" (2:39).

This remark is revealing. The romanticism we tend to remember – Blake, the Cockney School, the Lakers, and the Godwin-Shelley circle – *was* a coterie phenomenon. Popular Spenserian verse was of a different and much more conservative cast, being written by the likes of Mary Tighe, Thomas Campbell, Felicia Hemans, Henry Kirke White, and the later Southey. The objection of the Edinburgh reviewer – Walter Scott's son-in-law and biographer John Gibson Lockhart (1794–1854) – typifies the repossession of Spenser by political conservatives. This marks a change: in the early romantic era, the "violent ravings" of Spenserian writers took a Whiggish, even republican cast in the odes of Akenside, Collins, and Gray and in the forgotten writings of Dublin Protestants like Philip Doyne and Samuel Whyte. Their Spenserian revival was heartily opposed by conservative writers like Johnson. The French Revolution changed all that. Wordsworth's early, pacifist "Salisbury Plain," for instance, already deploys Spenserian stanzas and allegory in opposition to the liberal creed of commerce and modernity. Before long, conservative journals like the *Anti-Jacobin*, the *British Critic*, and *Blackwood's* were enlisting Spenser – appropriately, it must be said – in the cause of throne-and-altar Tory politics. In 1829 Newman's Oxford friend (and the future poetry professor) the Rev. John Keble wrote in the *Quarterly* that Spenser is "pre-eminently the sacred poet of his country" (32:231); as decades passed, the nineteenth century would "sucke spright" from an increasingly Christian and patriotic Spenser. This was the commonplace view in the Victorian era, when in 1879 Dean Church could find in Spenser "a great and sustained effort of rich and varied art, in which one main purpose rules – loyalty to what is noble and pure" (165).

If the early verse of laureate Warton marks an official beginning of the romantic movement, the early verse of laureate Tennyson marks an official close. The five opening stanzas of "Lotos-Eaters" (1833) are written in Spenserians and slyly evoke Keats and a certain kind of post-Beattie romantic Spenserianism:

> "Courage!" he said, and pointed toward the land,
> "This mounting wave will roll us shoreward soon."
> In the afternoon they came unto a land
> In which it seemed always afternoon.
> All round the coast the languid air did swoon,
> Breathing like one that hath a weary dream.
> Full-faced above the valley stood the moon;
> And like a downward smoke, the slender stream
> Along the cliff to fall and pause and fall did seem.
>
> (Poetical Works, 51)

This metaphorical stream of verse echoes and burlesques Thomas Gray's "Progress of Poesy," written in imitation of the hero-praising Pindar:

> Now rolling down the steep amain,
> Headlong, impetuous, see it pour:
> The rocks and nodding groves rebellow to the roar.
>
> (1757; ed. Lonsdale, 163)

For too long, British poetry had neglected its epic quest to linger idly in the paths of pleasure. To set British poetry once more on the high road to progress, Tennyson, like Thomson's Knight of Industry, signals an intent to reverse the spiritual acrasia of a downward-drifting romanticism. In Victorian criticism, a grave and moral Spenser returns, dimly remembered, to Ithaca.

Works Cited

Akenside, Mark. *Odes on Several Subjects*. London, 1745.

"The Apotheosis of Milton: A Vision," *Gentleman's Magazine* 8 (May 1738): 232–34.

Bathurst, Charles. "The Poetical Triumvirate: Spenser, Shakespeare, Milton. *Poems*. London, 1849.

Beattie, James. *The Minstrel; Or, The Progress of Genius*. London, 1771, 1774. In *Poetical Works*, ed. Alexander Dyce. London: Bell, 1894.

Boswell, James. *The Life of Samuel Johnson*. 2 vols. London, 1791. Ed. G. B. Hill, revised by L. F. Powell. 6 vols. Oxford: 1934–64.

Breval, John Durant. *Henry and Minerva. A Poem*. London, 1729.

Burns, Robert. "The Cotter's Saturday Night," *Poems, Chiefly in the Scottish Dialect*. Edinburgh, 1786.

Campbell, John. *The Polite Correspondence: or Rational Amusement*. London, 1741.

Campbell, Thomas. *Specimens of the British Poets*. London, 1819; quoted in The *Monthly Review* 90 (1819): 403.

Chudleigh, Lady Mary. "To Mr. Dryden," *Poems on Several Occasions*. London, 1703. In *Poems*, ed. Margaret J. M. Ezell. New York: Oxford UP, 1993.

Church, R. W. *Spenser* ["English Men of Letters."] London, 1879.

Cobb, Samuel. *Poetae Britannici. A Poem Satyical and Panegyrical, Upon our English Poets*. London, 1700.

Coleridge, S. T. "Effusion XXIV. In the Manner of Spenser," *Poems*. London, 1796. *Poems*, ed. Ernest Hartley Coleridge. London: Oxford UP, 1912.

———*Christabel; Kubla Khan: a Vision; The Pains of Sleep*. London, 1816. In *Poems*, ed. Ernest Hartley Coleridge. London: Oxford UP, 1912.

———*Biographia Literaria*. London, 1817. Ed. James Engell and W. Jackson Bate. 2 vols. Princeton: Princeton UP, 1983.

———Lecture Notes, *Literary Remains,* ed. H. N. Coleridge. 4 vols. London, 1836–39.

Collins, William. *Odes on Several Descriptive and Allegorical Subjects*. London, 1746. In *Poems of Gray, Collins, and Goldsmith*, ed. Roger Lonsdale. London: Longmans, 1969.

———"An Ode on the Popular Superstitions of the Highlands of Scotland, considered as the subject of poetry," *Transactions of the Royal Society of Edinburgh* (1788). In *Poems of Gray, Collins, and Goldsmith*, ed. Roger Lonsdale. London: Longmans, 1969.

Cooke, Thomas. *An Ode on the Powers of Poetry*. London, 1751.

Dennis, John. "Epistle Dedicatory," *The Advancement and Reformation of Modern Poetry*. London, 1701. In *Works*, ed. Edward Niles Hooker. 2 vols. Baltimore: Johns Hopkins UP, 1939, 1:197–278.

Dodd, William. "Moral Pastorals," *Poems*. London, 1767.

Downman, Hugh. *The Land of the Muses: A Poem in the Manner of Spenser*. London, 1768.

Drake, Nathan. *Literary Hours or Sketches Critical and Narrative*. London, 1798.

———*Shakespeare and his Times*. 2 vols. London, 1817. 1 vol. London, 1838.

Fergusson, Robert. "The Farmer's Ingle," *Poems*. Edinburgh, 1773.

Gray, Thomas. "The Progress of Poesy," *Odes, by Mr. Gray*. Strawberry Hill, 1757. In *Poems of Gray, Collins, and Goldsmith*, ed. Roger Lonsdale. London: Longmans, 1969.

Hayley, William. *An Essay on Painting, In Two Epistles to Romney.* London, 1778.

———*The Triumphs of Temper: a Poem in Six Cantos.* London, 1781.

Hazlitt, William. *Lectures on the English Poets.* London, 1818.

Home, Henry, Lord Kames, *Elements of Criticism.* Edinburgh, 1762.

Hume, David. *History of England, Vol. IV.* London, 1759. *History of England,* ed. William B. Todd. 6 vols. Indianapolis: Liberty Classics, 1983.

Hunt, Leigh. "A New Gallery of Pictures," The *Indicator* (1833); *Leigh Hunt's Literary Criticism,* ed. Lawrence Huston Houtchens and Carolyn Washburn Houtchens. New York: New York UP, 1956.

Hurd, Richard. *Letters on Chivalry and Romance.* London, 1762.

Irving, Washington. Untitled poem, *Salmagundi; or the Whim-Whams and Opinions of Launcelot Langstaff, esq.* 2 vols. London, 1807–8. In *Works.* 27 vols. New York: Putnam's, 1880–83.

Johnson, Samuel. The *Rambler* (1750–52). Ed. W. J. Bate and Albrecht B. Strauss. 3 vols. New Haven: Yale UP, 1969.

———Letter to Thomas Warton, July 16, 1754 in *The Letters of Samuel Johnson,* ed. Bruce Redford. 5 vols. Princeton: Princeton UP, 1992–94.

———*A Dictionary of the English Language.* 2 vols. London, 1755.

———*Lives of the Poets.* 10 vols. London, 1779–81. Ed. G. B. Hill. 3 vols. Oxford: Clarendon Press, 1905.

Jortin, John. *A Hymn to Harmony.* London, 1729.

———*Remarks on Spenser's Poems.* London, 1734.

Keats, John. "On First Looking into Chapman's Homer," "Specimen of an Induction," "Calidore, A Fragment," in *Poems.* London, 1817. *Poetical Works,* ed. H. W. Garrod. London: Oxford UP, 1956, 1970.

———Letter to Charles Brown, November 1818. *Letters of John Keats,* ed. Maurice Buxton Forman. London: Oxford UP, 1947.

———"Eve of Saint Agnes," *Lamia, Isabella.* London, 1820. *Poetical Works,* ed. H. W. Garrod. London: Oxford UP, 1970.

Keble, John. Review of Condor, Star in the East, *Quarterly Review.* 32 (1825): 211–32.

Lamb, Charles. "Popular Fallacies: 'That great Wit is allied to Madness,'" The *New Monthly Magazine* (May 1826). *Works,* ed. E. V. Lucas. 7 vols. London: Methuen, 1903–05.

Lloyd, Robert. "On Rhime: A Poetical Epistle to a Friend," Poetical *Works.* 2 vols. London, 1774.

Lockhart, J. G. "The Cockney School of Poetry," *Blackwood's Edinburgh Review* 2 (1817): 38–40.

———*Memoirs of the Life of Sir Walter Scott*. 7 vols. 1837–38. 5 vols. Boston: Houghton Mifflin, 1901.

Mason, William. *The English Garden: A Poem*. London, 1772.

Mickle, William Julius. *The Concubine: A Poem in Two Cantos. In the Manner of Spenser*. Oxford, 1767. Reprinted in 1777 as *Syr Martyn*.

Millar, John. *The Origin of the Distinction of Ranks*. Edinburgh, 1771. Fourth edition, Edinburgh, 1806.

Mitford, Mary Russell. Letter to her father, 1811. *The Life of Mary Russell Mitford in a Selection from her Letters*, A. G. L'Estrange, ed. 3 vols. New York: 1870.

The Muses' Library, ed. Elizabeth Cooper. London, 1737.

Neele, Henry. "Lectures on English Poetry," *The Literary Remains*. London, 1829; quoted in The *Gentleman's Magazine* NS 41 (1829): 42.

Newcomb, Thomas. *Bibliotheca: A Poem*. London, 1712. In *A Select Collection of Poems,* ed. John Nichols. 8 vols. London, 1782, 3:19–74.

Newman, John Henry. "Poetry, With References to Aristotle's Poetics," The *London Quarterly Review* (1829). *Critical Essays of the Early Nineteenth Century,* ed. Raymond MacDonald Alden. New York, 1921.

Pinkerton, John. *Letters of Literature, by Robert Heron Esq*. London, 1785.

Review of Tighe's Psyche, *Quarterly Review* 5 (1811): 471–85.

Review of Byron's *Childe Harold* in The *British Review* 3 (1812): 275–302.

Review of Tighe's *Psyche* in The *Eclectic Review* 9 (1813): 217–29.

Reynolds, J. H. "Popular Poetry – Periodical Criticism," The *Champion* (1816). In *Selected Prose,* ed. Leonidas M. Jones. Cambridge: Harvard UP, 1966.

Scott, John, of Amwell. *Moral Eclogues*. London, 1778.

Scott, Walter. Review of Southey's edition of *Pilgrim's Progress*, The *Quarterly Review* 43 (1830).

Shelley, Percy Bysshe. "A Defense of Poetry, *Works,* ed. Mary Shelley. 2 vols. London, 1840. In *Shelley's Prose,* ed. David Lee Clark. Albuquerque: U of New Mexico P, 1954.

Shenstone, William. "The School-Mistress," *Poems Upon Various Occasions*. Oxford, 1737.

———Correspondence on *The School-Mistress*, 1741–49. In *The Letters of William Shenstone, Arranged and Edited with Introduction, Notes, and Index, by Marjorie Williams*. Oxford: Blackwell, 1939.

Southey, Robert. "English Eclogues," *Poems*. Bristol, 1799.

Spence, Joseph. *Polymetis: or, An Enquiry concerning the Agreement Between the Works of the Roman Poets, and the Remains of the Antient Artists. Being an Attempt to illustrate them mutually from one another*. London, 1747.

Letter in The *Talisman* (August 12, 1820): 59.

Tennyson, Alfred, Lord. "The Lotos-Eaters." *Poems*. London, 1833. *Poetical Works*. Oxford: Oxford UP, 1953.

Thompson, William. *Sickness: A Poem in Three Books*. London, 1745.

———"On Spenser's Faerie Queene," *The Poetical Calendar*. 12 vols. London, 1763.

Thomson, James. *The Castle of Indolence: An Allegorical Poem. Written in Imitation of Spenser*. London, 1748.

Tighe, Mary. *Psyche, or the Legend of Love*. Privately printed, 1805. London, 1811.

Upton, John. *A New Canto of the Fairy Queen*. London, 1747.

Upton, John ed. *Spenser's Faerie Queene*. 2 vols. London, 1758. Preface in *John Upton: Notes on the Fairy Queen*, ed. John G. Radcliffe. 2 vols. New York: Garland, 1987.

The Village Sunday, a Poem, Moral and Descriptive, in the Manner of Spenser. London, [1809]; the preface quoted from the *Critical Review*, Series 3, 18 (1809): 218.

Walpole, Horace. Letter to Cole, March 17, 1765. *Correspondence with The Rev. William Cole,* ed. W. S. Lewis and A. Dayle Wallace. 2 vols. New Haven: Yale UP, 1937.

Warton, Joseph. *Odes on Various Subjects*. London, 1746.

———*An Essay on the Writings and Genius of Pope*. 2 vols. London, 1756, 1782.

Warton, Thomas the elder. *Poems on Several Occasions*. London, 1748.

Warton, Thomas. *Five Pastoral Eclogues: the Scenes of Which are Supposed to Lie Among the Shepherds, Oppressed by the War in Germany*. London, 1745.

———*The Pleasures of Melancholy*. London, 1747. In *Poetical Works*, ed. Richard Mant. 2 vols. Oxford: Oxford UP, 1802, 1:68–95.

———*Observations on The Fairy Queen of Spenser*. London, 1754; 2 vols, 1762.

———*The History of English Poetry*. 3 vols. London, 1774–81.

———*Verses on Reynolds's Painted Window at New College.* Oxford, 1782. In *Poetical Works*, ed. Richard Mant. 2 vols. Oxford: 1802.

West, Gilbert. West, Gilbert. *A Canto of the Fairy Queen. Written by Spenser. Never Before Published.* London, 1739.

Wordsworth, William. Preface, "Nutting," in *Lyrical Ballads, with other Poems, in Two Volumes.* London, 1800. "Nutting" in *Poems*, 2 vols, ed. John O. Hayden. New Haven: Yale UP, 1981. Preface in *Lyrical Ballads, 1798*, ed. W. J. B. Owen. Oxford: Oxford UP, 1969.

———Preface to *Poems.* 2 vols. London, 1815. *Literary Criticism of William Wordsworth*, ed. Paul M. Zall. Lincoln: U of Nebraska P, 1966.

3: English Studies

Spenser in the National Context

In the nineteenth century, English poetry at last became part of the official curriculum taught in British and American colleges. As *grammar* schools evolved into *high* schools, teachers gradually yielded up the Latin classics, partly because historicism was undermining the authority of Cicero and Virgil but mostly because Victorian schools needed to attend to more immediate business. With the rapid expansion of the franchise in Britain and the growing and diverse immigrant population in America, it seemed desirable, even necessary, to offer more advanced instruction in the vernacular language. This was not a new idea; educational reformers had been resisting the Latin curriculum since the seventeenth century and the way to English studies was long preparing in dissenting academies, New England schoolhouses, and institutions with modern curriculums like the Scottish universities and Thomas Jefferson's University of Virginia. In the new, highly specialized capitalist economies, persons in authority often had neither the need nor the opportunity to practice the older aristocratic virtues; with the triumph of liberalism and the consolidation of the professions into a middle class, heroism became the purview less of the high-minded man than of the great-hearted state. In the English-speaking nations the state saw to it that even those who were not assuming positions of professional authority received instruction in the more modern forms of morality and civic virtue that patriotism required. Learning a vernacular literature was not only more pleasurable to young readers; it encouraged them to adopt the national spirit needed to hold together a diverse and rapidly changing commercial society. Rote drilling in the Greek and Latin classics no longer seemed like such a "liberal" art.

The aims of the new English studies are succinctly outlined in the 1867 introduction to the first textbook edition of the *Faerie Queene*, edited by the dean of Durham, G. W. Kitchin (1827–1912):

> The teacher, who sets the book before the young, will remember that his pupil may benefit by it in four ways at least.

> 1. By obtaining an insight into the genius of a great poet, and thereby purifying and ennobling his taste, as well as exercising his imagination. This is the first lesson to be learnt – the training of the poetic faculty.

2. Next, the teacher will find in it plentiful texts on which to hang historical instruction; and what period of the history of England is so likely to arouse a boy's sympathies and interest as the latter half of the sixteenth century?

3. Then, from the peculiarities of its language, it is well suited to teach learners to look carefully into the meaning of words, the forms of inflexion, and the construction of sentences in their mother-tongue.

4. Lastly, from the singularly clear and vivid descriptions of human qualities contained in the book, from the pictures of true nobility in man and woman, and from the opposite views of the intrinsic baseness and misery of selfishness and vice, the student may learn lessons of religious and moral truth, of no small value at the time of life at which education ought to set before the young and fervent imagination the beauty and chivalrous elevation of what is good, and the degradation of evil. Let us welcome whatever tends to turn into right channels the boy's sense of honour, and instinctive preferences for what is gallant and truthful.

(1901; xxi-xxii)

Here are four cardinal points for fashioning a gentleman or public-spirited citizen in virtuous and gentle discipline: aesthetic perception, historical and political understanding, philology, and moral rectitude. Kitchin's object is to direct the student's affections toward a democratized, nineteenth-century culture with strong roots in Elizabethan literature, Protestantism, and imperial ambition. The significance of Spenser's poetry to such a program is readily apparent. Or is it? One notes the very un-Spenserian word "preference" applied to gallantry and truth, a word closer to our market-place notion of "values" than to vocabulary of moral discipline Spenser preached to an aristocracy. In the capitalist economy, the old humanist theme of a "choice of Hercules" reemerges as an aesthetic preference for, say, Milton as opposed to Shakespeare.

Spenser wrote for courtly and highly educated readers who were very different from nineteenth-century schoolmasters and their pupils; Kitchin deemed it necessary to expurgate some of the more memorable stanzas in the *Faerie Queene* — the very passages to which a school boy would "instinctively" turn. Teachers regarded the difficulties of Spenser's language and the supposed difficulties of his allegory as another daunting obstacle to young or semiliterate readers. Lecturing at the Working Men's College in 1864, F. D. Maurice (1805–72) worried that readers of the *Faerie Queene* "have heard strange rumours about certain hidden meanings in it which they must guess at, and which, after taking great pains, they may perhaps never discover" (1874; 219). While I have found no chapbook *Faerie Queene* (obviated, perhaps, by Richard Johnson's 1596 *Seven Champions of Christendom*), prose renditions for unlettered readers began to appear with *Prince Arthur, an Allegorical Romance* (1779) by the novelist Alexander Bicknell (d. 1796). Bicknell complains in his preface that

"the Beauties of SPENSER'S FAIRY QUEEN, lie hid like Diamonds in a
Mine; or rather, in their rough and unpolished state: The Learned World
alone are able to enjoy them; a very small part of the great World, from the
Antiquity of the Language, and the Quaintness of the Expressions, being
qualified to share in that Pleasure" (1:vi). In the nineteenth century the great
world was not generally prepared to accept Spenser on his own terms. Dis-
cussing Hazlitt's *Lectures on the English Poets*, in 1820 an anonymous reviewer
suggests that while the *Faerie Queene* was rather a botch, "some selection of the
prominent parts, connected by prose-narrative, would be a welcome substitute
for the entire work, and might tend to preserve its beauties from desertion and
oblivion" (92:64). Several writers followed up on this suggestion; Leigh Hunt
offered extended commentary on elegant extracts in *Imagination and Fancy*
(1844) encouraging timid readers to explore this "divine poet": "when ac-
quaintance with him is once begun, he repels none but the unpoetical. Others
may not be able to read him continuously; but more or less, and as an en-
chanted stream 'to dip into,' they will read him always" (71). For those who
needed a story, publishers supplied various kinds of prose redactions. In 1793
Lucy Peacock, bookseller and writer for children, published *The Knight of the
Rose*, a prose paraphrase of the *Faerie Queene* for the young. The Scottish novel-
ist George MacDonald (1824–1905) adapted characters and episodes from the
Faerie Queene in *Phantastes: A Faerie Romance for Men and Women* (1858) while re-
casting Spenserian narrative as popular romance. If common readers seldom
warmed to Spenser – one nineteenth-century editor suggested that for every
reader of Spenser, there were twenty for Shakespeare and Milton – it was not
for want of trying. Editions of Spenser, learned and popular, appeared at regu-
lar intervals and were often reprinted.

Victorian attempts to bring Spenser to a wider readership began in earnest
with a series of seven long essays John Wilson (1785–1854) contributed to
Blackwood's in 1833–35. The shaggy-maned "Christopher North," one of the
more colorful characters produced in the romantic era, was the friend of fellow
conservatives Walter Scott, Robert Southey, and William Wordsworth.
When not entertaining famous writers, sailing his yacht, or hunting grouse on
his estates, he taught moral philosophy – a discipline from which English stud-
ies was emerging – at Edinburgh University. The general tenor of Wilson's
criticism resembles Hazlitt's lectures, though Wilson himself regards Spenser
first and foremost as a sacred poet. The series appears intended for a female
readership – "young and fair thou art – so whispers our Genius" – though
not exclusively so. It begins with a biography of the poet illustrated with ex-
tracts from the minor poems, followed by a discussion of the eighteenth-
century criticism reprinted in Todd's variorum. This consists mostly of ad
hominem abuse directed toward the likes of "Tom Warton," "Old Polymetis,"
and "Upton Sage." By this time, or at least for this readership, the verbal criti-

cism practiced by classically trained philologists had become a closed book. Warton, trying to make grammatical sense of a wayward text, had complained that Spenser never neglected the opportunity of a good description. This charge Wilson finds "absurdly unjust . . . the old woman's charge against every great poet who delights to walk in the realms of imagination. His imagination overwhelms his judgment, as used to be said of Shakespeare . . . . There is not an inopportune description in the *Faery Queen*." Better that Spenser should overwhelm *our* judgments; "We must peruse poetry in a kindred spirit" (November 1834; 695, 681). Like those who were translating the *Faerie Queene* into prose, Wilson was more concerned with the spirit than the letter of his text.

Blackwood's disrespect for the London critical establishment – which was both liberal and elitist – is expressed through constant appeals to a *common* sense: "For a spurt, Glorious John [Dryden] might have been safely backed at odds against any poet of his own century; but he has given no proof of being able to conceive unity of design in any extensive work, and must very soon have been bewildered in the woods of Faery Land. He knew but street-scenery; and was ignorant of all manner of trees" (September 1834, 423). Such prose exhibits what Hazlitt described as "gusto," a breezy, spirited tastefulness that won *Blackwood's* many admirers even on the opposing side of the political fence. Wilson affects fond regard for old Tories like Dryden and Warton, but for real authority he looks to the "pure" poetry of Spenser, Milton, and Wordsworth. Despite his foolery, Professor Wilson was a cagey critic who knew the Spenserian poetical tradition as well as Hazlitt or Hunt and the critical tradition rather better; he acknowledges that "we owe to Hurd the vindication of Spenser," gives a discriminating list of the chief imitations, and recognizes that among modern poets, Wordsworth is the legitimate heir of Spenser. Not only does Wilson accept Spenser's use of allegory, but he goes so far as to express the minority opinion that "till all distinctions of ranks have been first confused and then destroyed, John Bunyan must stand far aloof from Edmund Spenser" (415).

Wilson favors Spenser's descriptions because he would like to harness romantic hedonism to the larger project of social and religious reformation: "And can it be thought that such Poetry, so picturing Purity to our eyes, that her image remains for ever after enshrined within our hearts, is of no avail to purify our earthly passions? . . . We have always, in speaking of Spenser, and in quoting from the *Faery Queen*, called Poetry religion" (December 1834; 716). An 1818 essay in *Blackwood's*, entitled "On the Revival of a Taste for our Ancient Literature," argues: "The living and creative spirit of literature is its nationality. Whatever is introduced into it from abroad, or added to it from within, should be, in harmony with its past greatness. It was the glory of the Greeks that their literature was native – it was the fatality of the Romans that theirs was imported. But when a nation reaches a high point of civilization, and when its literature is highly refined and perfect, it must then either turn itself to the study, and consequently the imitation, of the literature of other nations, or it must revert to the ancient spirit of its own" (4:266). As in the writings of Hume, Beattie, and Scott, such historicism was typical of the Scottish Enlightenment and often took a politically conservative tack. The high-flying Toryism of *Blackwood's* aroused resistance from a liberal press committed to rationality in all things. Thus the *Westminster Review* states in 1824: "They are the mere creatures of sentimental sympathy and antipathy; their heart tells them this, and their heart tells them that; their love and hatred, their approbation and disapprobation, are measured by no intellectual standard. Their fine feelings supply them instinctively with all the rules of morality. In their view, logic has indeed a closed fist and a scowling aspect . . . . They love to carry us back to days of yore, when the mind of man was still cradled in infantine weakness; and appear almost to regret the passing away of the blessed days of chivalry, with all their darkness and *donjons*, violence and insecurity" (1:19). Most romantic critics did indeed believe in an order higher than reason. Like Coleridge, Wilson specifies a narrow canon of great geniuses whose poetry "we must peruse . . . in a kindred spirit," and like Coleridge, he approaches this literary canon as a body of divinity: "By that spirit expanded and elevated, Intellect and Imagination create within themselves conceptions and emotions of the sublime and beautiful, the spiritual and the everlasting. Poetry is the produce of Love in its delight – Philosophy of Love in its wonder – Religion of Love in its gratitude – and thus in all higher moods the Three in One." In the interest of forming an empathetic bond with genius, the Augustan "beauties and blemishes" school of empirical criticism is left far behind; the issue is not good or bad poetry but pure or impure spirit: "false philosophy, false poetry, and false religion – all arise from self-willed ignorance, or misconception of the intimations nature gives us of her own laws. 'Truth and pure delight' are inseparable, because cognate . . . . Hence, all great poets have been good men" (November 1834; 681).

Wilson's five remaining essays are taken up with a redaction of book 1 of the *Faerie Queene* addressed to the "moral imagination" of nineteenth-century readers. Adopting a pulpit manner, Wilson interpolates commentary into extensive quotations, guiding his periodical readership through the troublesome allegory: "Was it not strange and suspicious to see such a Palace there? Yet we may not say it was; for the Knight had already encountered marvelous adventures, and the House of Pride was beautiful, in the architecture of enchantment, as Error's Wood with its colonnades and canopies of the seemingly harmless umbrage of earth's natural trees. The poet shows it to us – as it was – unsubstantial on sand" December 1834; 717). At the same period Professor Wilson's essays were appearing in *Blackwood's*, John Keble, then professor of poetry at conservative Oxford, was defending Spenser and allegory in his lectures on classical literature, originally delivered in Latin: "It makes little difference whether the result is produced by an allegorical symbolism or by the transference of the poet's own passion and disposition to actual characters. For either way, the reader who once surrenders himself to the poet's real meaning, will have little leisure for mere ornament and pettiness" (1844; trans. Francis, 2:36). In an essay appearing in the *Quarterly Review* (1825), Keble had described the *Faerie Queene* as "a continual, deliberate endeavour to enlist the restless intellect and chivalrous feeling, of an inquiring and romantic age, on the side of goodness and faith, of purity and justice" (225–26). Wilson's book-length commentary on Spenser does indeed resemble the religious aspirations of the Oxford movement, and it is perhaps not entirely beside the point that the Scottish Wilson was an Oxford graduate himself. It is a pity that he did not annotate the later books and that his essays were not collected and reprinted.

Nonetheless, if Spenser was admired by high church Anglicans, he was not a favorite of Roman Catholics, who could be yet more conservative than Oxford Tories. Just as nineteenth-century Catholics were challenging the New England "common" schools, so in Old England they were challenging the secular canon of Protestant nationalism. In 1856 Cardinal Nicholas Patrick Stephen Wiseman (1802–1865) criticized Chaucer and Spenser in *On the Perception of Natural Beauty by the Ancients and the Moderns*, an essay that drew the ire of Leigh Hunt, by then a pensioned elder statesman of the liberal cause. Wiseman objects to Spenser's "wantonness, voluptuousness, and debauchery; so as almost to drive one to the fear, that, after all, virtue may well disdain to feed its thoughts even on the most innocent of earthly contemplations, and fly to the wilderness or the hermitage, and there habitually nourish penitential ideas" (8). Replying in *Fraser's Magazine* (1856), Hunt reminds the cardinal that Chaucer himself had a good Catholic education; conceding that Spenser's natural descriptions are often connected to love, he insists that "when the allegory itself does not lead the poet to set forth the perils of temptation, none of the scenes lie open in the least degree to the Cardinal's imputations." Much of Hunt's dyspeptic essay is merely a venomous attack on a Catholic who dared to criticize "*our* great poets" (752, 759, my emphasis), though it may be that later in life Hunt was himself responding to a grave and moral Spenser. He did not have the last word in this dispute, however. Dean Kitchin's textbook edition of the *Faerie Queene* provoked bitter words from Thomas Arnold in 1880; writing in the *Dublin Review,* he regrets "Milton's foolish saying that Spenser was 'a better teacher than Scotus of Aquinas.' "To Arnold, the liberal Hunt typifies an England in which "it is felt to be of more importance that the spirit and tone of a work used in teaching should be Protestant, or at least non-Catholic, than that it should be pure from moral taint." Catholic students are better served by the Latin classics than vernacular poetry with "a virulent anti-

Catholic bias" composed by an author "whose mind was so deeply tainted by licentiousness and whose moral sense in some directions was so perverted" (325, 327, 328, 325). In 1879 Thomas Gallwey, another Dublin writer, presumably Catholic, wrote of Spenser's *View of Ireland*: "Edmund Spenser has written poems which have immortalized his memory . . . and he has written one prose work . . . which ought to render his name infamous wherever Christianity is professed" (19). While their assessments of Spenser's doctrines break down along party lines, Wilson, Wiseman, Hunt, Kitchen, and Arnold all regard verbal descriptions like those in the *Faerie Queene* as a useful instructional device.

Early Nineteenth-Century Editions of Spenser's Works

Spenser was also undergoing trials and tribulations in editions intended for adult readers. The 1805 variorum produced by the Reverend Henry James Todd was criticized by Walter Scott in the *Edinburgh Review* with lasting effect. In addition to comparing Spenser's allegory unfavorably to Bunyan's, Scott voiced the antiquarian's complaint that Todd had failed to identify enough of the contemporary allusions. In 1805 Wordsworth wrote to Scott, "Like you, I had been sadly disappointed with Todd's Spenser . . . three parts of four of the Notes are absolute trash. That style of compiling notes ought to be put an end to" (1: 641). In an edition of Spenser's *Works* published in 1839, George Stillman Hillard (1808–79) complained that "the merits of this [Todd's] edition are not commensurate with Spenser's rank in English literature. There is a great deal of learned rubbish in it (1:iv). Nonetheless, whatever its demerits as a reading text, Todd's edition was a landmark in the study of Spenser's reception that gathers in one place more than two centuries of verbal glosses, critical remarks, commendatory verse, and lists of imitations. It reprints at length the essays by Hughes, Spence, Warton, Upton, and Hurd that set the agenda for Spenser criticism down to modern times – John Wilson made copious use of these remarks, even as he ridiculed eighteenth-century criticism. Todd, who must have held the record for multiple livings in the Church of England, was well connected and had access to manuscript notes by Warton, Upton, and Church, which belatedly found their way into print. The biography in his variorum is much more complete than its predecessors, demolishing much of the mythology surrounding Spenser and contributing new information about Spenser's career in Cambridge and his life in Ireland. Todd turned up and reprinted the valuable early commentary on the *Faerie Queene* by Sir Kenelm Digby, as well as that in Lodowick Bryskett's *Discourse of Civill Life* (1606); he also identified Bryskett as the author of two pastoral elegies previously attributed to Spenser. While it is true that the variorum contained little original criticism, Todd's labors – performed at a time when library catalogues were in a primitive state and bibliographies were scarce – made no small contribution to scholarship. With the assistance of a bevy of learned corespondents, he uncovered most of what was to be found and laid the foundation for the mountain of philological scholarship yet to come. The Todd *Variorum* remains a very useful tool for anyone studying the role of Spenser in shaping British literature.

It was not reprinted for many decades, however, and most nineteenth-century readers encountered Spenser in the collections of *British Poets* edited by Anderson, Chalmers, or Aikin or in one of the many less scholarly editions. Frederic Ives Carpenter's 1923 *A Reference Guide to Edmund Spenser*, the indispensable source for Victorian criticism, lists twenty-four nineteenth-century editions of Spenser's collected works, and it is far from complete. One suspects that in many cases these collected editions were purchased more for library furniture than reading material. The conspicuous consumption of books was becoming an object of comment; in *The Eden of the Imagination* (1814) John Hamilton Reynolds writes:

> My books must find a resting-place, for they
> Can cheer my dreams by night, my thoughts by day.
> Let Shakespeare, Milton, Spenser, and the rest,
> Who glad the fancy and instruct the breast,
> Lie on my table, negligently free,
> To charm my friends, or yield their worth to me:
> Not with gilt leaves, and letter'd backs, arrang'd,
> On some high shelf, and ne'er disturb'd, nor chang'd;
> Plac'd there as size demands, or fancy rules,
> A prey to dullness, worms, and dust, and fools.

(24)

And in 1823 Leigh Hunt amplifies: "Sitting, last winter, among my books, and walled round with all the comfort and protection which they and my fireside afford me; to wit, a table of high-piled books at my back, my writing-desk one side of me, some shelves on the other, and the feeling of the warm fire at my feet; I began to consider how I loved the authors of these books: how I loved them, too, not only for the imaginative pleasures they afforded me, but for their making me love the very books themselves, and delight to be in contact with them. I looked sideways at my Spenser, my Theocritus, and my Arabian Nights; then above them at my Italian poets; then behind me at my Dryden and Pope, my romances, and my Boccaccio; then on my left side at my Chaucer, who lay on a writing-desk; and thought how natural it was in C[harles] L[amb] to give a kiss to an old folio, as I once saw him do to Chapman's Homer" (ed. Johnson, 77). The private library, along with the billiard room, was a relatively recent addition to genteel domestic life. Books were much less

expensive in the nineteenth century than they had been in Dryden's or War-
ton's time, but more than that, they came to serve Victorian readers as icons of
culture. In the previous century book collecting had been mostly the province
of eccentric virtuosi, persons who savored a black-letter ballad in much they
same way and for much the same reasons that they valued a rare shell or a
Roman coin. In the period from 1750 to 1850, as aesthetic education was
gradually incorporated into the schools and journals, "taste" became a moral
and even a political matter of the sort we have seen in Kitchin's remarks. Mid-
dle-class drawing rooms, bedecked with books, prints, musical instruments,
and the inevitable periodicals, began to resemble the curiosity cabinets of an
earlier age. A library fitted out with gothic wallpaper, pointed windows, and
engraved images of ruined cathedrals would hardly be complete without the
Faerie Queene proudly displayed as a reminder of the glory that was Elizabeth
(never mind that those ruins were of Tudor making). Even so, the commen-
tary one finds in such nineteenth-century editions expresses more than a little
doubt about the aesthetic value of Spenser's poetry as well as reiterating the
usual complaints that Spenser is going unread.

The Pickering edition of 1825 contains an essay by Philip Masterman (oft
reprinted) that indicates the direction Hurd's kind of historicist criticism was
taking: "In founding his poem on the manners and customs of chivalry,
Spenser consulted the taste of his age; for the genius of that singular institution
had not then taken flight, but hovered over the land like the genius of an Ara-
bian story, half enveloped in clouds, and rendered more gigantic and imposing
from its partial obscurity. Of this fleeting form Spenser has drawn a lasting pic-
ture, which he has adorned with the richest hues of an unequaled fancy" (1839
1:xxii). As fuel for the visionary imagination, chivalry was thus quite accept-
able; as a moral guide for modern readers of the liberal persuasion, however,
Spenser's political views were neither effective nor trustworthy: "It was evident
that the honors and practices of chivalry must soon terminate a reign which,
whatever may be the romantic interest attached to it, had already been pro-
longed to a greater period than was desirable; and as Spenser was writing for
the future, he might have cast his poem in a more useful mold. The image of a
perfect knight could be no more profitable as an example, than the pictorial
representations of our armed ancestors. It might excite admiration by its an-
tiquity, by the skill of the imitation and the accuracy of the resemblance, but it
could not serve for actual use" (1:xxiii). Romance and admiration versus profit
and use: these were the terms in which Spenser, and indeed poetry generally,
would be debated throughout the Victorian era. This issue was the more prob-
lematic because, as we have seen in Hurd's criticism, it was no easy matter to
work out a plausible connection between the historical and timeless qualities of
poetic experience, between the often opposing claims of history and the imagi-
nation. On the one hand, Masterton follows Warton in tracing Spenser's alle-

gory to the peculiarities of his age ("allegorical personages must have been as familiar to Spenser as real ones: hardly any festival was held without pageants and spectacles"); on the other, following Hazlitt, he declares that allegory is what is peculiar to Spenser's character as a poet ("his imagination poured out its creations from stores which seemed inexhaustible, and of all shapes and colours, ever rich and various" 1:xxvii). Was the poetry to be regarded as historically created or imaginatively creative? How one came down on this issue had (and has) broad implications for how Spenser was to be edited, read, and criticized in the postromantic era; was Henry J. Todd or William Wordsworth to be the guide here?

While most nineteenth-century readers regarded historical writing as a source of imaginative pleasure, they plainly felt that Spenser fell something short of Walter Scott in that department. As Hawthorne's friend G. S. Hillard, put it in 1839, "who can have much interest in the solution of the questions of whether the rebellion of the O'Neals be imaged in the episode of the babe with bloody hands, in the Second Book? or whether or not Sir Satyrane is a representative of Sir John Perrott? What are Sir John Perrott and the rebellion of the O'Neals to us? 'What's Hecuba to him, or he to Hecuba?'" Passions needed to be aroused, continues the American editor: "The poet starts with giving form and substance to certain abstractions of the mind; but, as he goes on, and kindles with the progress of the narrative, he either forgets or voluntarily departs from the allegorical character. It is Sir Guyon or Britomart, the man or the woman, with senses, organs, dimensions, that he is thinking of, and not Temperance or Chastity. The interest, too, which the reader feels, is a warm, flesh-and-blood interest, not in the delineation of a virtue, but in the adventures of a knight or lady." If this is so, of course, the *Faerie Queene* is to be measured by standards familiar from other kinds of poetry, and Spenser, not surprisingly, is found lacking: "He had not that variety of power which belonged to Shakespeare so preeminently, and, in an inferior degree, to Chaucer . . . . We look in vain in *The Faerie Queene* for flashes of wit and humor, for profound observations on life and manners, for the varied lights and shades of character, or the pungent flavor of satire" (1:liii, lii-liii, liv). This (supposedly) first American edition of Spenser's poems is very lightly annotated, the editor choosing to gingerly take up the allegory in a plot summary, leaving the verse to stand on its own merits. Reviewing Hillard's edition of Spenser, in 1840 H. K. Cleveland remarked in the *North American Review* that "there is another kind of terror equally to be guarded against, which makes us slaves of the allegory, and engages us in a busy search for hidden meanings where there are none; so that, while we are grasping at the shadow, we lose sight of the real and substantial beauties of the poem" (189).

"J. C.," in a London edition of Spenser published the following year, arrived at a similar conclusion: "This complication of meanings may render the

Faerie Queene doubly valuable to the antiquary who can explore its secret sense; but it must always be an objection to Spenser's plan, with the common reader, that the attempt at too much ingenuity has marred the simplicity of the allegory, and deprived it in great degree of consistency and coherence" (1840; Philadelphia 1857, 14). In 1853 the Scottish critic David Masson (1822–1907) put it rather trenchantly: "Why is Spenser the favourite poet of poets, rather than a popular favourite like Byron? For the same reason that a Court is crowded during a trial for life or death, but attended only by barristers during the trial of an intricate civil case" (1856, 436). One of the most endearing passages in Spenser criticism occurs in arch-liberal Thomas Babington Macaulay's 1830 complaint about Spenser's allegory: "Nay, even Spenser himself, though assuredly one of the greatest poets that ever lived, could not succeed in the attempt to make allegory interesting. It was in vain that he lavished the riches of his mind on the House of Pride and the House of Temperance. One unpardonable fault, the fault of tediousness, pervades the whole of the Fairy Queen . . . . Of the persons who read the first canto, not one in ten reaches the end of the first book, and not one in a hundred perseveres to the end of the poem. Very few and weary are those who are in at the death of the Blatant Beast" (1880 1:560). Very few readers indeed, for no such event occurs! Despite the best efforts of popular taste makers like Hazlitt, Lamb, and Hunt, one cannot but suspect that many of those handsome library editions of Spenser's works merely gathered dust.

Spenser and the Victorian Reader

Such was not the case with *Spenser and his Poetry* (3 vols, 1845) by the Rev. George L. Craik (1798–1866). Craik's condensation of the *Faerie Queene* is still read; I have seen undergraduate marginalia in a 1971 facsimile bearing witness to its continued value as a crib. A prolific writer, Craik was active in the Society for the Diffusion of Useful Knowledge and was one of the first professors of English Literature (at Belfast, 1849–66). As a critic of Spenser, he can be vaporous to the point of vacuity; sucking spirit from the *Shepheardes Calender* he writes, "The bright green herbage seems ready to burst forth everywhere, as from a soil of inexhaustible fertility and moisture" (1871, 1:93). Here Craik presents Spenser as a "naive" poet in Schiller's sense of the word, prone to error and excess yet characterized by "what we may call his perfect sincerity, or at least air of sincerity" (3:128). As so often in nineteenth-century criticism, an appeal is made to the pictorial imagination: "The charm of the *Fairy Queen* resides more than that of any other great poem in single passages – which stand out from the general ground of the verse almost as framed pictures do from the wall on which they are hung. It is, in truth, a great picture gallery, with this advantage – among others which a painting by words has, in the hands of so great a master, over other painting – that it addresses itself to the ear as well as to the eye, and is at once colour and music" (1:110). Craik sees to it that Spenser's pigments are properly scrubbed and varnished, for his text is thoroughly modernized, this despite an admonition that "in all writing the thought and language are inseparable, or rather one and the same thing" (3:126). He reprints about two-thirds of the *Faerie Queene* which with the addition of his prose synopsis renders this redaction quite as long as the original. *Spenser and his Poetry* was reprinted and read for a long time as much for what was excised as what was included: "The story, besides being somewhat shortened, is certainly clearer, and more easily followed . . . and all superfluities likely on any account to be found wearisome or offensive have been quietly omitted" (3:123). Among the quiet omissions are all the naughty bits. Craik's commentary does not meddle with the allegory.

Though also Bowdlerized, The Rev. John S. Hart's *An Essay on the Life and Writings of Edmund Spenser, with A Special Exposition of The Fairy Queen* (1847) sets a somewhat higher standard. Hart (1810–77) was principal of the Philadelphia High School and the State Normal School at Trenton, New Jersey; he was founder and editor of the *Sunday School Times* (1859–71). Hart employs Spenser to inculcate ethical principles: quoting extended passages, he explicates the moral sense and italicizes the lessons students are to *store away in their memories*. In a fine phenomenological explication of design in the *Faerie Queene*, he seizes an opportunity to lecture on astronomy: Prince Arthur "does not occupy so large a space in the reader's attention as Saint George, for the same reason that, to an ignorant man, the Sun seems a smaller, though a brighter object than the Earth. Yet could an inhabitant of this globe visit successively the different planets, and while he saw the Earth gradually shrinking to the size of Mars or Jupiter, the Sun still maintaining its unrivaled splendour and its enormous dimensions, he would gradually awaken to the conviction of the grand unity of the Solar System" (157). Hart's best criticism comes in a concluding stricture on Spenser's lack of popularity. The usual explanations will not do: Bunyan proves that allegory can be popular; the Bible indicates that Elizabethan vocabulary need be no impediment to understanding; Scott's novels demonstrate readers' tolerance for antiquarian lore and convoluted plots. The real explanation is that "*He does not tell his story well, because he has too much imagination*" (510, author's emphasis). Thomas Warton would probably agree. Coming after a full century of romantic criticism, this remark might seem to testify to the survival of humanist attitudes, at least in the grammar schools, at least in the provinces. But it also bears witness to the inroads newer, novelistic standards were making into criticism of verse romance; Spenser's "imagination is so completely engrossed with the present object, that the wants of the reader are forgotten. The reader is precipitated from one scene to another without any sufficient warning or preparation. He consequently gets bewildered"

(509). For all its didacticism, Hart's redaction of the narrative concentrates sin-gle-mindedly on the literal sense, meeting the expectations of a novel-reading public.

Up to this time, and for some while afterward, English literature was used, sometimes in conjunction with moral philosophy, as a basis for training in ora-tory; as one would expect from clerical schoolmasters, there was much em-phasis on logical arguments and rhetorical figures. Apart from Hugh Blair's *Lectures on Rhetoric and Belles Lettres*, the primary textbook in the early nineteenth century was *Elegant Extracts* (1784, 1805, many later editions) by Vicemus Knox (1752–1821), the famous master of Tunbridge School. The title of Knox's anthology is somewhat misleading since it consists mostly of complete poems "extracted" from the works of popular writers. It includes copious se-lections from the *Faerie Queene*, which of course was an ideal text for teaching the niceties of humanist discourse. *Elegant Extracts* did not, however, contain commentary of the sort one finds in Craik or Hart; subjective response was less an issue and schoolteachers could manage the rhetorical figures without assistance. In 1848 two English literature textbooks appeared that did include commentary pointing to new directions in education. Charles D. Cleveland (the name "Diabolus" is penciled below in my battered copy) based *A Compen-dium of English Literature* on lectures given to a school for young ladies in Phila-delphia. The construction and much of the matter of his book derives from *Chambers's Cyclopedia of English Literature*, consisting as it does of extracts (selected with an eye for useful knowledge) combined with biographical and historical facts and critical commentary. Students, dragged in tow behind a rather dreary docent, are introduced to English literature as a gallery of pictures. The com-mentary in this textbook indicates that poetry was now being used to teach history and that "taste" was beginning to require something more than a knowledge of rhetoric. Thomas B. Shaw (1813–62), professor of English litera-ture in far-away Saint Petersburg, omitted the extracts but included much more history in his *Outlines of English Literature*. Neither commentator is very re-liable – recalling Ben Jonson, Shaw can write that Spenser's "language was considered pedantic by his contemporaries. His peculiarities have affected the language less than those of any other great writer" (1884, 83). Because these books strive to teach "appreciation" by quoting copiously the bon mots of ear-lier critics, they are invaluable pointers to who was shaping Spenser's popular reception – apparently not Warton, Upton, and Hurd (or even Keats and Hunt), but rather Hazlitt, Campbell, Wilson, Hallam, and D'Israeli. Coleridge's lectures began to appear only in 1836, and Wordsworth's views were still being assimilated. Over the course of several decades, various editors contributed their own apparatus to Shaw's *Outlines* – some calculated to train the memory, others to cultivate sensibility.

Wilson, Craik, Hart, Cleveland, and Shaw all try to make Spenser "interesting" to nineteenth-century readers by approaching the poetry through biography. This was not so easily done; despite the best efforts of Todd, Spenser remained, like Shakespeare, a rather shadowy figure, not at all what was required in the great age of literary personality and gossip. Where the historical record was meager, however, it could be eked out by imaginative reconstruction, as in *Imaginary Conversations*. (1824, etc.) by Walter Savage Landor (1775–1864). Thomas Fuller, in *The History of the Worthies of England* (1662), told the story of how Queen Elizabeth, moved by Spenser's verses, awarded the poet "an hundred pound," but Lord Cecil "was so busied, belike, about matters of high concernment, that Spencer received no reward" (1840, 2:379). Landor draws upon this anecdote to supply what any reader of the *Faerie Queene* would like to have, the Queen's private response to Spenser's praises: "I advise thee again, churlish Cecil, how that our Edmund Spenser, whom thou callest most uncourteously, a whining whelp, hath good and solid reason for his complaint. God's blood! shall the lady that tieth my garter and shuffles the smock over my head, or the lord that steadieth my chair's back while I eat, or the other that looketh to my buck-hounds lest they be mangy, be holden to me in higher esteem and estate, than he who hath placed me among the bravest of past times, and will as safely and surely set me down among the loveliest of the future." Landor's themes and characters derive from Shakespeare's historical pageants, while his skillful use of the details of common life owes something to Sir Walter Scott. In Landor's hands, Cecil becomes a prototype for nineteenth-century liberals (like that writer for the *Westminster Review*) who had small use for the obsolete ways of chivalry: "So small a matter as a page of poesy shall never stir my choler nor twitch my purse-string." Elizabeth, thrilled by Spenser's amorous compliments, delivers a stirring monologue on fame and human mortality, acknowledging the greater wisdom of her grave and moral Spenser: "Edmund, if perchance I should call upon him for counsel, would give me as wholesome and prudent as any of you." Since imaginary conversation can render history the way it ought to have been, Landor transmutes the "hundred pound" into a gift rather more wonderful and strange: "Go, convey unto him those twelve silver spoons, with the apostles on them, gloriously gilded; and deliver unto his hand these twelve large golden pieces, sufficing for the yearly maintenance of another horse and groom. Beside which, set before him with due reverence this Bible, wherein he may read the mercies of his God toward those who waited in patience for his blessing; and this pair of crimson silk hose, which thou knowest I have worne only thirteen months, taking heed that the heel-piece be put into good and sufficient restoration, at my sole charges, by the Italian woman nigh the pollard elm at Charing-cross" (1846, 1:27–29).

The "dialogue of the dead" was a common genre in the Renaissance, though as derived from Lucian and his imitators, it favored a kind of satire that tended to render character with all the subtlety and nuance of a Punch and Judy show. The genre was revived and reinvented by Gilbert West's patron, George, Baron Lyttelton (1709–73), whose *Dialogues of the Dead* (1760) use the dramatic resources of the form to link critical discourse to taste and manners, as when Spenser appears in a remark Pope addresses to Boileau: "I understand you mean Spenser. He had a great Poetical Genius. There is a Force and Beauty in some of his Images and his Descriptions, equal to any in the best of those Writers you have seen him converse with. But he had not always the art of Shading his Pictures. He brings the minute and disagreeable Parts too much into sight; and with many sublime and noble Ideas mingles too frequently vulgar and mean" (127). This is an accurate rendition not only of Pope's views but of neoclassical criticism generally. "Pope's" comment on Spenser's rusticity and pictorialism may be compared to "Southey's" in another of Landor's dialogues: "He continues a great favourite with me still, although he must always lose a little as our youth declines. Spenser's is a spacious but somewhat low chamber, hung with rich tapestry, on which the figures are mostly disproportioned, but some of the faces are lively and beautiful; the furniture is part creaking and worm-eaten, part fragrant with cedar and sandal-wood and aromatic gums and balsams; every table and mantelpiece and cabinet is covered with gorgeous vases, and birds, and dragons, and houses in the air" (1:80). Here Landor taps into Spenser's own resources of descriptive allegory, at one and the same time rendering pictorially an impression of the verse and an expression of the laureate's character. The extended metaphor transforms Spenser's verses into the furniture they had literally become in nineteenth-century households. The aesthetic imagination mingles historical objects, events, and characters to the extent that they become interchangeable parts of the larger cultural whole in which they float suspended. Yet Landor's heroic characters sometimes burst the historical frames cleverly woven around them; they then speak directly to after times. Like Elizabeth apostrophizing fame, characters struggle to overcome the historical shelf on which they repose. "Edmund Spenser," appearing with Essex in a later dialogue, strives for a vital immortality: "The first seeds I sowed in the garden, ere the old castle was made habitable for my lovely bride, were acorns from Penshurst. I planted a little oak before my mansion at the birth of each child" (2:241). Landor then brings the destruction of Kilcolman to life in all its fictional horror: "Burned alive! burned to ashes! The flames dart their serpent tongues through the nursery-window. I can not quit thee, my Elizabeth! I can not lay down our Edmund. Oh those flames! they persecute, they enthrall me, they curl round my temples, they hiss upon my brain, they taunt me with their fierce foul voices, they carp at me, they wither me, they consume me, throwing back to me a little of life, to roll and suffer in, with their fangs upon me" (2:242). Adrift in London, mad as any romantic poet properly ought to have been, Edmund Spenser hurls imprecations into the void.

A woodcut of Spenser fleeing Kilcolman illustrates *Homes and Haunts of the Most Eminent English Poets* (1847) by the popular and prolific William Howitt (1792–1879). If seventeenth- and eighteenth-century poems and essays already linked poets to places, the Victorian literary pilgrimage brought a new dimension to the quest for character. Domestic tourism flourished in the heyday of the picturesque movement, when the Napoleonic wars made foreign travel difficult. Later, steam transportation made even remote parts of the islands readily accessible, and those who did not travel in person could travel in books. *Homes and Haunts* combines travel narrative with literary biography in a new form of criticism. Howitt visited scenes associated with the British poets and collected what oral history he could. The results could be adventuresome; a rude rebuff from the relatives of Mary Tighe leads to a splendid account of a modern-day House of Pride. Howitt was more successful investigating Spenser's Ireland: "The place was fit for Spenser's Pan, with all his fauns and sylvans. In the meadow, which extended to the banks of the river, grazed the fine herd of cattle, and amid them the sturdy bull; and all around us, above us on the rocks, in the meadow itself, and on the banks and green slopes of the other side of the river, grew the most prodigal trees. The whole scene told of ancient possession and a most affluent nature. At the foot of the precipice under the [modern] house, laurels and filberts, which must have been planted long ago, and probably by Spenser himself, had attained the most enormous size . . . . All was one scene of Arcadian greenness, and excess of growth (31–32). Landor too alludes to the project of cultivating Ireland. But Kilcolman castle itself is a desolate ruin, a reminder of how tenuous Spenser's foreign possession really was: "Here the poet was startled at midnight from his dreams by the sound of horse's hoofs beating in a full gallop the stony tracks of the dale, and by a succeeding burst of wild yells from crowding thousands of infuriated Irish. Fire was put to the castle, and it was soon in flames. Spenser, concealed by the gloom of one side of the building, contrived to escape with his wife, and most probably his three boys and girl, as they were saved, and lived after him, but the youngest child in the cradle perished in the flames, with all his property and unpublished poems" (41). The local peasants knew nothing of the poet, only that a Spenser "lived and died there, and was buried just below the castle, which used to be a church-yard" (43). Perhaps Howitt's own imaginative reconstruction of the flight from Kilcolman is not much more accurate.

An even more thoroughgoing attempt to integrate the life with the poems is Anne Manning's "Immeritus Redivivus," which appeared in *The Masque at Ludlow and Other Romanesques* (1866). Best known for fictionalizing the married life of Milton's Mary Powell, Manning (1807–79) novelizes Spenser's failure to win a puritanical Rosalind. The poet's love life was, of course, the object of intensive biographical research; where evidence was sparse, ingenuity was applied. In 1850, for example, Nathaniel Halpin in the *Proceedings of the Royal Irish Academy* had used anagrammical evidence to argue that Rosalind was "Rose Daniel," sister of the poet Samuel Daniel, and that Spenser's wife was Elizabeth Nagle, anagram for "angel" (445–51). Anne Manning simply invents the missing details in a series of fictional epistles from "Edmund" to his friend Harvey. She too fills out the lapses in the historical record, though with less reliance on recorded anecdote than Landor or Howitt. She interrupts her pastoral idyll to introduce occasional digressions into literary criticism, as when Spenser writes of his north-country kin: "They have a peculiar Doric of their own, wherein gate stands for goat, sicker for sure, ken for know, greet for weep, and so forth, *ad infinitum*, whereby I am but just beginning to see my way through the difficulties of an unknown dialect. As I sit at the casement, conning Theocritus by the rays of the setting sun, Whar's Hobby? says one" (101–2). Manning's narrative touches base with the texts through paraphrase, as when we first meet Rosalind: "a fair young lady, all in black bedight, mounted on a silver-gray ass; at whose heels followed a deformed urchin of some ten or twelve summers" (107). Rather than simply reduce the *Faerie Queene* to prose, as Bicknell had done, Manning introduces changes (like the dun color of Una's mount) to dramatize how Spenser's creative imagination transforms the scenes presented by everyday life. Readers not familiar with the texts could simply enjoy her work as a sentimental tale.

The novelist and reformer Charles Kingsley (1819–1875) takes up Spenser's biography at a slightly later period in *Westward Ho!* (1855). Raleigh and Spenser ("one was in complete armour; the other wrapt in the plain short cloak of a man of pens and peace") discourse on hexameter verse while lobbing shells at the besieged Spaniards:

> "Tut, tut, Colin Clout, much learning has made thee mad. A good old fishwives' ballad jingle is worth all your sapphics and trimeters, and 'riff-raff thurlery bouncing.' Hey? have I you there, old lad? Do you mind that precious verse?"
>
> "But, dear Wat, Homer and Virgil — -"
>
> "But, dear Ned, Petrarch and Ovid — -"
>
> "But, Wat, what have we that we do not owe to the ancients?"
>
> "Ancients, quotha? Why, the legend of King Arthur, and Chevy Chase too, of which even your fellow-sinner Sidney cannot deny that every time he hears it even from a blind fiddler it stirs his heart like a trumpet-blast. Speak well of the bridge that carries you over, man! Did you find your Redcross Knight in Virgil, or such a dame as Una in old Ovid? (*Works*, 6:179–10)

To compare these treatments of British literary and political history to their more decorous equivalents in the verse of Spenser and Drayton is to get a sense of how completely novels and popular essays were transforming the status of "literature" among a democratic reading public. Yet they upheld the reputation of the poet: if the *Faerie Queene* was known first-hand by relatively few nineteenth-century readers, its author was known to all who read.

Charles Kingsley's characters reappear in nonfictional form in *Spenser* (1879), written for John Morley's *English Men of Letters* series by Richard William Church, Dean of St. Paul's (1815–90). Church draws upon all the literary resources of Whig historiography to bring the Elizabethan era to urgent life: "The Wars of the Roses had left the crown powerful to enforce order, and protect industry and trade. The nation was beginning to grow rich. When the day's work was done, men's leisure was not disturbed by the events of neighboring war. They had time to open their imaginations to the great spectacle which had been unrolled before them, to reflect upon it, to put into shape their thoughts upon it . . . . In such a state there is everything to tempt poetry" (31–32). Spenser, moreover, was a poor boy of independent mind capable of playing a great part on such a stage: "In spite of opinions and fashions round him, in spite of university pedantry and the affectations of the court, in spite of Harvey's classical enthusiasm, and Sidney's Areopagus, and in spite of half-fancying himself converted to their views, his own powers and impulses showed him the truth" (29). Notice the absence of a language of ethical choice; as in a novel by Walter Scott, events acquire a life of their own. Meanwhile, such "powers and impulses" were driving the empire westward; in Ireland Spenser "accepted the conditions of the place and scene, and entered at once into the game of adventure and gain which was the natural one for all English comers, and of which the prizes were lucrative offices and forfeited manors and abbeys . . . . He saw only on all sides of him the empire of barbarism and misrule which valiant and godly Englishmen were fighting to vanquish and destroy – fighting against apparent but not real odds." While Church does not condone Spenser's politics, he regards them as typical of such unenlightened times: "All wise and good men thought so: all statesmen and rulers acted so" (69, 70).

Church criticizes Spenser's poetry in a similar spirit of historical condescension: "Spenser's art . . . has been praised by some of his critics. But the art, if there is any, is so subtle that it fails to save the reader from perplexity. The truth is that the power of ordering and connecting a long and complicated plan was not one of Spenser's gifts" (125). Dean Church devotes many pages to harsh criticisms of Spenser's design, allegory, diction, and lack of decorum, but like Warton before, he finds "the general effect is almost always lively and rich." Despite its manifest disorderliness, Spenser's poetry is tempered by a quick and sympathetic "perception of beauty of all kinds" (144, 145). This combination of ruggedness and sensibility is in keeping with the doctrine of the *Faerie Queene*: "All Spenser's 'virtues' spring from a root of manliness.

Strength, simplicity of aim, elevation of spirit, courage are presupposed as their necessary conditions. But they have with him another condition as universal. They all grow and are nourished from the soil of love; the love of beauty, the love and service of fair women" (152–53). In such criticism the power of empathy outweighs any strict concern for judgment, on the part of the critic as much as on that of the poet. Spenser – and, one infers, Spenser's civilization – "appears with a kind of double self. At one time he speaks as one penetrated and inspired by the highest and purest ideas of love, and filled with aversion and scorn for the coarser forms of passion – for what is ensnaring and treacherous, as well as what is odious and foul. At another, he puts forth all his power to bring out its most dangerous and even debasing aspects in highly coloured pictures, which none could paint without keen sympathy with what he takes such pains to make vivid and fascinating" (156). Surely Dean Church had noticed similar highly coloured pictures in Holy Scripture.

The commentary in Church's *Spenser* develops around pairs of contrasts found throughout nineteenth-century criticism: male and female, sacred and profane, idleness and industry, reason and passion, innocence and experience. The theme of youthfulness and maturity is particularly significant in light of the historicizing imagination of nineteenth-century criticism: "With a kind of unconsciousness and innocence, which we find now hard to understand, and which perhaps belongs to the early childhood or boyhood of a literature, he passes abruptly from one standard of thought and feeling to another; and is quite as much in earnest when he is singing the pure joys of chastened affections, as he is when he is writing with almost riotous luxuriance what we are at this day ashamed to read" (157). Two things are gained by regarding Spenser as a child. It becomes possible to treat his negligence and lack of propriety with benign tolerance, and it becomes possible to locate his poetry in a developmental narrative of English literature. Before Spenser, there was mere infancy: "We have forgotten all these preliminary attempts, crude and imperfect, to speak with force and truth, or to sing with measure and grace . . . . They were the necessary exercises by which Englishmen were recovering the suspended art of Chaucer, and learning to write" (3). Of the great things to come, "Spenser was the harbinger and announcing sign. But he was only the harbinger . . . . To the last [he] moved in a world which was not real, which never had existed, which, any how, was only a world of memory and sentiment . . . . He never threw himself frankly on human life as it is" (35–36). We recognize in this the story that James Beattie had told of the boy minstrel, Edwin. Lacking the "power of ordering and connecting" that comes with maturity, Church's Spenser, like Beattie's young and enthusiastic Edwin, could not tell a well-constructed story. But by virtue of this very immaturity, as it was supposed, critics like Church could find a place for Spenser in their own clearly plotted narrative of the progress of letters and civilization. While Church's is the official Victorian biography of Spenser, it should be read alongside the life in A. B. Grosart's unfinished edition of the *Works* (1882–84), which makes for more entertaining reading – it is lively, speculative, opinionated, and in the less pretentious antiquarian tradition. The writer has a disarming habit of printing the word FACTS in caps. If Church resembles George Eliot, Grosart is Charles Dickens.

Women, Children, and Culture

While nineteenth-century readers did not generally think of Spenser as child-ish, many attempts were made to render Spenser suitable for children. After all, Cowley, Pope, Wordsworth, Southey, and many others had testified to the power of youthful encounters with the *Faerie Queene*. Prose redactions of the *Faerie Queene*, like nineteenth-century periodicals, were often aimed at specific groups of readers. The anonymous *Holiness; or The Legend of St. George: a Tale from Spenser's Faerie Queene, by A Mother* (1836) was inspired by Charles and Mary Lamb's *Tales from Shakespeare* (1807): "Spencer needs translation; his obsolete dialect throwing him out of the reach of children, whom it is so desirable to interest in the elder writers of English literature" (iii). A series of questions appended to the narrative indicates that religious allegory was still respected as an educational device, in Puritan Boston anyway: "Does not this Italian name glance at the influence of Rome in England? St. George has not yet repented of the pride of the flesh, from whose dominions he had just escaped. He was therefore weak, an easy prey to the pride of a spiritual hierarchy. Thus ever does animal self indulgence betray man to spiritual bondage" (179). It seems that Catholicism was regarded as a threat to New England values even prior to the great Irish immigration of the 1840s. It is tempting to see in Massachusetts a survival or the radical Protestantism embraced by Spenser's early admirers; Anne Bradstreet, the immigrant daughter of one of the Colonial governors, had once praised "Phoenix Spenser" in an elegy on Sir Philip Sidney. But as New England Protestantism came under the influence of Unitarianism a more liberal view of childhood and religion was also coming into play. In 1840 J. S. Dwight, Harvard graduate and soon-to-be member of the experimental community at Brook Farm, remarked in the *Christian Examiner*: "*The Faerie Queene* brings back the long Elysian days of boyhood. No poetry is so engaging to the young imagination; it is so sensuous and full of vivid pictures, so fanciful and free, jumping the obstacles of literal facts so easily, yet always true to the facts of the soul, always gratifying simple hope. It leaves a lasting sweetness upon the tongue to have fed upon this manna in the days before care came" (208).

Spenser received more attention from writers for children later in the century, though by then religious instruction was less common than simple didactic storytelling of the sort found in Hart's *Essay*. "The Children's Library" reprinted *Tales from Shakespeare*, a "*Golden Key*" to Chaucer, and *Spenser for Children* by M. H. Towry (1885). Because young readers will not attend to allegory, the editor writes, "the finest descriptive parts [which] have little or no action . . . have, therefore, been necessarily omitted" (v). Towry relates the stories of "Sir Guy in Search of the Bower of Bliss" and "The Fair Florimell; or, The Sea King's Palace." In *Tales from Spenser* (1892), Sophia H. Maclehose chooses to relate her stories "simply as stories, and therefore only those episodes in the poem most interesting and most complete in themselves have been chosen" (iii). Such simplified retellings provoked something of a reaction from Clara L. Thomson, editor of many popular classics; in *Tales from the Faerie Queene* (1900) she complains that "they treat the original with somewhat greater freedom than is advisable when it is taken as the subject of the first literature lessons" (vii). Thomson's volume appends a bibliography of criticism for the use of schoolteachers. Spenser's biography receives detailed attention in Gertrude Ely's contribution to the *English Men of Letters for Boys and Girls* series (1894), though the author recommends "a little patience in conquering the style and laying aside the thought of [*The Faerie Queene*] as allegory" (73). In *Spenser's Britomart* (1896), Mary E. Litchfield produced a modernized textbook edition in which "the scattered portions of Spenser's interesting narrative" of the lady knight are "taken out and reunited" in a continuous story for young readers (iii). Such books seem to indicate that Spenser had a very broad reach in the Victorian era, yet here too the evidence for his popularity is equivocal: while his appearance in so many books for children indicates very high esteem, none of these books did for Spenser what the Lambs had done for Shakespeare. In contrast to the attention Spenser receives in Vicemus' Knox's *Elegant Extracts* (1805, etc.) in most Victorian anthologies he is awarded considerably less space than Chaucer, Shakespeare, Milton, Dryden, Pope, Wordsworth, and Byron; the lack of compelling characters and story plainly remained an impediment to readers young and old. The "best judges," even among writers for children, continued to admire him, however. The novelist George MacDonald, who praised Spenser's religious verse and bemoaned the lack of interest in Spenser's moral teachings, reinvented the fairy story for young readers, and Elizabeth Barret Browning, a great admirer of Spenser, drew upon his allegory and diction in verse that recalls Ambrose ("Namby-Pamby") Philips. In "A Vision of Poets" (1844) she writes:

> And Spenser drooped his dreaming head
> (With languid sleep-smile you had said
> From his own verse engendered.)
> On Ariosto's till they ran
> Their curls in one.

> (1900, 2:323).

At the turn of the twentieth century, poetry was often regarded as the high road to culture; for this reason, perhaps, attempts were made to present Spenser as a total aesthetic experience, whether for children or adults. In *The Red Cross Knight: Scenes from Spenser's Faerie Queene* (1913), William Scott Durrant, M.A. – author of *Chaucer Redivivus: A Playlet* (1912) and *Cross and Dagger: The Crusade of the Children* (1910) – presents Spenser to children in dramatic form, with actors, costumes, and stirring music by Wagner, Gounod, and Sir Edward German. Redactions for children were usually illustrated, including most of those I have mentioned as well as Mary Macleod's *Stories from the Faerie Queene* (London, 1897), N. G. Royde-Smith's *Una and the Red Cross Knight* (London, 1905), C. D. Wilson's *The Faerie Queene, Book I, Rewritten in Simple Language* (Chicago, 1906), R. W. Grace's *Tales from Spenser* (London, 1909), L. H. Dawson's *Stories from the Faerie Queene* (London, 1910), and Emily Underdown's *Gateway to Spenser* (London, 1911). Books of this kind continued to appear down to the Second World War. Nor were adult readers denied their gallery of pictures in the great age of illustrated books: Spenser's "Epithalamion" was illustrated by G. W. Edwards in 1895 and by Edwin Blashfield in 1902; the *Faerie Queene* was done by L. F. Muckley in 1896; the Kelmscott Press issued the *Shepheardes Calendar* illustrated by A. J. Gaskin in 1896; it was illustrated by Walter Crane in 1897, along with the *Faerie Queene*. Spenser's busy complexity found appropriate echoes in neogothic and art nouveau pictorialism – perhaps also in attempts by contemporary philologists to "illustrate" Spenser in their own form of neogothic criticism – by twining together vast skeins of sources, topics, and intertextual allusions. Spenser was much a presence in Victorian medievalism than he had been in Strawberry Hill gothick, but no doubt his gorgeous imagery and allegorical characters contributed something to design and themes of pre-Raphaelite painting.

The emphasis Victorian apostles of culture give to womanhood led to innovative interpretations of Spenser. Traditional humanism, centered around Latin grammar and literature, had been a largely masculine enterprise. With the shift to the vernacular, nineteenth-century programs for aesthetic education increasingly involved both sexes. It is surely no accident that most of the prose redactions were written by women acting in their feminine capacity as moral instructors of young children. Prior to the romantic era, women writers displayed slight and sporadic interest in Spenser; female readers inclined much more to untutored Shakespeare and to mannerly Pope. The first Spenser critics to address the issue of gender had been, as one would expect, Addison and Steele. Their *Spectator* papers on manners and morals in the *Faerie Queene* found echoes in Pope's "Rape of the Lock," Prior's "Colin's Mistakes," Samuel Wesley's "Battle of the Sexes," and in Spenserian sonnets by Thomas Percy of *The Reliques*. Yet women writers, having been spared grammar-school drilling in verbal mechanics, preferred the language of the day to the mannered artifice of imitation. Many knew the *Faerie Queene*; prior to 1770, one finds allusions to Spenser by Katherine Phillips, Anne Finch, Mary Chudleigh, Elizabeth Thomas, Hester Mulso Chapone, Mary Leapor, and Judith Cowper Madan. But such writers cultivated verse epistle and devotional poetry, leaving narrative poetry mostly to men. Then as now, Spenser and Milton attracted the attention of mostly university-educated readers; eighteenth-century women writers pursuing politeness through sexual commerce had little to gain by appearing as pedantic Goths. All of this changed after 1770, when James Beattie's *Minstrel* demonstrated a nonhumanist approach to imitating the *Faerie Queene* that emphasized description and sentimentality rather than ethical action. Even before that, Beattie's patron Elizabeth Montagu had defended a gothic Shakespeare against the strictures of Voltaire. As domestic life and sentimentality displaced politics and martial exploits in eighteenth-century romances, romance-writing became an important genre for female writers. Once aesthetic education began to seriously challenge traditional humanism, sexual difference became a foundational matter that women writers could turn to their (seeming) advantage. As women took an ever-greater interest in romance, the Spenserians Mary Tighe and Felicia Hemans set new standards for female poets, though the very hyper-feminine qualities that once attracted such admiration would later harm their reputations.

In contrast to the martial epic, the modern romance centered attention on themes of erotic love, domestic life, and religious experience. As Hurd pointed out, one of the marks of this "modern" and Christian genre was a higher regard for women than is found in classical epic. The case for romance as an alternative to epic was made with great force and eloquence by the novelist Clara Reeve (1729–1807) in *The Progress of Romance* (1785). As though to demonstrate the importance of romance to the woman writer, Reeve's spokeswoman overgoes Cowley, Dryden, and Pope in asserting Spenser's power to make poets of readers:

> *HORTENSIUS:* There is a kind of enthusiasm, that is inspired by these Poets, which seizes the head, and engages the heart, in their favour. — I have heard it observed that Spencer has made more poets than any other writer of our country.
>
> *SOPHRONIA:* I know one instance of it myself, in a lady, who never before dreamed of writing Poetry, she was not young at the time when she first met with Spencer; and reading some of the finest Cantos in it, the impression was so strong, that she could not sleep all the night after, and before the morning she composed a very pretty piece of poetry in honour of Spencer. — and from that time forward, she continued to write whenever a subject fell in her way, and all her writings are above mediocrity. (55–56)

I have not identified the writer discussed in this dialogue, though in the 1780s Reeve's friend Anna Seward (1747–1809) began writing short poems in Spenserians; soon afterward the romantic "Perdita" Robinson (1758–1800) would adopt the stanza in longer narratives. Whatever influence Spenser might have had on changing concepts of gender in women's writing would most likely have come through the prose fiction of novelists like Clara Reeve.

But influence was even more likely to work in the other direction; as we have seen, novels and prose romances had a profound influence on nineteenth-century interpretations of Spenser's poetry. Edward Dowden's "Heroines of Spenser," the major Victorian statement about gender in the *Faerie Queene*, first appeared in *Cornhill* in 1879 and was several times reprinted. Reeve would have approved of Dowden's emphasis: "Behind each woman made to worship or to love rises a sacred presence – womanhood itself." Spenser's heroines prevent the *Faerie Queene* from becoming "a frigid moral allegory or a mere masque of the fancy" (663, 664). Like other nineteenth-century critics, Dowden attempts to evoke the magical effects of Spenser's landscapes and characters through his own virtuosic prose descriptions. But he also makes some shrewd interpretations. Dowden notes how Spenser departs from the traditional story of St. George: "Una is never exposed to the monster; she devotes herself to the delivery of her parents, and the part which she plays in the adventure is far from being a passive one. To her the champion of her cause owes the sword which fights her battle, and hope, and courage, and forgiveness, and love, and even life itself" (668). Una thus becomes a shining example of Victorian womanhood, a Christian soldier in her own right. Dowden takes up the topic of gender and allegory in a rejoinder to Coleridge, who had demoted a feminine Spenser to a rank below Shakespeare. While it may be that "the perfection of woman is to be characterless," this should be construed positively as "a well developed harmonious nature" (665, 666). Spenser's men and women are different kinds of being; if in the heroes "the unity of personal character is broken by the allegory," the heroines "are not parceled out into fragments." They thus stand above and behind the male figures, assuming a superiority like that of Arthur over the lesser knights, or like Shakespeare over his invented characters. Una, Belphoebe, Amoret, and Britomart sustain the reader's interest throughout the story, and so assume a higher didactic purpose. Like Coleridge, Dowden insists on unity that draws distinctions without differences. In a series of character sketches, he singles out Amoret as *ewig Weibliche*, the eternal feminine while developing an argument in which all (feminine) women are finally Una. Consequently, Duessa, Acrasia, Radigund, and their likes are huddled together and dismissed, leading to a predictable conclusion that yet again demotes Spenser below Shakespeare: allegory lauds the ideal, but "does not make an imaginative inquest into complex problems of life and character"; in the last analysis, romance is judged and found lacking (672, 680). The "well developed, harmonious nature" pre-supposed by the feminine ideal in nineteenth-century arguments about culture remained problematic, for the same critics were also upholding a more mascu-line individualism, liberty, and civilization. Victorian attempts to identify femi-ninity with an eternal or transcendental culture could be as limiting as their opposite, the earlier attempt to identify femininity with a progressive and ma-terial refinement. The romantic habit of reducing distinctions between a multi-plicity of genres to distinctions between a pair of genders did little to clarify matters.

Dowden's gallery of female portraits was realized graphically in *Heroines of the Poets* (Boston, 1886) which illustrates the several characters of Victorian womanhood in poetry and woodcuts (the *Faerie Queene* is represented by Una with her lion). The beauty contest motif was also taken up in Gamaliel Brad-ford's *Elizabethan Women* (posthumously published in 1936). Bradford (1863–1932) explores the character of womanhood in the Elizabethan playwrights and in the *Faerie Queene* as a means of tracing Yankee civilization back to its vigorous cultural roots in Tudor England. In turn-of-the-century criticism, "culture" could be construed in a biological, Darwinian sense more materialist than anything in neoMarxist criticism today; throughout, Bradford implies strong connections between race, sexuality and culture. In a second Judgment of Paris, "Women of *The Fairy Queen*" presents Una, Britomart, and Florimell before the discerning imaginations of Bradford's readers. Like many Victorian critics, Bradford regards allegory as an impediment to aesthetic perception; in his character sketches the three damsels appear "as simple flesh and blood, af-ter all the stiff and unnatural garment of allegory has been plucked off them" (214). It is not really much of a contest; Una is "too saintly" and Britomart "too militant"; Florimell wins the prize "simply by being lovable – the best way to win love, after all, and the surest way to keep it" (223). While the con-cept of such a beauty contest derives from book 3 of the *Faerie Queene*, one notes that the criteria of judgment have certainly changed. In contrast, Dorot-hea Beale (1831–1906) promotes the ideals of New Womanhood in "Britomart, or Spenser's Ideal of Woman," a lecture delivered to graduates of the Ladies' College of Cheltenham and published in *Literary Studies* (1902). Beale was the leading woman educator of Victorian England; she was head teacher at Casterton, (the "Lowood" in *Jane Eyre*), established the first training college for women schoolteachers, and later founded Saint Hilda's Hall at Ox-ford. Beale too adopts the gallery motif, illustrating Britomart's life in six "stained glass windows," each of which addresses dilemmas facing contempo-rary women: Una and the magic mirror, Una arming herself, the defense of Red Cross, passing through the fire, the encounter with Artegall, and Una's resignation of authority. A second Merlin, Beale uses the mirror strategy to rouse her students to battle: the "true woman" is "no mere appendage of a knight" (27): she is motivated by love, suffers by and for love, and challenges the erotic norms typified by Gamaliel Bradford's treatment of Florimell. Britomart delivers Amoret from something very like Bradford's condescension: "Glozing lies must be proved to be such, then only can his victim be delivered from his snares" (39). Unlike any other critic I have considered, Beale treats Radigund seriously, though in the end with firm moral condemnation.

While Beale was lecturing in Cheltenham, Columbia University professor George Edward Woodberry (1855–1930) was lecturing on "race power" to the Lowell Institute in Boston. *The Torch: Eight Lectures on Race Power in Literature Delivered Before the Lowell Institute of Boston* appeared in 1905 and was several times reprinted. The reference in Woodberry's title is really to the *human* race; the lecturer, who wrote for the *Atlantic Monthly* and the *Nation*, was not a biological determinist but a social constructivist arguing that civilizations are shaped by a mutable mental culture in service to the broader ends of democracy and progress. Though forgotten today, Woodberry's popular book is invaluable as an eclectic summary of nineteenth-century concepts of education. Two preliminary lectures establish "mythology, chivalry, the Scriptures [as] the tongues of the imagination"; these are followed by two lectures on the Prometheus myth in romantic poetry and philosophy and separate lectures on Spenser, Milton, and Wordsworth (48). Woodberry's lecture on the *Faerie Queene* underscores historical continuity; Spenser confronts "the very problem before each of us in education: 'to fashion a gentleman'" (121). Woodberry's historicism precludes a direct application of Spenser's doctrines to modern life, yet he does believe that Spenser's backward-looking medievalism suggests how Americans might make use of a European civilization now passing into the dustbin of history: "The *Faerie Queene* depicts and contains a receding world, a dying culture." But in what sense might a poem contain a culture? This is a problem "Milton, Gray, Shelley, and Tennyson in their time met; the problem of how to reduce this miscellaneousness of matter to some order, to reconcile it with his own mind; to build up out of it his own world." We have seen how Hurd and Beattie first formulated this issue; similar to them in other ways, Woodberry gives gender a much larger role in the process of culture formation and aesthetic education. Faulting earlier nineteenth-century accounts of Spenser as either a moralist or a sensualist, he concludes that the poet "blended the two in a new worship of womanhood" (119, 120). The great achievement of the *Faerie Queene* is to foreshadow the cultural synthesis Woodberry expects from modern Bostonians; Spenser's "presentation of moral character" is more spiritual, and thus more complete, than even those of modern novelists like Scott, Thackeray, Dickens, and George Eliot (134).

Woodberry's identification of romanticism with the spirit of progress may be compared to that of Vida Scudder (1861–1954), who for many years taught English at Wellesley College. Both of these progressives were social Darwinists, but where Woodberry inclines towards biology and gender as motive forces, Scudder, a Christian socialist, looks to class. Her appropriation of British romanticism for American social values, with its double emphasis on science and democracy, would become normative in twentieth-century academia. "It was in the French Revolution that the idea of Progress entered" she writes in *The Life of the Spirit in the Modern English Poets* (1895, 15). This would have been news to Addison! While William Wordsworth had looked to nature as an anchor of permanence in changeful times, in Scudder's creative misreading he typifies, in contrast to Spenser, a new openness to "Mutabilitee": "to us moderns, the deeper meditation on Nature brings joy, not pain. For we have learned to recognize beneath her ceaseless ebb and flow, so often seemingly cruel, a steady onward movement towards fullness of life unguessed. In the light of science, change has become the symbol, no longer of decay but promise" (17). Speaking of "the force idea" in poetry, she condemns the motionlessness of Spenser's landscapes (along with those of Cowper, Thomson, and Gray); to such pseudo-romantics "nature's charm was a hidden secret." Speaking of "the unity idea" she laments "the absence of cause and effect in those old epics and romances where naive charm and childishness spring alike from the lack of wholeness of vision." In speaking of "the realistic temper" by which the modern romantics learned to see nature for what it is, she writes, "Spenser is certainly the most prodigal author of the time. His very name calls to the mind a gorgeous and brilliant pageant. But the means by which he produces this effect is certainly not through the use of color. His scale is the old conventional limited one; his allusions are few and commonplace. In the first book of the 'Faerie Queene' there are only ten color epithets. His only really powerful work in this line is in the chiaroscuro of which he is a master" (29, 49–50). Judged by the standards of modern realists like Wordsworth or Browning, the fantastic Spenser seems not to have had much to say to American readers.

But Scudder does not, quite, banish the Poets' Poet from Parnassus. In a later book, *Social Ideals in English Letters* (1898), she historicizes Spenser in much the way that Woodberry does in *The Torch*: Americans have done away with aristocracy, but not with high ideals: "Spenser's poetry is the very mirror of the times at their best. Its bright and chivalric spirit scorns money as much as it cherishes what money brings. Listen to Sir Guyon, knight of Temperance, tempted in the cave of Mammon by piles of glistening lucre." On the other hand, there is the encounter between Sir Artegall and the "giant of Communism, who wishes to weigh the sea and land in his balances, and distribute them more evenly . . . . Sir Artegall has no trouble at all in answering his arguments; and as with much satisfaction to himself the knight demonstrates that equality produced to-day would be inequality to-morrow, he utters a line which shows the attitude of Spenser and his age to all radical social changes. 'All chance is perilous and all change unsound,' says Sir Artegall" (83–84).

This episode had been more troubling to the republican Wordsworth than it is to the democratic Scudder; working through its murky and unpleasant implications in the unpublished "Salisbury Plain," he seems to have argued himself to a standstill. But Wordsworth – no historical relativist he – was more inclined to regard Spenser, as had his fellow republican Milton, as a grave moral teacher. Vida Scudder, more confident in the transformative powers of social evolution, is less challenged by Spenser's hauteur. So far from being a threat to American democracy, Spenser's aristocratic values helped to bring it about: "no one can read the 'Faerie Queene,' no one can know the Elizabethans, and regret the pride of rank in that great period. It had a work to do: to exalt the ideal of character higher than ever before; to raise such a standard of magnificent manhood that the English-speaking race could never be content with a vulgar average life. We in America have unconsciously higher intuitions because Sidney lived and Spenser flashed his vision of Arthur the Magnificent, of St. George, and of Sir Artegall, upon the world. The work was done, and the ideal of courtliness is one which social evolution, though it develop in forms of the most advanced democracy, can never afford to lose" (85–86). Just what higher ideal of character had democratic America inherited through "social evolution"? By what mechanisms might traits of moral and literary character be passed down to unconscious beneficiaries? Like Matthew Arnold's famous definition of culture as the best that has been thought and said, Victorian concepts of progress remained little more than intuitions awaiting philosophical specification. For all its inaccuracies and speculativeness, the literary criticism of Woodberry and Scudder was fruitful in intellectual problems; as we shall see in the next chapter, such questions of inheritance became foundational matters for twentieth-century academic criticism.

Russell, Dowden, and De Vere

Spenser, of course, was being discussed in colleges and universities even before the era of modern philology. The question of how students might best respond to Spenser is the subject of a famous pair of essays by James Russell Lowell (1819–91) and Edward Dowden (1843–1913). Both were poets and public men of letters in the grandest Victorian sense, but also scholars and professors – Lowell at Harvard and Dowden at Trinity College, Dublin. While many of the writers discussed above were teachers, tutors, or even college professors, a new era of academic criticism of Spenser might properly be said to begin with these two writers: Lowell was an early president of the Modern Language Association of America; Dowden, a tireless proselytizer, lectured on English literature to students at Oxford, Cambridge, and Princeton. If Lowell's Spenser criticism derives from Coleridge and Dowden's from Wordsworth, both writers looked to Spenser as an example of the general culture that might make whole a civilization threatened by professional specialization. Paradoxically, by striving to establish English studies as an academic subject, Lowell and Dowden contributed to making literary studies the professional specialization it is has since become. The original aim of college English was to offer training in the *liberal* arts as a hedge against the very *liberalism* that was transforming modern, capitalist society into a network of interlocking specializations: as one degree among others, the liberal arts degree could be regarded as a kind of specialization in generalities. As formulated in the critical prose of Wordsworth and Coleridge, "culture" was the alternative to "civilization." The Victorian habit of opposing the universals of culture from the particulars of civilization made it possible for Sir Edward Tylor to write his groundbreaking book in anthropology, *Primitive Culture* (1871).

Lowell's "Spenser" first appeared in 1875 as a long essay in the *North American Review*; it was subsequently revised and collected in *Among My Books*. The essay is written in the form of a public lecture, beginning with a long introduction on the drudgery of metrical romance and antiquarian criticism, followed by discussions of Spenser's career and works, concluding with the poet's character illustrated through pictorial analogies, aesthetic impressions, and rhapsodic appreciation. Lowell ventures a substantially new account of the poet's character that emphasizes Spenser's preoccupation with poetical craft. "Rosalind," for instance, is seen not as a biographical event but as a literary pretext: "I very much doubt whether Spenser ever felt more than one profound passion in his life, and that luckily was for his *Faery Queen*" (2:153). While written for publication, "Spenser" is thoroughly oratorical, studded with the audience-pleasing asides that made Lowell a legendary Harvard professor. Taking aim at Thomas Warton (misidentified as Joseph), Lowell praises Spenser's prolix astronomical similes: "His way of measuring time was perfectly natural in an age when everybody did not carry a dial in his poke as now. He is the last of the poets, who went (without affectation) by the great clock of the firmament . . . . Time itself becomes more noble when so measured; we never knew how precious a commodity we had the wasting" (2:180–81). Spenser's "natural" sense of temporality, akin to that of savages in Polynesia, represents a kind of pastoral otium. Telling time was a not unimportant topic, as Lowell's students would have recognized: the efficient control of time was the hallmark of industrial production and the new theories of management. Two such quotable remarks have made Lowell's essay notorious. Of Spenser's allegory he writes, "whenever you come suddenly on the moral, it gives you a shock of unpleasant surprise, a kind of grit, as when one's teeth close on a bit of gravel in a dish of strawberries and cream" (2:184). Allegory was Spenser's way of showing "Master Bull his new way of making fine words butter parsnips, in a rhymed moral primer" (2:175). Just as Lowell tries to outdo Hazlitt on allegory, so he overgoes Hunt on the gallery conceit: Spenser "makes one think always of Venice . . . as at Venice you swim in a gondola from Gian Bellini to Titian, and from Titian to Tintoret, so in him, where other cheer is wanting, the gentle sway of his measure, like the rhythmical impulse of the oar, floats you lullingly along from picture to picture" (2:177–78). Such intense enjoyment of timeless leisure was the reward of the intense control of timely labor pursued by the future captains of industry who were Lowell's students. These virtuoso passages have led some to mistakenly dismiss Lowell as a dilettante and a lightweight. In fact, the Harvard professor was firing the opening rounds in a long, hard-fought, and ultimately successful attempt to divorce aesthetic appreciation from the sad remains of a humanist education that in Lowell's time consisted largely of memory drilling.

Lowell's nuanced discussion of Spenser's supposed Puritanism was surely intended to speak to the immediate concerns of New England readers. He concedes that when Spenser "wrote the *Shepherd's Calendar* he was certainly a Puritan, and probably so by conviction rather than from any social influences or thought of personal interests." Yet, after all his early labors, the poet mellowed with age: "The bent of his mind was toward a Platonic mysticism, a supramundane sphere where it could shape universal forms out of the primal elements of things, instead of being forced to put up with their fortuitous combinations in the unwilling material of mortal clay" (2:166–68). Lowell's own Platonism, derived from Emerson out of Coleridge, leads to a penetrating if one-sided insight into Spenser's poetics: "He was soon convinced of his error, and was not long in choosing between an unreality which pretended to be real and those everlasting realities of the mind which seem unreal only because they lie beyond the horizon of the every-day world and become visible only when the mirage of fantasy lifts them up and hangs them in an ideal atmosphere" (2:141). The Choice of Hercules here becomes a choice between labor and leisure, a grubby materialism and an uplifting culture. In this passage and the elaborate simile of the "magic glass" and its "shadowy echoes of actuality" developed in Lowell's peroration (2:196), nineteenth-century aestheticism modulates into something like the cult of literariness that would later dominate twentieth-century classrooms. The imagery Lowell pits against contemporary Philistinism often comes directly from the *Faerie Queene*.

Edward Dowden's "Spenser, the Poet and Teacher" first appeared in Grosart's edition of Spenser in 1882 and was collected in *Transcripts and Studies* (1888, 1896). It takes aim at the romantic characterization of the poet as the dreaming hedonist one finds in both Keats and Lowell: "Shall we accept this view, or that of Milton — 'a better teacher than Scotus or Aquinas?' Was Spenser such a teacher 'sage and serious' to his own age? If so, does he remain such a teacher for this age or ours?" (271). Shadowing Lowell almost topic by topic, Dowden draws upon Aristotle's *Nichomachian Ethics* to make the case for Spenser as a moral teacher. If Lowell's Platonism foregrounds an informing *logos*, Dowden follows Aristotle in stressing a narrative *ethos*; in contrast to contemporary aestheticism, he underscores the place of Spenser's poetry in history and the place of history in Spenser's poetry. As far as I know, Dowden's use of Aristotle to explicate the several legends is the earliest application of hermeneutic method in Spenser criticism – a major contribution to Spenser studies and an indication that Professor Dowden was keeping abreast of the "higher criticism" then developing on the Continent. In Dowden's view, Spenser's moral teachings exemplify the distinctions Sir Philip Sidney makes between the ends of history, philosophy, and poetry in *Defence of Poetry*: "are we merely to gaze on with wide-eyed expectancy as at a marvelous pageant or procession . . . or are these visible shows only a rind or shell, which we must break or strip away in order to get at that hidden wisdom which feeds the spirit? Neither of these things are we to do" (286). The *Faerie Queene* fuses precept and example into "a living creature of the imagination" teaching "self-culture, the formation of a complete character for the uses of the earth, and afterwards, if need be, for the uses of heaven" (302, 293). This emphasis on "use" is aimed at Lowell's aestheticizing: "Spenser breathes into us a breath of life, which has an antiseptic power, which kills the germs of disease, and is antagonistic to the relaxed fibre, the lethargy, the dissolution, or disintegrating life-in-death of sensuality"; in support of this position Dowden cites a letter of Wordsworth to John Wilson insisting on the power of poetry to "rectify men's feelings" (285).

Yet this vocabulary of feeling, health, and organic wholeness undergirds a *cultural* program that in the end is closer to Lowell's contemplations than to Aristotle's or Sidney's emphasis on poetic "making." Aristotle spoke of habits, Sidney of ideas, but Dowden pursues what is finally a morality of aesthetic sensation: "To render men's *feelings* more sane, pure, and permanent – this was included in the great design of the *Faery Queen*" (285–6, my emphasis). Dowden's formulation recalls Dean Kitchin's "instinctive preferences for what is gallant and truthful." The substitution of habits of feeling for habits of doing – the change wrought by aesthetic education – takes us back to the split between sentiment and action we noted in Bishop Hurd's *Letters on Chivalry and Romance*; like Hurd, though less explicitly, Dowden distinguishes between the formal artistry that renders Spenser "a teacher for this age of ours" from the ethical and political doctrines that made Spenser "a teacher 'sage and serious' to his own age." Dowden papers over the difference, but a creeping historicism in his criticism threatens to divide what humanists had always striven to unite, self-discipline and political order: "what Spenser's political faith would be, if he were now living, we may surmise, but cannot assert. Living in the age of great monarchies, he was monarchical and aristocratic" (294). If we must historicize Spenser's doctrines, in what sense can he be called a teacher for all time? Like Vida Scudder and other liberal Victorians, Dowden shifts the discussion to personal character; with "none of the meanness of the libertine, none of the

meanness of the precision," Spenser's personality expresses and embodies the
political equilibrium Whig historians had long identified with the reign of
Elizabeth. But this golden age was not to last: "contending parties of the Eng-
lish nation went their ways – one party to moral licentiousness and political
servility, the other to religious intolerance and the coarse extravagances of the
sectaries. Each extreme ran its course" (303).

These two extremes are plainly the Hellenism and Hebraism that Matthew
Arnold, in *Culture and Anarchy* (1869), had used to subordinate politics to
"culture." Like Arnold, Dowden looks to poetry for a transhistorical, personal
culture that might unify a nation divided by political prejudice and factional-
ism. But in lifting "culture" above the sublunary realm of politics, Victorian
sages made it very unclear how culture might contribute *to* politics. Spenser
himself was no such disinterested creature as Dowden has in mind, as his po-
litical allegories and dedicatory sonnets demonstrate. Spenser's political and re-
ligious program was recognized in the nineteenth century, as the many
complaints about his topical references testify. It could even become an object
of admiration, as when John Ruskin celebrates Spenser's organic powers in a
dazzling theological analysis of book 1 of the *Faerie Queene* appended to *The
Stones of Venice* (1851–53). Yet the ideal of aesthetic education adopted by writ-
ers on culture was not generally receptive to political engagement. If Aristotle,
Sidney, and Spenser recommended practicing of aristocratic virtues, Lowell
and Dowden are typical of their age in recommending the contemplation of
bourgeois feelings. Victorians sometimes praised Spenser's teachings, but they
could hardly embrace them whole-heartedly without abandoning democracy.
Full-blown, literal attempts to revive chivalry were made in the nineteenth cen-
tury – Kenelm Digby's *Broad Stone of Honour* (1822) went through many edi-
tions – but such nostalgia was rejected by the liberal consensus.

Although Lowell and Dowden address contemporary social issues, their
views fall within long-standing critical paradigms. Lowell's cool, disinterested
cosmopolitanism recalls Dryden and Pope, while Dowden's urgent didacticism
derives from the patriotic criticism of Addison, Steele, and Hughes. Insofar as
Lowell and Dowden were still lecturers speaking to a general public rather
than scholars addressing specialists in departments of English, they both fall
within the tradition of belle lettres that begins with the *Tatler*, the *Spectator*, and
the *Guardian*. That tradition was coming under sustained criticism in the nine-
teenth century, even from the men of letters who were its heirs and beneficiar-
ies. Coleridge decried the commercial values that gave rise to the periodical
essay and its republic of polite readers; whether liberal or conservative, many
romantics rejected Augustan norms of civility as shallow and ephemeral. As
ideals of genius displaced ideals of common sense, the lecturer at the rostrum
supplanted the conversationalist in the coffeehouse. Victorian sages opposed
literature and culture to the commerce and civilization upheld by the earlier

generation of Whigs: Lowell's Venice is a museum rather than a bustling commercial republic; Dowden locates Britain's political synthesis in the Tudor monarchy rather than in the revolution of 1689. Like Coleridge and Hazlitt before him, Dowden expresses disdain for the earlier generation of Whig writers. These changes resulted from the middle eighteenth-century romantic turn that recast the contest between Ancients and Moderns criticism as the new opposition between a unifying but static culture and a divisive but progressive civilization. Consequently, Victorian critics faced difficult choices. Advocates of English studies like Lowell and Dowden looked to literature, and especially to Elizabethan literature, for a spirit at once unifying in its appeal to the passions and progressive in its celebration of personality and individual character.

A more traditional humanism remained an option for bringing Spenser to bear on contemporary issues, though it was an option seldom pursued. The most attractive nineteenth-century humanist essay on Spenser appears in Grosart's edition (1882–84), printed alongside Dowden's "Spenser as Poet and Teacher." Like Dowden, Aubrey De Vere (1814–1902) was Irish and a professor, but whereas Dowden taught at Protestant Trinity, De Vere taught at Catholic Dublin University. In 1851 he had followed Newman into the Roman Church; as one might expect, his criticism does not locate Spenser in a historical march of liberty and progress: "So far from being true that his poetry is deficient in human interest, there is a sense in which he was especially a poet of the humanities. More than any predecessor he was the poet of beauty; but he sought that beauty in the human relations even more than in that world of ideal thought which was his native land. This truth seems little recognized, and is yet momentous if we would understand Spenser. Spenser was a great thinker, but he seldom writes in a speculative vein; and deep and sound as was his philosophy, he knew that poetry must express it in a strain 'simple, sensuous, and impassioned,' or not at all" (1:257–58). This "truth" was indeed little recognized by either the Lowells or the Dowdens among nineteenth-century critics. While De Vere's essay unfolds as a series of descriptive appreciations, it departs from the Victorian consensus in important ways. De Vere, for instance, interprets from within rather than against the allegory: "Embodied Vices are but abstractions, and do not constitute human characters, because the Vices are themselves but accidents of human nature when disnatured. It is otherwise with the Virtues: they belong to the essence of human nature; and in a large measure they create by the predominance now of this virtue, now of that, the different types of human character, each type drawing to itself by a gradual accretion the subordinate qualities most in harmony with that fundamental virtue" (1:261). This moral conception of human *nature* differs fundamentally from the nineteenth-century naturalism, an affair of "forces" taking rise from biology and sociology, and it leads to insights not available to the progressives. De Vere expresses admiration for Dowden's "Heroines of

Spenser," and he is typically Victorian in his praises of Una, but his neo-Aristotelian understanding of character does not reduce the heroines to Una: "Belphoebe is his great type of Purity, as her twin sister Amoret is of Love. Britomart is as eminently a type of Purity as Belphoebe, but notwithstanding, she is an essentially different character; and while Belphoebe glides like a quivered Dian through the forests, and sends shaft on shaft after the flying deer, Britomart cannot be contented except when she rides forth on heroic enterprise. Amoret, Belphoebe's sister, is equally unlike both: she can love only, love always, endure all things for love, and love but one. The woodland sport and the war field are alike alien to her. Britomart, who unites both those sister types of character, loves as ardently as Amoret, but she cannot, like her, love only; her life must be a life of arduous action and sustained endeavour" (1:262).

This emphasis on sustained endeavor amid difference restores a landscape of moral choice to Spenser's poem; De Vere does not represent these allegorical characters as intimations of an eternal feminine; they figure forth human virtues to both sexes, made attractive in their very beauty. Similarly, De Vere does not see Spenser as coincident with the genius of his age or regard the Elizabethan era as the great organic synthesis championed by Dowden: "The age in which Spenser lived was one full of what may be called anachronisms, so inconsistently did it bring together what it had inherited, and what it had produced and was producing. The luckless incoherency could not but reflect itself in [Spenser's] poetry." De Vere instances the episode of the Palace of Mercilla, in which Elizabeth passes judgment on Catholic Mary: "The greater our disappointment when it turns out that though the days described are those of the 'Round Table,' the Goddess of Justice is the daughter of Anne Boleyn, and that queenly lady 'of great countenance and place' who stands at her bar for judgment, and is successively convicted of immorality, of treason, of transgressing the law of nations, and of murder, is Mary Queen of Scotland" (1:275, 276). Despite its poetic artifice, the passage reveals a Spenser divided between the Middle Ages and the Renaissance, displaying feudal fealty to a coolly calculating Machiavellian monarch. De Vere exhibits considerable skill in casuistry as he brings Spenser before the bar of moral judgment. Illustrating the kind of moral restraint Artegall learned to his cost, De Vere holds out aestheticism and historical relativism as possible ways of softening the blow, even as he makes clear what he really thinks of the episode: "I cannot but believe that those stains on the surface of Spenser's poetry which, though not snares to moral principle, are yet insults to moral taste, and need to be stepped over like bad spots on a road, came to him from the coarseness of the age in which he lived, and to which the great Elizabethan drama, excepting in the main Shakespeare, bears so deplorable a witness" (1:277). In contrast to Thomas Arnold's 1880 essay in the *Dublin Review*, De Vere does not argue that the *Faerie Queene* is a threat to the moral principles upheld by Catholic readers; regarding human nature as fallible, Christians will make allowances even as they make discriminations. Such skills are what, after all, the humanist reader hopes to take away from the study of poetry. Even as he is more critical of Spenser than Dowden, De Vere surpasses Dowden in restoring Spenser's claim to be a moral teacher; as a humanist, De Vere can be more adept at mediating the opposing claims of history and philosophy: Spenser "is the philosophic poet of his age, as Wordsworth is of ours; and the philosophy of those two great poets, though in no sense at variance, was as different, the one from the other, as the character of their genius" (1:303).

Literary History

De Vere is the exception, however. More common are the critics like George Woodberry and Vida Scudder who look to literature for an example of the historical development that will bridge the opposing conservative and liberal tendencies in nineteenth-century social thought. Conservatives (Catholics excepted) hoped to find in Spenser a transhistorical and unifying expression of the Anglo-American Protestant tradition. Liberals desired to bring Spenser before a wider readership, extending the social reach of literature and furthering historical progress through aesthetic education. Since both identified national prowess with personal initiative, it was a foregone conclusion that attempts would be made to find in the *Faerie Queene* a synthesis of collective enterprise and individual freedom. Nor was warrant lacking in the text; by trimming between humanist traditionalism and vernacular innovation, Spenser set a precedent for what postromantic English and American educators were trying to achieve with English studies. English-speaking critics differed from both the German habit of defining culture from below through philological study of language and custom, and the French habit of defining culture from above though standards set by an academy. While there was a range of opinion, the consensus among Victorian liberals and conservatives alike was to regard poetry as the expression of a tradition of individual genius rather than an upwelling of communal forces or the product of rationalizing state institutions. This middle way accorded with Anglo-American political values but proved to be an impediment to the "scientific" study of literature being developed in Germany and France.

As a result, critical literary history, to which we now turn, was a late growth in Britain and the United States. In part, this was a legacy of the Ancients-Moderns debate, which instilled and sustained an abiding antipathy between antiquarianism and aestheticism; critical history remained impossible so long as British writers regarded writing history and writing criticism as different and opposing activities. Moreover, in the romantic era both modes tended to treat poetry piecemeal, the antiquarians drawing up indexes of curious words and the aestheticians assembling galleries of elegant extracts and memorable images. Critical history requires forms of narrative and argumentation equally foreign to the virtuoso collector of scattered facts and the Longinian collector of scattered beauties. Alternatives were always available, even in English; Continental literary history itself was much influenced by Thomas Blackwell's *Life of Homer* (1735), Richard Hurd's *Letters on Chivalry and Romance* (1762), Hugh Blair's *Critical Dissertation on the Poems of Ossian* (1763), and "Estimate" Brown's *Dissertation on Poetry and Music* (1763). Later on, literary histories by German and French writers were translated and widely read in Britain. These alternatives were rejected because they involved a historical determinism that did not accord easily with liberal social thought. It was long before anyone bothered to complete Thomas Warton's *History of English Literature*, which broke off with the Elizabethans; for the modern era English and American readers were left with periodical essays, anthology prefaces, lectures, biographies, and the extraordinary collections of anecdotes compiled by John Nichols and Isaac D'Israeli. Materials for historical study were abundantly available; Victorian readers with an interest in Spenser and his contemporaries had copious access to poems, documents, biographies, and bibliographies, but little narrative literary history.

Before the middle of the nineteenth century, the history of literature remained the province of antiquarians, book collectors, persons of taste, or the occasional philosophe like Adam Smith or William Godwin. While various attempts were made to bridge the social gap between Tom Warton and Bishop Hurd, most of these were carried out in specialist periodicals catering to book collectors: the *Retrospective Review* and the *Censura Literaria, British Bibliographer*, and *Restituta*, edited by Sir Samuel Egerton Brydges (1762–1837) in collaboration with other bibliophiles. The most notable piece of such criticism is *The Poetical Decameron, or Ten Conversations on English Poets and Poetry, Particularly of the Reigns of Elizabeth and James I* (1820), by the future Shakespeare forger and editor of Spenser, John Payne Collier (1789–1883). Collier's stated purpose is "to treat an antiquarian subject in a popular way" (1:v); he imitates the form and substance of Dryden's *Essay on Dramatic Poesy*. The significance of this work lies in its replaying the Ancients-Moderns debate entirely within the sphere of British literature:

> I understand your sarcasm (added Elliot, smiling), but though I may not be quite so deeply read in old poets as yourselves, you must not fancy that you engross all faculty of judging of the productions of the "divine infusion." I take it that the moderns know quite as well what good poetry is as the ancients (I mean the ancients of our own country), and write much better, with two or three exceptions.

"With two or three exceptions!" Indeed! (said Bourne) is that all you al-
low? Omitting Spenser and Shakespeare as out of the question, what say you
to Fletcher and Jonson, to Chapman, Drayton, and Nash, to Greene, Lodge,
Hall, Marston, Peele, Marlow, Daniel, and perhaps a hundred others? (1:xvii-
xviii)

With Bourne leading the charge, this reconstituted Ancients faction makes the
case that Elizabethan poetry may be enjoyed by persons of even the most re-
fined tastes. In its personated characters, the *Decameron* brings together the
"facts" and "beauties" schools of criticism, but Collier's narrative is not a his-
tory of British literature; rather, it takes the form of a fictional boat trip from
Westminster to an estate in the country. This line of criticism culminates in
Collier's *Bibliographical and Critical Account of the Rarest Books in the English Language*
(1866), a four-volume alphabetical catalogue of obscure Renaissance poems
and pamphlets that remains a useful tool for book collectors. It is "critical"
only in the sense of offering opinions as well as information.

The oft-reprinted *Introduction to the Literature of Europe during the Fifteenth, Six-
teenth, and Seventeenth Centuries* (1837–39) by the antiquarian Henry Hallam
(1777–1859) likewise combines information with appreciation, but in the form
of a chronicle. Hallam takes "literature" in its broadest, premodern sense, to
include theology, scientific writings, and even mathematics. Spenser, the only
nondramatic Elizabethan writer to receive serious attention, is marched
through the usual topics: design, allegory, archaisms. Hallam studiously ig-
nores the Cockneys Leigh Hunt and William Hazlitt, regarding Thomas
Campbell, John Wilson, and Samuel Taylor Coleridge as the modern critics
worth engaging. Sardonically cataloguing Spenser's beauties and blemishes,
Hallam observes, "Notwithstanding the more imaginative cast of poetry in the
present century, it may be well doubted whether the *Faery Queen* is as much
read or as highly esteemed as in the days of Anne. It is not perhaps very diffi-
cult to account for this: those who seek the delight that mere fiction presents to
the mind (and they are the great majority of readers) have been supplied to the
utmost limit of their craving by stores accommodated to every temper, and far
more stimulant than the legends of Faeryland" (1882, 1:237). While Spenser
remains "the third name in the poetical literature of our country" – bawdy
Chaucer had slipped by this point – Hallam fears that his elaborate fictions
were no match for the quick-paced modern novel. Craik's *Sketches of the History
of Literature and Learning in England* (1844–45) was another compendium of facts
and appreciations – larger, but no more a critical literary history than Hallam's
effort.

But George L. Craik's later work illustrates the coming change. In 1849 he
was appointed professor of English literature and history at Belfast; this eleva-
tion to official status brought with it a change in the way Craik wrote criticism.
In 1866 the professor recast his earlier "sketches" as *A Compendious History of*

English Literature, and of the English Language, from the Norman Conquest, with Numerous Specimens. In this work literature is presented as an adjunct to the larger philological subject of the history of languages; literary history must be "compendious" because it is necessary to include many minor figures as historical context for the major ones. Craik's move from "sketch" to critical history is imperfectly made, however, for his text remains a patchwork of philology, aesthetics, and social history, its specimens arranged in separate drawers: the "Norman Period," "Second English," "Third English," the "Middle and Latter part of the Seventeenth Century," the "Century between the English Revolution and the French Revolution," the "Latter Part of the Eighteenth Century," "The Nineteenth Century." Edmund Spenser receives much the longest entry. While the Spenser chapter still adopts the biography-and-appreciation format, there is a new emphasis on "development," personal and national. Craik's discussion of the *Shepheardes Calender* compares Spenser's prosody to that of Langland and Chaucer: "It might seem to echo, and, as it were, continue and prolong, the strain of the old national minstrelsy; thus at once expressing his love and admiration of the preceding poets who had been his examples, and, in part, his instructors and inspirers, and making their compositions reflect additional light and beauty upon his own." Not the first poetical bird of spring, Spenser is no longer represented by Craik as the naive or primitive versifier he had been in the 1845 *Spenser and His Poetry*. Spenser's pastoral verse signifies a stage in personal development: the *Calendar* is a "very unequal composition" to be followed by "Mother Hubberds Tale," which belongs to "the middle age of Spenser's genius, if not of his life — the stage in his mental and poetical progress when his relish and power of the energetic had attained perfection, but the higher sense of the beautiful had not yet been fully developed" (1:516, 519). That culmination comes, of course, in the *Faerie Queene*, which Craik introduces by way of a long digression on aesthetics and "pure poetry." This chronology ignores the evidence in Harvey's letters that Spenser was working on the *Faerie Queene* contemporaneously with the *Shepheardes Calendar*.

In Craik's writings one again sees the different stains of Victorian criticism gathered but not assimilated. Poetry, as such, is said to approach the condition of music; standing apart from the limits imposed by morality and history, it exists in its own "proper region." And so, "these peculiarities [of *The Faerie Queene*] — the absence of an interesting story or concatenation of incidents, and the want of human character and passion in the personages that carry on the story, such as it is — are no defects in the Fairy Queen. On the contrary, the poetry is only left thereby so much the purer. Without calling Spenser the greatest of poets, we may still say that his poetry is the most poetical of all poetry. Other poets are all of them something else as well as poets, and deal in reflection, or reasoning, or humor, or wit, almost as largely as in the proper product of the imaginative faculty; his strains alone, in the Fairy Queen, are poetry, all poetry, and nothing but poetry" (1:531, 528–29). Few Victorian critics would go so far, leaving us rather unprepared for Craik's peroration on Artegall and the Giant, one of only two "specimens" taken from the poem: it "might seem to be a satire written in our own day on the folly and madness of the seventy years ago, and it is difficult to believe that it was published two centuries before the events which it so strikingly prefigures." Craik reprints the entire episode, concluding the chapter on Spenser by praising the poet's prophetic "anticipation and refutation of the Liberty and Equality philosophism of the end of the eighteenth century in the end of the nineteenth" (1:541, 546). By exposing "the almost mechanical methods human legislation has alone at its command" Spenser's poetry transcends the historical conditions of its production and speaks directly to the social issues confronting nineteenth-century policy makers who were looking for something stronger than laws to bind together an empire threatened by Irish nationalism and class warfare. Ultimately, this desire for a unifying culture was the common goal of those who professed English studies, be they conservative or liberal.

While British literary history was driven by the empirical urge to accumulate biographical facts, bibliographical information, and appreciations by authoritative readers, Continental critics were developing a more scientific approach to culture barely visible in Craik's nods in the opposing directions of philology and Kantian aesthetics. Professor Craik's very political conservatism owes something to the German romantics. *Lectures on the History of Literature Ancient and Modern* by Friedrich Schlegel (who was likewise no lover of the French Revolution) decries Spenser's "lifeless Allegory" in contrast to "such as breathes and moves throughout the older chivalric poesy, revealing lofty conceptions of spiritual heroism and the secrets of exalted devotion by means of outward adventure and symbolical tales" (1818, 1889, 273). While Schlegel's notion of a spirit that "breathes and moves" recalls Montesquieu and Hurd, his remark seems to paraphrase John Millar's criticism in *Origin of the Distinction of Ranks* (1771). There was an active exchange going on between Germany and Scotland; Craik himself, like many of the early professors of English, was a Scot. Schlegel's lectures were translated in 1818 and published in Edinburgh by John Gibson Lockhart, the tormentor of Keats and Hunt. If Walter Scott and Thomas Carlyle were much influenced by Germany, German philology itself owed much to the Edinburgh enlightenment, from which precedents can be found for the thoughts about the diction of British poetry expressed by Schlegel: "In a language of mixed derivation, like the English, there is a twofold ideal, according as the poet inclines to one or other of the components of his language. Of all English poets, Spenser is the most Germanic in diction, whilst Milton, on the other hand, has given the preponderance to the Latin element" (273–74). Yet the linguistic emphasis here is properly that of German philology, in which language and race become more fundamental categories than politics, religion, or nationhood. Schlegel's passing remarks on Spenser presage what would later become a specialty of American Ph.D. programs constructed on the German model.

Literary science was also making great strides in France, following the sway of the philosopher Auguste Comte (1798–1857), the original "positivist." The great monument of positivist literary history is Hippolyte Taine's influential *History of English Literature* (1863), a grand attempt to synthesize empirical psychology with the cultural theories developed by Herder, Hegel, and Comte: modern critics "perceived that a literary work is not a mere individual play of the imagination, the isolated caprice of an excited brain, but a transcript of contemporary manners, a manifestation of a certain kind of mind" (1874, 1:1). While literary works make their appeal directly to the aesthetic imagination, historians should approach them methodically, working from the text of a document, to the mental state that produced it, to the culture that produced that mental state. As science demonstrates, literary works, though records of mind, are finally manifestations of material history: "The idea ever expresses the actual situation, and the creatures of the imagination, like the conceptions of the mind, only manifest the state of society and the degree of its welfare; there is a fixed connection between what man admires and what he is" (1:230). In Taine's system literature is reconstructed as the joint product of three causal forces: race, milieu, epoch. Despite this formal adherence to historical determinism, Taine attempts to find a place for both artistic freedom and material causality, though he no more than any other critical historian was able to overcome the conundrums posed by the German metaphysics. While Taine's theories proved more fruitful for posing questions than finding solutions, his skills as a writer and propagandist made him a memorable literary historian; in more ways than one, Taine is to history what Dickens is to fiction. The great positivist decried his own novelistic age: "We are the descendants of M. Jordain .... Hence our shoppy and realistic novels. I pray the reader to forget them, to forget himself, to become for a while a poet, a gentleman, a man of the sixteenth century. Unless we bury the M. Jourdain who survives in us, we shall never understand Spenser." To enjoy Spenser is to escape the paradoxes bedeviling nineteenth-century history and philosophy; Spenser is "not yet shut in by that species of exact common sense which was to found and cramp the whole of modern civilization" (1:289, 301). The *Faerie Queene* is a "poetic and shadowy land" in which "the poet has ceased to observe the differences of races and civilizations." Bewailing the "feverish raving" of "de Musset, Heine, Edgar Poe, Burns, Byron, Shelley, Cowper," Taine (much like his contemporary the Swiss historian Jacob Burckhardt) yearns nostalgically for the unbridled energy of the Renaissance: "This was Europe's grand age, and the most notable epoch of human growth. To this day we live from its sap" (1:302, 269, 230). Note how the metaphors for culture shift away from seventeenth-century notions of planting and grafting: from being something that we make, culture has become something that makes us.

In parallel with this confusing discussion of the place of free will and determinism in literary composition, Taine's discussion of the *Faerie Queene* is vehemently enthusiastic and vehemently contradictory. On the one hand, Spenser is the naive poet: "No modern is more like Homer . . . . He is always simple and clear; he makes no leaps, he omits no argument, he robs no word of its primitive and ordinary meaning, he preserves the natural sequence of ideas. Like Homer he is redundant, ingenuous, even childish"; "he shows no appearance of astonishment at astonishing events; he comes upon them so naturally, that he makes them natural" (1:294, 304). Where seventeenth- and eighteenth-century critics regarded Chaucer and Spenser as rude, nineteenth-century critics like Craik, Church, and Taine regarded them as childish, representing "progress" as a natural and largely unconscious growth rather than an outcome of artful, civilizing choices. On the other hand, Taine's concluding stricture praises Spenser's poetry as "modern in its perfection": in it "art has made its appearance: this is the great characteristic of the age, which distinguishes the *Faerie Queene* from all similar tales heaped up by the middle age. Incoherent, mutilated, they lie like rubbish, or rough-hewn stones." Taine then bestows the highest accolade a French critic can give: "His ruling idea is stamped upon the work which it produces and controls. Spenser is superior to his subject, comprehends it fully, frames it with a view to its end" (1:320, 321). Neither position accurately characterizes the *Faerie Queene*, though this arabesque on freedom and restraint does characterize the kind of criticism Taine opposes to prosaic common sense: reading Spenser, "our emotion is raised and purified . . . . We find ourselves happy in being extricated from a belief which was beginning to be oppressive" (1:299).

It will be noted that in criticizing Spenser, Taine fails to develop his argument about historical determinism. This omission would be rectified by Taine's successor, J. J. Jusserand (1855–1932), in *A Literary History of the English People* (1895). Milieu is densely realized in a literary history that situates Spenser's career among scores of Elizabethan writers, courtiers, and politicians and Spenser's works among almost as many contemporary readers, critics, and imitators. Much as other critics would sketch an impression based upon scattered passages in the *Faerie Queene*, Jusserand reconstructs the Elizabethan world picture by using social facts like tesserae in a glittering mosaic: "Often, during the winter of 1590, and later in 1596, during their idle hours, when they were not occupied at tennis, or detained at Greenwich by their court duties, or seated on the stage of those theatres, the fame of which went increasing, the noble personages for whom Spenser had written, stretched themselves on cushions, in the large bay-windows of their palaces bordering the Thames, and opened the pretty volume just published by William Ponsonby, one of the fashionable booksellers" (2:481). Innocent of modern niceties, Spenser's first readers relished the repulsive description of the Cave of Error: "Thick-laid paint was not considered unacceptable; these satin-garbed, frizzled and gilded young noblemen were accustomed to applaud even less reserved scenes in the Southwark play-houses; realism and lyricism combined pleased them. Was not the portrait, besides, that of Error, that is to say, of those wretches who did not believe as the queen or as they themselves did? those papists, those dissenters whose carcasses swung from every gibbet? The description was decidedly 'a matter pleasant'" (2:483). Historicism and a commitment to science free a reincarnated Voltaire to range in territories where British critics hardly dared venture. Spenser's moral "is an aristocratic moral, good to look at; a well-bred moral, that knows how to condone weaknesses . . . . No Leicester would be excluded from Spenser's paradise" (2:492). Not just the *Faerie Queene*, but the whole Elizabethan milieu is at once shocking and amusing. Jusserand's dry wit is the more effective because his criticisms are often just: "It happens to the reader sometimes to lose his way, which is humiliating; but Spenser occasionally loses his too"; "This dragon is enormous, and the description life-size"; "The variety is wonderful; Saracens of the time of the Crusaders meet nymphs of the time of Homer; abstractions in flowing garments of John de Meun's period bow to great ladies in Elizabethan gold gowns" (2:478, 487, 489). Noting the endless succession of seductions and rapes, Jusserand concludes that "Spenser's women are, as a rule, chiefly bodies"; "Guyon, doubtless, will reduce to naught the more dangerous of these beauties; but who knows whether the fragile reader will not preserve a more lively remembrance of them than of him?" (2:494). Jusserand concludes that while moderns may prefer Shakespeare, in his time Spenser appealed to "learned, wealthy, and powerful England, ready for a great poem, and who, till then, had lacked it" (2:504).

One begins to suspect why England was resistant to *critical* literary history. Yet Taine and Jusserand were read and admired, despite the fact that British critics were much less inclined than their French counterparts to interpret great works of genius as products of anonymous social forces: while minor writers might reflect the genius of the age, writers of genius were a law unto themselves. As Shelley declared so memorably in the "Defense of Poetry," they were makers and not followers of the laws upholding society. British historians were more receptive to positivism than the literary critics; even before Taine, in *A Popular History of England* (1856–62) Charles Knight (1791–1873), publisher and member of the Society for the Diffusion of Useful Knowledge, declares that "the poet, by his creative power, may in some degree shape the character of an age, instead of being its mirror; but in the relations of a great writer to his readers there is a mutual action, each inspiring the other. The

tone of Spenser's poetry must at any rate have been in accordance with the
mental condition of those with whom the *Faery Queen* became at once the most
popular of all books" (3:300). In his *History of the English People* (1877), the for-
midable J. R. Green (1837–1883) uses Spenser to illustrate the chivalric origins
of the quest for progress and empire: "In the age of Cortes and of Raleigh
dreamland had ceased to be dreamland . . . . The very incongruities of the
story of Arthur and his knighthood, strangely as it had been built up out of the
rival efforts of bard and jongleur and priest, made it the fittest vehicle for the
expression of the world of incongruous feeling which we call the Renascence"
(2:464–65). Spenser's "irreconcilable impulses" toward dreamy refinement and
practical energy denote "an awakening sense of human power." While stress-
ing cultural forces, Green's narrative of progress underscores the accomplish-
ments of heroic individuals: "The appearance of the *Faerie Queen* in 1590 is the
one critical event in the annals of English poetry; it settled in fact the question
whether their would be such a thing as English poetry or no" (2:466, 464).
This claim has seldom been stated so boldly.

Thomas Warton's *History of English Poetry* (1774–81) was reprinted for the
last time in 1875, finally superseded at the turn of the twentieth century by *A
History of English Poetry* by William John Courthope (1842–1917). Courthope
began his career with a prize essay, "The Genius of Spenser," published in
1868, and concluded it by contributing the Spenser chapter to the *Cambridge
History of English Literature* (1909). In the preface to *A History of English Poetry*
(1895) Courthope echoes Taine and Jusserand, undertaking "to treat poetry as
an expression of the imagination, not simply of the individual poet, but of the
English people; to use the facts of political and social history as keys to the
poet's meaning, and to make poetry clothe with life and character the dry rec-
ord of external facts" (1:xv). Courthope pegs the progress of poetry to the
great themes of Whig historiography; to be treated historically, poetry "must
exhibit the principle of its growth and movement. Movement in political his-
tory is measured by the achievements of arms and commerce; in constitutional
history by changes in laws and institutions . . . in poetry . . . by the simultane-
ous appearance in the nation of new modes of thought, fresh types of composi-
tion, improved methods of harmony" (2:240). In practice, however,
Courthope's staunch liberalism undercuts the emphasis critical history ordinar-
ily places on a narrative of underlying social forces. His melange of history and
appreciation is neither systematic nor original, nor is it very different from the
chronicles written by Hallam and Craik. While Spenser is denominated "the
poet of allegory," allegory needs be stripped away to find anything of interest
or value: "The motive of every one of his greater compositions, when de-
tached from the cloudy words with which he chooses to cover it, is found to
be primarily poetical" (2:258). It is disconcerting to discover a biographer of
Pope describing Upton as Spenser's "earliest commentator in the eighteenth

century"; yet Courthope's familiarity with the Augustans does appear in (mostly hostile) critical remarks plainly paraphrased from Rymer and Dryden, Warton and Hurd. Courthope's appreciation is finally another instance of damnation by faint praise, an early indication of a coming slippage in Spenser's reputation as poet: "He wanted no quality required to place him in the same class with Homer, Virgil, Dante, Shakespeare, Milton, and, perhaps, I may add Chaucer, but that supreme gift of insight and invention which enables the poet to blend conflicting ideas into an organic form" (2:234). Spenser, that is, lacked naught but that one quality which would be all-in-all to modernist criticism.

Courthope's essay on Spenser in the *Cambridge History of English Literature* (1909) struggles to make historical sense of Spenser's poetry. So far from exhibiting youthful naiveté, the "eclectic treatment which he bestowed upon his material [in the *Shepheardes Calender*] is a sign – as eclecticism is in all the arts – of exhaustion in the natural sources of inspiration" (3:255). Spenser's nostalgia sets him profoundly at odds with the genius of his age: "the knight, as such, no longer, in any real sense, formed part of the social organism . . . . So long as it was possible to believe in his existence, men pleased their imaginations with reading of the knight's ideal deeds in the romances; but the time was close at hand when the romances themselves were, necessarily, to be made the subject of just satire. Absolutism had everywhere crushed the energies of feudalism; the knight had been transformed into the courtier" (3:266). Courthope's "necessarily" points to the dilemma confronting critical history: what to do with specimens that fail to conform to the laws of social science? What to do if one cannot find the genius of the age in its foremost poet? Courthope sometimes speaks of Spenser in such terms. At the beginning of the essay, we are told that "Spenser's genius [responded] to each of the separate influences by which it was stirred. His mind was rather receptive than creative. All the great movements of the time are mirrored in his work" (3:240). Source study demonstrates this: in contrast to Wordsworth, whose "imaginative reasoning is his own," Spenser's "sole contribution to the poetry is the beautiful and harmonious form of English verse which he makes the vehicle of the thought" (3:240, 250). In summarizing his chapter on Spenser, however, Courthope declares that "it will be seen that he differed from the great European poets who preceded or immediately followed him, in that he made no attempt to represent in his verse the dominant moving spirit in the world about him" (3:277). Plainly, the assumptions of cultural history do not easily account for the phenomenon. In the end, Courthope again tries to settle upon allegory as a unifying principle: "To fuse irreconcilable principals in a directly epic or dramatic mould was impossible; but it was possible to disguise the essential oppositions of things by covering them with the veil of allegory. This was the method that Spenser adopted. The unity of his poetical creations lies entirely in the imaginative medium through which he views them." This can hardly be a satisfactory resolution if one accepts Coleridge's view of allegory as lacking in imaginative wholeness, which Courthope evidently does. He concludes by stressing Spenser's organic relationship to tradition: "to have been the poetical ancestor of the poetry of these illustrious writers [Thomson, Keats, Shelley, Byron] shows how deeply the art of Spenser is rooted in the imaginative genius of his country" (3:278, 279).

It seems appropriate to conclude with the *Cambridge History of English Literature*, in many ways the fit monument to Victorian scholarship. It is not critical history in the Continental sense; with two senior editors and a host of contributors, it could hardly be a thesis-driven project. Yet it has its own kind of coherence, reflecting the anonymous tastes and sometimes contradictory beliefs of a century's worth of clerics, lawyers, gentlemen, and officials whose accumulated hoard of facts and opinions lends the broad row of green volumes their considerable substance. In its pages the exceptional voices of the nineteenth-century sages, lecturers, and prophets are melted down into something like a common sense. Like its equivalent, the eleventh edition of the *Encyclopedia Britannica*, the *Cambridge History* is resolutely empirical, little troubled by the questions of value judgment and methodology that would render such a project nigh unthinkable today. While Victorian scholarship had its blind spots, its liberal consensus could be remarkably inclusive, so much so that the *Cambridge History*, like the *Britannica*, remains a standard reference today. Eclecticism and comprehensiveness have virtues not always realized in the more methodical products of institutional scholarship. As a piece of collaborative writing, the *Cambridge History* instances something rather like the spirit of the age so much talked about in Victorian criticism – an organic tradition in good working order. And while Courthope's remarks on Spenser are not flattering, Spenser, with a big chapter to himself, does maintain his place of honor in the national story. This monument of Victorian scholarship also points to significant changes that will be the theme of the next chapter: its essays, as opposed to the materials going into them, were produced not by common readers, but by professional scholars, Americans prominent among them.

Works Cited

Arnold, Thomas. "Spenser as a Textbook," *Dublin Review* S3, 4 (1880): 321–32.

Beale, Dorothea. "Britomart, or Spenser's Ideal of Woman," in *Literary Studies of Poems, Old and New*. London, 1902, 25–51.

Bicknell, Alexander. *Prince Arthur, an Allegorical Romance*. 2 vols. London, 1779.

"On the Revival of a Taste for our Ancient Literature," *Blackwood's Edinburgh Magazine* 4 (December 1818): 264–66.

Bradford, Gamaliel. "Women of the *Fairy Queen*," *Elizabethan Women*, ed. Harold O. White. Cambridge: Riverside Press, 1936, 207–26.

Browning, Elizabeth Barrett. *Poems*. 2 vols. London, 1844; ed. Charlotte Porter and Helen A. Clarke, 6 vols. New York: Crowell, 1900.

Carpenter, Frederic Ives. *A Reference Guide to Edmund Spenser*. Chicago: U of Chicago P, 1923.

Church, R. W. *Spenser* ["English Men of Letters."] London, 1879.

Cleveland, H. K. Review of Hillard's edition of Spenser, *North American Review* 50 (1840): 174–206.

Cleveland, Charles D. *A Compendium of English Literature*. Philadelphia, 1848.

Collier, John Payne. *The Poetical Decameron, or Ten Conversations on English Poets and Poetry, Particularly of the Reigns of Elizabeth and James I*. 2 vols. Edinburgh, 1820.

———*A Bibliographical and Critical Account of the Rarest Books in the English Language*. 4 vols. London, 1866.

Courthope, William John. *A History of English Poetry*. 6 vols. London: Macmillan, 1895–1910.

———"The Poetry of Spenser," *The Cambridge History of English Literature*. Vol. 3. New York: Putnam, 1909, 239–80.

Craik, George L. *Sketches of the History of Literature and Learning in England from the Norman Conquest to the Accession of Elizabeth*. 6 vols. London, 1844–45.

———*Spenser and His Poetry*. 3 vols. London, 1845, 1871. Facsimile, New York: AMS Press, 1971.

———*A Compendious History of English Literature, and of the English Language, from the Norman Conquest, with Numerous Specimens*. 2 vols. London: 1866; New York, 1877.

Dawson, L. H. *Stories from the Faerie Queene.* London, 1910.

De Vere, Aubrey. "Characteristics of Spenser's Poetry," in Edmund Spenser, *Complete Works*, ed. A. B. Grosart. 10 vols. London: privately printed, 1882–84.

Dowden, Edward. "Heroines of Spenser," *Cornhill* 39 (1879): 663–80.

———"Spenser, the Poet and Teacher," in Edmund Spenser, *Complete Works*, ed. A. B. Grosart. 10 vols. London: privately printed, 1882–84. Reprinted in *Transcripts and Studies.* London, 1888, 1896.

Durrant, William Scott. *The Red Cross Knight: Scenes from Spenser's Faerie Queene.* London: Year Book Press, 1913.

Dwight, J. S. Review of Hillard's edition of Spenser, *The Christian Examiner* 28 (1840): 208–23.

Ely, Gertrude H. "Spenser," in *Chaucer, Spenser, Sidney.* New York: Kellogg, 1894, 37–76.

Fuller, Thomas. *The History of the Worthies of England* . London, 1662. Ed. Austin Nutall, 2 vols. London, 1840.

Gallwey, T. "Spenser in his Relations with Ireland," *Monitor* 2 (1879): 19–27.

Grace, R. W. *Tales from Spenser.* London, 1909.

Green, J. R. *A History of the English People.* 4 vols. London, 1877–80.

Grosart, A. B. Life of Spenser, Edmund Spenser, *Complete Works*, ed. A. B. Grosart. 10 vols. London: privately printed, 1882–84.

Hallam, Henry. *Introduction to the Literature of Europe in the Fifteenth, Sixteenth, and Seventeenth Centuries.* 4 vols. London, 1837–39. Reprinted London, 1882.

Halpin, Nathaniel. "On Certain Passages in the Life of Edmund Spenser," *Proceedings of the Royal Irish Academy* 4 (1850): 445–51.

Hart, John S. *An Essay on the Life and Writings of Edmund Spenser, with A Special Exposition of The Fairy Queen.* New York, 1847.

Heroines of the Poets: Drawings by Fernand Lyngren. Boston: D. L. Throp, 1886.

Holiness; or The Legend of St. George: a Tale from Spenser's Faerie Queene, by A Mother. Boston, 1836.

Howitt, William. "Edmund Spenser," *Homes and Haunts of the Most Eminent British Poets.* New York: Harper, 1847.

Hunt, Leigh. "Among My Books," *Literary Examiner* (July 5, 1823). Reprinted in *Essays of Leigh Hunt*, ed. R. B. Johnson (London: Oxford UP, 1906, 1928).

———*Imagination and Fancy; or Selections from the English Poets.* London, 1840.

———"English Poetry versus Cardinal Wiseman," *Fraser's Magazine* 60 (1856): 747–66.

Jusserand, Jean J. *A Literary History of the English People* [1894]. London: Unwin, 1895. 3 vols. 1907, 1925.

Keble, John. Review of Condor, Star in the East, *Quarterly Review*. 32 (1825): 211–32.

———*Praelectiones poeticae*. London, 1844. *Keble's Lectures on Poetry, 1832–1841*, translated by Edward Kershaw Francis. 2 vols. Oxford: Oxford UP, 1912.

Kingsley, Charles. *Westward Ho!* London, 1855. *Works*. 28 vols. London: Macmillan, 1880–85.

Kitchin, G. W. ed. *Spenser: Faerie Queene, Book I*. Oxford: Clarendon Press, 1867.

Knight, Charles. *A Popular History of England*. 8 vols. London, 1856–62.

Knox, Vicemus, ed. *Elegant Extracts: or Useful and Entertaining Passages in Poetry*. 1770; 4 vols. London, 1805, etc.

Landor, Walter Savage. *Imaginary Conversations of Literary Men and Statesmen*. 2 vols. London, 1824. In *Works*, 2 vols. London, 1846.

Litchfield, Mary E. *Spenser's Britomart*. Boston: Ginn, 1896.

Lowell, James Russell. "Spenser," *North American Review* (1875). In *Among My Books*. 2 vols. Boston: Houghton Mifflin, 1889, 2:125–200.

Lyttelton, George. *Dialogues of the Dead*. London, 1760. Facsimile, New York: Garland, 1970.

Macaulay, Thomas Babington. Review of Southey's edition of *Pilgrim's Progress*, *The Edinburgh Review* (December 1830); reprinted in *Essays and Poems*, 3 vols. New York, 1880. 1:558–70.

MacDonald, George. *Phantastes: A Faerie Romance for Men and Women*. London, 1858.

Maclehose, Sophia H. *Tales from Spenser*. Glasgow: James Maclehose, 1892.

Macleod, Mary. *Stories from the Faerie Queene*. London, 1897.

Manning, Anne. "Immeritus Redivivus," *The Masque at Ludlow and Other Romanesques*. London: Sampson Low, and Son, 1866, 1–96.

Masson, David. "Theories of Poetry," *North British Review* (1853); in *Essays, Biographical and Critical, Chiefly on English Poets*. Cambridge, 1856.

Maurice, John Frederick Denison. *The Friendship of Books and Other Lectures*, ed. Thomas Hughes. London, 1874.

Review of Hazlitt's *Lectures on the English Poets*, *Monthly Review* 92 (1820): 53–68.

Peacock, Lucy. *The Knight of the Rose.* London, 1793.

Reeve, Clara. *The Progress of Romance.* London, 1785.

Reynolds, J. H. *The Eden of the Imagination. A Poem.* London, 1814.

Royde-Smith, N. G. *Una and the Red Cross Knight.* London, 1905.

Ruskin, John. "Theology of Spenser," *The Stones of Venice.* 3 vols. London, 1851–53.

Schlegel, Friedrich. *Lectures on the History of Literature Ancient and Modern,* translated J. G. Lockhart. Edinburgh, 1818. London: Bell, 1889.

Scudder, Vida D. *The Life of the Spirit in the Modern English Poets.* Boston: Houghton Mifflin, 1895.

——*Social Ideals in English Letters.* Boston: Houghton Mifflin, 1898.

Shaw, Thomas B. *Outlines of English Literature.* London, 1848; reprinted as *Shaw's New History of English Literature; Together with a History of English Literature in America,* ed. Truman J. Backus. New York: Sheldon and Company, 1884.

Spenser, Edmund. *Poetical Works,* ed. H. J. Todd. 5 vols. London, 1805.

——*Poetical Works.* 5 vols. London, 1825. The prefatory essay by Philip Masterman is reprinted in Spenser, *Works,* ed. Hillard, 1839.

——*Poetical Works,* ed. G. S. Hillard. 5 vols. Boston, 1839.

——*Works, with Observations on his Life and Writings* [by J. C.] London, 1840; new edition, Philadelphia, 1857.

——*Epithalamion, with Illustrations by G. W. Edwards.* New York, 1895.

——*The Shepheardes Calender.* Illustrated by A. J. Gaskin. Kelmscott, 1896.

——*The Faerie Queene and Epithalamion.* Illustrated by L. Fairfax Muckley. London, 1897.

——*The Shepheardes Calender.* Illustrated by Walter Crane. London, 1897.

Taine, Hippolyte. *History of English Literature* [1863], translated by H. Van Laun. 2 vols., Edinburgh, 1871; 4 vols., Edinburgh, 1873–74.

Thomson, Clara L. *Tales from the Faerie Queene.* London: Horace Marshall, [1902].

Towry, M. H. *Spenser for Children.* London: Chatto and Windus, 1885.

Underdown, Emily. *Gateway to Spenser.* London, 1911.

Wilson, C. D. *The Faerie Queene, Book I, Rewritten in Simple Language.* Chicago, 1906.

Wilson, John. Essays on Spenser in *Blackwood's Edinburgh Magazine* (1833–35). "Spenser and His Critics," in *Critical Essays of the Early Nineteenth Century*, ed. Raymond MacDonald Alden. New York, Scribners, 1921.

Wiseman, Cardinal Nicholas Patrick Stephen. *On the Perception of Natural Beauty by the Ancients and the Moderns: Two Lectures.* London, 1856.

Woodberry, George Edward. *The Torch: Eight Lectures on Race Power in Literature Delivered Before the Lowell Institute of Boston MCMIII.* New York: McClure, 1905.

Wordsworth, William. Letter to Sir Walter Scott, 1805. *The Letters of William and Dorothy Wordsworth: The Early Years, 1787–1805.* Second Edition. Ed. E. de Selincourt, revised by Chester L. Shaver. 4 vols. Oxford: Clarendon Press, 1967.

4: Groves of Academe

Modern Philology

Twentieth-century wits, journalists, and clergymen have not busied themselves much about Spenser, nor have eager ticket holders thronged to hear famous personalities lecture on Guyon, Britomart, and the defects of allegory. Even as more people were reading the *Faerie Queene* than ever before, the study of Spenser became once more a largely academic matter. But circumstances had changed since Spenser was being taught in seventeenth- and eighteenth-century grammar schools. Heroic poetry was no longer regarded as the highest expression of intellectual and national achievement; it was not even a respectable literary genre. Religious poetry fared even worse; even Milton's reputation went into serious decline. The "best judges" no longer expressed enthusiasm for England's Arch-Poet — Tennyson and Arnold, Pound and Eliot said next to nothing about Spenser. Yet even as Spenser was no longer a force in contemporary literature, his verse was being taught to millions of young students, often unwilling conscripts. This state of affairs both departs from and grows out of the nineteenth-century concerns with culture discussed in the last chapter. The Victorian effort to include English studies in high school and college curricula was completely successful; Kitchin's pioneering textbook editions of the first two books of the *Faerie Queene* were the first of many to come. At a time when Spenser's name seldom appeared in general-interest periodicals, his verse became a staple of scholarly publication. The Victorian origins of the these phenomena have not always been apparent, partly because school texts create the misleading impression that the classroom is the native domain of literature and partly because the twentieth-century zeal for professionalism encourages modern scholars to ignore the efforts of their amateur predecessors. Yet considered in a long perspective, twentieth-century notions of literature, criticism, and education plainly derive from the nineteenth-century invention of "culture" and the forms of writing associated with it. In refining and institutionalizing those paradigms, academic criticism exploited the ways of commerce and specialization Victorian writers on culture strove to resist. In what ways could or should an academy committed to preserving older literature act as a force for progressive social change? While scholars and educators have adopted a wide range of positions on this issue, the general tendency has been to oppose literature to criticism as art to science, situating the former in a timeless, historical, or ideal realm of imagination, the latter in a progressive and modish marketplace of ideas. The attempts by Dowden and his contemporaries to present Spenser as both a repository of traditional values and an authority for change continue throughout much of twentieth-century academic criticism. As a result, the kinds of institutional conflict that began a century ago with the creation of English studies are still very much alive. The postromantic division of the kingdom of literature between art and science was never very satisfactory and has lately come to seem very problematic indeed.

Since the United States has generally led the way in academic scholarship on Elizabethan literature, it might be useful to review the historical context of American criticism. Spenser, Shakespeare, and the Elizabethans were particularly important here; as cultural founders they served to anchor American identity in European origins; as liberal-minded men of the Renaissance, they also stood for American independence from the dead weight of tradition. Prior to 1875, literary study in American colleges was still based on humanist principles; it was addressed less to private readers than to public speakers – future clergy and orators, lawyers and politicians. With the subsequent development of the research university and the importation of the doctoral degree from Germany, college English often abandoned what remained of its humanist foundations, becoming a specialized department distinct from general instruction in rhetoric, history, and moral philosophy. One of the first German-trained American scholars was Harvard professor Francis James Child (1825–96), who edited Spenser's works (1855), wrote *Observations on the Language of Chaucer* (1863), and published the famous collection *English and Scottish Popular Ballads* (1882–98). These projects all bear witness to the German interest in archaic language and folk literature. Philology was taken up quickly in the United States, as witnessed by the founding of *PMLA* (1886), *Modern Language Notes* (1886), the *Journal of English and Germanic Philology* (1897) and *Modern Philology* (1903). By the end of the nineteenth century, ethics- and rhetoric-based literary study was steadily losing ground to more specialized forms of critical scholarship; in the early decades of the twentieth-century the research university added vast new territories to the college curriculum, each staffed by credentialed and certified experts. The stage was set for yet another battle of Ancients and Moderns, with the non-specialist "man of letters" squaring off against the professional student of literature.

"Modern" philology was German philology, the bastion of conservatism deployed against the French Enlightenment by Herder, the Grimms, and the Schlegels. German scholars used philological research to establish historical foundations for cultural identity by studying languages, folk tales, and literary history. In the United States, German-based philology undermined the republican humanism taught in American colleges – a cosmopolitan enterprise with roots in both the ancient world and the European Enlightenment, a tradition that served to hold together a young, ethnically and religiously diverse country. The professional philologists displacing the oratorical tradition established their new discipline by taking over the American Founders' rhetoric of science and progress. The collectivist ideals of American philology undermined the older republicanism, but it did so by appealing, curiously enough, to liberal democracy. Fearing a threat to Enlightenment principles of government from Catholic and later Jewish immigration, philologists sought to cultivate the roots of American liberalism by teaching Anglo-Saxon (regarded by Thomas Jefferson as the true language of liberty) and a unifying Protestant tradition of British literature. As we have seen, turn-of-the-century students of Spenser were vitally concerned with issues of race, gender, and cultural origins. Just as Dowden bypassed the English Revolution in order to promote an Elizabethan origin for British liberalism, so American students of culture bypassed the American Revolution, discovering the seeds of the American spirit in Spenser, Shakespeare, and Milton. While the European founders of modern philology were romantics who bitterly opposed Enlightenment rationalism, American disciples like Woodberry and Scudder identified the romantic movement itself with the Enlightenment critique of social institutions. Almost all of the new American universities were constructed in a neoromantic, revivalist style, though there was disagreement over what the architecture of knowledge should be classical or gothic. This was largely a moot point, for the kinds and dispositions of spaces within these steel and concrete edifices were those of the factories and offices shaping (and funding) the new curriculum. Like the *Faerie Queene* itself, and for not-dissimilar reasons, a thoroughly modern creation was concealed behind a facade of antiquity. So strong was the modernist desire to anchor material progress in an organic tradition that at a time when originality was the chief yardstick for poetic genius, literary criticism focused squarely on source study as the chief means of cultivating a tradition of genius. No doubt the torturous argument of "Tradition and the Individual Talent" owes much to the up-to-date training in philology and literary history T. S. Eliot encountered at Harvard.

Despite the high value it placed on tradition, American philology was profoundly liberal. "Appreciations" of the Lowell variety relied implicitly on the peculiar character and insight of the lecturer standing at the rostrum, whereas philological work employed an impersonal methodology that with the proper expenditure of time and effort could be mastered by anyone. Twentieth-century scholarship has often been compared to factory production. At the same time that Henry Ford was transforming Detroit, Spenser scholarship was setting up shop in such unlikely places as Baltimore, Maryland; Chapel Hill, North Carolina; Austin, Texas; Norman, Oklahoma; and Seattle, Washington. As with the automobile industry, the rapid growth of college English was made possible by the specialization and standardization that were hallmarks of the new industrial technology. Academic research demanded specialized skills and knowledge that required years of professional training; the dissertation requirement and peer-review process raised standards even as they imposed a kind of uniformity on the means of production. Prior to 1875, college professors were neither required nor expected to publish; under the new system, the increased production of knowledge led to the establishment of scores of university presses and thousands of academic journals. Philology encouraged competition and a merit system of promotion that eventually advanced the careers of Catholic and Jewish professors who could never have taught at Lowell's Harvard; philology also leveled the playing field for women scholars, who in the prewar era did much groundbreaking work in Spenserian studies. These changes were not brought about without a great deal of contention; even as academic progressives argued the necessity of history, modernity, and innovation, the more conservative humanists stubbornly refused to roll over and die – they too could claim the mantle of liberty and freedom. While the research universities obviously dominated scholarly publication, they were not able to monopolize higher education until the Ph.D. became a general requirement for college teaching, a very recent development.

While twentieth-century Spenser criticism is hardly limited to philology or to the United States, the founding of the American research university is in a sense the most massive fact in the history of Spenser criticism. In the first three decades of the twentieth century, more was written about Spenser than in the previous three hundred years. William Sipple's bibliography, which is not comprehensive, lists over 1400 items, mostly American, published between 1900 and 1936 – that is to say, even before academic publishing really began to boom. Almost as significant is what Spenser's poetry did for college English within the American university system: in the decades prior to 1965, more dissertations were written on Spenser than any other writer save Shakespeare. It is difficult to believe that Spenser was a more admired writer than Milton or Pope or Wordsworth; Swift or Scott or Dickens. Nor can the volume of Spenser studies be attributed solely to the desire to root American identify in Elizabethan literature. Something of a philologist himself, Edmund Spenser was simply God's gift to American philology. The classic problems in Spenser studies – the origin and qualities of his stanza; his use of archaisms and regional dialect; his reliance on classical, Italian, and vernacular sources; his modifications of Platonic, Aristotelian, and Christian doctrines; the identity of E. K. and the historical personages in the allegories; Spenser's shadowy presence in Tudor history – these were exactly the kinds of problems that philological scholarship was best able to address. Considered in such terms, Spenser becomes a very difficult poet. Difficulty brought prestige to college English, still frowned upon as dilettantish as late as the 1920s. Moreover, Spenser's archaic poetry resembled the Anglo-Saxon and early English texts being used to make the case for English studies as an academic discipline.

Professional scholarship wrought changes in the genres used to criticize Spenser. The nineteenth-century essay, typified by Hazlitt's *Lectures on the English Poets* and Hunt's *Imagination and Fancy*, emphasized character and personality: a general exordium on Spenser's significance would be followed by a biographical sketch, discussions of archaism, allegory, stanza, and design, concluding with an appreciation that would foreground the personality and taste of the critic. Depending on the writer's bent, Spenser's "character" would be used to illustrate concepts of poetical genius, Elizabethan civilization, or British culture. The philological article placed much less emphasis on the character of either the poet or the critic; it pursued impersonal regularity and opposed the impressionism typical of the lectures of professors Lowell and Dowden, still only one remove from Coleridge and Hazlitt; the words "sketch" and "impression" gradually dropped out of critical usage. Essays in scholarly journals would focus on a particular problem – grammatical, exegetical, stylistic, or historical – treated in isolation and often in great particularity, with careful documentation of sources and authorities. Just as the character of the poet disappeared into a nexus of sources, analogs, and facts it supposedly reflected, so the personality of the critic dissolved into a nexus of supportive footnotes and citations that lent institutional authority to the argument. Spenser criticism repudiated the civil norms of oral presentation appropriate to drawing room and lecture hall, and adopted the scholastic norms of print presentation appropriate to research libraries and conference proceedings. Thomas Warton triumphed over Bishop Hurd.

In the nineteenth century, book-length treatments of Spenser were mostly prose paraphrases or excerpts with commentary; the modern university press book on Spenser usually consists of collections of articles or a monograph-length treatment of a specialized subject; because academic criticism presupposes familiarity with the professional literature, it cannot usually stand alone or speak to a common reader. Nineteenth-century critics returned again and again to a short list of topics that served as pretexts for appreciation: we have Coleridge's Spenser, Hunt's Spenser, Lowell's Spenser, Dowden's Spenser. By contrast, the philological article covered, one at a time, a wider range of topics in criticism that was impersonal, cumulative, and mostly nonjudgmental. Monographs, too, became more specialized: over the course of the century the trend evolved from studies of English literature, to studies of Spenser, to studies of particular poems, to studies of single books of the *Faerie Queene*. The piecemeal nature of such scholarship precluded the traditional summary stricture; the task of integration was largely left to the scholarly reader, who might spend years working up "Spenser" with the assistance of bibliographies, review essays, handbooks, anthologies of criticism, and encyclopedias – or histories of criticism like this one. Academic genres reinforced regularity of presentation even as they demanded innovation of matter. In the period between the wars, scholars developed uniform standards of evidence, print presentation, and argumentation for the scholarly note, essay, monograph, and textual edition. There were contrary pressures to innovate: the uniform standards were largely formal, affording a kind of integration that was in some ways little more than that of a card catalogue. The task of assembling the matter exhumed by empirical research into a coherent design became more daunting with each passing decade. Spenser scholars soon found themselves threading a labyrinth as daunting the *Faerie Queene* itself; by the 1950s Spenser criticism was becoming a subject of academic research in its own right.

Prewar Academic Criticism

The nature of specialized academic criticism does not lend itself to narrative literary history: the scholarly genres have changed relatively little, while the matter handled within the thousands of articles, dissertations, and monographs on Spenser is too various to be easily summarized, much less explained. Institutional pressures have been such that, despite large changes in critical practices and beliefs, the note, the article, the review, and the monograph have remained the dominant forms since the beginning of the century; twentieth-century scholars do not, like their humanist predecessors, present their criticism in the form of drama, dialogue, epigram, satire, or verse epistle. Because there are many intersecting critical conversations taking place at any given moment, with topics of research dropped and resumed at irregular intervals, a short, chronological presentation can hardly do justice to the complexity of academic writing on a major writer. In his useful 1971 dissertation, "A History of the Criticism of the *Faerie Queene*, 1910–1947," Bernard J. Vondersmith adopted a categorical approach, devoting chapters to studies of classical influences (Plato, Aristotle, Virgil, Ovid, Lucretius), Italian influences (Dante, Boccaccio, Boiardo, Ariosto, Tasso), and vernacular influences (Malory, historians, Celtic mythology, Chaucer, Sidney). There is a chapter on style (diction, figurative language, narrative technique, stanza), a chapter on general studies (Renwick, Jones, Davis) and another on studies of the political and historical allegory. There are two chapters on studies of the structure of the *Faerie Queene*. These categories themselves tell part of the story: philology tended to be conservative in its choice of topics; while new information was always being added, the kinds of broad questions being investigated were still largely those first addressed by Warton, Upton, and Hurd.

Two of Vondersmith's chapters, however, are devoted to substantially new topics: genetic criticism and reception history, both related to the modernist concern with organicity. Nineteenth-century studies of the genesis of poems

emphasized memory and associationist psychology, like this account, from A.
B. Grosart's 1882 life of Spenser, describing the effect of the queen's corona-
tion on the impressionable mind of young Spenser: as Elizabeth "took her way
through the tapestried and pageant-decked streets, one bright-eyed boy stood
gazing at the gorgeous procession, which was to him a vision of Fairy Land; . .
. among those crowds which lined the three miles of the triumphant way,
there *he* stood, who thirty years after was to make the same *Gloriana* famous to
all ages" (1:10–11). The poem takes rise from the spectacle impressed on the
mind of the writer, an image the biographer recreates for us in an impression-
istic sketch of what the scene must have looked like – the same "speculative"
procedure was at work in Anne Manning's fictional biography. One recalls
Arthur's vision of Gloriana, and the mark left behind on the "pressed gras"
(1.9.15.2). By contrast, philological criticism strives to trace the genesis of a text
to another text, a source of influence, or an earlier state of the poem. The
Harvey-Spenser correspondence led nineteenth-century critics to suspect that
parts of the *Faerie Queene* began as independent poems, but in the absence of
direct evidence, sophisticated arguments about the textual genesis of the poem
were not possible until the deployment of advanced textual criticism devel-
oped by modern students of Renaissance drama and the Bible. Janet Spens ini-
tiated a new area of research and speculation with *Spenser's Faerie Queene: An
Interpretation* (1934), which argues that the "Epithalamion Thamesis" men-
tioned in the correspondence was incorporated into book 4 of the *Faerie Queene*.
Spens argues that the disparities between the poem as we have it and the poem
as described in the letter to Raleigh indicate that an Aristotelian scheme of alle-
gorizing the virtues was imposed on an earlier, eight-book structure allegoriz-
ing the seven deadly sins: "The laying bare of this earlier ground plan permits
us to trace a more consistent philosophic and ethical scheme, and this new per-
spective in turn enables us to deal more successfully with other difficulties in
the appreciation of the poet" (11–12). The notion of a hidden "ground plan"
follows from applying a critical method to ostensible irregularity, as when
Hurd posits a spirit of romance to explain Spenser's unruly design. The proj-
ect of identifying and reconstructing a hidden structure typifies twentieth-
century academic criticism, though the structures themselves are quite various;
it might be a prior state of the text or formal figure-in-the-carpet; an authorial
intention or secret pathology; an ideological program or a cultural unity.

These kinds of investigation could not be undertaken so long as critics re-
garded the *Faerie Queene* as merely an irregular gallery of beautiful images. In
fact, this new genetic criticism led to the first major investigations of Spenser's
design since Hurd's study almost two centuries earlier. There were difficulties,
however. The variations in Spenser's texts are not so substantial as those
found in biblical narratives or between the quarto and folio versions of Shake-
speare's plays. As may have been intended, the destruction of Spenser's manu-

scripts limited possibilities for interpretation. And, given the fragmentary state of the *Faerie Queene*, inferences about the intended design of the poem, the necessary starting point for interpreting narrative inconsistencies, are themselves problematic. Much of Spens's interpretation seems speculative or forced, though less so than the efforts by some of her contemporaries who used similar "textual" evidence to attribute Spenser's poems to Francis Bacon – most notoriously E. G. Harman, who in 1914 attributed to Bacon not only Spenser's verse but that of Gascoigne, Sidney, Raleigh, Daniel, and others. The Baconians, ever fond of "ciphers," were amateur sleuths and conspiracy buffs who applied the higher criticism in ways repudiated by professional scholars who otherwise shared the same passion for unearthing new discoveries. If her conclusions have not been accepted, Spens did make a convincing case that irregularities in the poem as we have it point not to a *furor poeticus* but to revisions made over a long period of composition. This advances philological study well beyond the point where Warton had left it. Further evidence for this position was gathered by J. H. Walter in "*The Faerie Queene*: Alterations and Structure" (1941), which assembles an imposing catalogue of narrative inconsistencies. Walter perceives traces of an earlier scheme based on the twelve months of the year. In *The Evolution of The Faerie Queene* (1942), Josephine Waters Bennett discerns an original design centered on the titular heroine, embedded in a later scheme involving Arthur and the Knights of the Order of Maidenhead; she proposes to examine "the poem as a growing and developing conformation of ideas and to examine the meager external evidence, and the abundant but hitherto uncorrelated internal evidence, in an attempt to discover how it might have grown in the course of many years, to its present state" (1). This emphasis on organic "growth" rather than authorial rejection of earlier versions is consistent with Victorian notions of culture. Dean Church had complained that Spenser's poem "carries with it no adequate account of its own story" (1879, 120); half a century later, textual criticism suggested how the seeming irregularity of the poem was itself evidence of a "growth" process. While these genetic studies generally arrived at mutually exclusive conclusions, they argued persuasively that the *Faerie Queene* was not composed seriatim, a discovery that casts considerable doubt on interpretations like those of Craik, Grosart, and Church that link the narrative in the poem to developments in the poet's career and mental states. While this possibility was not foreclosed, later critics could ignore the evidence of philological research only at their peril. And they often did ignore it, as we shall see.

The other new area being investigated was reception history. While the amount of such research was insignificant compared to traditional source study, it had potentially more important and challenging implications for literary history. William Lyon Phelps's *The Beginnings of the English Romantic Movement* (1893) and Henry A. Beers's *A History of English Romanticism in the Eighteenth*

Century (1899) devoted chapters to eighteenth-century Spenserianism that sparked the controversy about "preromanticism" mentioned above. Beers was perhaps the first to observe that English romanticism took rise from Spenser rather than Shakespeare; he took Spenser and Pope as the romantic and classical poles between which English poetry oscillates: "we weary, in time, of the absence of passion and intensity in Spenser, his lack of dramatic power, the want of actuality in his picture of life, the want of brief energy and nerve in his style; just as we weary of Pope's inadequate sense of beauty. But at a time when English poetry had abandoned its true function – the refreshment and elevation of the soul through the imagination – Spenser's poetry, the poetry of ideal beauty, formed the most natural corrective" (78). The conventional wisdom that Augustan critics harbored strong distaste for romantic Spenser was challenged by the discovery of scores of "neoclassical" imitations. Early contributors to this debate saw little value in imitation and pointed to the burlesques by Pope, Shenstone, and Richard Owen Cambridge as indications of Augustan contempt. In the series of books and essays published 1910–17 by Herbert E. Cory, neoclassical criticism began to receive a grudging respect. Harko G. DeMaar stressed the continuity of romanticism across the centuries in *A History of Modern English Romanticism* (1924): "it will not suffice to say that the eighteenth-century was 'classical' and the nineteenth 'romantic'"; "the pseudo-Spenserians should be looked upon in the same light as those who imitated and consciously or unconsciously burlesqued other English authors. The Augustans parodied not only Chaucer, Spenser, and Milton, but nearly all the ancient masters as well" (3, 45). The historical continuity of romanticism received massive documentation in Raymond Dexter Havens's *The Influence of Milton on English Poetry* (1922), Francis Gallaway's *Reason, Rule, and Revolt in English Classicism* (1940), and Earl R. Wasserman's *Elizabethan Poetry in the Eighteenth Century* (1947). Yet as sometimes happens, the discovery of historical evidence failed to make a difference in critical practice. The discovery of an Augustan romanticism did not accord with the belief that the romantic revolt was a manifestation of the spirit of the French Revolution. Humanist deprecators of romanticism like Irving Babbitt and their progressive opponents like Arthur Lovejoy alike derived British romanticism from Continental sources; others disregarded any debt the romantic movement might have owed to monarchical Spenser while foregrounding the influence of the republican Milton. The New Critics who rehabilitated Dryden and Pope took little interest in philology or Spenserianism; the new champions of the romantic movement in the 1960s and 1970s took little interest in Augustan verse. A later generation of philologists gave less attention to source study, concentrating instead on issues of periodization. In the end, scholarly investigation of Spenser's reception had a negligible effect on narrative literary histories of British literature; it became a specialization even among Spenserians.

A topical overview of Spenser criticism tells us little about why so much was written about Spenser in the early twentieth century or why philology became such an American concern. While the notable career of Edwin Greenlaw (1874–1931) is more exemplary than representative, it will help to explain why a general drop in critical estimation had so little effect on the institutional importance of Spenser criticism. Greenlaw was a Harvard Ph.D. who taught at the University of North Carolina from 1913 before he moved to Johns Hopkins in the 1920s; he edited and significantly improved two journals closely associated with Spenser scholarship, *Studies in Philology* (at North Carolina) and *Modern Language Notes* (at Johns Hopkins). Late in life, Greenlaw was the moving force behind the Johns Hopkins *Variorum* Spenser, and he founded a monograph series that made the Johns Hopkins University Press a leader in literary history. Greenlaw's influence survived his death when another Hopkins journal, *ELH*, was for decades the chief outlet for scholarship on Spenser. With Arthur Lovejoy, Greenlaw participated in the influential History of Ideas Club at Johns Hopkins; several important publications on Spenser began as student papers delivered in his once-famous Seminary C. If one may compare small things to large, Edwin Greenlaw was to American scholarship what Edmund Spenser was to British Poetry.

In Greenlaw's work Victorian notions of culture and progress enter directly into professional scholarship and modern pedagogy. In 1912 he published *A Syllabus of English Literature*, one of the earlier college texts in English studies. This characteristically innovative book invented still another way to combine facts with appreciation: Greenlaw frees lecturers and pupils from the chore of recording names, facts, and dates by printing these on the verso pages of the textbook; the recto pages are left blank, awaiting the "actual experience with literature itself" to be entered by the student's own hand (v). In contrast to earlier textbooks, the *Syllabus* encourages students to develop and record their own personal responses to literature, a development that has since become standard procedure. While at North Carolina, Greenlaw published a companion volume, *An Outline of the Literature of the English Renaissance* (1916), impressive in its scope, that hints at the kind of experience with literature that might be recorded on the tabula rasa: "No other period in our literary history is so rich [as the age of Elizabeth] in what may be called symbols of racial experience," symbols that in the *Faerie Queene* "shadow forth a mighty panorama, an infinitely varied succession of dissolving views, and interpretation through symbol of the life that pulsed so intensely through the veins of Elizabethan England" (3, 5). While the notion of a panorama of symbols points to modernist understandings of culture – one might compare T. S. Eliot's more plangent ruminations in "The Waste Land" (1922) – Greenlaw's program for aesthetic education recalls the associationist allegories taught in eighteenth-century grammar schools: students will imbibe from the imaginative spectacle of

Spenser's verse the love of liberty that Spenser imbibed from the imagery of Elizabeth's coronation. Like his predecessors, Greenlaw looked to Tudor literature for cultural guidance; in translating "facts" into "symbols," however, he explored innovative and practical means to further progress by acculturating the young.

Literature and Life (1922–24), a widely-emulated series of high school readers conceived by Greenlaw, tackles the Victorian issue of preserving freedom in an organic society by using normative arguments about culture to support critical ideals of liberty: "The relation between literature and life in this series is no fanciful relation. It is organic, interwoven in many different ways into the body of the book and its method" (1:iv). Greenlaw and his co-editors are confident that an innovative "method" will improve on stale traditions in education. This is the legacy of Enlightenment rationalism; at the same time, the idea that tradition sustains the "relation between literature and life" derives from nineteenth-century romanticism. "Organicity," a property common to rationalist systematizing and irrationalist naturalizing, was the great aim of progressive educators; it appears, for example, in Vida Scudder's belief that Wordsworth had reconciled science with nature. "Organicity" also characterizes the methodized irregularity of the philological enterprise, already bearing fulsome fruit in the scholarly journals. It enters into Greenlaw's textbook through complex and sequentially developed readings in literary, social, and political history. Where earlier textbooks anthologized edifying poems and stories popular with nineteenth-century common readers, Greenlaw lays the foundations of modern progressive pedagogy by adopting a much more interventionist approach – readings are selected to tell a particular story about the rise of democracy. Yet he encourages students to think critically about a set of readings selected to convey the differing "points of view" afforded by different eras and different kinds of writing – collective experience is to be interpreted in individual ways. This accords with the aims of education being formulated by the philosopher John Dewey (1859–1952), Greenlaw's contemporary, whose influence also appears in the extensive use of graphic illustrations, another invention intended to acculturate children. *Literature and Life* underscores the transmigration of liberty from Elizabethan England to democratic America; despite its rationalizing tendencies, the series everywhere emphasizes romance and romanticism.

The ideals of progressive politics are even more explicit in the college reader Greenlaw developed with his younger colleague, the Miltonist James Holly Hanford. *The Great Tradition: A Book of Selections From English and American Prose and Poetry, Illustrating the National Ideals of Freedom, Faith, and Conduct* (1919) narrates the "march of the Anglo-Saxon mind from the beginning of the modern period." This widely imitated anthology departs from the stolid sequence of facts and appreciation in textbooks like Cleveland's *Compendium*; the editors

attempt to engage students' intellect with selections that present opposing per-
ceptions of key events in the progress of democracy. The influence of Arnold
and Dowden is apparent in the introduction: "Spenser, the poet's poet, the
embodiment of the qualities which seem to make of poetry a thing apart, nev-
ertheless stated that his aim in writing the *Faerie Queene* was 'to fashion a gen-
tleman or noble person in virtuous and gentle discipline.' Milton summed his
idea of Spenser, whose disciple he was, in the statement that he was 'a better
teacher than Aquinas,' and Milton's own writings bear abundant witness to his
wish to be regarded as a teacher . . . . Wordsworth illustrated his faithfulness
to the ideal which he professed: 'Every poet is a teacher; I wish to be consid-
ered as a teacher or as nothing.' "The roll call of visionary republicans con-
cludes with Shelley, who teaches that "poets are the unacknowledged
legislators of the world." Greenlaw believed that modern educators faced un-
precedented social conditions. If America in 1919 confronted "the dawn of a
new day" not unlike England in 1588, it could no longer rely on an outworn
classicism; now that "all the world is to be the inheritance of democracy,"
teachers must rely on "a new humanism, competent to guide through doctrine
and discipline . . . a racial tradition as rich and as clearly defined as that of clas-
sical antiquity" (xviii). Anglo-American literature is a "bible of democracy . . .
set forth as a unity and with the cumulative effect of a mighty tradition";
"Rightly or wrongly, we have substituted modern culture for ancient as the
material of humane discipline." In a ringing peroration, Greenlaw and Han-
ford contrast Anglo-American liberty, "inherited and written in our blood," to
German celebrations of "the savagery of war, the savagery of industrialism,
the savagery of intolerance, the savagery of the mob" (p. xiii, xiv, xix, xx, xxi).
One cannot but note the irony that their very progressivism – the anthology
concludes with Woodrow Wilson's appeal for a league of nations – took rise
from an understanding of racial tradition developed out of a reactionary Ger-
man philology.

Greenlaw's program for English studies was firmly rooted in his academic
research on the use of history for political purposes in Tudor poetry. In a se-
ries of articles, he demonstrated how Spenser's treatment of Arthurian legends
represented one side of a contemporary debate over historiography and con-
temporary politics. By relating the place of history within the *Faerie Queene* to
the place of the *Faerie Queene* in history, he invented what in retrospect might
be regarded as an early form of ideology critique: Spenser "was not merely a
dreamer, an idle singer in an empty day, a poet's poet, but a far-sighted stu-
dent of government who saw clearly the great destiny of his nation" (1932,
135). Greenlaw admired Tudor ideology, of course: Spenser's mythological
use of Arthur could become the prototype for Greenlaw's own pedagogical
use of Spenser because the imperial ambitions of Elizabethan Protestantism are
his model for the imperial ambitions of American democracy. More than this,

Spenser's use of vernacular sources in his heroic poetry reinforced the authority of English departments that were challenging the entrenched status of classics. This was still a bone of contention; in the 1920s the "Ancients versus Moderns" debate played out yet once more in an acrimonious academic dispute about classicism and romanticism. In 1919 Greenlaw was calling for a "new humanism"; by the time he had moved to Johns Hopkins, he was abandoning any pretense to humanism in favor of a more scientific approach to literary history. Johns Hopkins, the first American university to offer the Ph.D. in English, was then the high temple of literary research. With both romanticism and philology under attack from Babbitt and the New Humanists, Greenlaw took up the cudgel in *The Province of Literary History* (1931), a polemic directed against his friend and former colleague at North Carolina, Norman Foerster, whose *American Scholar: A Study in Litterae Inhumaniores* (1929) championed Babbitt's attacks on romanticism and philology. Greenlaw's argument revolves around the critical reception of Spenser, setting up John Dryden (classicism) as whipping-boy and upholding Thomas Warton (romanticism) as the exemplar of the proper aims of literary history. Spenser is called in to defend philology: himself "an antiquary who delved in the old documents and records, compiled from many sources his own history of Britain, studied folk customs, old etymologies, monuments and tapestries[,] his scholarship and poetic imagination united to produce his own epic of the meaning of British history"; Greenlaw concludes that "scholarship, and not criticism, whether in Elizabethan days or ours, produces readers of the poet, which is the end and aim of literary investigation" (60, 59).

The massed forces of professional philology easily won the contest with New Humanism, as indeed the Moderns had won similar triumphs over the Ancients in every debate of this kind since the time of Dryden himself. By the 1920s, the institutional dominance of the Ph.D. in American literary studies and progressivism in American politics were much too strong to be beaten back by a few high-minded reactionaries. Though Greenlaw did not live to supervise the publication of the Johns Hopkins *Variorum* Spenser, he was the force behind this high-water mark of American philology; with tongue only slightly in cheek, in 1933 the Briton W. L. Renwick paid tribute to the thicket of notes and appendixes compiled by the industrious Yanks: "Spenser has long engaged the fealty of American scholars – was, indeed, all but abandoned to them – and many notable studies have resulted. Now appears the *magnum opus*, the complete edition of his works, with abundant apparatus compiled by a team of specialists, and produced in full form by a University Press" (508–9). Several scholarly editions of Spenser had recently been published in Britain, but nothing like this. The *Variorum* was a quarter-century in the making; its handsomely printed quarto volumes are a monument not only to Edmund Spenser but to the importance of Spenser to the American academy. And yet the *Variorum* proved to be something of a mixed blessing: in the wake of its appearance, the flood tide of notes and articles temporarily slowed a bit – hadn't everything already been said? – while its bristling scholarship only reinforced Spenser's reputation for fearsome difficulty. Despite the large typeface and broad margins accorded Spenser's prolix verse, the notes and essays appended by the editors, in small print at the back of the volumes, occupied even more space. More than ever before, in the 1930s and 1940s Spenser became the province of literary history, the province of academic specialists. Greenlaw's wish that historical research would attract readers to Spenser was fulfilled in the manner of the old fairy stories he reprinted in *Literature and Life*: the mob of scholars unintentionally frighted away the very common readers that Greenlaw most wanted to reach. He himself has suffered the common fate of progressives: his textbooks, his scholarship, and his politics, long superseded by others more progressive still, came to seem hopelessly dated. The legacy survives, nonetheless, in the institutional structures he did so much to promote.

Spenser in Britain

The American Ph.D. mills were not the whole story, however. By the late nineteenth century, modern philology and English studies were already established in Edinburgh, Dublin, and London; by the early twentieth century even Oxford and Cambridge followed suit. The transformation of scholarship and higher education was less dramatic in Britain than in the United States, in part because reforms began earlier, and in part because the prestige of tradition-minded Oxford and Cambridge acted as a kind of ballast. The more understated British approach is visible in the still-reprinted 3 volume edition of Spenser's works edited by J. C. Smith and Ernest de Selincourt (1909–10), which lacks explanatory notes, and even in the 8 volume *Works* edited by W. L. Renwick (1930–32). Neither of these Oxford productions displays the cultural ambitions of the incomplete Grosart edition of 1882–84 or of the Hopkins *Variorum*. Not that Oxford lagged behind in its traditional championship of our Cambridge-educated poet: of all the American and British scholars writing on Spenser before the war, the only one generally remembered or consulted today is C. S. Lewis, who in 1925 became a fellow of Magdalen College, Oxford. Lewis wrote very much in the tradition of the Oxford Spenserians chronicled in previous chapters: he was an unrepentant Christian humanist of conservative views. Though a learned man and a university professor, Lewis resisted the sway of academic specialization and wrote and lectured on a wide range of topics, literary and nonliterary. Like Lowell or Dowden, he addressed common readers in writing that paid little heed to the great divide between literature and science. As a moralist and religious apologist he can seem almost Victorian, though Lewis's humanism was not Arnoldian, nor was he an "apostle of culture" in any modern sense. Though their doctrines were antithetical, Lewis shared with Greenlaw the conviction that Spenser's wisdom had a direct bearing on modern life. Lewis wrote on Spenser throughout his career, down to the course of lectures posthumously published as *Spenser's Images of Life* (1967), but it is the Spenser chapter in *The Allegory of Love: A Study in Medieval Tradition* (1936) that has had the greatest impact on later criticism. Lewis's literary history of courtly love cedes nothing to the Americans in the depth or range of its learning, yet it differs from the philological ideal by rejecting pretensions to scientific objectivity in history and criticism: "Spenser is not so much part of my subject as one of my masters or collaborators .... The story he tells is therefore part of my story: the final struggle between the romance of marriage and the romance of adultery" (298, 340). Just as Greenlaw the progressive was wielding Spenser against the humanists, so Lewis the humanist was wielding Spenser against the progressives.

Implicit in the topic and handling of *The Allegory of Love* is an attack on Bloomsbury modernism and Bloomsbury morality: "a young lady whom I once had the honour to examine advanced the view that Charissa sucking her babes was a figure, in its own way, no less disgusting than Error vomiting. If there is any lingering sympathy with this attitude in us, we shall do well to leave the *Faerie Queene* unread" (316). Lewis traces the ills of modernity to the failures of nineteenth-century morality the moderns were reacting against. The post-romantic habit of opposing Spenser the moralist to Spenser the hedonist is typical. Spenser, Lewis argues, reconciles Pleasure and Virtue in an ideal of wedded love undervalued by Victorians and modernists alike: "The synthesis which he helped to effect was so successful that this aspect of his work escaped notice in the last century: all that Britomart stands for was platitude to our fathers. It is platitude no longer" (360). It is probably fair to say that Lewis's chapter makes more original observations about the *Faerie Queene* – sources, prosody, philosophy, and design – than all of nineteenth-century criticism laid end to end. Lewis was not, like Lowell, an aesthete, nor was he, like Dowden, a historicist; as a Christian humanist, he could interpret the *Faerie Queene* on something like its own terms: "The Bower of Bliss is not a picture of lawless, that is, unwedded, love as opposed to lawful love. It is a picture, one of the most powerful ever painted, of the whole sexual nature in disease. There is not a kiss or an embrace in the island: only male prurience and female provocation" (332). Lewis's dissatisfaction with nineteenth-century prudery goes hand in hand with his distaste for Bloomsbury's lascivious affection for Freud. Like the humanist De Vere he does not regard "nature" as an organic or evolutionary force but the ethical process by which men and women fulfill their potential, a process of consciously seeking the mean for their kind. Unlike Greenlaw, Lewis ignores or disparages Spenser's political ambitions: "He becomes a bad poet because he is, in certain respects, a bad man" (357). Lewis criticizes the man and not the culture, judging the poet against an ideal that is the human telos and not the social system that he supposedly reflects. If Lewis is not the kind of humanist who limits their reading to a few "great books," neither is he a typical literary historian: he lapses into the older rhetorical mode, even to a concluding stricture that is one of the best in the tradition. While Lewis's skill as a philologist made him a central figure in Spenser studies, his opposition to modernism rendered him otherwise a somewhat marginal figure in twentieth-century academic criticism. Lewis addressed his many books to a kind of common reader that seems to have been more numerous in Britain than in an America where high culture was rapidly becoming the province of specialists. One gets the impression that, on the whole, the high modernists on both continents took Lewis's advice and left the *Faerie Queene* unread.

One exception was W. B. Yeats, whose most extensive commentary on Spenser appears in an introduction composed for a selection of the verse published in 1906. It is in many respects a Victorian document. Though they agree about little else, Yeats shares Lewis's distaste for Spenser's politics: "Spenser had learned to look to the State not only as the rewarder of virtue but as the maker of right and wrong, and had begun to love and hate as it bid him. He was the first of many Englishmen to see nothing but what he was desired to see" (1961, 371–72). Formally, Yeats's essay harkens back to Campbell and Hazlitt, being a biography-cum-appreciation directed to a general readership, but also in its fervent romantic hedonism: Spenser "is a poet of the delighted senses, and his song becomes most beautiful when he writes of those islands of Phaedria and Acrasia, which angered 'that rugged forehead' [of Burleigh], as it seems, but gave to Keats his *Belle Dame sans merci* and his 'perilous seas in faery lands forlorn' to William Morris in his 'Water of the Wondrous Isles'" (370). Yeats does not share Lewis's assessment of Spenser as an ethical poet: "One is persuaded that his morality is official and impersonal – a system of life which it was his duty to support – and it is perhaps a half understanding of this that has made so many generations believe that he was the first Poet Laureate, the first salaried moralist among the poets. His processions of deadly sins, and his houses, where the very cornices are arbitrary images of virtue, are an unconscious hypocrisy, an undelighted obedience to the 'rugged forehead,' for all the while he is thinking of nothing but lovers whose bodies are quivering with the memory or the hope of long embraces." The presence of the critic as poet falls very much in the nineteenth-century tradition of subjective appreciation, yielding a partial view of Spenser that broadly illuminates the character of the critic. Yeats is one of the few moderns who make an issue of Spenser's unhappy experience in Ireland; the bitterness of the late poetry reflects the poet's inability to "understand the people he lived among or the historical events that were changing all things around him" (369, 361).

These, the great themes of Yeats's own career, appear in a long perspective applied to race, nationality, and history in Spenser's poetry that was intended to illuminate issues in the politics of Irish nationalism. Spenser's contemporaries "lived in the last days of what we may call the Anglo-French nation, the old feudal nation that had been established when the Norman and the Angevin made French the language of court and market. In the time of Chaucer English poets still wrote much in French, and even English labourers lilted French songs over their work; and I cannot read any Elizabethan poem or romance without feeling the pressure of habits of emotion, and of an order of life, which were conscious, for all their Latin gaiety, of a quarrel to the death with the new Anglo-Saxon nation that was arising amid Puritan sermons and Marprelate pamphlets" (364–65). We have seen the same emphasis on race and "habits of emotion" in Taine and other Victorian cultural criticism; yet Yeats differs from the Anglo-Irishness of Dowden, or the Anglo-Americanism of Gamaliel Bradford in his acute awareness of the cultural heterogeneity and historical contingency of Elizabethan England. Speaking as an Irishman, he could hardly regard this as the cradle of liberty: Spenser "was, I think, by nature altogether a man of that old Catholic feudal nation, but, like Sidney, he wanted to justify himself to his new masters. He wrote of knights and ladies, wild creatures imagined by the aristocratic poets of the twelfth century, and perhaps chiefly by English poets who had still the French tongue; but he fastened them with allegorical nails to a big barn door of common sense, of merely practical virtue" (367). Yeats's essay has not found favor among scholars, partly because the London-born, ultra-Protestant Spenser simply fails to conform to the political character attributed to him. Yeats's inspired impressionism cannot stand comparison with the diligent research of an Edwin Greenlaw. Then, too, there is the antipathy Yeats expresses towards the tradition underlying liberal criticism, a tradition that had long championed Tudor Protestantism and was already beginning to subordinate poetry to criticism in Yankee institutions of higher learning: "Because poetry belongs to that element in every race which is most strong, and therefore most individual, the poet is not stirred to imaginative activity by a life which is surrendering its freedom to ever new elaboration, organization, mechanism" (380). Though no humanist, Yeats would agree with Norman Foerster that modern philology is not a "liberal" art. In this respect, his cultural criticism is no more in harmony with the naturalist consensus than that of C. S. Lewis.

Virginia Woolf's essay "The Faery Queen," posthumously published in 1947, also takes rise from nineteenth-century aestheticism. Ostensibly, she appeals to the eighteenth-century notion of a "common reader," abandoning the lectern and reintroducing norms of politeness into criticism: "dare we then at this time of day come out with the remark that *The Faery Queen* is a great poem? So one might say early rising, cold bathing, abstention from wine and tobacco are good; and if one said it, a blank look would steal over the company as they made haste to agree and then to lower the tone of the conversation" (25). The *Faerie Queene* was not, as Lewis would have surmised, a favorite topic of conversation in Bloomsbury, and in fact Woolf read it only late in life. She makes little pretense of trying to make historical sense of the poem, nor does she, like Yeats, read it against a backdrop of political controversy. Nonetheless, she follows Yeats (and Pater) into impressionistic appreciation, concentrating squarely on her own introspective response to a poem she describes as a meditation. The common-reader posture drops away, for the point is that Woolf is a most uncommon reader in her ability to suck sweets where her contemporaries found only dusty morality. She even updates the painterly approach to the *Faerie Queene* for a postimpressionist age: "As we read, we half consciously have the sense of some pattern hanging in the sky, so that without referring any of the words to a special place, they have that meaning which comes from their being parts of a large design, and not an isolated fragment of unrelated loveliness. The mind is being perpetually enlarged by the power of suggestion" (26). One notes the modernist desire to savor the symbolism, though the passage otherwise recalls Thomas Campbell in 1819: "The clouds of his allegory may seem to spread into shapeless forms, but they are still the clouds of a glowing atmosphere. Though his story grows desultory, the sweetness and grace of his manner still abide by him." One reason romantic criticism favored fragments is that fragmentary works permit and indeed require completion by an empathetic responder. Wandering in the wood of subjective criticism, Woolf recasts an observation made earlier by Bishop Hurd: "At no point is Spenser under the necessity of bringing his characters to the surface; they lack the final embodiment which is forced so drastically upon the playwright. They sink back into the poet's mind and thus lack definition" (29). And like Hurd or Scott or Yeats, she regards Spenser as a last minstrel, trembling on the cusp of modernity: "Spenser's ability to use despair in person depends on his power to create a world in which such a figure draws natural breath, living breath. He has his dwelling at the centre of a universe which offers him the use of dragons, knights, magic; and all the company that exist about them; and flowers and dawn and sunset. All this was still just within his reach. He could believe in it, his public could believe in it, sufficiently to make it serviceable." Like her fellow modernist T. S. Eliot, Woolf bemoans the passing of the Elizabethan ability to *think* sensually and holistically: "We have lost our power to create symbols" (28).

Both Yeats and Woolf betray something of an aristocratic nostalgia for a courtly Spenser that sets them at odds with the democratic and progressive impetus behind Spenser studies in the modern era. Among the other high modernists, Joyce seems to have had little sympathy for the Protestant oppressor, while Spenser hardly existed for Pound and Eliot, exponents of a Browning tradition that preferred Dante. The double onus of Victorian appreciation and modern philology lead Eliot in 1932 to dismiss Spenser with telling condescension: "Who, except scholars, and except the eccentric few who are born with a sympathy for such work, or others who have deliberately studied themselves into the right appreciation, can now read through the whole of *The Faerie Queene* with delight?" (443). It is difficult to describe a critical void, to account for the motives of those who wrote not. One searches in vain for modernist equivalents of remarks by Ruskin, Macaulay, Kingsley, J. R. Green, E. B. Browning; apart from Yeats, Woolf, and Eliot, the bibliographies include little nonacademic commentary. Perhaps the chronicler of "Lit. Eng.," Stephen Potter, speaks for the silent majority in *The Muse in Chains* (1937): "I had always known the name of Spenser. Knew that he was 'great poet,' ancient, romantic; and the one line of his I knew – 'A gentle knight was pricking on the plain' – lovely. Here was I about to read his first poem, work of a young great poet, known, I knew, as the poet's poet.... My disappointment was complete. It may be that this is a unique experience, but for me, nothing I have read has been more irrevocably damping to my poetic appetite. Instead of breath-taking images, there was smooth poetistical language. Instead of apprehensions of nature (making me see something for the first time), there was talk of *oaten stop*, and the shepherds' *fleecy care*" (41). Potter describes his reaction as a product of "lit," the Victorian doctrine of appreciation still thriving in the tweedy refuges of undergraduate classroom teaching.

New Critics and College Readers

While most professional scholars turned their backs on the reading public, attempts to attract and mold the common reader were being made by several modernists hostile to the academy. The Arnoldian project of infusing a liberal society with elitist ideals of culture was taken up by critics associated with the journal *Scrutiny* (1932–53). Where Dowden hailed Spenser as the wellhead of British liberal values, F. R. Leavis of Cambridge University (1895–1978) ejected Spenser and his followers from a Great Tradition that separated organically minded sheep from bloodless and intellectual goats. In *Revaluation, Tradition and Development in English Poetry* (1936), Leavis constructs a genealogy of modernism through Shakespeare and Donne: Milton's "influence is seen in Tennyson as well as in Thomson, and to say that he groups with Tennyson and Spenser in contrast to Shakespeare and Donne is to say something more important about him than that he latinized" (55). Writing in the Leavisite journal *Scrutiny*, D. A. Traversi was even more explicit: "Puritanism, as embodied in Spenser, is nothing else than the disembodied and destructive intellect preying on the body to kill the soul. That is the importance of Spenser and Milton, and their relation to the development of the English tradition. Their pallid successors are seen in the age of Tennyson and after, producing a dead poetry out of a dead 'poetic' language – sterile emotions issuing in a sterilized speech" (1936, 291). While such criticisms had been made by generations of neoclassical writers, these modernists innovate by explicitly setting out to define and evaluate traditions on the basis of contemporary practice rather than the other way about. Dismantling Joseph Warton's triumvirate – Spenser, Shakespeare, Milton – the project of "revaluation" attempted to make over the whole poetic landscape. For such purposes academic philology – generally hostile to contemporary writing anyway – was useless at best. While the *Scrutiny* group was at least as much concerned with continuity as were Greenlaw and company, they seemed to believe that tradition was much too important to be left to the vagaries of historical contingency. This Leavisite desire to shape a canon by rewriting literary history to meet present-day cultural standards has only gained strength in recent critical practice.

Spenser suffered a double humiliation among the modernists: not only was his tradition under attack by the champions of Shakespeare and Donne, in the criticism of Eliot and Leavis he was supplanted by Milton as the romantic poet worth quarreling with. In *Reason and Beauty in the Poetic Mind* (1933), Charles Williams (1886–1945) regards Spenser, compared to Shakespeare and Milton, as a trifler: "We are sometimes told that we need not bother about Spenser's allegory; that he did not bother about it himself. The second assurance is to some extent true; but he thought he did – poor darling! . . . Whatever the luxury of loveliness needs, must be provided at the expense of the pure abstract thought which has also been invoked, and the dark conceit is made doubly dark by its own forgetfulness. Abstractions have destroyed poetry often enough; it is perhaps now but a fair revenge" (54, 61). René Wellek's *History of Modern Criticism* bears silent witness to the slip in Spenser's reputation; in striking contrast to earlier installments, he is not so much as indexed in the volume on twentieth-century English criticism. The American New Critics shared the *Scrutiny* view of Spenser. In 1936 Allen Tate (1899–1979) professes respect for "that great poem" but like Charles Williams bemoans its lack of Coleridgean organicism: "The action has no meaning apart from the preconceived abstractions . . . the ideas suffer no shock and receive no complication in contact with the narrative" (91). In *Modern Poetry and the Tradition* (1939), Cleanth Brooks objects to "an allegorical construct, an abstract framework of statement which was to be illustrated and ornamented by overlaying the framework with concrete detail" (220). In 1956 Yvor Winters (1900–68) is more scathing still: "The dragon in general and in all its details, and merely as a dragon, is a very dull affair: it is poorly described and poorly characterized. I do not, frankly, know what one might do to make a dragon more interesting, but it seems to me that unless one can do better than this one had better not use a dragon" (44). There is no entry for Spenser in Wellek's volume on American criticism either.

By mid-century the academics were beginning to respond, attacking modernist prejudices against romantic Spenser even as they began to incorporate elements of modernist literary criticism into their own scholarship. In 1953 the Miltonist Merritt Y. Hughes defended Spenser by pointing to the biological foolishness of the *Scrutiny* charge of impotence: "We would suspect a theory of sterility as a typically heritable trait, and in literature we should hesitate to attribute it to a poet whose distinctive qualities appear for three centuries after his death as dominant characteristics of his tribe" (6). By mid-century aesthetic judgments begin to appear more frequently in academic writing; in contrast with the "appreciations" of old, they eschew subjectivity for the close textual analysis and comparison expected from scholarly criticism. In *Elizabethan and Metaphysical Imagery: Renaissance Poetic and Twentieth-Century Critics* (1947), Rosemond Tuve took the fight directly to the enemy: "Modern poets fled with Yeats from painted symbolic object to symbol; modern criticism fled from Spenser as the painter of the poets to Donne. We have been given the same reasons for both flights, with how much justice I am not entirely sure." Combining the "scrutiny" of close reading with the historicist's contextual awareness, Tuve contends that Elizabethan imagery is both organic and functional, fulfilling all the requirements of modern criticism and others since forgotten: "the more we tend simply to assume in earlier poems purposes which now happen to be congenial to us, the more we shall overlook in the rest of the poem those subtler indications of purpose which explain why the imagery is as it is. The more willfully we misread earlier imagery, the fewer fields of poetic pleasure we leave open to ourselves" (6, 21). Tuve's long and dense argument set new critical standards for literary historians. *Elizabethan and Metaphysical Imagery* was published in Chicago, where at this time the "Chicago Critics" were beginning to introduce "theory" into literary history, a process that in a mere twenty-five years would transform the venerable discipline of philology almost beyond recognition.

It is probably fair to say that, despite the appearance of the Hopkins *Variorum* and some thousands of books, articles, and dissertations, Spenser's reputation among the general reading public was never lower than in the 1950s: he was not Wordsworth; he was not Yeats. And yet Spenser had more readers then than ever before or than he is likely to have ever again. College English expanded rapidly after the war and still retained much of the "lit" curriculum developed by Lowell, Dowden, and their successors. Victorian opinions about Spenser (pro and con) enjoyed a long after-life in college textbooks; in *A History of English Literature,* updated and reprinted over five decades, William Vaughan Moody (1869–1910) opines that "Spenser had the great gift of the poet, the power to create the illusion of a different world, a world of magic where the imagination and the senses are satisfied. With all his morality, Spenser shared the rich sensuous life which the Renaissance had thrown open to men" (1943, 85). In 1918 Walter S. Hinchman, master of English in Groton School, complains that Spenser "never portrays characters like Shakespeare's; he is rarely sublime, like Milton; his allegory is too involved to be pointed; his pastoral poetry, an accepted convention in his own day, is no longer popular" (88–89). In "Spenser's *Faerie Queene* and the Student of To-Day" (1916) H. W. Peck complains about the encroachments of Kipling and Jack London, declaring that "the problem of preserving interest in *The Faerie Queene* is one of the live problems of the modern teacher of literature. The most common advice as to the best method of accomplishing this is to ignore the allegory, and to emphasize the pictorial and imaginative qualities, and the metrical beauty . . . . [But] the best method of meeting this condition is, in my opinion, the purely historical method. The best preparation for the study of the *Faerie Queene* is a thorough course in mediaeval history" (347, 348). Spenser's works may not have been liked in all quarters, but they continued to be taught; while absent from the Elizabethan section of Atwood Townsend's *Student's Guide to Good Reading: A List of Six Hundred Books Which are Enjoyable, Well Worth Reading, and Inexpensive* (1933), the *Faerie Queene* does make Mortimer J. Adler's list of 113 "great books" in his best-selling *How to Read a Book: The Art of Getting a Liberal Education* (1940).

In the post-war era, renewed efforts were made to make liberal education available to all citizens. Enrollments swelled throughout the English-speaking world; in the United States half the population began to attend colleges of one sort or another. Spenser's continued presence in college English may be inferred from the flurry of cribs appearing in the 1960s: *Monarch Review Notes* (1963), *Study Master* (1963), *Bar-Notes* (1966), *Barnes & Noble Book Notes* (1968), *Cliffs Notes* (1968). The background-plot-theme-character analysis offered by such guides, like their appended "appreciations," carries over from the pedagogical methods of the nineteenth-century founders of English studies. Yet there are differences. Gone is the Victorian emphasis on morality; in the wake of philology and New Criticism the cribs emphasize the history of ideas and literary formalism. The "essay discussion" section in *Monarch Notes* poses the questions: How effective is Spenser's allegorical method? What is meant by neoplatonism in Spenser? What are Spenser's religious views? What characterizes Spenser as a narrative artist? Does Spenser have a sense of humor? (92–95). Students are not instructed in temperance, chastity, or friendship, but in Spenser's "life and environment" – a phrase recalling the methodology used by Taine and the nineteenth century naturalists to historicize poetry. But the philological focus on race, religion, and nationality was passing in response to cultural pluralism and changes in college demographics. Spenser's stature in American college English was accordingly diminished; fashioning gentlemen and noble persons was no longer the point and racial theories were discredited. Believing that "culture" was a matter of environmental adaptation, progressive educators argued that the curriculum should be modified to reflect the life experiences of contemporary readers. While the number of new Spenser dissertations remained about constant, their proportion declined as Joyce and Faulkner, Yeats and Eliot became the choice subjects for a new generation of college readers with a penchant for difficulty. The marketplace of ideas responded enthusiastically to a modernism that did not always share Greenlaw's reverence for literary history and cultural tradition.

In a 1975 essay entitled "The Aesthetic Experience of Reading Spenser," S. K. Heninger comments that "Spenser suffered what must surely be the most demeaning of fates for a poet. His high reputation survived intact, while the taste for his poetry rapidly declined. As a consequence, he continued to be read, but for the wrong reasons and in the wrong way, and therefore with less and less understanding (79). Heninger is (mistakenly) describing eighteenth-century Spenser criticism, but his remark accurately describes how postwar critics were beginning to regard their immediate predecessors. Fearful of what philological pedantry was doing to Spenser's reputation, academic critics sought to recover the aesthetic experience of reading Spenser by following the lead suggested by Rosemond Tuve; amalgamating elements of literary history and New Criticism, they strove to harmonize historicism and aestheticism, or if not bring them into harmony, at least into some form of fruitful exchange. The surprising result was a "rediscovery" of Spenser in the 1960s comparable to that launched by the Wartons two centuries before. But in this instance, and for the first time, a revival of Spenser was not accompanied by significant changes in the genres of criticism: as New Criticism penetrated the academy, it sprouted the footnotes, bibliographies, and commitment to science and progress demanded by the scholarly journals and university presses. Despite the new focus on criticism, the formal qualities of academic writing changed very little.

The reasons for this have much to do with the institutional structures of the modern research university; the peer-review process demanded mastery of prior scholarship even as it demanded innovations in methodology – like comparable commercial enterprises, the Spenser industry maintained its system of production even as it developed new products for new customers. There were more models of criticism to choose from as the marketplace of ideas benefited from efficiencies and economies of scale. By the 1950s and 1960s, academic careers depended less on an ability to muster historical facts and more on an ability to propose original interpretations. While Spenser continued to attract learned critics, with the assimilation of New Criticism scholarly journals began to put a premium on the novelty of critical insight. While this emphasis derives, via the New Criticism, from the nineteenth-century "appreciation," postwar scholarship differed from the old paradigms, at least at first, by circumscribing subjectivity. Academic formalism made its way into the research program by laying claim to a coolly rational objectivity. The new sciences of criticism served the immediate needs of rapidly expanding American and British universities better than traditional philology; they did not require the time necessary to master classical languages and the minutiae of intellectual and social history. Yet competition for places within the system raised standards elsewhere; scholars were expected to publish sooner and to publish more. The pressure to innovate also changed the nature of literary research. Within a generation, critical modes became so various and complex as to require a training in "theory" as rigorous as the older training in philological skills. In the 1960s there was a noticeable uptick in the number of dissertations written on Spenser, though nothing compared to the abundant "research" being done on modern novelists and poets. Older kinds of scholarship continued under the aegis of academic pluralism; philology achieved new standards in Paul E. McLane's *Spenser's Shepheardes Calendar: A Study in Elizabethan Allegory* (1961) and Robert Ellrodt's *Neoplatonism in the Poetry of Spenser* (1960). A younger generation of literary historians adopted more strictly literary approaches based on symbolism, myth, numerology, iconology, narrative analysis, psychoanalysis, and phenomenology.

This proliferation of new readers and critical methods underscores the extent to which, in certain respects, the research university really was value-neutral. Scholarly research continued unabated when Spenser was out of favor with modernist taste; it continues today, despite the fact that Spenser's moral and political commitments are abhorrent to most of the academic establishment. If Spenser's original rise to academic prominence came in response to British fears of class conflict and American fears for traditional values in a time of rapid immigration and social change, it survived the demise of the Victorian ruling class and Protestant, Anglo-Saxon dominance. In fact, opening the research universities to members of other traditions revitalized Spenser scholarship: Catholic scholars contributed their familiarity with traditional understandings of moral virtues and vices (not always a strong point of Protestant criticism), while Jewish scholars contributed highly developed exegetical skills. In other respects scholarship was not value-neutral: academic formalism made Spenser respectable to a diverse readership by ignoring or dismissing the political implications of his writings; as if to compensate, the more radically egalitarian criticism of recent years has attended to little else. Yet the more scholarship changes, the more it remains the same; these shifts in focus and methodology fulfilled institutional demands for specialization and productivity that began with philological criticism and the Ph.D. in literature.

Postwar Criticism

If the ideal of prewar philology was extensive historical coverage, the distinguishing mark of postwar criticism was intensive argumentative complexity; to do any justice to this phase of Spenser criticism requires treating in some detail only a sample of representative work. *The Allegorical Temper: Vision and Reality in Book II of Spenser's Faerie Queene* (1957) is hardly Harry Berger Jr.'s last word on Spenser, but it is probably his most influential book. Berger undertook to demonstrate to Spenserians how to read "the poem as a poem" (9), that is, to illustrate how it could be read within the Dante-Browning-Eliot paradigm. *The Allegorical Temper* began as a Yale dissertation written under the tutelage of William Wimsatt; formally, it is an extended New Critical essay. Berger begins by questioning why Guyon would faint after his encounter with Mammon, weaving around this crux a gyre of reflections in which the swoon becomes central to book 2, book 2 becomes central to the poem, and the poem becomes central to an understanding of how modern literary criticism ought to function. *The Allegorical Temper* was easily the most complex piece of extended Spenser criticism to date, a linked argument long drawn out that took direct aim at both the historicist habit of treating the *Faerie Queene* as a document and the earlier New Critical inclination to dismiss it as a bloodless didactic allegory.

To understand poetry as poetry, Berger argues, it is above all necessary to reconsider the nature of a fictionality by no means simple: "for unless we know how the limits of poetry are conceived in the *Faerie Queene* it will be difficult to understand the relation of poetry to history, fiction to reality, drama to allegory; and this too is dependent on Elizabeth's position inside and outside of the poem; on the light she throws on Belphoebe and the light Belphoebe throws on her, on what Belphoebe as well as Elizabeth is doing in a poem about Guyon" (114). Berger coaxes intrinsic significance out of a complex sequence of internal allusions, presenting the poem as a self-reflexive hall of mirrors: "It is only in this context that the problems of British history assume a poetic, rather than a merely political or didactic, function" (90). Rather than look for analogies to texts or events outside the poem, like the historicist Greenlaw, one should look for analogies to texts and events as they appear inside the poem: "Like the two terms of a simile, Britain and Faery confront each other to produce a third entity compact of their similarities and differences . . . a situation in which Faery must be defined by Britain and Britain by Faery." Greenlaw erred less in his conclusions than in his understanding of the nature of poetic allegory: "He takes the poem's personifying images as disguises of historical realities rather than as incarnations of concepts or qualities abstracted from those realities" (168–69, 202–03).

Berger uses the word "incarnation" advisedly; for him it implies the primacy of the poem as poetry, but also, more problematically, a literary identity of res and verba: "The *Faerie Queene* in fact raises in a special and pressing manner the general problem of poetic unity. Precisely how is it a poem? How is it *one?*" (121). Very few of Spenser's admirers, from Dryden on down, had regarded the poem as unified; formal unity was not even an issue for most nineteenth-century critics. It was a prime concern for the New Critics, though their efforts had been previously concentrated on lyric and drama, not on verse narratives. Berger's task was thus a formidable one; he does not, like Rosemond Tuve, attempt to reconstruct what Renaissance poets understood by poetry; rather, he attempts to "save the phenomenon" for contemporary aesthetics by foregrounding the lyric qualities in Spenser's narrative: as opposed to novels, "the epic poem is closer to the lyric (in which the poetic experience is centered in the speaker's own soul) because its subject is more explicitly transformed by the narrative speaker" (131). As in Dante or Browning, the "ethical speaker" is himself a character who participates in a "poetic action" parallel to and involved with the fable itself. Spenserian allegory is not a matter of external reference, but a "dual perspective produced by his manipulation of fable and poetic action, on the consequent difference between the world the characters see and the world the readers see." Not only is the poet "in" the poem; its readers are too: "As long as the poet and his audience (Everyman) are part of the poetic world and in the poetic vision, the questions of intention, didacticism, and allegory must be approached within the fiction" (163, 160, 172). No prior discussion of design in the *Faerie Queene* begins to approach the intricacy of Berger's argument.

As "poetic action," Guyon's faint points to a meaningful failure, one comprehensible in novelistic terms. But to see why it is meaningful, it is not enough to heed Hazlitt's injunction to ignore the allegory. In parallel with Guyon's haughty idealism, modern readers are inclined to mistake Spenser's elevated abstractions for embodied meanings: "Our insufficiency mirrors his own. So far as our consciousness of the poem's world is concerned, we too are in a kind of metaphoric swoon" (174). Rather, it is in the context of allegorical abstraction that poetic action becomes significant. Nineteenth-century readers comparing the *Faerie Queene* to the *Pilgrim's Progress* invariably found fault with courtly Spenser; *The Allegorical Temper* defends the *Faerie Queene* by discovering a this-worldly, novelistic critique of the official allegory. Just as Spenser can render the haughty Guyon a fallible Everyman, so, Berger argues, critics should extend their charity to Spenser's unfashionable poem, which is not such a period piece as it has been taken to be: "Modern, and particularly 'new,' criticism tends to look on the *Faerie Queene* as a special and inferior mode of poetry which is inaccessible to the usual modern techniques of reading. Such a judgment ultimately springs from the failure to consider a general principle of distinction: that though modern criticism (in any age) is generated by the nature of modern literature, its techniques have little value if they cannot be applied to any work in terms of the work's individual problems, and without the implicit judging of that work by the standards of modern literature." Here again is the modernist understanding of "tradition" one finds, for example, in Leavis: the past waits upon the present. To the extent that New Criticism can broaden its horizons by universalizing its principles, "it breaks away from the confines of literary history" (175). Berger differentiates himself from both old historicism and the New Criticism, yet his emphasis on a demotic liberalism at the expense of aristocratic virtue places *The Allegorical Temper* in the Whig tradition of Addison, Hazlitt, Dowden, and Greenlaw.

In Harry Berger's book New Criticism retains much of its earlier edginess; in A. C. Hamilton's *The Structure of Allegory in The Faerie Queene* (1961) it merges almost seamlessly into academic criticism. Rather than present the *Faerie Queene* as a difficult critical challenge to modern readers, Hamilton strives to refamiliarize it: "Despairing of the complicated puzzle which has been made of the poem, many readers respond: 'I read Spenser because I enjoy him, and don't pretend to understand him.' My real quarrel with modern criticism is that very little of what it has said is relevant to such a reader's response, or can extend and intensify that enjoyment through the understanding of its continued allegory" (13). *The Structure of Allegory* will not bristle with argument; rather, Hamilton presents himself as a kind of docent, leading the reader through the poem in an attempt to see it whole: "My own approach to the allegory of *The Faerie Queene* involves a simple yet radical re-orientation. In this study I shall focus upon the image itself, rather than seek the idea hidden behind the image" (12). Like Berger, Hamilton decries extrinsic interpretations of the allegory; unlike Berger, he stresses the "internal harmony" of Spenser's poem. In striving to make the *Faerie Queene* accessible and pleasurable to modern readers, Hamilton repeatedly underscores that he and we should not give undue heed to its philological difficulties: one does not read Spenser to learn about Tudor historiography, Aristotelian ethics, or Protestant theology. We should strive to relate the poem to "our" world by grasping "the inner coherence which binds all the parts of the poem" (14, 34). And yet Hamilton devotes at least half the book to philological explication of just the kinds of issues readers need not attend to; if he does so in the spirit of putting them "out of the way," it is probably true that *The Structure of Allegory* retains its popularity because it expounds them so clearly. Thirty years on, the book retains its place of honor on the reserve shelf.

Nevertheless, the arguments about the internal coherence of "the image itself" are sometimes less clear than the philological exposition. Hamilton addresses the "unity" of the *Faerie Queene* in a close reading that pointedly sets aside the substantial objections raised by three centuries of earlier critics. Rather than defend the poem as a narrative history, Hamilton expounds it as an "image." The warrant for this is Sidney's neoplatonic notion of an "imaginative groundplot," which Hamilton assimilates with a New Critical understanding of poetic unity based on the norms of lyric poetry. This attempt to identify Renaissance Platonism with post-Kantian aesthetics results in a torturous passage in an otherwise lucid book: "Our sense of that other reality to which the poem points, by first pointing to itself, grows from our sense of the poem's reality. We may be said to understand – literally to under-stand – the poem because we bear the whole poem in our response. That response is integrated because the intense delight given by the poem determines, at the same time, our understanding of its meaning" (43). The shifting locus of "reality" in this passage stems from the ambiguous connotations of "image": a fore-conceit above or behind the poem, the literal narrative that yields aesthetic delight, a perception formed by a reader. Hamilton attempts to steer between the Scylla and Charybdis posed by ethical and historical interpretations of the allegory, avoiding either form of extrinsic reference by interpreting the poem as a self-referential pattern of imagery. From the perspective of a Kantian belief in the transhistorical nature of art, to seize on Aristotelian ethics or Tudor politics would be to deny the pleasure that is poetry: "What is so perverse about this effort to identify historical allusions is that Spenser has laboured so carefully to conceal them . . . . He does so in order to turn the reader from the particular to the universal" (45). This is plainly a tendentious argument. Like Berger (or Greenlaw, for that matter), Hamilton rejects older humanist understandings of gender- and class-specific models of virtue "imaged" in a mimetic poem that was addressed to a complex, socially and sexually differentiated readership; the idea is that a disinterested and universal poetry should appeal equally to all readers, and to all readers conceived as equals.

Rather than discriminating social and historical differences, Hamilton uses his concept of imagery to explore organic unity through analogy. The "integration of multiple meanings into a perfect whole" is implicit even in the poem's smallest units: "the separate stanzas form a mosaic whose pattern is organic rather than mechanical, and spatial rather than temporal. They form larger images which expand into that total image which is the poem. That total image is its own world, the faery land which is the poet's fiction. Though this image may be sustained by moral ideas, it insists too strongly upon its own reality ever to be dissolved into them" (14). This optical metaphor for poetic unity, reducing ethical action to aesthetic image, recalls Hobbes's comments on Davenant's *Gondibert,* and the attempts by cultural critics to define an image of society in which the diversely specialized parts are subsumed within an informing "spirit" of the whole. Like Berger, Hamilton sees the poem as a hall of mirrors: the first half of book 1 is repeated in the second half; book 1 contains, in "the four stages of the Red Cross Knight's action," the design of the whole: "The first stage is described in book 2 which shows, as we have seen, how virtue aided by grace may prevent the knight's fall. The second stage is shown in book 3 in the redeeming power of chaste love displayed in the female Arthur, Britomart, who descends into the dungeon to save Amoret. The third stage is treated in books 4 and 5. In book 4 there is displayed the 'regeneration' of the flesh . . . in book 5 the 'regeneration' of England. The fourth stage is reached in book 6 which projects the vision of the restored lovers joined in delight" (60, 79, 129). It might be objected that to locate the meaning of the poem in its formal patterning is to strip it of meaning altogether. Yet Hamilton is not so pure a Kantian as that; as this synopsis indicates, *The Structure of Allegory* is very much about ethics, politics, and theology. In a dialectical procedure ultimately closer to Renaissance Neoplatonism than modern criticism, Hamilton works his way up from the welter of differences addressed by Spenser's ethics, politics, and theology to the transcendental harmony represented by his poetry-as-such. This characteristically Platonic move may be contrasted with Berger's characteristically Aristotelian insistence on the place of agon and history within poetry-as-such. Berger's emphasis on ethical striving in the *Faerie Queene* looks back to Dowden's concept of Spenser as teacher, just as Hamilton's emphasis on effortless pleasure recalls Lowell's concept of Spenser as aesthete. The very tone of their writing – Berger's argumentative thorniness versus Hamilton's Olympian objectivity – recalls their Victorian predecessors. Nor should this be surprising, for New Criticism sustained more than it challenged the foundational dilemmas of romantic aesthetics.

A similar dialectic informs Northrup Frye's seminal 1961 article, "The Structure of Imagery in The Faerie Queene." Frye was one of the few nonspecialists who were writing about Spenser in the postwar era and one of the few professors whose criticism found a general readership. In this respect he was like Lewis: not just a critic of humanist writing, but a critic writing as a humanist. Like Lewis, Frye finds in Spenser a potential mentor, a writer to be used rather than merely researched or enjoyed. Spenser's poetry, as Frye describes it, resembles nothing so much as Frye's own archetypal criticism: Spenser "thinks inside regular frameworks – the twelve months, the nine muses, the seven deadly sins – and he goes on filling up his frame even when his scheme is mistaken from the beginning, as it certainly is in *The Tears of the Muses*." Frye does not describe how a such a scheme could be mistaken, though presumably this would involve a failure to achieve the satisfying closure of the Mutabilitie Cantos: "If Mutability could be cast out of the world of ordinary experience, lower and upper nature would be reunited, man would re-enter the Golden Age, and the reign of 'Saturn's son' would be replaced by that of Saturn" (1963, 69–70, 72). Like Hamilton, Frye pursues a patterning that is ultimately "organic rather than mechanical, and spatial rather than temporal."

Frye's article strives to put Mutability in her place, not only within Spenser's philosophy, but within Spenser's poem itself. It is a mistake to regard the *Faerie Queene* as an unfinished fragment; while the poem might have been continued, it is complete as it stands; while the poem contains "dropped stitches" in its plots, "they do not interfere with our sense of their unity." Like the other postwar critics we have been considering, Frye shares Coleridge's unhappiness with allegory. Like them, he gives an account of Spenser's design that subordinates the supposed duality of allegory to the monism of analogy: "To demonstrate a unity in *The Faerie Queene*, we have to examine the imagery of the poem rather than its allegory." Frye differs from Berger and Hamilton, however, in the way he situates his structure of imagery: rather than using the imagery to mediate between a formal structure and an aesthetic response, he uses it to mediate between the poem and an elaborate scale of differentiated ethical and ontological levels, the "axioms and assumptions which Spenser and his public shared" (70, 71, 72). Unlike most other postwar critics, Frye does not regard attention to Spenser's teachings as a historicizing enterprise: as a Christian humanist, he can accept much of the doctrine of the *Faerie Queene*, or something very similar, as valid for all poetry, at least for all romantic poetry (in postromantic criticism this tends to become a distinction without a difference). Since, in Frye's criticism, poetry as such works by appealing to desire through imagination, the norms of romantic criticism are universalized: human beings as such share a timeless desire to transcend time.

While Frye devalues the explicit allegory of Spenser's poem, in parsing the *Faerie Queene* as "natural cycle" and "moral dialectic," his own procedure for interpreting Spenser is plainly allegorical; the poetry is made to say one thing while implying another – Fryvian romantic humanism. Because Spenser's characters do not display the "complicated behavior" of Shakespeare's heroes or Milton's Satan, we look for meaning not in agency or action but in a "framework" where "symbols of virtue are parodied by their vicious or demonic counterparts" (74). Displacing Spenser's narrative onto Frye's system of cycles and epicycles disposes of the problems of design that have always troubled Aristotelian critics of Spenser; like Hurd, he gets around them by elaborating a system appropriate to a romantic poetics that resolves ethical discord into the unity of an aesthetic response to fiction. Frye's framework, elegantly simple yet capable of complex elaboration, is based on a distinction between the private virtues of fidelity Spenser expounds in the first three legends and the public virtues of concord he treats in the three latter: "In the first two books the symbolism comes to a climax in what we may call a 'house of recognition,' the House of Holiness in Book I and the House of Alma in Book II. In the third the climax is the vision of the order of nature in the Gardens of Adonis. The second part repeats the same scheme: we have houses of recognition in the Temple of Venus in Book IV and the Palace of Mercilla in Book V, and a second *locus amoenus* vision in the Mount Acidale canto of Book VI, where the poet himself appears with the Graces. The sequence runs roughly as follows: fidelity in the context of human nature; fidelity in the context of physical nature; fidelity in the context of nature as a whole; concord in the context of physical nature, concord in the context of human nature; concord in the context of nature as a whole" (76–77).

If Frye's pursuit of a unifying structure of imagery is similar to the aims of the books by Berger and Hamilton, his treatment of ethical and ontological themes resembles the more traditional humanism of C. S. Lewis. Yet to state the parallel is to underscore the difference. In Lewis's *Allegory of Love* (1936) Spenser speaks from within Mutability's reign: as an agent in history, this Renaissance poet deconstructs an earlier courtly love tradition in a manner that makes claims upon modern readers *now*. Frye's universalized Spenser speaks from a transcendental platform above the reach of time's baleful tooth. Lewis underscores the occasional moral failures of the poet and his characters; Frye's emphasis is elsewhere: "Spenser means by 'Faerie' primarily the world of realized human nature . . . . The vision of Faerie may be the author's dream . . . but what the poet dreams of is the strenuous effort, physical, mental, and moral, of waking up to one's humanity" (73). In Frye's version of Christian humanism, ethical striving is ultimately illusionary; it is difficult to imagine him dismissing book 5 as a bad poem by a bad poet. Lewis opposes a fallible art to a fallible nature; in his criticism, poetry is the human means by which fallible poets strive to fulfill their human nature. Frye sees something altogether different: "The distinction between art and nature is disappearing because nature is taking on a human form. In the Bower of Bliss the *mixing* of art and nature is what is stressed: on Mount Acidale the art itself is nature" (86). Frye's philosophy of redemptive monism leads to conclusions similar to those of the New Critics, while his spirit of inclusiveness accords with the general tenor of academic criticism in the 1960s. As critics resisted an earlier humanism's insistence on ethical, historical, and generic discriminations, romantic holism, like renewed taste for romantic poetry, became the order of the day.

Romanticism Reconstructed

The rising tide of neo-romantic criticism elevated Spenser's academic reputation along with the reputations of Blake, Wordsworth, Coleridge, Byron, Shelley, and Keats. The one romantic who did not benefit was Sir Walter Scott, whose fascination with history did not appeal to students of myth and archetype. Such might easily have been Spenser's fate, had not Burger and the others demonstrated how to read Spenser as a poet of images. Instead, with Chaucer, Spenser was once more haled as a foundational figure in a romantic genealogy of English literature neatly adumbrated by the essays collected in Joseph Anthony Wittreich Jr.'s *Milton and the Line of Vision* (1975): Chaucer, Spenser, Sidney, Milton, Blake, Wordsworth, the Shelleys, Wallace Stevens. The reputations of those Wittreich describes as "the line of wit" (xiv) suffered a relative decline; these had been the New Critical favorites: Donne and Jonson, Dryden, Swift, and Pope. The Canadian critics Hamilton and Frye follow Kant and Coleridge in laying great stress on formal patterns and historical continuity. As neoromantics, they conceive of literature as an imaginative realm in which desire finds fulfillment in poems conceived as patterns of vision, poems that themselves participate in a yet larger pattern called "literature." Harry Berger's later essays on the green worlds of Renaissance poetry were among the high points of the era. True to its Longinian origins, neoromantic criticism regarded readerly response as something of a creative act; as a result, the New Critical "heresy of paraphrase" ceased to be heretical. Not only were later poems regarded as re-visions of earlier poems, but critical utterance itself became a matter of re-envisioning aesthetic experience in analogical or allegorical interpretations that refracted the poem-as-image through the "curious perspective" of the several critical methodologies. The acrimony typical of an earlier and more objective formalism subsided into a comfortable, kaleidoscopic pluralism. This variety of approaches and tolerance for subjectivity led to a situation resembling the original romantic cult of personality. The results for Spenser criticism were extraordinary: where prior criticism yielded only two or three accounts of the design of the *Faerie Queene*, in the 1960s and 1970s scores of "patterns" were discovered or inferred – thematic, narrative, imagistic, numerological. The multiplicity of Spensers appearing in the critical literature began to raise the kinds of questions posed by the multiplicity of facts and influences in the earlier philological criticism. How did it all add up? Was there a figure in the carpet, a pattern underneath the patterns discerned by Spenser's interpreters?

The romantic paradigm for reducing multiplicity to unity had always been Shakespeare's creative imagination. In *Spenser's Allegory: The Anatomy of Imagination* (1976), Isabel G. MacCaffrey applies the logic of Coleridge's Shakespearean epistemology to Spenser's landscape of psychology: "Mental space is Coleridge's identifying phrase for the locale of *The Faerie Queene*: it is liberated from 'all material obstacles'; 'it is truly a land of Fairy, that is, of mental space . . . .' *The Faerie Queene* mirrors the mind's very structure, as well as its principalities and powers; it is at once a treatise upon, and a dazzling instance of, the central role that imagination plays in human life" (6–7). Though she does not address the problem of the multiplicity of interpretations, MacCaffrey's exposition of visionary power does touch on the epistemological question they raise: "The relationships between ontology and imagining were not always clearly discerned or spelled out [in the history of ideas]. Before proceeding to the particulars of Spenser's poem, it will be necessary to unravel some complications of the imagination's life with respect to certain philosophical principles . . . . [The ambiguity of dreams] is a vividly focused instance of a larger problem, the central issue of epistemology. Does the mind (or the imagination) make or merely apprehend what it perceives?" Following Harry Berger, MacCaffrey regards Spenser's allegory as self-reflexive in the manner of lyric poetry: "The relation assumed in allegory between reader and fiction entails a degree of identification between fictive and 'real' events that seems to blur the lines we normally draw between these two realms. If we wish to save appearances in order to maintain a Kantian aesthetic, we can say that the fiction invites us to enter into its world and become for the time being a fictional character" (5). But MacCaffrey does not, like Hamilton, assert the closure typical of the verbal icon: "The position I have outlined is an ingenious but sophistical solution to some theoretical problems, and I do not insist upon it, except intermittently . . . . What is peculiar to allegory is the frankness with which the invitation [to reflect] is extended, and a congruence of patterning whereby the correspondence between invented and experienced reality is demonstrated." There is a certain tautology about this: what interpreters interpret in the poem is its peculiar power to elicit interpretation: "By calling attention to the process of whereby we understand the fiction itself, it sheds light upon the process whereby all understanding takes place" (58, 59).

Angus Fletcher uses a psychology of archetypes to lay out the epistemological problem in *The Prophetic Moment: An Essay on Spenser* (1971), accepting indeterminacy as a given: "Spenser pursues each action to the point at which it is clear how energies are distributed. Few incidents have a discursive interest of their own, as they might in a novel. But every ornament in the tapestry implies a power. It is exactly because the poem is so 'overdetermined' in this way that it needs, and gets, an exceedingly complex structure. Its stability comes largely from its multiplication of sources and its deep strain of imagistic relativism. The mythic surface of *The Faerie Queene* arises from its multiplication of sources in such a way that their separateness is at once both affirmed and denied" (55–56). Like Berger, Fletcher develops a phenomenological interpretation by locating the reader in the poem; like Frye, he discovers a "mythological grammar" structuring the reader's experience of the poem: "Together the temple and the labyrinth encompass the archetypal universe of *The Faerie Queene* and in that sense their meaning is more than allegorical. It is a narrative reality within the epic. Heroes come to temples, which they may enter and leave, and they pass through a labyrinthine faerieland" (6, 13). Fletcher's reading rings many dialectical changes on these two archetypes, considered separately or together. Hovering indeterminately between the stability of the temple and the uncertainty of the labyrinth yields the negative capability and visionary power that neoromantic criticism expects from poetic experience: "The structure of the prophetic moment is given by the dialectic of the temple and the labyrinth, between which there is a theoretical threshold, corresponding spatially to the temporal crossover defined as a moment. Thresholds are openings or doorways between two spaces or places. Moments are doorways between two spaces of time. These metaphors diagram the emergence of vision. At the theoretical meeting place between the temple and the labyrinth there bursts forth a higher order, which the great synchretist of ancient allegory, Philo Judaeus, would call 'the Immanent Logos'" (45–46). Fletcher's mythological grammar ultimately yields before the rhetoric of the unspeakable. Here is a modern elaboration of a romantic, Longinian reading of the *Faerie Queene* at least as old as the Wartons: Spenser's richness and indeterminacy overwhelm the judgment and inspire sublime emotions.

As though in response to this multiplication of interpretations, the 1970s saw two impressive and monumental efforts at synthesis: A. C. Hamilton's Longman edition of *The Faerie Queene* (1977) and James Nohrnberg's *The Analogy of The Faerie Queene* (1976). Hamilton reported on his editorial labors in a clever 1975 essay on the seven sins of annotation. He decries the emphasis Greenlaw and the philologists placed on source study; older criticism "interpreted the poem through abstract ideas and general moral background," while postwar criticism "interprets it either through a direct and immediate response to the words in the experience of reading or through a growing recognition of the larger structure or patterning of the episodes." If now "the poem is understood more clearly as a '*continued* Allegory,'" nonetheless individual studies of imagistic patterns and close readings of episodes "fragment the poem and violate its unity" (42, 54). In his preface to the Longman edition, Hamilton proposes to correct this deficiency: "The one critical 'fact' which matters is that, the more fully we understand *The Faerie Queene*, the more clearly we see the essential rightness of each part in the present order . . . . The assumption behind the present edition is that only by understanding precisely and fully each detail of the poem in the context of the whole may we understand the allegory (3, 4). Hamilton's annotated edition undertakes to demonstrate the integrity of Spenser's sprawling poem by integrating the disparate discoveries of several decades of formalist interpretation. A desire to "clarify [the reader's] immediate response" (4) leads Hamilton, like Greenlaw before him, to reconsider the structure of the text used by students. In contrast to the Clarendon edition (no notes) and Johns Hopkins edition (too many notes), the Longman volume introduces beginners to the peculiarities of Spenser's poetics and the history of Spenser criticism. A table listing the major characters assists readers in moving about within the narrative, and a substantial bibliography does the same for the criticism. Since this is a teaching edition, all of the contents are contained within a single paperback volume; ample margins provide space for students to record their own annotations and cross-references. Where earlier variorums, from the Hughes to the Hopkins, gathered appreciations and critical essays as separate appendixes, Hamilton prefaces each book with his own synthesis of criticism.

His chief innovation, however, is to supply glosses and annotations in columns parallel to the text, placing interpretation plainly in the reader's line of sight. While it is a large volume, the Longman edition is physically and conceptually compact. The result is ease of use and critical clarity, though one might object that the reader's "immediate response" is less clarified than controlled: it is a bold gesture to print criticism in parallel columns rather than demoting it to the bottom of the page or the back of the book. Hamilton's annotations achieve some of their clarity through exclusion: they register minor critical disagreements about points of interpretation but not major disagreements about how and why the poem should be read. The source and background study that preoccupied earlier annotators is largely absent here; if Greenlaw and colleagues strove to present Spenser as an Elizabethan, for Hamilton he is a poet for all times. Discussions of the political allegory are annotated only when, as in book 5, they are absolutely necessary; mythological allusions are noted, though otherwise Spenser's imitations of earlier writers go largely unglossed. So do most of the narrative inconsistencies, despite the large body of twentieth-century criticism that had grown up around them; if genetic criticism of the text required the presence of inconsistencies, their absence assisted interpretations of the design based on ideas of formal unity and closure. The result of these exclusions is a textbook admirably suited to the aims of college English in the 1960s and 1970s, when literary history and critical controversy were deemphasized. For that very reason, in the 1990s the Longman edition now begins to seem as dated as the Hopkins *Variorum*, which emphasized little else.

James Nohrnberg's *Analogy of The Faerie Queene* is a truly monumental book – its nine hundred closely printed pages make it not only the largest commentary on Spenser but one of the largest commentaries ever written on a British poem. It "began as a study of the 'unity of design' in the *Faerie Queene*," which, as ever, proved to be a fertile topic. Though a student of Frye, Nohrnberg owes as much to Coleridge in his desire to wed comprehensiveness to analysis within a single complex argument. Under the auspices of "Pan," the *Analogy* pursues mythopoeia, "that analogical coherence that obtains over any congregation of vaguely homologous forms considered as a whole"; under the auspices of "Proteus," the *Analogy* pursues invention, "the conspicuous heterogeneity of its matter" (ix). The copiousness of design and invention Nohrnberg discerns in the poem are mirrored in the construction and adumbration of his commentary, which thus becomes an "analogy" of the *Faerie Queene* in more senses than one. Nohrnberg takes as his point of departure Frye's contentions that the poem is complete as we have it and that the second half was written as a symmetrical complement to the first. Thus "the legend of friendship is conceived as both a sequel to, and a partner book for, the legend of chastity . . . . Next there is an analogy of private and public order, in the legends of temperance and justice . . . . Last there is an analogy of grace, especially gracious speech, in the legends of holiness and courtesy" (285). Nohrnberg's argument does not follow the sequence of Spenser's narrative; in a *refacciamento* of Spenser's own design, it proceeds phenomenologically from the middle outward by analogy to a reader's process of discovery: "each of Spenser's books forms a completed rhetorical period; subsequent installments reveal the membership of a book in a more inclusive pattern. The coherence of a given unit is not obscured by the addition of a counterpart, but clarified by the analogy between them" (86).

Clarity is not always the chief virtue of analogical reasoning, as the *Faerie Queene* itself instances well enough; in the *Analogy* tenor and vehicle sometimes go their independent ways, while criss-crossings of metaphor and metonymy lead readers into dense webs of signification, as when the "poem becomes a true phenomenology of allegory, a treatise on the manifestations of allegory that is itself yet a further manifestation" (xii). Nohrnberg is not a critic to let such beauties escape; under the sign of Proteus his commentary swells with matter. As is often the case in Coleridgean arguments, parts come to stand for the whole, and parts for other parts. As we have seen, by the 1970s, the problem for Spenserians was less to discern a unity of design in an unruly poem, than to discover unity among an unruly set of possible designs. In addition to its principle analogies, Nohrnberg's *Analogy* reads the poem as a sequence of three diptychs (1–2, 3–4, 5–6), two triptychs (1–2–3, 4–5–6), and a series of alternating books (1, 3, 5, 2, 4, 6). The commentary enters into still further allegory and analogy: "a clock face has some advantages over a calendar for illustrating the mechanics of the whole design. Spenser planned to run through a twelve-part cycle twelve times, his cantos passing at the rate of the minute hand, his books at the rate of the hour hand. The two hands cross once an hour: the corresponding event in the poem is a given knight's meeting with Prince Arthur, a kind of 'golden intersection' of each protagonist with his greater self" (36). The incontinent brilliance of these studies of "analogical coherence" is paralleled by (and opposed to) discussions of Spenser's "conspicuous heterogeneity" in particular episodes. The presiding influences here are the iconographer Edgar Wind and the developmental psychologist Erik Erikson. This unlikely pairing yields yet another analogy, since in amplifying, illustrating, and applying their insights Nohrnberg is able to fold the insights of prewar philology into the insights of postwar psychologism. And so the field of analogies becomes even wider, embracing the classical, biblical, medieval, and Renaissance literatures studied by an older generation of critics, and the equally wide swatch of post-Elizabethan writing that has been the cynosure of modernist criticism.

Nohrnberg's command of languages and literatures is quite beyond what even Spenser could muster; indeed it is a match for the best Renaissance philosophical synchretists, the most proximate analogy to Nohrnberg's way with a text (see the sixty page double-column index). Burton's *Anatomy of Melancholy* comes to mind. In content as in form, the *Analogy* rewrites Spenser's text, applying pagan, Hebrew, and Christian mysteries to educational doctrines and dilemmas familiar to any twentieth-century parent. *The Analogy of the Faerie Queene* is a challenging book, not only for its daunting size and formidable complexity but because Nohrnberg's play with order and disorder threatens a reductio ad absurdum of modern academic criticism. His analogies stretch intentionality to the limit and beyond: could Spenser really have meant all that? At what point does the virtuosity of a reader's response begin to obscure rather than clarify? Nohrnberg's *refacciamento* of the *Faerie Queene* tests the limits of "relevance" in several ways and in several senses, not least by citing ephemera such as *Pace: The Inflight Magazine of Piedmont Airlines* (295n). In such analogical criticism, the inclusiveness favored by the postwar academy is taken to an extreme: any document, any argument, is potentially pertinent (can the clock-face metaphor be used as part of an interpretation that requires the poem be complete in six books?). Here Hamilton's open handed gesture toward pluralism – "no genuine response to the poem is ever entirely wrong, only incomplete" (1977, 8) finds a just illustration.

A New Historicism

If *The Analogy of the Faerie Queene* takes rise from Northrup Frye, Jonathan Goldberg's *Endlesse Worke: Spenser and the Structures of Discourse* (1981) follows in the footings of Harry Berger, emphasizing the irregularity and obscurity of a demanding text. Curiously, where Nohrnberg pursues unity and discovers multiplicity, Goldberg pursues multiplicity and finds uniformity. *Endlesse Worke* begins by asserting what Frye and Hamilton had taken such pains to deny: "The poem is not merely unfinished, but frustratingly incomplete and inconclusive throughout, even when it encourages readers to expect conclusions" (1). Since Goldberg does not believe that the poem is a whole, he does not discuss the poem as a whole; the consistent inconsistencies of book 4 can be taken as representative of the rest: "These radical disturbances of narration, I would argue, lay bare the nature of narration throughout *The Faerie Queene*" (6). Here the postwar discussion of Spenser's design takes an interesting turn: like the formalist critics, Goldberg perceives a uniform "nature" in the poem, yet unlike the formalist critics, he does not argue that the different books are structured in different ways. Earlier monographs on the individual books of the *Faerie Queene* began from the assumption that the several virtues required several kinds of narrative and allegorical presentation, but Goldberg resists such teleological links between narrative ends and means: "In its groups and in its motion, book IV reveals that narration in *The Faerie Queene* functions as a grid on which different positions define an actor from moment to moment.... Heroism and distinct individuality are eroded by these matrices, for they allow endless shifting and substitution." Spenser's "structures of discourse" are not orderly: "The writerly text is infinite, replete, broken, empty, arbitrary, structured and deconstructed in its reading, which is its rewriting, produced by reader and author at once" (8–9, 11). Behind this Barthesian language stands Longinus and two centuries of romantic exegesis; Goldberg's emphasis on the reader's collaboration in constructing the text is something we have seen before in Coleridge, Hazlitt, and Lowell, as well as in Berger, MacCaffrey, and Fletcher. There is a difference of emphasis; where those critics regard formal irregularity as an expression of liberty, for Goldberg it is more likely to be a sign of constraint. His analysis of "substitution" leads to results very different from Nohrnberg's quest for "analogy"; in *The Analogy of The Faerie Queene* metaphorical interpretation playfully ramps over three millennia of writing while in *Endlesse Worke* metonymic interpretation costively limits itself to reshuffling the components of book 4.

Rather than ignore the narrative ruptures or explain them as errors introduced in revision, Goldberg argues persuasively if somewhat inconsistently that in the case of book 4 they do play a functional role in the reflections on loss, desire, and substitution that Spenser pursues in an intertextual exchange with Chaucer: "This paradigmatic story about the text as a replacement for loss and about the necessity of a lack for the production of a text is not merely another ending for and undoing of that crucial lost text that book IV keeps replacing. We have seen that Timias's story intersects with one squire's tale, Chaucer's; but that is not all. It also crosses another squire's tale, the one Spenser's narrator is telling when Timias's story interrupts" (xi). This argument about substitution in the *Faerie Queene* is replayed in Goldberg's own critical refashioning. Just as Spenser returns to Chaucer's text without completing it, so *Endlesse Worke* returns to Spenser's text without completing it. The argument resists closure by repetitively "substituting" one topic for another, ringing obsessive changes on themes of loss and blockage. Despite its thoroughgoing resistance to ideals of progress, *Endlesse Worke* can perhaps be regarded as a decadent scion of the Whig tradition, for its central concerns are freedom and constraint. If "much that is valuable in Spenser criticism is conservative in nature" Goldberg argues, post-structuralists can also contribute something of value by attending to what conservatives have neglected, Spenser's structures of discourse. Unconventional readers "like Bourdieu, are intent upon arguing that the subject-in-process answers the menace of the subject subjected and that language is the key to the liberation of the subject.... *The Faerie Queene* is a revolutionary text, even if what it glimpses is an impossible revolution and the limits of possibility which force it into silence" (137n). Like Longinus contemplating the decline of oratory, Goldberg laments restrictions on freedom of discourse and contemplates the subversive possibilities afforded by Spenser's sublimely fragmentary and disruptive language. Though *Endlesse Worke* is hardly optimistic, it does emphasize the figural freedom of language that Berger and the academic formalists regarded as liberating: "Social judgment confronts not the difference between truth and falsity, between reality and illusion, but true and false representation, masks of various kinds, all of which are, nonetheless, masks (149). Goldberg reconceives Berger's Green World as a fictional dystopia red in tooth and claw, but the debt is apparent and acknowledged.

In developing its argument about figural transpositions, *Endlesse Worke* returns to the themes of an earlier generation of historicists: "How did the chivalry of Elizabeth's court serve its real power in the world? How did the veneration of Elizabeth as goddess operate practically? . . . Power depends upon certain potent fictions . . . . The discourse that shapes the text has its place in the wider text of society" (135). This theme is common to Taine, Dowden, and Greenlaw; but where earlier historicists regarded the *Faerie Queene* as instrumental in the progressive development of Western liberalism, Goldberg reads the poem, like Yeats before him, as a regressive turn toward feudalism. Its potential for liberation, however, can be unlocked by a contemporary rereading that subverts the poem and conservative criticism. *Endlesse Worke* was written in the 1970s, a time when Renaissance studies was undergoing an Ovidian mutation from literary formalism to poststructuralism. This shift is plainly visible in the fissures of Goldberg's book, which moves from textual *jouissance* in the early chapters to ideology critique in the later ones. In reacting against the criticism of the 1960s, interpretations like *Endlesse Work* return to historicism of the philologists and the wit of the New Critics. Edwin Greenlaw's study of the role of fiction in Tudor ideology is a telling absence in *Endlesse Worke*: as though to play out the theme of return and substitution, Johns Hopkins not only published Goldberg's "new" historicist interpretation of Spenser but also offered him Greenlaw's old job.

One of the striking features of these postwar interpretations of Spenser is the extent to which they are self-reflexive, identifying their own way of reading with procedures for interpretation supposedly found in the text itself. In Harry Berger Jr.'s formulation, we can learn from Spenser how "problems of British history assume a poetic, rather than a merely political or didactic, function" (1957, 90). In Hamilton, Frye, MacCaffrey, Fletcher, Nohrnberg, and even in Goldberg, Spenser's poetry is held forth as a paradigm for one or another kind of critical reading. While these scholars often use historical evidence to illustrate how Spenser intended his poetry to be read, the mode of interpretation being read out of the text is not itself historicized – it is this, after all, that makes Spenser a living author for the academic reader. But, as such readers multiplied ways of reading Spenser, the claims of any one to be Spenser's came to seem problematic, resulting in the kind of argument being made in *Endlesse Worke* – that while "unconventional" readers are free to reconstruct texts at will, this particular willful misreading is warranted by Spenser's "revolutionary" text. With this, the idea that a successful poem exists as a kind of heterocosm with its own implied way of reading reaches the breaking point. By the 1980s, Hamilton's proposition that "no genuine response to the poem is ever entirely wrong, only incomplete" (1977, 8) could seem very hollow, for critical relativism had gone so far that academic readers could no longer even pretend to agree on what might be considered genuine. One condition for a return to historicism was the acceptance that readings of Renaissance poetry are "genuinely" different and that such differences need to be explained rather than explained away. Rather than postulate an internal, implied, informed, typical, or transcendental reader, critics began to consider particular, historical readers of Spenser and to make sense of their interpretations by giving up neo-Kantian aesthetics in order to discriminate between social, political, and sexual differences. This book itself has used such differences to explain historical changes in Spenser criticism while also invoking a concept of a historical tradition rather different from historicist periodization narrowly conceived. Since Spenser's readers invariably speak from within one or more ongoing critical traditions, they do not simply "reflect" the norms of their immediate time and place – any more than they are able to wholly escape from them. As writers, they often *take* from Spenser even as they *make* something appropriate to their own social and historical circumstances.

In *Milton's Spenser: The Politics of Reading* (1983), Maureen Quilligan raises this point by citing Dryden's comment in the preface to *Fables*: Milton "has acknowledged to me that Spenser was his original." She uses the example of Milton's use of Spenser to question the propositions that writers are able transcend their times, or that they are reducible to historical circumstances: "The reader whose activities are interrogated in the following pages is not then a critical tool for abstracting the text to a different level of discourse by turning a consumer of literature through critical fiat into a 'producer' of the text. Rather he or she is a historically real and representative reader of allegory, for whom reading was assumed to be a protopolitical act" (19). Despite political and historical differences, Milton's readings of Spenser originate in Spenser's text and Spenser's concerns; the very rejection of allegory as a vehicle for epic narration was a response to Spenser: "The presence of allegory in *Paradise Lost* posed interesting questions for Milton's poetic – and that is the enduring heresy firing the central thesis of this book: as an allegory, self-consciously interrogating its own status as fiction, *The Faerie Queene* intentionally offers strategies for interpretation which, when Milton incorporates them into his specifically non-allegorical *Paradise Lost*, form part of his text's self-consciousness about its necessary (intentional) interpretation by the reader's reading – not merely as a

fictive but, revisionarily, as a true text" (30). The issue of allegory as an inter-
pretative mode and its relation to fiction and history is one addressed by most
of the postwar critics we have considered. Quilligan differs from their ap-
proaches by treating the reader's text – *Paradise Lost* – not as a mirror or ful-
fillment of the text being read but as a modification of it that addresses a
changed set of historical circumstances. She is quick to make the connection
between Milton as a "heretical" reader of Spenser and her own desire to re-
historicize literary criticism by violating the rules of New Criticism: "My pres-
ent heresy, in concretizing reading in a certain way, leaves the realm of critical
abstractions and moves back into politics and history. Although to ask ques-
tions about the gender of the reader may seem merely the next logical ques-
tion to pose in current theoretical concern over the reader, I in fact came upon
it instructively enough not by way of querying reader theory (of any school),
but actually by sitting down to read a Renaissance text, as I had been taught to
read. In a sense, I simply took seriously for the first time Spenser's dedications
and rededications to Elizabeth throughout *The Faerie Queene*" (15–16). What
our generation can learn from reading Renaissance poetry (and from studying
its reception) is that reading is a gendered and political act. While *Milton's
Spenser* does put "the next logical question" in terms of the trajectory in critical
theory we have been tracing, it is also true that politics and gender were cen-
tral concerns not only of Renaissance readers, but of Spenser criticism gener-
ally, down to the middle twentieth century.

What goes around comes around, though not without change: the new
historicism differs from the old in laying much greater emphasis on
"opposition" as a constituent element of culture. Oppositions, both political
and literary, were less visible in prewar criticism because the operative notions
of culture led critics to seek a unifying principle in an oeuvre, a period, or a
tradition. The new historicism absorbed from the French structuralism popu-
lar in the 1970s the idea that such collective entities are constituted not around
substantive "patterns of culture" but around formal oppositions among sys-
tems of signs. Richard Helgerson brings this idea to bear on Spenser's oeuvre
in *Self-Crowned Laureates: Spenser, Jonson, Milton, and the Literary System* (1983). A
career is shaped by a *system*, while the system itself is shaped by oppositions
among competing possibilities for contemporary poetry, as well as competition
with earlier exemplars. Helgerson observes of his poets, "Theirs was to be a
role apart. But apart from what? A 'different' kind implies other kinds. Indeed,
it implies the existence of a system whose individual elements take meanings
from their relationship to the whole" (2). *Self-Crowned Laureates* takes from
structuralism the idea of opposing synchronic and diachronic relationships
while at the same time Anglicizing this by laying greater stress on the dia-
chronic pole and allowing for personal agency in history: "A generation is the
temporal location in which a certain language is spoken. 'I am laureate' is the

statement each of our poets wanted to make. The problem that faced them was whether the statement could be convincingly made in the language of their own particular generation. An appreciation of the problem can only make their accomplishment more humanly important, more relevant to the struggle of men and women in any age to achieve a position of individual authority and preeminence" (15). Helgerson bases his analysis of Spenser's work on oppositions between amorous and heroic poetry, private and public voices, and amateur and professional status that give the oeuvre its peculiar form: "Spenser's idea of a poet was finally an unstable but necessary union of two ideas, embodied in two roles — shepherd and knight, Colin and Calidore — neither of which could be renounced in favor of the other. The first gained him a place in the genus *poetae* as it was understood by his generation. The second defined him as the unique English member of the species of professed national poets. Without the first he would have been no poet at all, however much verse he had written. Without the second he, like Sidney, Harington, or Lodge, would have been able to make of poetry no more than a diversion of youth" (99–100). In this analysis, the nature of poetry is historicized while the matter of writing from within a system of social and literary oppositions is universalized.

Both American New Historicism and to a lesser extent British Cultural Materialism owe debts to the French culture-critics Bourdieu and Foucault, and behind them to the literary sociology of Taine, Jusserand, and Legouis. It is an axiom of this Francophone tradition that "power" resides not in individuals but in the social institutions dominant in a given era. Recent American studies emphasize Spenser's unweeting participation in the discursive contest for political authority and imperial power. Or they chastise him for his courtly ambition; Goldberg notes that Spenser's "complaints" were part of a deliberate strategy for institutional preferment: "There are some palpable ironies here, not the least of which was that Spenser had more success as a professional poet than any other poet of his time. No other poet was granted so large a pension" (1981, 171). The new generation of literary sociologists differ from their nineteenth-century counterparts in their greater sophistication about symbolic representation — rather than using literary works to illustrate social forces, they regard literature as a social force in its own right. As did Spenser, who elected to publish his poems. If New Historicism is eclectic in aims and methods (the name itself suggests its unstable amalgamations of New Criticism and old historicism), it is at least consistent in bringing a plurality of interpretive discourses to bear on a plurality of discursive structures being interpreted. Rejecting the positivism of the older generation of sociologists, "new" historicists enter into active engagement, friendly or hostile, with the texts they interpret. New Historicist criticism has been very institutional and very oppositional, bristling with terminology derived from a wide spectrum of academic disciplines. Its own striving for institutional preferment bears more than a casual relationship to the Renaissance documents serving as pretexts for academic debate.

While Shakespeare and theatricality have been its favorite themes, recent criticism resembles the discourse of the public theater less than the quasi-private discourses of the Inns of Court. The best recalls John Donne in displays of logic-chopping and technical jargon, prurient fascination with sex and violence, hard-nosed contempt for beauty and sentimentality, and virtuosic display of novelty and paradox. New Historicist writing began as coterie criticism exchanged between a small but influential group for whom subversive utterance commanded a circumscribed but potent kind of status. Ever adaptable, the essay genre once again served writers as a medium for bringing Renaissance verse to bear on contemporary critical practice; in the 1980s literary criticism became ever less patient with long or logically-structured arguments. It would be strange if Spenser, like Shakespeare and Donne, did not have something to contribute to the resulting "theory wars." In 1980 Louis Montrose argued that "the shepherd's *gift* – both his *talent* and his *offering* – is the power to create symbolic forms, to create illusions which sanctify political power; his expectation is a reciprocal, material benefit" (168). Such insights stem from cultural anthropology, but also from a cagey awareness of how the crabbed and oblique diction of academic utterance might be bent to material ends – things learned from the *Shepheardes Calender* and "Lycidas." But perhaps Stephen Greenblatt's ironic reflections on subversion and containment ring even truer to the common experience of both court poets and academic politicians: "Talus's violence, in destroying the Giant, exorcises the potentially dangerous social consequences – the praxis – that might follow from Spenser's own eloquent social criticism. The cosmological vision and the moral outrage remain, but the 'great expectations' of a radical reordering of wealth and power are shattered" (1983, 22). Like Spenser's poetry, Greenblatt's famous essay, "Murdering Peasants," speaks from a position of palpable irony: hermeneutic attempts to exorcise social demons attract admiration while keeping their safe, metaphorical distance. Unlike Kilcolman, the ivory tower has yet to be put to the torch, though the Philistines are said to be arming.

Since the literary reputation of a classic is "a function of the circumstances in which it was read," Jane Tompkins has argued that "the 'durability' of the text is not a function of its unique resistance to intellectual obsolescence; for the text, in any describable, documentable sense, is not durable at all. What endures is the literary and cultural tradition that believes in the idea of the classic, and that perpetuates that belief from day to day and from year to year .... For classic texts, while they may or may not have originally been written by gen-iuses, have certainly been written and rewritten by the generations of pro-fessors and critics who make their living by them. They are the mirrors of cul-

ture as culture is interpreted by those who control the literary establishment"
(1985, 5, 37). Spenser criticism bears witness to the idea that classics are con-
stantly being rewritten within a tradition that believes in classics: seventeenth-
century Moderns regarded Spenser as a navigator in uncharted seas; eight-
eenth-century Whigs regarded him as the sounding voice of ancient liberty; in
romantic criticism he is a visionary dreamer; in Victorian criticism he is a
Christian soldier; in the twentieth century, Spenser has appeared as a philolo-
gist, a spokesman for the common man, and an apologist for absolutism and
genocide. Without a doubt, critics rewrite the text they read in accordance
with the priorities at hand, among which is usually the desire to preserve the
monuments of literature for use by future imitators. Among those imitators
have been writers of literary criticism, who have followed the *Shepheardes Cal-
ender* in writing critical dialogues in which poets and readers discourse as shep-
herds, and followed the *Faerie Queene* by variously adopting its techniques of
allegory, ecphrasis, character description, genealogy, and storytelling. Of
course these devices have been put to use in ways very different from those
they originally served. Yet it would be misleading to suggest that they are sim-
ply a function the cultural norms of their own time: while critical reconstruc-
tions of Spenser's verse have been both interested and partial, the best of
Spenser's critics and imitators – Dryden, Hughes, Warton, Hurd, Beattie,
Coleridge, Wilson, Dowden, Greenlaw, Lewis, Berger, Frye – did not reflect
the dominant critical consensus of their eras; they shaped a new consensus
through a process of thoughtful rereading carried out against the grain of what
earlier readers had said. Even a consensus view can be no better than "partial"
for, as we have seen, other views are always in circulation, including the views
of critics long dead. Because the idea of a classic implies a tradition, the idea of
what makes a work "classic" will itself change over time, for traditions foster
change as well as continuity. Unlike many Victorians, Spenser's contemporar-
ies shared Tompkins's view that literatures are not natural growths and that,
to be sustained, literary traditions require a belief in the concept of a classic.
Like the Victorians, but unlike Tompkins, they believed that a classic work
can speak to more than one set of circumstances. In large part, E. K.'s
"vncouthe" poet achieved his classic status by design, skillfully taking up and
recasting images, arguments, and genres that the experience of earlier literature
indicated would be of enduring interest. Spenser's writings subsequently be-
came the quarry from which much poetry and not a little criticism has been
hewn. While the Prince of Poets has seldom been a popular favorite, the tradi-
tions of Spenser criticism have proven extremely lasting.

Works Cited

Adler, Mortimer J. *How to Read a Book: The Art of Getting a Liberal Education.* New York: Simon and Schuster, 1940.

[Bar-Notes.] Neuville, H. Richmond Jr. *Spenser's The Faerie Queene.* New York: Bar-Notes, 1966.

[Barnes & Noble.] Myers, Catherine R. *Edmund Spenser: The Faerie Queene.* New York: Barnes & Noble Book Notes, 1968.

Beers, Henry A. *A History of English Romanticism in the Eighteenth Century.* New York: Henry Holt, 1899.

Bennett, Josephine Waters. *The Evolution of the Faerie Queene.* Chicago: U of Chicago P, 1942.

Berger, Harry Jr. *The Allegorical Temper.* New Haven: Yale UP, 1957.

Brooks, Cleanth. *Modern Poetry and the Tradition.* Chapel Hill: U of North Carolina P, 1939.

Campbell, Thomas. *Specimens of the British Poets.* London, 1819.

Church, R. W. *Spenser* ["English Men of Letters."] London, 1879.

[Cliffs Notes.] Priest, Harold M. *The Faerie Queene.* Lincoln: Cliffs Notes, 1968.

Cory, Herbert E. "The Influence of Spenser on English Poetry from 1579 to the Death of Keats." Ph.D. diss., Harvard University, 1910.

———"The Golden Age of Spenserian Pastoral," *PMLA* 25 (1910): 241–67.

———"Browne's 'Britannia's Pastorals' and Spenser's 'Faerie Queene,'" *University of California Chronicle* 13 (1911): 189–200.

——— *The Critics of Edmund Spenser.* University of California Publications in Modern Philology, 1911.

———"Spenser, Thomson, and Romanticism," *PMLA* 26 (1911): 51–91.

———"Spenser, The School of the Fletchers, and Milton," *University of California Publications in Modern Philology* 2 (1912): 311–73.

——— *The Critics of Edmund Spenser.* Berkeley: U of California P, 1917.

DeMaar, Harko G. *A History of Modern English Romanticism.* London: Oxford UP, 1924.

Eliot, T. S. *Selected Essays, 1917–1932.* New York: Harcourt, Brace, 1932.

Ellrodt, Robert. *Neoplatonism in the Poetry of Spenser.* Geneva: Library Droz, 1960.

Fletcher, Angus. *The Prophetic Moment: An Essay on Spenser*. Chicago: U of Chicago P, 1971.

Foerster, Norman. *The American Scholar: A Study in Litterae Inhumaniores*. Chapel Hill: U of North Carolina P, 1929.

Frye, Northrup. "The Structure of Imagery in The Faerie Queene," *Fables of Identity: Studies in Poetic Mythology*. New York: Harcourt, Brace, & World, 1963, 69–87.

Gallaway, Francis. *Reason, Rule, and Revolt in English Classicism*. New York: Scribners, 1940.

Goldberg, Jonathan. *Endlesse Worke: Spenser and the Structures of Discourse*. Baltimore: Johns Hopkins UP, 1981.

Greenblatt, Stephen. "Murdering Peasants: Status, Genre, and The Representation of Rebellion," *Representations* 1 (1983): 1–29.

Greenlaw, Edwin. "The Shepheards Calender," *PMLA* 26 (1911): 419–51.

———*A Syllabus of English Literature*. Chicago: Sanborn, 1912.

———*An Outline of the Literature of the English Renaissance*. Chicago: Sanborn, 1916.

Greenlaw, Edwin and James Holly Hanford. *The Great Tradition: A Book of Selections From English and American Prose and Poetry, Illustrating the National Ideals of Freedom, Faith, and Conduct*. Chicago: Scott, Foresman, 1919.

Greenlaw, Edwin, William Elson, Christine Keck, eds. *Literature and Life*. 4 vols. Chicago: Scott, Foresman, 1922–24.

Greenlaw, Edwin. *The Province of Literary History*. Baltimore: Johns Hopkins UP, 1931.

———*Studies in Spenser's Historical Allegory*. Baltimore: Johns Hopkins UP, 1932.

Greenlaw, Edwin, Charles Grosvenor Osgood, Frederick Morgan Padelford, Roy Heffner, eds. *The Works of Edmund Spenser: A Variorum Edition*. 12 vols. Baltimore: Johns Hopkins UP, 1932–55.

Grosart, A. B. Life of Spenser, Edmund Spenser, *Complete Works*, ed. A. B. Grosart. 10 vols. London: privately printed, 1882–84.

Hamilton, A. C. *The Structure of Allegory in The Faerie Queene*. Oxford: Clarendon Press, 1961.

———"On Annotating Spenser's Faerie Queene: A New Approach to the Poem," in *Contemporary Thought on Edmund Spenser*, ed. Richard C. Frushell and Bernard J. Vondersmith. Carbondale and Edwardsville: Southern Illinois UP, 1975, 41–60.

———, ed. Edmund Spenser, *The Faerie Queene*. London: Longmans, 1977.

Harman, Edward G. *Edmund Spenser and the Impersonations of Francis Bacon.* London, 1914.

Havens, Raymond Dexter. *The Influence of Milton on English Poetry.* Cambridge: Harvard UP, 1922.

Helgerson, Richard. *Self-Crowned Laureates: Spenser, Jonson, Milton, and the Literary System.* Berkeley: U of California P, 1983.

Heninger, S. K. "The Aesthetic Experience of Reading Spenser," in *Contemporary Thought on Edmund Spenser,* ed. Richard C. Frushell and Bernard J. Vondersmith. Carbondale and Edwardsville: Southern Illinois UP, 1975, 79–98.

Hinchman, Walter S. *A History of English and American Literature.* New York, 1918.

Hughes, Merritt Y. "Spenser, 1552–1952," *Transactions of the Wisconsin Academy* 42 (1953): 5–24.

Leavis, F. R. *Revaluation, Tradition and Development in English Poetry.* London: Chatto and Windus, 1936.

Lewis, C. S. *The Allegory of Love: A Study in Medieval Tradition.* Oxford: Clarendon Press, 1936.

———*Spenser's Images of Life,* ed. Alastair Fowler. Cambridge: Cambridge UP, 1967.

MacCaffrey, Isabel. *Spenser's Allegory: The Anatomy of Imagination.* Princeton: Princeton UP, 1976.

McLane, Paul E. *Spenser's Shepheardes Calender: A Study in Elizabethan Allegory.* Notre Dame: U of Notre Dame P, 1961.

[Monarch Notes.] Grace, William J. *The Faerie Queene and Other Works by Spenser.* New York: Monarch Notes, 1963.

Montrose, Louis. "'Eliza, Queene of Shepheardes,' and the Pastoral of Power," *English Literary Renaissance* 10 (1980): 153–82.

Moody, William Vaughan. *A History of English Literature.* New York, 1902. Many later editions.

Nohrnberg, James. *The Analogy of the Faerie Queene.* Princeton: Princeton UP, 1976.

Peck, H. W. "Spenser's *Faerie Queene* and the Student of To-Day," *Sewanee Review* 24 (1916): 340–52.

Phelps, William Lyon. *The Beginnings of the English Romantic Movement.* Boston: Ginn, 1893.

Potter, Stephen. *The Muse in Chains: A Study in Education.* London: Jonathan Cape, 1937.

Quilligan, Maureen. *Milton's Spenser: The Politics of Reading.* Ithaca: Cornell UP, 1983.

Renwick, W. L. Review of the Hopkins *Variorum, Modern Language Review* 28 (1933): 508–11.

Sipple, William L. *Edmund Spenser 1900–1936: A Reference Guide.* Boston: G. K. Hall, 1984.

Spens, Janet. *Spenser's Faerie Queene: An Interpretation.* London: Arnold, 1934.

Spenser, Edmund. *Poetical Works,* ed. F. H. Child. 5 vols. Boston, 1855.

———*Poetical Works,* ed. J. C. Smith and Ernest de Selincourt. 3 vols. Oxford: Clarendon Press, 1909–10.

———*Works,* ed. R. L. Renwick. 8 vols. Oxford: Clarendon Press, 1930–32.

———*The Faerie Queene,* ed. A. C. Hamilton. London: Longmans, 1977.

[Study Master.] Wertheim, Lee Hilles. *The Faerie Queene: Canto by Canto Analysis with Critical Commentary.* New York: Study Master, 1963.

Tate, Allen. "Three Types of Poetry," *Reactionary Essays on Poetry and Ideas.* New York, 1936, 83–112.

Tompkins, Jane. "Masterpiece Theater: The Politics of Hawthorne's Literary Reputation," *Sensational Designs: The Cultural Work of American Fiction, 1790–1860.* New York: Oxford UP, 1985, 3–39.

Townsend, Atwood H. *Student's Guide to Good Reading: A List of Six Hundred Books Which are Enjoyable, Well Worth Reading, and Inexpensive.* NP, 1933.

Traversi, D. A. "Revaluation (X): *The Vision of Piers Plowman,*" *Scrutiny* 5 (1936): 276–91.

Tuve, Rosemond. *Elizabethan and Metaphysical Imagery: Renaissance Poetic and Twentieth-Century Critics.* Chicago: U of Chicago P, 1947.

Vondersmith, Bernard J. "A History of the Criticism of the *Faerie Queene,* 1910–1947." Ph.D. diss., Duquesne University, 1971.

Walter, J. H. "*The Faerie Queene*: Alterations and Structure," *Modern Language Review* 36 (1941): 37–58.

Wasserman, Earl R. *Elizabethan Poetry in the Eighteenth Century.* Urbana: U of Illinois P, 1947.

Wellek, René. *A History of Modern Criticism, 1750–1950.* Vol. 5. *English Criticism, 1900–1950.* New Haven, Yale UP, 1986.

———*A History of Modern Criticism, 1750–1950.* Vol. 6. *American Criticism, 1900–1950.* New Haven, Yale UP, 1986.

Williams, Charles. *Reason and Beauty in the Poetic Mind.* Oxford: Clarendon Press, 1933.

Winters, Yvor. "Problems for the Modern Critic of Literature," *Hudson Review* 9 (1956): 325–86. Reprinted in *The Function of Criticism: Problems and Exercises.* Denver: Alan Swallow, 1957, 9–78.

Wittreich, Joseph Anthony Jr., ed. *Milton and the Line of Vision.* Madison: U of Wisconsin P, 1975.

Woolf, Virginia. "The Faery Queene," *The Moment and Other Essays.* London: Harcourt, Brace, 1947, 25–29.

Yeats, W. B, ed. *The Poems of Spenser Selected and with an Introduction by W. B. Yeats.* London, 1906. The introduction is reprinted in *Essays and Introductions.* New York: Collier, 1961, 256–83.

Works Cited

E. K. "Dedicatory epistle," Edmund Spenser, *The Shepheardes Calender*. London, 1579.

Harvey, Gabriel. *Three Proper, and Wittie, Familiar Letters*. London, 1580.

Peele, George. *The Araygnement of Paris. A Pastorall*. London, 1584.

Webbe, William. *A Discourse of English Poetrie*. London, 1586.

Fraunce, Abraham. *Arcadian Rhetorick: Or the Praecepts of Rhetorick Made Plain by Examples*. London, 1588.

———*The Lawiers Logick, Exemplifying the Praecepts of Logicke by the Practise of the Common Lawe*. London, 1588.

Puttenham, George. *The Arte of English Poesie*. London, 1589.

Marlowe, Christopher. *Tamburlaine the Greate*. London, 1590.

Raleigh, Walter et al. "Commendatory verses," *The Faerie Queene*. London, 1590.

Spenser, Edmund. "Letter to Raleigh," *The Faerie Queene*. London, 1590.

Drayton, Michael. *Idea. The Shepheards Garland*. London, 1593.

Lodge, Thomas. "Induction," *Phillis: Honoured with Pastorall Sonnets, Elegies, and Amorous Delights*. London, 1593.

Daniel, Samuel. "To the Right Honourable, The Lady Marie, Countess of Pembroke," *Delia and Rosamond augmented*. London, 1594.

Barnfield, Richard. *Cynthia; certaine sonnets; the legend of Cassandra*. London, 1595.

Edwards, Thomas. *Cephalus and Procris. Narcissus*. London, 1595.

Sidney, Sir Philip. *The Defence of Poesie*. London, 1595.

W. S. *The Lamentable Tragedie of Locrine*. London, 1595.

Fitzgeffrey, Charles. *Sir Francis Drake*. Oxford, 1596.

Smith, William. "To the Most Excellent and learned Shepheard Collin Clout," *Chloris*. London, 1596.

Hall, Joseph. "His Defiance of Enuy," *Virgidemiarum*. London, 1597.

Meres, Francis. *Palladis Tamia. Wits Treasury. Being the Second part of Wits Common wealth*. London, 1598.

Rous, Francis. *Thule, or Vertues Historie*. London, 1598.

Greene, Robert. *The Comicall Historie of Alphonsus King of Aragon*. London, 1599.

Cutwode, Thomas. *Caltha Poetarum: or The Bumble Bee*. London, 1599.

Tourneur, Cyril. *The Transformed Metamorphosis*. London, 1600.

Chapman, George. *Monsieur D'Olive: a Comedie*. London, 1606.

Anon. *The Returne from Parnassus*. London, 1606.

Dekker, Thomas. *The Whore of Babylon, As it was Acted by the Princes Servants*. London, 1607.

Stradling, Sir John. Untitled, *Epigrammatum Libri Quatuor*. London, 1607.

Fletcher, Giles the younger. *Christs Victorie and Triumph on Heaven and Earth*. London, 1610.

Drayton, Michael. *Poly-Olbion*. London, 1612–22.

Browne, William. *Britannias Pastorals*. London, 1613–16.

Norden, John. *The Labyrinth Of Mans Life, or Vertues Delight and Envies Opposite*. London, 1614.

Gill, Alexander. *Logonomia Anglica. Qua gentis sermo facilius addiscitur conscripta*. London, 1619.

Jonson, Ben. Untitled, Shakespeare, *Works*. London, 1623.

Fletcher, Phineas. *The Locusts, or Apollyonists*. Cambridge, 1627.

Reynolds, Henry. *Mythomystes, Wherein a Short Survey Is Taken of the Nature and Value of True Poetry*. London, 1632.

Fletcher, Phineas. *The Purple Island, or the Isle of Man: together with Piscatorie Eclogs and other Poetical Miscellanies*. London, 1633.

Johnson, Edmund. "A Quare with a Quare concerning Iohn Quis," John Gower, *Pyrgomachia*. London, 1635.

Milton, John. *A Maske Presented at Ludlow Castle* [Comus]. London, 1637.

Jonson, Ben. "Timber; or Discoveries," Works. 2 vols. London, 1640.

More, Henry. *Psychodia Platonica: or a Platonical song of the Soul, Consisting of Foure Severall Poems*. London, 1642.

Digby, Sir Kenelm. *Observations on the 22. Stanza in the 9th Canto of the 2d. Book of Spencers Faery Queene*. London, 1643.

Milton, John. *Areopagitica*. London, 1644.

Milton, John. *Poems of Mr. John Milton, Both English and Latin, Compos'd at Several Times*. London, 1645.

Anon. *The Faerie Leveller: or, King Charles his Leveller descried and deciphered*. London, 1648.

Beaumont, Joseph. *Psyche, or Loves Mysterie*. London, 1648.

Davenant, William. *A Discourse upon Gondibert*. London, 1650.

Hobbes, Thomas. *The Answer of Mr. Hobbes to Sr. Will. D'Avenant's Preface Before Gondibert*. London, 1650.

Vaughan, Thomas. "Epistle Dedicatory," *The Man Mouse taken in a Trap*. London, 1650.

R. C. "Epistle Dedicatory," William Bosworth, *The Chast and Lost Lovers*. London, 1651.

Aylett, Robert. *Divine and Moral Speculations in Metrical Numbers*. London, 1653.

Denham, Sir John. "To Daphne: On his Incomparable In[c]omprehensible Poem Gondibert," Certain *Verses Written By several of the Authors Friends; to be re-printed with the Second Edition of Gondibert*. London, 1653.

More, Henry. *Conjectura Cabbalistica*. London, 1653.

Sheppard, Samuel. *The Faerie King Fashioning Love and Honour*. Ca. 1655. Ed. P. J. Klemp. Salzburg, 1984.

Fuller, Thomas. *The History of the Worthies of England*. London, 1662. Ed. Austin Nutall. 2 vols. London, 1840.

Denham, Sir John. "On Mr. Abraham Cowley His Death and Burial," *Poems and Translations*. London, 1668.

Rymer Thomas. "Preface of the Translator," René Rapin, *Reflections on Aristotle's Treatise of Poesie*. London, 1674.

Phillips, Edward. *Theatrum Poetarum, or A Compleat Collection of the Poets*. 2 vols. London, 1675.

Spenser, Edmund. *The Works of that Famous English Poet, Mr. Edmund Spenser*. London, 1679.

Dryden, John. Dedication, *The Spanish Fryar*. London, 1681.

Soame, William and John Dryden. *The Art of Poetry, written in French by The Sieur de Boileau*. London, 1683. In *The Continental Mode*, ed. Scott Elledge and Donald Schier. Ithaca: Cornell UP, 1960.

Dryden, John. Preface, *Sylvae: or, the Second Part of Poetical Miscellanies*. London, 1685.

Howard, Edward. *Spencer Redivivus Containing the First Book of the Fairy Queen*. London, 1687.

Atterbury, Francis. Preface, *The Second Part of Mr. Waller's Poems*. London, 1690.

Temple, Sir William. "Of Poetry," *Miscellanea. The Second Part*. London, 1690.

Dryden, John. "Dedication To the Right Honourable Charles Earl of Dorset," *The Satires of Decimus Junius Juvenalis. Translated into English Verse*. London, 1693.

Addison, Joseph. "An Account of the Greatest English Poets," *The Annual Miscellany for the Year 1694*. London, 1694.

Blackmore, Sir Richard. *Prince Arthur. An Heroick Poem. In Ten Books*. London, 1695.

———*King Arthur. An Heroick Poem. In Twelve Books*. London, 1697.

Dryden, John. Dedication to Clifford, *The Works of Virgil Translated into English Verse*. London, 1697.

Wesley, Samuel the elder. "The Essay on Heroic Poetry," *The Life of our Blessed Lord.* London, 1697.

Cobb, Samuel. *Poetae Britannici. A Poem Satyical and Panegyrical, Upon our English Poets.* London, 1700.

Dryden, John. Preface, *Fables Ancient and Modern.* London, 1700.

Dennis, John. "Epistle Dedicatory," *The Advancement and Reformation of Modern Poetry.* London, 1701. In *Works*, ed. Edward Niles Hooker. 2 vols. Baltimore: Johns Hopkins UP, 1939, 1:197–278.

Bysshe, Edwin. *The Art of English Poetry.* London, 1702.

Chudleigh, Lady Mary. "To Mr. Dryden," *Poems on Several Occasions.* London, 1703. In *Poems*, ed. Margaret J. M. Ezell. New York: Oxford UP, 1993.

Swift, Jonathan. *A Full and True Account of the Battel . . . Between the Antient and the Modern Books.* London, 1704. In *A Tale of a Tub*, ed. A. C. Guthkelch and D. Nichol Smith. Oxford: Clarendon Press, 1965, 211–58.

Prior, Matthew. *An Ode Humbly Presented to the Queen.* London, 1706. In *Works*, ed. H. Bunker Wright and Monroe K. Spears. 2 vols. Oxford: Clarendon Press, 1971.

Philips, Ambrose. "Preface to Pastorals," *Poetical Miscellanies: The Sixth Part.* London, 1709. Pastorals in "A Variorum Text of Four Pastorals by Ambrose Philips," ed. R. H. Griffith, Texas University Studies in English 12 (1932): 118–57.

Pope, Alexander. Pastorals, *Poetical Miscellany . . . . Sixth Part.* London, 1709. Reprinted in *Pastoral Poetry and An Essay on Criticism*, ed. E. Audra and Aubrey Williams. London: Methuen, 1961.

Evans, Able. "Six Pastorals" (ca. 1710), in *A Select Collection of Poems*, ed. John Nichols. 8 vols. London, 1782, 5:87–143.

Cooper, Anthony Ashley, Lord Shaftesbury. "Soliloquy, or Advice to an Author," *Characteristicks.* London, 1711. Ed. John M. Robertson. Indianapolis: Bobbs-Merrill, 1964, 103–234.

Addison, Joseph. *Spectator* (1711–14). Ed. Donald F. Bond. 5 vols. Oxford, Clarendon Press, 1965.

Pope, Alexander. An Essay on Criticism. London, 1711. Reprinted in *Pastoral Poetry and An Essay on Criticism*, ed. E. Audra and Aubrey Williams. London: Methuen, 1961.

Newcomb, Thomas. *Bibliotheca: A Poem.* London, 1712. Reprinted in *A Select Collection of Poems*, ed. John Nichols. 8 vols. London, 1782, 3:19–74.

Diaper, William. *Nereides: or Sea-Eclogues.* London, 1712.

Tickell, Thomas. Essays in *The Guardian* (1713). Ed. John Calhoun Stephens. Lexington: University of Kentucky, 1982.

Croxall, Samuel. *An Original Canto of Spencer: Design'd as Part of his Fairy Queen, but Never Printed.* London, 1713.

Theobald, Lewis. *The Mausoleum. A Poem. Sacred to the Memory of Her Late Majesty Queen Anne*. London, 1714.

Croxall, Samuel. *An Ode Humbly Inscrib'd to the King*. London, 1714.

Pope, Alexander. *The Rape of the Lock. An Heroi-comical Poem. In Five Canto's*. London, 1714.

Gay, John. *The Shepherd's Week*. London, 1714. Reprinted in *Poetry and Prose*, ed. Vinton A. Dearing. 2 vols. Oxford: Clarendon Press, 1974.

Hughes, John, ed. *Works of Mr. Edmund Spenser*. 6 vols. London, 1715.

Purney, Thomas. *Pastorals, After the Simple Manner of Theocritus*. London, 1717.

Pope, Alexander. "Discourse on Pastoral Poetry," *Works*. London, 1717. *Prose Works*, ed. Norman Ault. Oxford: Blackwell, 1936, 297–302.

Gildon, Charles. *The Complete Art of Poetry. In Six Parts*. London, 1718.

Ramsay, Allan. Richy and Sandy: A Pastoral on the Death of Mr. Joseph Addison. 1719.

Prior, Matthew. *Colin's Mistakes. Written in Imitation of Spenser's Style*. London, 1721.

Ramsay, Allan. *Robert, Richy, and Sandy: A Pastoral on the Death of Matthew Prior*. 1721.

Wesley, Samuel the younger. *The Battle of the Sexes. A Poem*. London, 1723.

Ramsay, Allan. *The Gentle Shepherd: a Scots Pastoral Comedy*. Edinburgh, 1725.

Pope, Alexander. "The Alley," *Miscellanies*. London, 1727.

——— *The Dunciad*. London, 1728–42.

Breval, John Durant. *Henry and Minerva. A Poem*. London, 1729.

Browne, Moses. *Piscatory Eclogues: an Essay to Introduce New Rules, and New Characters, into Pastoral*. London, 1729.

Jortin, John. *A Hymn to Harmony*. London, 1729.

Gentleman's Magazine (1731–1914).

Manning, Francis. *The British Hero, or the Vision: A Poem, Sacred to the Immortal Memory of John, Late Duke of Marlborough*. London, 1733.

Jortin, John. *Remarks on Spenser's Poems*. London, 1734.

The Muses' Library, ed. Elizabeth Cooper. London, 1737.

Shenstone, William. "The School-Mistress," *Poems Upon Various Occasions*. Oxford, 1737.

Anon. "The Apotheosis of Milton: A Vision," *Gentleman's Magazine* 8 (May 1738): 232–34.

West, Gilbert. *A Canto of the Fairy Queen. Written by Spenser. Never Before Published*. London, 1739.

Campbell, John. *The Polite Correspondence: or Rational Amusement*. London, 1741.

Akenside, Mark. *Odes on Several Subjects*. London, 1745.

Thompson, William. *Sickness: A Poem in Three Books*. London, 1745.

Warton, Thomas. *Five Pastoral Eclogues: the Scenes of Which are Supposed to Lie Among the Shepherds, Oppressed by the War in Germany*. London, 1745.

Collins, William. *Odes on Several Descriptive and Allegorical Subjects*. London, 1746. In *Poems of Gray, Collins, and Goldsmith*, ed. Roger Lonsdale. London: Longmans, 1969.

Warton, Joseph. *Odes on Various Subjects*. London, 1746.

Relph, Josiah. "Poems in the Cumberland Dialect," *A Miscellany of Poems*. Glasgow, 1747.

Spence, Joseph. *Polymetis: Or, an Enquiry Concerning the Agreement Between the Works of the Roman Poets, and the Remains of the Antient Artists*. London, 1747.

Warton, Thomas. *The Pleasures of Melancholy*. London, 1747. In *Poetical Works*, ed. Richard Mant. 2 vols. Oxford: Oxford UP, 1802, 1:68–95.

Thomson, James. *The Castle of Indolence: An Allegorical Poem. Written in Imitation of Spenser*. London, 1748.

Upton, John. *A New Canto of Spenser's Fairy Queen. Now First Published*. London, 1748.

Warton, Thomas the elder. *Poems on Several Occasions*. London, 1748.

Johnson, Samuel. *Rambler* (1750–52). Ed. W. J. Bate and Albrecht B. Strauss. 3 vols. New Haven: Yale UP, 1969.

Cooke, Thomas. *An Ode on the Powers of Poetry*. London, 1751.

West, Gilbert. *Education: A Poem in Two Cantos*. London, 1751.

Johnson, Samuel. Letter to Thomas Warton, July 16, 1754 in *The Letters of Samuel Johnson*, ed. Bruce Redford. 5 vols. Princeton: Princeton UP, 1992–94.

Warton, Thomas. *Observations on The Fairy Queen of Spenser*. London, 1754; 2 vols, 1762.

Johnson, Samuel. *A Dictionary of the English Language*. 2 vols. London, 1755.

Warton, Joseph. *An Essay on the Writings and Genius of Pope*. 2 vols. London, 1756, 1782.

Gray, Thomas. *Odes, by Mr. Gray*. Strawberry Hill, 1757. In *Poems of Gray, Collins, and Goldsmith*, ed. Roger Lonsdale. London: Longmans, 1969.

Upton, John, ed. *Spenser's Faerie Queene*. 2 vols. London, 1758. In *John Upton: Notes on the Fairy Queen*, ed. John G. Radcliffe. 2 vols. New York: Garland, 1987.

Hume, David. *History of England, Vol. IV*. London, 1759. *History of England*, ed. William B. Todd. 6 vols. Indianapolis: Liberty Classics, 1983.

Lyttelton, George. *Dialogues of the Dead*. London, 1760. Facsimile, New York: Garland, 1970.

Denton, Thomas. *The House of Superstition. A Poem*. London, 1762.

Home, Henry, Lord Kames. *Elements of Criticism*. Edinburgh, 1762.

Hurd, Richard. *Letters on Chivalry and Romance*. London, 1762.

Churchill, Charles. *The Prophecy of Famine*. London, 1763. In *Works*, ed. Douglas Grant. Oxford: Clarendon Press, 1956.

Thompson, William. "On Spenser's Faerie Queene," *The Poetical Calendar*. 12 vols. London, 1763.

Walpole, Horace. Letter to Cole, March 17, 1765. *Correspondence with The Rev. William Cole*, ed. W. S. Lewis and A. Dayle Wallace. 2 vols. New Haven: Yale UP, 1937.

Dodd, William. "Moral Pastorals," *Poems*. London, 1767.

Mickle, William Julius. *The Concubine: A Poem in Two Cantos. In the Manner of Spenser*. Oxford, 1767. Reprinted in 1777 as *Syr Martyn*.

Downman, Hugh. *The Land of the Muses: A Poem in the Manner of Spenser*. London, 1768.

Beattie, James. *The Minstrel; Or, The Progress of Genius*. London, 1771, 1774. In *Poetical Works*, ed. Alexander Dyce. London: Bell, 1894.

Millar, John. *The Origin of the Distinction of Ranks*. Edinburgh, 1771. Fourth edition, Edinburgh, 1806.

Mason, William. *The English Garden: A Poem*. London, 1772.

Fergusson, Robert. "The Farmer's Ingle," *Poems*. Edinburgh, 1773.

Lloyd, Robert. *Poetical Works*. 2 vols. London, 1774.

Warton, Thomas. *The History of English Poetry*. 3 vols. London, 1774–81.

Paine, Thomas. *Common Sense*. Philadelphia, 1776. In *Complete Writings*, ed. Philip S. Foner. 2 vols. New York: Citadel Press, 1945.

Hayley, William. *An Essay on Painting, In Two Epistles to Romney*. London, 1778.

Scott, John, of Amwell. *Moral Eclogues*. London, 1778.

Johnson, Samuel. *Lives of the Poets*. 10 vols. London, 1779–81. Ed. G. B. Hill. 3 vols. Oxford: Clarendon Press, 1905.

Bicknell, Alexander. *Prince Arthur, an Allegorical Romance*. 2 vols. London, 1779.

Hayley, William. *The Triumphs of Temper: a Poem in Six Cantos*. London, 1781.

Warton, Thomas. *Verses on Reynolds's Painted Window at New College*. Oxford, 1782. In *Poetical Works*, ed. Richard Mant. 2 vols. Oxford: 1802.

Pinkerton, John. *Letters of Literature, by Robert Heron Esq*. London, 1785.

Reeve, Clara. *The Progress of Romance*. London, 1785.

Burns, Robert. "The Cotter's Saturday Night," *Poems, Chiefly in the Scottish Dialect*. Edinburgh, 1786.

Boswell, James. *The Life of Samuel Johnson*. 2 vols. London, 1791. Ed. G. B. Hill, revised by L. F. Powell. 6 vols. Oxford: 1934–64.

Peacock, Lucy. *The Knight of the Rose*. London, 1793.

Coleridge, S. T. *Poems*. London, 1796. *Poems*, ed. Ernest Hartley Coleridge. London: Oxford UP, 1912.

Drake, Nathan. *Literary Hours or Sketches Critical and Narrative*. London, 1798.

Southey, Robert. "English Eclogues," *Poems*. Bristol, 1799.

Wordsworth, William. Preface to *Lyrical Ballads*. London, 1800. *Lyrical Ballads, 1798*, ed. W. J. B. Owen. Oxford: Oxford UP, 1969.

Knox, Vicemus, ed. *Elegant Extracts: or Useful and Entertaining Passages in Poetry*. 4 vols. London, 1805.

Spenser, Edmund. *Poetical Works*, ed. H. J. Todd. 5 vols. London, 1805.

Tighe, Mary. *Psyche, or the Legend of Love*. Privately printed, 1805. London, 1811.

Wordsworth, William. Letter to Sir Walter Scott, 1805. *The Letters of William and Dorothy Wordsworth: The Early Years, 1787–1805*. Second Edition. Ed. E. de Selincourt, revised by Chester L. Shaver. 4 vols. Oxford: Clarendon Press, 1967.

Scott, Walter. Review of Todd's *Spenser*. *Edinburgh Review* 7 (1806): 203–17.

Irving, Washington. Untitled poem, *Salmagundi; or the Whim-Whams and Opinions of Launcelot Langstaff, esq.* 2 vols. London, 1807–8. In *Works*. 27 vols. New York: Putnam's, 1880–83.

Campbell, Thomas. *Gertrude of Wyoming; a Pennsylvanian Tale*. London, 1809.

Anon. *The Village Sunday, a Poem, Moral and Descriptive, in the Manner of Spenser*. London, [1809].

Anon. Review of Tighe's *Psyche*, *Quarterly Review* 5 (1811): 471–85.

Mitford, Mary Russell. Letter to her father, 1811. *The Life of Mary Russell Mitford in a Selection from her Letters*, A. G. L'Estrange, ed. 3 vols. New York: 1870.

Anon. Review of Byron's *Childe Harold* in *British Review* 3 (1812): 275–302.

Byron, Lord. *Childe Harold's Pilgrimage: A Romaunt*. London, 1812–18.

Anon. Review of Tighe's *Psyche*, *Eclectic Review* 9 (1813): 217–29.

Reynolds, J. H. *The Eden of the Imagination. A Poem*. London, 1814.

Wordsworth, William. Preface to *Poems*. 2 vols. London, 1815. In *Literary Criticism of William Wordsworth*, ed. Paul M. Zall. Lincoln: U of Nebraska P, 1966. "Nutting" in *Poems*, ed. John O. Hayden. 2 vols. New Haven: Yale UP, 1977.

Coleridge, S. T. *Christabel; Kubla Khan: a Vision; The Pains of Sleep*. London, 1816. In *Poems*, ed. Ernest Hartley Coleridge. London: Oxford UP, 1912.

Reynolds, J. H. "Popular Poetry – Periodical Criticism," *Champion* (1816). In *Selected Prose*, ed. Leonidas M. Jones. Cambridge: Harvard UP, 1966.

–––"On Egotism in Literature," The *Champion* (1816). *Selected Prose*, ed. Leonidas M. Jones. Cambridge: Harvard UP, 1966.

Coleridge, S. T. *Biographia Literaria*. London, 1817. Ed. James Engell and W. Jackson Bate. 2 vols. Princeton: Princeton UP, 1983.

Drake, Nathan. *Shakespeare and his Times*. 2 vols. London, 1817. 1 vol. London, 1838.

Keats, John. "On first looking into Chapman's Homer," "Specimen of an Induction" in *Poems*. London, 1817. In *Poetical Works*, ed. H. W. Garrod. London: Oxford UP, 1970.

Lockhart, J. G. "The Cockney School of Poetry," *Blackwood's Edinburgh Review* 2 (1817): 38–40.

Anon. "On the Revival of a Taste for our Ancient Literature," *Blackwood's Edinburgh Magazine* 4 (December 1818): 264–66.

Hazlitt, William. *Lectures on the English Poets*. London, 1818.

Keats, John. Letter to Charles Brown, November 1818. *Letters of John Keats*, ed. Maurice Buxton Forman. London: Oxford UP, 1947.

Schlegel, Friedrich. *Lectures on the History of Literature Ancient and Modern*, translated by J. G. Lockhart. Edinburgh, 1818. London: Bell, 1889.

Campbell, Thomas. *Specimens of the British Poets*. London, 1819.

Anon. Review of Hazlitt's *Lectures on the English Poets*, *The Monthly Review* 92 (1820): 53–68.

Anon. Letter in *Talisman* (August 12, 1820): 59.

Keats, John. "Eve of Saint Agnes," *Lamia, Isabella*. London, 1820. *Poetical Works*, ed. H. W. Garrod. London: Oxford UP, 1970.

Collier, John Payne. *The Poetical Decameron, or Ten Conversations on English Poets and Poetry, Particularly of the Reigns of Elizabeth and James I*. 2 vols. Edinburgh, 1820.

Hunt, Leigh. "Among My Books," *Literary Examiner* (July 5 1823). In *Essays of Leigh Hunt*, ed. R. B. Johnson. London: Oxford UP, 1928.

Anon. Review of More, *Fables for the Holy Alliance*, *Westminster Review* 1 (1824): 18–27.

Landor, Walter Savage. *Imaginary Conversations of Literary Men and Statesmen*. 2 vols. London, 1824. In *Works*. 2 vols. London, 1846.

Spenser, Edmund. *Poetical Works*. 5 vols. London, 1825. The prefatory essay by Philip Masterman is reprinted in Spenser, *Works*, ed. Hillard, 1839.

Keble, John. Review of Condor, "Star in the East," *Quarterly Review* 32 (1825): 211–32.

Lamb, Charles. "Popular Fallacies: 'That great Wit is allied to Madness,'" *New Monthly Magazine* (May 1826). In *Works*, ed. E. V. Lucas. 7 vols. London: Methuen, 1903–5.

Neele, Henry. "Lectures on English Poetry," *The Literary Remains*. London, 1829.

Newman, John Henry. "Poetry, With References to Aristotle's Poetics," *Quarterly Review* (1829). In *Critical Essays of the Early Nineteenth Century*, ed. Raymond MacDonald Alden. New York, 1921.

Macaulay, Thomas Babington. Review of Southey's edition of *Pilgrim's Progress, Edinburgh Review* (December 1830). In *Essays and Poems.* 3 vols. New York, 1880. 1:558–70.

Scott, Walter. Review of Southey's edition of *Pilgrim's Progress, Quarterly Review* 43 (1830).

Wilson, John. Essays on Spenser *Blackwood's Edinburgh Magazine* (1833–35). "Spenser and His Critics," reprinted in *Critical Essays of the Early Nineteenth Century,* ed. Raymond MacDonald Alden. New York, Scribners, 1921.

Hunt, Leigh. "A New Gallery of Pictures," *Indicator* (1833). In *Leigh Hunt's Literary Criticism,* ed. Lawrence Huston Houtchens and Carolyn Washburn Houtchens. New York: New York UP, 1956.

Tennyson, Alfred, Lord. "The Lotos-Eaters." *Poems.* London, 1833. In *Poetical Works.* Oxford: Oxford UP, 1953.

Anon. *Holiness; or The Legend of St. George: a Tale from Spenser's Faerie Queene, by A Mother.* Boston, 1836.

Coleridge, S. T. Lecture Notes, *Literary Remains,* ed. H. N. Coleridge. 4 vols. London, 1836–39.

Hallam, Henry. *Introduction to the Literature of Europe in the Fifteenth, Sixteenth, and Seventeenth Centuries.* 4 vols. London, 1837–39.

John Gibson Lockhart. *Memoirs of the Life of Sir Walter Scott.* 7 vols. 1837–38. 5 vols. Boston: Houghton Mifflin, 1901.

Spenser, Edmund. *Poetical Works,* ed. G. S. Hillard. 5 vols. Boston, 1839.

Dwight, J. S. Review of Hillard's edition of Spenser, *Christian Examiner* 28 (1840): 208–23.

Cleveland, H. K. Review of Hillard's edition of Spenser, *North American Review* 50 (1840): 174–206.

Hunt, Leigh. *Imagination and Fancy; or Selections from the English Poets.* London, 1840.

Shelley, Percy Bysshe. "A Defense of Poetry, *Works,* ed. Mary Shelley. 2 vols. London, 1840. In *Shelley's Prose,* ed. David Lee Clark. Albuquerque: U of New Mexico P, 1954.

Spenser, Edmund. *Works, with Observations on his Life and Writings* [by J. C.]. London, 1840. New edition, Philadelphia, 1857.

Browning, Elizabeth Barrett. *Poems.* 2 vols. London, 1844; ed. Charlotte Porter and Helen A. Clarke, 6 vols. New York: Crowell, 1900.

Craik, George L. *Sketches of the History of Literature and Learning in England from the Norman Conquest to the Accession of Elizabeth.* 6 vols. London, 1844–45.

Keble, John. *Praelectiones poeticae.* London, 1844. *Keble's Lectures on Poetry, 1832–1841,* translated by Edward Kershaw Francis. 2 vols. Oxford: Oxford UP, 1912.

George L. Craik. *Spenser, and his Poetry.* 3 vols. London, 1845.

Landor, Walter Savage. "Essex and Spenser," *Works*. 2 vols. London, 1848.

Hart, John S. *An Essay on the Life and Writings of Edmund Spenser, with A Special Exposition of The Fairy Queen*. New York, 1847.

Howitt, William. "Edmund Spenser," *Homes and Haunts of the Most Eminent British Poets*. New York: Harper, 1847.

Cleveland, Charles D. *A Compendium of English Literature*. Philadelphia, 1848.

Shaw, Thomas B. *Outlines of English Literature*. London, 1848; reprinted as *Shaw's New History of English Literature; Together with a History of English Literature in America*, ed. Truman J. Backus. New York: Sheldon and Company, 1884.

Bathurst, Charles. "The Poetical Triumvirate: Spenser, Shakespeare, Milton. *Poems*. London, 1849.

Halpin, Nathaniel. "On Certain Passages in the Life of Edmund Spenser," *Proceedings of the Royal Irish Academy* 4 (1850): 445–51.

Ruskin, John. "Theology of Spenser," *The Stones of Venice*. 3 vols. London, 1851–53.

Masson, David. "Theories of Poetry," *North British Review* (1853). In *Essays, Biographical and Critical, Chiefly on English Poets*. Cambridge, 1856.

Spenser, Edmund. *Poetical Works*, ed. F. H. Child. 5 vols. Boston, 1855.

Kingsley, Charles. *Westward Ho!* London, 1855. In *Works*. 28 vols. London: Macmillan, 1880–85.

Hunt, Leigh. "English Poetry versus Cardinal Wiseman," *Fraser's Magazine* 60 (1856): 747–66.

Knight, Charles. *A Popular History of England*. 8 vols. London, 1856–62.

Wiseman, Cardinal Nicholas Patrick Stephen. *On the Perception of Natural Beauty by the Ancients and the Moderns: Two Lectures*. London, 1856.

MacDonald, George. *Phantastes: A Faerie Romance for Men and Women*. London, 1858.

Taine, Hippolyte. *History of English Literature* [1863], translated by H. Van Laun. 2 vols., Edinburgh, 1871. 4 vols., Edinburgh, 1873–74.

Collier, John Payne. *A Bibliographical and Critical Account of the Rarest Books in the English Language*. 4 vols. London, 1866.

Craik, George L. *A Compendious History of English Literature, and of the English Language, from the Norman Conquest, with Numerous Specimens*. 2 vols. London: 1866; New York, 1877.

Manning, Anne. "Immeritus Redivivus," *The Masque at Ludlow and Other Romanesques*. London: Sampson, Low, and Son, 1866, 1–96.

Kitchin, G. W. ed. *Spenser: Faerie Queene, Book I*. Oxford: Clarendon Press, 1867.

Mitford, Mary Russell. *The Life of Mary Russell Mitford in a Selection from Her Letters,* ed. A. G. L'Estrange. 3 vols. New York: 1870.

Maurice, John Frederick Denison. *Friendship of Books and Other Lectures*, ed. Thomas Hughes. London, 1874.

Lowell, James Russell. "Spenser," *North American Review* (1875). In *Among My Books*. 2 vols. Boston: Houghton Mifflin, 1889, 2:125–200.

Green, J. R. *A History of the English People*. 4 vols. London, 1877–80.

Church, R. W. *Spenser* ["English Men of Letters."] London, 1879.

Dowden, Edward. "Heroines of Spenser," *Cornhill* 39 (1879): 663–80.

Gallwey, T. "Spenser in his Relations with Ireland," *Monitor* 2 (1879): 19–27.

Arnold, Thomas. "Spenser as a Textbook," *Dublin Review* S3, 4 (1880): 321–32.

De Vere, Aubrey. "Characteristics of Spenser's Poetry," Edmund Spenser, *Complete Works*, ed. A. B. Grosart. 10 vols. London: privately printed, 1882–84.

Dowden, Edward. "Spenser, the Poet and Teacher," Edmund Spenser, *Complete Works*, ed. A. B. Grosart. 10 vols. London: privately printed, 1882–84. Reprinted in *Transcripts and Studies*. London, 1888, 1896.

Grosart, A. B. Life of Spenser, Edmund Spenser, *Complete Works*, ed. A. B. Grosart. 10 vols. London: privately printed, 1882–84.

Towry, M. H. *Spenser for Children*. London: Chatto and Windus, 1885.

Heroines of the Poets: Drawings by Fernand Lyngren. Boston: D. L. Throp, 1886.

Maclehose, Sophia H. *Tales from Spenser*. Glasgow: James Maclehose, 1892.

Phelps, William Lyon. *The Beginnings of the English Romantic Movement*. Boston: Ginn, 1893.

Ely, Gertrude H. "Spenser," *Chaucer, Spenser, Sidney*. New York: Kellogg, 1894, 37–76.

Courthope, William John. *A History of English Poetry*. 6 vols. London: Macmillan, 1895–1910.

Jusserand, Jean J. *A Literary History of the English People* [1894]. London: Unwin, 1895. 3 vols, 1907, 1925.

Scudder, Vida D. *The Life of the Spirit in the Modern English Poets*. Boston: Houghton Mifflin, 1895.

Spenser, Edmund. *Epithalamion, with Illustrations by G. W. Edwards*. New York, 1895.

Spenser, Edmund. *The Shepheardes Calender*. Illustrated by A. J. Gaskin. Kelmscott, 1896.

Litchfield, Mary E. *Spenser's Britomart*. Boston: Ginn, 1896.

Macleod, Mary. *Stories from the Faerie Queene*. London, 1897.

Spenser, Edmund. *The Faerie Queene and Epithalamion*. Illustrated by L. Fairfax Muckley. London, 1897.

——— *The Shepheardes Calender*. Illustrated by Walter Crane. London, 1897.

Scudder, Vida D. *Social Ideals in English Letters*. Boston: Houghton Mifflin, 1898.

Beers, Henry A. *A History of English Romanticism in the Eighteenth Century*. New York: Henry Holt, 1899.

Thomson, Clara L. *Tales from the Faerie Queene*. London: Horace Marshall, [1902].

Moody, William Vaughan. *A History of English Literature*. New York, 1902. Many later editions.

Beale, Dorothea. "Britomart, or Spenser's Ideal of Woman," *Literary Studies of Poems, Old and New*. London, 1902, 25–51.

Royde-Smith, N. G. *Una and the Red Cross Knight*. London, 1905.

Woodberry, George Edward. *The Torch: Eight Lectures on Race Power in Literature Delivered Before the Lowell Institute of Boston MCMIII*. New York: McClure, 1905.

Wilson, C. D. *The Faerie Queene, Book I, Rewritten in Simple Language*. Chicago, 1906.

Yeats, W. B, ed. *The Poems of Spenser Selected and with an Introduction by W. B. Yeats*. London, 1906. The introduction reprinted in *Essays and Introductions*. New York: Collier, 1961, 256–83.

Courthope, W. J. "The Poetry of Spenser," *The Cambridge History of English Literature*. Vol. 3. New York: Putnam, 1909, 239–80.

Spenser, Edmund. *Poetical Works*, ed. J. C. Smith and E. de Selincourt. 3 vols. Oxford: Clarendon Press, 1909–10.

Grace, R. W. *Tales from Spenser*. London, 1909.

Dawson, L. H. *Stories from the Faerie Queene*. London, 1910.

Cory, Herbert E. *The Critics of Edmund Spenser*. University of California Publications in Modern Philology, 1911.

———"Spenser, Thomson, and Romanticism," *PMLA* 26 (1911): 51–91.

Underdown, Emily. *Gateway to Spenser*. London, 1911.

Greenlaw, Edwin. "The Shepheards Calender," *PMLA* 26 (1911): 419–51.

———*A Syllabus of English Literature*. Chicago: Sanborn, 1912.

Baskervill, C. R. "The Early Fame of the Shepheards Calender," *PMLA* 28 (1913): 291–313.

Durrant, William Scott. *The Red Cross Knight: Scenes from Spenser's Faerie Queene*. London: Year Book Press, 1913.

Harman, Edward G. *Edmund Spenser and the Impersonations of Francis Bacon*. London, 1914.

Greenlaw, Edwin. *An Outline of the Literature of the English Renaissance*. Chicago: Sanborn, 1916.

Cory, Herbert E. *The Critics of Edmund Spenser*. Berkeley: U of California P, 1917.

Peck, H. W. "Spenser's *Faerie Queene* and the Student of To-Day," *Sewanee Review* 24 (1916): 340–52.

Hinchman, Walter S. *A History of English and American Literature*. New York, 1918.

Greenlaw, Edwin and James Holly Hanford. *The Great Tradition: A Book of Selections from English and American Prose and Poetry, Illustrating the National Ideals of Freedom, Faith, and Conduct*. Chicago: Scott, Foresman, 1919.

Greenlaw, Edwin, William Elson, Christine Keck, eds. *Literature and Life*. 4 vols. Chicago: Scott, Foresman, 1922–24.

Havens, Raymond Dexter. *The Influence of Milton on English Poetry*. Cambridge: Harvard UP, 1922.

Carpenter, Frederic Ives. *A Reference Guide to Edmund Spenser*. Chicago: U of Chicago P, 1923.

DeMaar, Harko G. *A History of Modern English Romanticism*. London: Oxford UP, 1924.

Renwick, W. L. *Edmund Spenser: An Essay on Renaissance Poetry*. London: Arnold, 1925.

Foerster, Norman. *The American Scholar: A Study in Litterae Inhumaniores*. Chapel Hill: U of North Carolina P, 1929.

Spenser, Edmund. *Works*, ed. R. L. Renwick. 8 vols. Oxford: Clarendon Press, 1930–32.

Greenlaw, Edwin. *The Province of Literary History*. Baltimore: Johns Hopkins UP, 1931.

Eliot, T. S. *Selected Essays, 1917–1932*. New York: Harcourt, Brace, 1932.

Greenlaw, Edwin. *Studies in Spenser's Historical Allegory*. Baltimore: Johns Hopkins UP, 1932.

Greenlaw, Edwin, Charles Grosvenor Osgood, Frederick Morgan Padelford, Roy Heffner, eds. *The Works of Edmund Spenser: A Variorum Edition*. 12 vols. Baltimore: Johns Hopkins UP, 1932–55.

Davis, B. E. C. *Edmund Spenser: A Critical Study*. Cambridge: Cambridge UP, 1933.

Renwick, W. L. Review of the Hopkins *Works of Edmund Spenser*, *Modern Language Review* 28 (1933): 508–11.

Townsend, Atwood H. *Student's Guide to Good Reading: A List of Six Hundred Books Which are Enjoyable, Well Worth Reading, and Inexpensive*. NP, 1933.

Williams, Charles. *Reason and Beauty in the Poetic Mind*. Oxford: Clarendon Press, 1933.

Boswell, James. *The Life of Samuel Johnson*, ed G. B. Hill, revised by L. F. Powell. 6 vols. Oxford: 1934–64.

Spens, Janet. *Spenser's Faerie Queene: An Interpretation*. London: Arnold, 1934.

Bradford, Gamaliel. "Women of the *Fairy Queen*," in *Elizabethan Women*, ed. Harold O. White. Cambridge: Riverside Press, 1936, 207–26.

Leavis, F. R. *Revaluation, Tradition and Development in English Poetry*. London: Chatto and Windus, 1936.

Lewis, C. S. *The Allegory of Love: A Study in Medieval Tradition*. Oxford: Clarendon Press, 1936.

Tate, Allen. "Three Types of Poetry," *Reactionary Essays on Poetry and Ideas*. New York, 1936, 83–112.

Traversi, D. A. "Revaluation (X): *The Vision of Piers Plowman*," *Scrutiny* 5 (1936): 276–91.

Potter, Stephen. *The Muse in Chains: A Study in Education*. London: Jonathan Cape, 1937.

Walpole, Horace. *Correspondence with The Rev. William Cole*, ed. W. S. Lewis and A. Dayle Wallace. 2 vols. New Haven: Yale UP, 1937.

Brooks, Cleanth. *Modern Poetry and the Tradition*. Chapel Hill: U of North Carolina P, 1939.

Shenstone, William. *The Letters of William Shenstone, Arranged and Edited with Introduction, Notes, and Index, by Marjorie Williams*. Oxford: Blackwell, 1939.

Adler, Mortimer J. *How to Read a Book: The Art of Getting a Liberal Education*. New York: Simon and Schuster, 1940.

Gallaway, Francis. *Reason, Rule, and Revolt in English Classicism*. New York: Scribners, 1940.

Walter, J. H. "*The Faerie Queene*: Alterations and Structure," *Modern Language Review* 36 (1941): 37–58.

Bennet, Josephine Waters. *The Evolution of the Faerie Queene*. Chicago: U of Chicago P, 1942.

Keats, John. *Letters of John Keats*, ed. Maurice Buxton Forman. London: Oxford UP, 1947.

Tuve, Rosemond. *Elizabethan and Metaphysical Imagery: Renaissance Poetic and Twentieth-Century Critics*. Chicago: U of Chicago P, 1947.

Wasserman, Earl R. *Elizabethan Poetry in the Eighteenth Century*. Urbana: U of Illinois P, 1947.

Woolf, Virginia. "The Faery Queene," *The Moment and Other Essays*. London: Harcourt Brace, 1947, 25–29.

Hughes, Merritt Y. "Spenser, 1552–1952," *Transactions of the Wisconsin Academy* 42 (1953): 5–24.

Winters, Yvor. "Problems for the Modern Critic of Literature," *Hudson Review* 9 (1956): 325–86. Reprinted in *The Function of Criticism: Problems and Exercises*. Denver: Alan Swallow, 1957, 9–78.

Berger, Harry Jr. *The Allegorical Temper*. New Haven: Yale UP, 1957.

Ellrodt, Robert. *Neoplatonism in the Poetry of Spenser*. Geneva: Library Droz, 1960.

Hamilton, A. C. *The Structure of Allegory in The Faerie Queene*. Oxford: Clarendon Press, 1961.

McLane, Paul E. *Spenser's Shepheardes Calender: A Study in Elizabethan Allegory*. Notre Dame: U of Notre Dame P, 1961.

Frye, Northrup. "The Structure of Imagery in The Faerie Queene," *Fables of Identity: Studies in Poetic Mythology*. New York: Harcourt, Brace, & World, 1963, 69–87.

Wertheim, Lee Hilles. *The Faerie Queene: Canto by Canto Analysis with Critical Commentary*. New York: Study Master, 1963.

Grace, William J. *The Faerie Queene and Other Works by Spenser*. New York: Monarch Notes, 1963.

Neuville, H. Richmond Jr. *Spenser's The Faerie Queene*. New York: Bar-Notes, 1966.

Lewis, C. S. *Spenser's Images of Life*, ed. Alastair Fowler. Cambridge: Cambridge UP, 1967.

Wordsworth, William. *The Letters of William and Dorothy Wordsworth: Second Edition*. Ed. E. de Selincourt and Chester L. Shaver. 4 vols. Oxford: Clarendon Press, 1967.

Myers, Catherine R. *Edmund Spenser: The Faerie Queene*. New York: Barnes & Noble Book Notes, 1968.

Priest, Harold M. *The Faerie Queene*. Lincoln: Cliffs Notes, 1968.

Fletcher, Angus. *The Prophetic Moment: An Essay on Spenser*. Chicago: U of Chicago P, 1971.

Vondersmith, Bernard J. "A History of the Criticism of the *Faerie Queene*, 1910–1947." Ph.D. diss., Duquesne University, 1971.

Hamilton, A. C. "On Annotating Spenser's Faerie Queene: A New Approach to the Poem," *Contemporary Thought on Edmund Spenser*, ed. Richard C. Frushell and Bernard J. Vondersmith. Carbondale and Edwardsville: Southern Illinois UP, 1975, 41–60.

Heninger, S. K. "The Aesthetic Experience of Reading Spenser," in *Contemporary Thought on Edmund Spenser*, ed. Richard C. Frushell and Bernard J. Vondersmith. Carbondale and Edwardsville: Southern Illinois UP, 1975, 79–98.

Wittreich, Joseph Anthony Jr., ed. *Milton and the Line of Vision*. Madison: U of Wisconsin P, 1975.

MacCaffrey, Isabel. *Spenser's Allegory: The Anatomy of Imagination*. Princeton: Princeton UP, 1976.

Nohrnberg, James. *The Analogy of the Faerie Queene*. Princeton: Princeton UP, 1976.

Spenser, Edmund. *The Faerie Queene*, ed. A. C. Hamilton. London: Longmans, 1977.

Montrose, Louis. "'Eliza, Queene of shepheardes,' and the Pastoral of Power," *English Literary Renaissance* 10 (1980): 153–82.

Goldberg, Jonathan. *Endlesse Worke: Spenser and the Structures of Discourse*. Baltimore: Johns Hopkins UP, 1981.

Greenblatt, Stephen. "Murdering Peasants: Status, Genre, and The Representation of Rebellion," *Representations* 1 (1983): 1–29.

Helgerson, Richard. *Self-Crowned Laureates: Spenser, Jonson, Milton, and the Literary System.* Berkeley: U of California P, 1983.

Quilligan, Maureen. *Milton's Spenser: The Politics of Reading.* Ithaca: Cornell UP, 1983.

Sipple, William L. *Edmund Spenser 1900–1936: A Reference Guide.* Boston: G. K. Hall, 1984.

Tompkins, Jane. "Masterpiece Theater: The Politics of Hawthorne's Literary Reputation," *Sensational Designs: The Cultural Work of American Fiction, 1790–1860.* New York: Oxford UP, 1985, 3–39.

Wellek, René. *A History of Modern Criticism, 1750–1950.* Vol. 5. *English Criticism, 1900–1950.* New Haven, Yale UP, 1986.

————*A History of Modern Criticism, 1750–1950.* Vol. 6. *American Criticism, 1900–1950.* New Haven, Yale UP, 1986.

Johnson, Samuel. *The Letters of Samuel Johnson,* ed. Bruce Redford. 5 vols. Princeton: Princeton UP, 1992–94.

Selected Studies of Spenser's Reception and Influence

Anon. "MS Notes to Spenser's 'Faerie Queen,'" *Notes and Queries* 202 (1957): 509–15.

Aldrich, Earl A. "James Beattie's Minstrel: Its Sources and Its Influence on English Romantic Poets." Ph.D. diss., Harvard University, 1927.

Atkinson, Dorothy F. *Edmund Spenser: A Bibliographic Supplement.* Baltimore: Johns Hopkins UP, 1937.

————"A Note on Spenser and Painting," *Modern Language Notes* 58 (1943): 57–58.

Baker, Carlos Heard. "Spenser, the Eighteenth Century, and Shelley's Queen Mab," *Modern Language Quarterly* 2 (1941): 81–98.

Baskerville, C. R. "The Early Fame of 'The Shepheards Calender,'" *PMLA* 28 (1913): 291–313.

Beatty, Elsie. "The Criticism of Spenser During the Eighteenth Century." Master's thesis, University of Illinois, 1925.

Beers, Henry Augustus. *A History of English Romanticism in the Eighteenth Century.* New York: Henry Holt, 1899.

Bell, Edna F. "Imitations of Spenser from 1706 to 1774." Master's thesis, University of Oklahoma, 1928.

Böhme, Traugott. *Spenser's literarisches Nachleben bis zu Shelley.* Berlin: Mayer & Muller, 1911.

Bouchier, Jonathan. "The Spenserian Stanza," *Notes and Queries,* 7th Series 3 (1887): 409, 525; 4 (1887): 137–38.

Bradner, Leicester. "The Latin Translations of Spenser's *Shepheardes Calender,*" *Modern Philology* 33 (1935): 21–26.

Bragg, Marion K. *The Formal Eclogue in Eighteenth-Century England.* Orono: U of Maine P, 1926.

Brinkley, Roberta Florence. *Arthurian Legend in the Seventeenth Century.* Baltimore: Johns Hopkins UP, 1932.

Brown, Peter Franklin. "The Influence of Edmund Spenser on the British Romantic Poets, 1800–1840." Master's thesis, University of Chicago, 1905.

Burgholzer, Sister Carolyn. "Edmund Spenser's The Faerie Queene: A History of Criticism, 1948–68. Ph.D. diss., Duquesne University, 1970.

Bush, Douglas. "Some Allusions to Spenser," *Modern Language Notes* 47 (1927): 314–16.

———"Marlowe and Spenser," *TLS* (January 1, 1938): 12.

Bushnell, Nelson Sherwin. "The Style of Keats's Spenserian Stanzas, Sonnets, and Odes." Ph.D. diss., Harvard University, 1927.

Campbell, Jeannette H. "The Influence of 'The Shepheardes Calender' upon the Formal Pastoral of the Period 1579–1602." Master's thesis, University of Chicago, 1928.

Carpenter, Frederic Ives. "Spenser's Cave of Despair, An Essay in Literary Comparison," *Modern Language Notes* 12 (1897): 257–73.

———*A Reference Guide to Edmund Spenser.* Chicago: U of Chicago P, 1923.

Case, Robert H. *English Epithalamies.* London: John Lane, 1896.

Congleton, James Edmund. *Theories of Pastoral Poetry in England 1684–1798.* Gainesville: U of Florida P, 1952.

Corson, Hiram. *A Primer of English Verse, Chiefly in Its Aesthetic and Organic Character.* Boston: Ginn, 1892.

Cory, Herbert E. "The Influence of Spenser on English Poetry from 1579 to the Death of Keats." Ph.D. diss., Harvard University, 1910.

———"The Golden Age of Spenserian Pastoral," *PMLA* 25 (1910): 241–67.

———"Browne's 'Britannia's Pastorals' and Spenser's 'Faerie Queene,'" *University of California Chronicle* 13 (1911): 189–200.

———*The Critics of Edmund Spenser.* University of California Publications in Modern Philology, 1911.

———"Spenser, Thomson, and Romanticism," *PMLA* 26 (1911): 51–91.

———"Spenser, The School of the Fletchers, and Milton," *University of California Publications in Modern Philology* 2 (1912): 311–73.

———*The Critics of Edmund Spenser.* Berkeley: U of California P, 1917.

Covington, F. F., Jr. "An Early Seventeenth-Century Criticism of Spenser," *Modern Language Notes* 41 (1926): 386–87.

Crane, Ronald S. "Imitation of Spenser and Milton in the Early Eighteenth Century," *Studies in Philology* 15 (1918): 195–206.

Cullen, Patrick. *The Infernal Triad: The Flesh, the World, and the Devil in Spenser and Milton.* Princeton: Princeton UP, 1974.

Cummings, R. M, ed. *Spenser, The Critical Heritage.* New York: Barnes and Noble, 1971.

Davies, Phillips G. "A Check List of Poems, 1595 to 1833, Entirely or Partly Written in the Spenserian Stanza," *Bulletin of the New York Public Library* 77 (1974): 314–28.

DeMaar, Harko Gerrit. *A History of Modern English Romanticism. Vol. 1. Elizabethan and Modern Romanticism in the Eighteenth Century.* New York: Oxford UP, 1924.

Dees, Jerome. "The Narrator's Voice in The Faerie Queene, Christs Victorie, and Triumph, and The Locusts, or Apollyonists." Ph.D. diss., University of Illinois, 1968.

Dodds, M. H. "Chaucer: Spenser: Milton in Drama and Fiction," *Notes and Queries* 176 (1939): 69.

Donow, Herbert S. *The Sonnet in England and America: A Bibliography of Criticism.* Westport: Greenwood Press, 1982.

Dryfus, Norman J. "Eighteenth-Century Criticism of Spenser." Ph.D. diss., Johns Hopkins University, 1938.

Emerson, Francis Willard. "The Spenser-Followers in Leigh Hunt's Chaucer," *Notes and Queries* 213 (1958): 284–86.

Evett, David Hal. "Nineteenth-Century Criticism of Spenser." Ph.D. diss., Harvard University, 1965.

Fowler, Alastair. "Oxford and London Marginalia to 'The Faerie Queene,'" *Notes and Queries* 206 (November 1961): 416–19.

Fox, Alice. "'What Right Have I, a Woman?' Virginia Woolf's Reading Notes on Sidney and Spenser," in *Virginia Woolf: Centennial Essays,* ed. Elaine K. Ginsberg and Laura Moss Gottlieb. Troy, N.Y.: Whitson, 1983.

French, J. Milton. "Lamb and Spenser," *Studies in Philology* 30 (1933): 205–07.

Frushell, Richard C. "Spenser and the Eighteenth-Century Schools," *Spenser Studies* 7 (1986): 175–98.

Frushell, Richard C. and Bernard J. Vondersmith, eds. *Contemporary Thought on Edmund Spenser, With a Bibliography of Criticism of the Faerie Queene, 1900–1970.* Carbondale: Southern Illinois UP, 1975.

Fujii, Haruhiko. "Lycidas and Spenser's Pastorals," *SEL* 19 (1972): 34–50.

Fulton, Edward. "Spenser and Romanticism," *Nation* 92 (1911): 445.

Gleckner, Robert F. *Blake's Prelude: Poetical Sketches.* Baltimore, Johns Hopkins UP, 1982.

———*Blake and Spenser.* Baltimore: Johns Hopkins UP, 1985.

Godschalk, W. L. "Prior's Copy of Spenser's Works, 1679," *Papers of the Bibliographical Society of America* 61 (1967): 52–55.

Good, John Walter. *Studies in the Milton Tradition*. Urbana: *University of Illinois Studies in Languages and Literature*; 1915. New York: AMS Press, 1971.

Greenlaw, Edwin. "Shakespeare's Pastorals," *Studies in Philology* 13 (1916): 122–54.

———"Spenser's Influence on Paradise Lost," *Studies in Philology* 17 (1920): 320–59.

Greg, Walter W. *Pastoral Poetry & Pastoral Drama: A Literary Inquiry, with Special Reference to the Pre-Restoration Stage in England*. London: Bullen, 1906.

Groom, Bernard. *The Diction of Poetry From Spenser to Bridges*. Toronto: U of Toronto P, 1966.

Grundy, Joan. *The Spenserian Poets: A Study in Elizabethan and Jacobean Poetry*. London: Edwin Arnold, 1969.

Guillory, John. *Poetic Authority: Spenser, Milton, and Literary History*. New York: Columbia UP, 1983.

Haller, William. *The Early Life of Robert Southey: 1774–1803*. New York: Columbia UP, 1917. New York: Octagon House, 1966.

Hamilton, A. C., general editor. *The Spenser Encyclopedia*. Toronto: U of Toronto P, 1990.

Hard, Frederick. "Lamb on Spenser," *Studies in Philology* 28 (1931): 124–38.

———"Lamb on Spenser Again," *Studies in Philology* 30 (1933): 533–34.

———"Two Spenserian Imitations by 'T. W.,'" *ELH* 5 (1938): 113–26.

Harris, Robert Brice. "The Beast in English Satire from Spenser to John Gay." Ph.D. diss., Harvard University, 1930.

Harrison, Thomas. P. "Spenser and Shelley's Adonais," *University of Texas Studies in English* 13 (1933): 54–63.

Harrison, Thomas P. "Jonson's The Sad Shepherd and Spenser," *Modern Language Notes* 58 (1943): 257–62.

Havens, Raymond Dexter. *The Influence of Milton on English Poetry*. Cambridge: Harvard UP, 1922.

Heffner, Ray. "The Printing of John Hughes's Edition of Spenser, 1715," *Modern Language Notes* 50 (March 1935): 151–53.

Hendricks, Ira K. "The Use of the Spenserian Stanza before 1798." Master's thesis, Stanford University, 1926.

Hieatt, A. Kent. *Chaucer, Spenser, Milton*. Montreal: McGill-Queen's UP, 1975.

Hoffman, Arthur W. "Spenser and The Rape of the Lock," *Philological Quarterly* 49 (1970): 530–46.

Hook, Julius Nicholas. "Three Imitations of Spenser," *Modern Language Notes* 55 (June 1940): 431–32.

———"Eighteenth-Century Imitations of Spenser." Ph.D. diss., University of Illinois, 1941.

Hudson, Hoyt H. "John Hepwith's Spenserian Satire upon Buckingham: With Some Jacobean Analogues," *Huntington Library Bulletin* 6 (1934): 39–71.

Huckaby, Calvin. *John Milton: An Annotated Bibliography, 1929–1968.* Pittsburgh: Duquesne UP, 1969.

Hunter, William B. *The English Spenserians: The Poetry of Giles Fletcher, George Wither, Michael Drayton, Phineas Fletcher and Henry More.* Salt Lake City: U of Utah P, 1977.

Irving, William Henry. "An Imitation of the Faerie Queene," *Modern Language Notes* 43 (1928): 80.

Jones, Frederick L. "Shelley and Spenser," *Studies in Philology* 39 (1942): 662–69.

Jones, Mabel Laverne. "Recent Interest in Edmund Spenser (1910–1930)." Master's thesis, University of Oklahoma, 1930.

Jones, Richard F. "Eclogue Types in English Poetry of the Eighteenth Century," *JEGP* 24 (1925): 33–60.

Judson, Alexander C. "Samuel Woodford and Edmund Spenser," *Notes and Queries* (November 3 1945): 191–92.

———"The Seventeenth-Century Lives of Edmund Spenser," *Huntington Library Quarterly* 10 (1946): 35–48.

———"The Eighteenth-Century Lives of Edmund Spenser," *Huntington Library Quarterly* 16 (1952–53): 161–81.

Kastor, Frank S. *Giles and Phineas Fletcher.* Boston: Twayne, 1978.

Kennedy, William Sloane. "Tennyson and Other Debtors to Spenser's Faerie Queene," *Poet Lore* 10 (1898): 492–506.

King, Everard H. *James Beattie.* Boston: Twayne, 1977.

Klein, Joan Larson. "Some Spenserian Influences on Milton's Comus," *Annuale Mediaevale* 5 (1964): 27–47.

Klemp, P. J., ed. Samuel Sheppard, *The Faerie King Fashioning Love and Honour.* Salzburg, Austria: Institut fur Anglistik und Amerikanistik, Universität Salzburg, 1984.

Koller, Katherine. "Abraham Fraunce and Edmund Spenser," *ELH* 7 (1940): 108–20.

Kucich, Greg. "Leigh Hunt and Romantic Spenserianism," *Keats-Shelley Journal* 37 (1988): 110–35.

———*Keats, Shelley, & Romantic Spenserianism.* University Park: Pennsylvania State UP, 1991.

Langdale, Abram Barnett. *Phineas Fletcher, Man of Letters, Science, and Divinity.* New York: Columbia UP, 1937.

Lavender, Andrew. "An Edition of Ralph Knevett's Supplement of the Faerie Queene (1635)." Ph.D. diss., New York University, 1958.

Lemmi, Charles W. "The Serpent and the Eagle in Spenser and Shelley," *Modern Language Notes* 50 (March 1935): 165–68.

Lievsay, John. "Braggadocchio: Spenser's Legacy to the Character-Writers," *Modern Language Quarterly* 2 (1941): 475–85.

———"Spenser in Low Company," *Shakespeare Association Bulletin* 19 (1944): 186–89.

McNeir, Waldo F., and Foster Provost. *An Annotated Bibliography of Edmund Spenser.* New York: Columbia UP, 1961.

Markland, Murray F. "A Note on Spenser and the Scottish Sonneteers," *Studies in Scottish Literature* 1 (1963): 136–40.

Marsh, George L. "Imitation and Influence of Spenser in English Poetry from 1765–1800." Master's thesis, University of Chicago, 1899.

Maxwell, J. C. "Milton in Wordsworth's Praise of Spenser," *Notes and Queries* NS 15 (1968): 22–23.

McCown, Gary Mason. "The Epithalamium in the English Renaissance." Ph.D. diss., University of North Carolina, 1968.

McKillop, Alan Dugald. *James Thomson: The Castle of Indolence and Other Poems.* Lawrence: U of Kansas P, 1961.

———"Some details of the Sonnet Revival," *Modern Language Notes* 39 (1924): 438–40.

Miller, Paul W. "The Decline of the English Epithalamion," *Texas Studies in Language and Literature* 12 (1970): 405–16.

Millican, C. Bowie. "Ralph Knevett, Author of the Supplement to Spenser's Faerie Queene," *Review of English Studies* 14 (1938): 44–52.

Monro, John. "Spenser Allusions 1637–1709," *Notes and Queries* 118 (1908): 121.

Moorman, F. W. *William Browne and the Pastoral Poetry of the Elizabethan Age.* Strassburg: Trubner, 1897.

Morris, Harry. *Richard Barnfield, Colin's Child.* Tallahassee: Florida State UP, 1963.

Morton, Edward Payson. "The Spenserian Stanza before 1700," *Modern Philology* 4 (1907): 1–16.

———"The Spenserian Stanza in the Eighteenth-Century," *Modern Philology* 10 (1913): 1–27.

Mounts, Charles E. "The Influence of Spenser on Wordsworth and Coleridge." Ph.D. diss., Duke University, 1941.

———"The Place of Chaucer and Spenser in the Genesis of Peter Bell," *Philological Quarterly* (1944): 108–15.

———"Coleridge's Self-Identification with Spenserian Characters," *Studies in Philology* 47 (1950): 522–33.

Muir, Kenneth. "Locrine and Selimus," *TLS* (August 12, 1944): 391.

Neuse, Richard. "The Virgilian Triad Revisited," *Journal of English Literary History* 45 (1978): 606–39.

Osgood, Charles G. "Epithalamion and Prothalamion: 'and theyr eccho ring,'" *Modern Language Notes* 76 (1961): 205–8.

Packard, Faith E. "Spenser's Influence on the Pictorial Landscape of Certain Eighteenth-Century Poets." Master's thesis, Wellesley College, 1931.

Padelford, Frederick M. "Robert Aylett," *Huntington Library Bulletin* 10 (1936): 1–48.

———"E. W. His Thameseidos," *Shakespeare Association Bulletin* 12 (1937): 69–76.

———"Anthony Copley's A Fig for Fortune: A Roman Catholic Legend of Holiness," *Modern Language Quarterly* 3 (1942): 525–33.

Parker, Patricia. "The Progress of Phaedria's Bower: Spenser to Coleridge," *ELH* 40 (1973): 372–97.

Phelps, William Lyon. *The Beginnings of the English Romantic Movement.* Boston: Ginn, 1893.

Pierce, Majorie Brand. "The Allusions to Spenser up to 1650." Master's thesis, University of Chicago, 1927.

Pitts, George Richard. "Romantic Spenserianism: *The Faerie Queene* and the English Romantics." Ph.D. diss., University of Pennsylvania, 1977.

Potts, Abbie Findlay. "The Spenserian and Miltonic Influence in Wordsworth's 'Ode' and 'Rainbow,'" *Studies in Philology* 29 (1932): 607–16.

Prettyman, Virginia F. "Shenstone's Reading of Spenser," *The Age of Johnson: Essays Presented to Chauncey Brewster Tinker,* ed. Frederick W. Hilles. New Haven: Yale UP, 1949, 227–37.

Quilligan, Maureen. *Milton's Spenser: The Politics of Reading.* Ithaca: Cornell UP, 1983.

Radcliffe, John G. *John Upton: Notes on the Fairy Queen.* 2 vols. New York: Garland, 1987.

Reaney, James. "The Influence of Spenser on Yeats." Ph.D. diss., University of Toronto, 1958.

Reschke, Hedwig. *Die Spenserstanze im neunzehnten Jahrhundert.* Heidelberg: Carl Winters, 1918.

Reuning, Karl. *Das Altertümliche Im Wortschatz Der Spenser-Nachahmungen Des 18. Jarhunderts.* Strassburg: Trubner, 1912.

———"'The Shepherd's Tale of the Powder Plot,' Eine Spenser-Nachahmung," *Beiträge zur Erforschung der Sprache und Kultur Englands und Noradamerikas* 4:2 (1928): 8–154.

Rinaker, Clarissa. *Thomas Warton: A Biographical and Critical Study.* Urbana: University of Illinois, 1916.

———"Percy as a Sonneteer," *Modern Language Notes* 35 (1920): 56–58.

Ringler, Richard N. "Dryden at the House of Busirane," *English Studies* 49 (1968): 224–29.

Ringler, William. "Spenser and Thomas Watson," *Modern Language Notes* 69 (1954): 484–87.

Sambrook, James. *English Pastoral Poetry*. Boston: Twayne, 1983.

Sanderlin, George. "A Bibliography of English Sonnets 1800–1850," *ELH* 8 (1941): 226–40.

Sandison, Helen E. "Three Spenser Allusions," *Modern Language Notes* 44 (1929): 159–62.

Sasek, Lawrence A. "William Smith and '*The Shepheardes Calender*,'" *Philological Quarterly* 39 (1960): 251–53;

Schulman, Samuel E. "Wordsworth's Salisbury Plain Poems and Their Spenserian Motives," *JEGP* 84 (1985): 221–42.

Schulze, Ivan I. "Blenerhasset's *A Revelation*, Spenser's *Shepheardes Calender*, and the Kenilworth Pageants," *ELH* 11 (1944): 85–91.

Scribner, Dora Anna. "The History of Spenser's Literary Reputation." Ph.D. diss., University of Chicago, 1906.

Sen, Dilip Kumar. *A Critical Study of Spenserian Imitations from 1700 to 1771*. Master's thesis, University of London, 1952.

–––– "William Thompson – the Spenserian," *Bulletin of the Department of English* (Calcutta University): (1968–69): 33–38.

Sensabaugh, G. F. "A Spenser Allusion," *TLS* (October 29, 1938): 694.

Sheehan, James Clement. "Form and Tradition in the English Epithalamion, 1595–1641." Ph.D. diss., University of Michigan, 1971.

Shih, Chung-Wen. "The Criticism of *The Faerie Queene*." Ph.D. diss., Duke University, 1955.

Sipple, William L. *Edmund Spenser 1900–1936: A Reference Guide*. Boston: G. K. Hall, 1984.

Sirluck, Ernest. "Milton Revises *The Faerie Queene*," *Modern Philology* 48 (1950): 90–96.

Smith, Audrey. "Richard Hurd's Letters on Chivalry," *ELH* 6 (1939): 58–81.

Spurgeon, Caroline. *Five Hundred Years of Chaucer Criticism and Allusion: 1357–1900*. 3 vols. Cambridge: Cambridge UP, 1925.

Stepanik, Karel. "The Problem of Spenserian Influence in Keats's Poetry," *Brno Studies in English* 2 (1960): 7–54.

Stewart, Randall. "Hawthorne and the *Faerie Queene*," *Philological Quarterly* 12 (1933): 196–206.

Strathman, Ernest A. "William Austin's 'Notes' on *The Faerie Queene*," *Huntington Library Bulletin* 11 (1937): 155–60.

—"Lycidas and the Translation of 'May,'" *Modern Language Notes* 52 (1937): 398–400.

—"A Scotch Spenserian: Patrick Gordon," *Huntington Library Quarterly* 1 (1938): 427–37.

Stroup, Thomas B. "'Lycidas' and the Marinell Story," *SAMLA Studies in Milton* (Gainesville: U of Florida P, 1953): 100–113.

Swedenberg, H. T. *The Theory of the Epic in England, 1650–1800.* Berkeley: U of California P, 1944.

Thompson, Elbert N. S. "Between *The Shepheard's Calender* and *The Seasons*," *Philological Quarterly* 1 (1922): 23–30.

Tilley, M. P. "The Comedy Lingua and the *Faerie Queene*," *Modern Language Notes* 42 (March 1927): 150–57.

Tillotson, Kathleen. "The Language of Drayton's *Shepheards Garland*," *Review of English Studies* 13 (1937): 272–81.

Truesdale, Calvin William. "English Pastoral Verse from Spenser to Marvell: A Critical Revaluation." Ph.D. diss., University of Washington, 1956.

Tucker, Herbert F. Jr. "Spenser's Eighteenth-Century Readers and the Question of Unity in the *Faerie Queene*," *University of Toronto Quarterly* 46 (1977): 322–41.

Turnage, Maxine. "Samuel Johnson's Criticism of the Works of Edmund Spenser," *SEL* 10 (1970): 557–67.

John A. Vance. *Joseph and Thomas Warton.* Boston: Twayne, 1983.

Vondersmith, Bernard J. "A History of the Criticism of the *Faerie Queene*, 1910–1947." Ph.D. diss., Duquesne University, 1971.

Wall, L. N. "Some Notes on Marvell's Sources," *Notes and Queries* NS 4 (1957): 170–73.

Wallace, Calvin Riley. "A Comparative Study of Church's Glosses and Annotations of Spenser's *Faerie Queene*." Master's thesis, University of Tennessee, 1930.

Wasserman, Earl R. "The Scholarly Origin of the Elizabethan Revival," *ELH* 4 (1937): 213–43.

—*Elizabethan Poetry in the Eighteenth Century.* Urbana: U of Illinois P, 1947.

Watkins, W. B. C. *Shakespeare and Spenser.* Princeton: Princeton UP, 1953.

Wellek, Réne. *The Rise of English Literary History.* 1941; New York: McGraw Hill, 1966.

Wells, Minnie E. "The Eve of St. Agnes and The Legend of Britomartis," *Modern Language Notes* 57 (1942): 463–65.

Wells, William, ed. *Spenser Allusions in the Sixteenth and Seventeenth Centuries.* Chapel Hill: U of North Carolina P, 1972.

White, H. O. "Thomas Purney: A Forgotten Poet and Critic of the Eighteenth Century," *Essays and Studies by Members of the English Association* 15 (1929): 66–97.

Wormell, Helen E. "Some Aspects of the Early Biographies of Spenser and Milton." Master's thesis, University of North Carolina, 1932.

Wurtsbaugh, Jewel. "Thomas Edwards and the Editorship of *The Faerie Queene*," *Modern Language Notes* 50 (1935): 146–50.

———"Digby's Criticism of Spenser," *Review of English Studies* 11 (1935): 192–95.

———*Two Centuries of Spenserian Scholarship (1609–1805)*. Baltimore: Johns Hopkins UP, 1936.

Zimmerman, Dorothy Wayne. "Romantic Criticism of Edmund Spenser." Ph.D. diss., University of Illinois, 1957.

INDEX

Addison, Joseph, 12, 31, 38, 39, 41, 43, 44, 46, 92, 98, 125, 130, 135
  and Whig Spenserianism, 32-36
  proposes a modernization of the *Faerie Queene*, 36
Adler, Mortimer, 198
  the *Faerie Queene* a Great Book, 175
Akenside, Mark, 68, 69, 97
allegory (see also under *Shepheardes Calender, Faerie Queene*), 30, 34-36, 44, 67, 68, 71-72, 76, 132, 142, 146-48, 193-94
  as a critical mode, 56, 69-70, 118, 133, 183, 193-94
Ancients and Moderns
  emulation between, 14, 19, 29, 60-61, 75
  controversy, 30, 36-38, 43-45, 78, 120, 136, 138
Aquinas, Thomas, 19, 24, 133
archaisms: see diction
Areopagus, 2
Ariosto, Ludovico, 17, 27
Aristotle, 23, 25, 45, 63, 65, 133-34, 137, 182
Arnold, Matthew, 131, 135, 165
Arnold, Thomas, 109-10, 137, 149
Atterbury, Bishop Francis, 46
  on Spenser's diction, 22
Aylett, Robert, 46; Selected Studies: Padelford, 225
  a Spenserian poet, 19, 20

Babbitt, Irving, 162, 166
Barnfield, Richard, 46; Selected Studies: Morris, 224
  first to imitate the *Faerie Queene*, 9
Barton, Bernard
  uses Spenserian stanza, 82
Baskervill, C. R., 46
  on the early fame of the *Shepheardes Calender*, 8
Bathurst, Charles, 74, 98
Beale, Dorothea, 149
  on Spenser's women, 128
Beattie, James, 20, 89, 90, 93, 95, 98, 108, 126; Selected Studies: Aldrich, 219; King, 223
  his *Minstrel*, 78-82, 88, 91, 122
Beaumont, Joseph, 46
  his *Psyche* imitates Spenser, 18

Bedell, William: Selected Studies: Reuning, 225
Beers, Henry, 46, 161-62, 198
  on neoclassical criticism of Spenser, 31
Bennett, Josephine Waters, 198
  on the design of the *Faerie Queene*, 161
Bentley, Richard, 30-31, 41, 57, 73, 85
Berger, Harry, Jr, 181, 182, 183, 185, 186, 190, 198
  his *Allegorical Temper*, 178-180
Bicknell, Alexander, 149
  his prose adaptation of the *Faerie Queene*, 105-06
Bidlake, John
  uses Spenserian stanza, 82
biography (see also under "Spenser, character") 117-23
Birch, Thomas, Selected Studies: Wurtsbaugh, 228
  editor of the *Faerie Queene*, 52
Blackmore, Sir Richard, 35, 46; Selected Studies: Brinkley, 220
  author of political Arthuriads, 27
Blackwell, Thomas, 139
Blackwood's Magazine, 84, 97, 106
Blair, Hugh, 116, 139
  ignores Spenser in *Lectures on Rhetoric*, 75
Blake, William, 97, 184; Selected Studies: Gleckner, 221
Blashfield, Edwin
  illustrates the "Epithalamion," 125
Blenerhasset, Thomas: Selected Studies: Schulze, 226
Boileau, Nicholas, 26, 118
Bowles, William Lisle, 52
  uses the Spenserian stanza, 83
Boyd, Henry
  uses Spenserian stanza
Bradford, Gamaliel, 149, 170
  on women in the *Faerie Queene*, 128
Bradstreet, Anne, 123
Bradner, Leicester
  on Latin translations of *Shepheardes Calender*
Breval, John Durant, 46, 98
  imitates Spenser, 35, 68
Brook, Christopher
  an Inns of Court poet, 10